THE AGE OF CONSEQUENCE

McGill-Queen's/Brian Mulroney Institute of Government Studies in Leadership, Public Policy, and Governance

Series editor: Donald E. Abelson

Titles in this series address critical issues facing Canada at home and abroad and the efforts policymakers at all levels of government have made to address a host of complex and multifaceted policy concerns. Books in this series receive financial support from the Brian Mulroney Institute of Government at St Francis Xavier University; in keeping with the institute's mandate, these studies explore how leaders involved in key policy initiatives arrived at their decisions and what lessons can be learned. Combining rigorous academic analysis with thoughtful recommendations, this series compels readers to think more critically about how and why elected officials make certain policy choices, and how, in concert with other stakeholders, they can better navigate an increasingly complicated and crowded marketplace of ideas.

1 Braver Canada
  Shaping Our Destiny in a Precarious World
  Derek H. Burney and Fen Osler Hampson

2 The Canadian Federal Election of 2019
  Edited by Jon H. Pammett and Christopher Dornan

3 Keeping Canada Running
  Infrastructure and the Future of Governance in a Pandemic World
  Edited by G. Bruce Doern, Christopher Stoney, and Robert Hilton

4 The Age of Consequence
  The Ordeals of Public Policy in Canada
  Charles J. McMillan

The Age of Consequence

The Ordeals of Public Policy in Canada

CHARLES J. MCMILLAN

McGill-Queen's University Press
Montreal & Kingston • London • Chicago

© McGill-Queen's University Press 2022

ISBN 978-0-2280-1093-7 (cloth)
ISBN 978-0-2280-1210-8 (ePDF)

Legal deposit second quarter 2022
Bibliothèque nationale du Québec

Printed in Canada on acid-free paper that is 100% ancient forest free (100% post-consumer recycled), processed chlorine free

Funded by the Government of Canada / Financé par le gouvernement du Canada Canada Council for the Arts / Conseil des arts du Canada

We acknowledge the support of the Canada Council for the Arts.

Nous remercions le Conseil des arts du Canada de son soutien.

Library and Archives Canada Cataloguing in Publication

Title: The age of consequence: the ordeals of public policy in Canada / Charles McMillan.

Names: McMillan, Charles J., author.

Series: McGill-Queen's/Brian Mulroney Institute of Government studies in leadership, public policy, and governance; 4.

Description: Series statement: McGill-Queen's/Brian Mulroney Institute of Government studies in leadership, public policy, and governance; 4 | Includes bibliographical references and index.

Identifiers: Canadiana (print) 20210366931 | Canadiana (ebook) 20210367105 | ISBN 9780228010937 (cloth) | ISBN 9780228012108 (ePDF)

Subjects: LCSH: Canada—Social policy. | LCSH: Canada—Economic policy—20th century. | LCSH: Canada—Foreign relations—1945– | LCSH: Canada—Politics and government—1945– | CSH: Canada—Economic policy—1945–

Classification: LCC HN107 .M45 2022 | DDC 320.6097109/045—dc23

This book was typeset by Marquis Interscript in 10.5/13 Sabon.

For Kazuyo

Contents

Figures and Tables ix

Preface: A Note to Readers xi

Acknowledgments xv

Abbreviations xix

Illustrations xxi

PART ONE – CANADA IN THE GLOBAL SYSTEM

1 From Colony to G7 Partner: Canada in a Global World 3

PART TWO – POLICY OUTCOMES: THE FOUR PILLARS OF GOVERNMENT

2 Setting a Policy Agenda: New National Policy Challenges 33

3 Social Justice and Defining Individual Rights and Responsibilities 87

4 National Reconciliation: Institutional Alignments 137

5 Constructive Internationalism in a Changing World Order 193

PART THREE – CANADA'S FUTURE

6 Aboriginal Peoples: Wards of the State or Full Citizens? 247

7 A Digression on Trade Policy 288

8 Successful Governments, Successful Prime Ministers 329

APPENDICES

A Contested Liberal and Conservative Leadership Conventions (1948–2003) 367

B Contested Liberal and Conservative Leadership Conventions (21st Century) 369

C Federal Cabinets, Size, and Committees since 1948 371

D A Performance Scorecard: Canada and Other Industrialized Countries 373

Source References by Chapter 375

Bibliography 383

Index 389

Figures and Tables

Author's analysis is source of figures and tables, unless otherwise specified.

FIGURES

1.1 International Comparison of Countries: Corruption and Well-Being   7
1.2 Two Role Sets: Party Leader and Prime Minister   21
1.3 The Mulroney Policy Process (14 June 1983–4 September 1984)   28
2.1 Industries and Dynamic Model of Competitive Advantage   35
2.2 The PMO Policy Unit   37
2.3 The Mulroney Competitive Agenda   37
2.4 Organization of the Ministry of Finance   41
2.5 The Components of a Wealth-Creating Economy   77
3.1 Observed and Projected Youth, Senior, and Total Demographic Dependency Ratios, Canada 1971–2056   92
3.2 The European Union: Social Justice Framework   100
3.3 Health-care Spending: Coverage, Benefits, and Payments   104
3.4 Health-Care Cost (1970–2016)   105
3.5 Cumulative Emissions of CO_2 and Future Non-CO_2 Radiative Forcing Determine the Probability of Limiting Warming to 1.5 C°   125
3.6 A General Framework Illustrating Climate Change, Infections Diseases, and Society   126
5.1 NATO Defence Spending as a Percentage of GNP   200
5.2 Comparison of Donor Countries for Foreign Aid   205

5.3   The Shifting Fortunes of Globalizatio   211
5.4   *Les routes maritimes polaires*   233
6.1   Rules of Governance: Four Views on Indigenous Independence and Self-Governance   250
7.1   Globalization over Five Centuries   290
7.2   Presidents, Protectionism, and Free Trade   300
7.3   Tariff Reductions in the Post-war Era   304
7.4   Share of Canadian SMEs That Export   313
7.5   Contributors to China's Asian Infrastructure Bank   328

TABLES

1.1   Timelines of Canadian Prime Ministers   19
2.1   The Evolution of Canadian Banking 1867–1967   48
2.2   Selected Privatization Initiatives, 1985–1988   72
3.1   Three Eras of Social Policy in Canada   90
3.2   Funding the 2004 Health Accord to Date   107
3.3   Social Justice: Evolution of Canadian Social Programs by Type   113
4.1   Gross Domestic Product (GDP), by Province, Mid-2010s   148
4.2   Five Rounds of Constitutional Negotiations (1971-1992)   168
5.1   Comparative Country Ranking of Soft Power   244
6.1   Aboriginal-Identity Population Canada, Provinces and Territories   252
6.2   Canada and the Indigenous Community: Key Dates   253
7.1   Exporters and Non-exporters among Canadian Manufacturers   311
7.2   Canada's Trade Strategies (1867–Date)   314
8.1   Quebec and Rest of Canada (ROC) in Federal-Election Victories (1949–2015)   332
8.2   Prime Ministers' Electoral Wins and Defeats (1949–2019)   343

Preface: A Note to Readers

The great economist John Maynard Keynes once remarked that there are only two types of opinions: "Not, as in former ages the true and the false, but the outside and the inside."[1] In an age of fake news, disruptive change, and an abundance of opinion and a scarcity of judgment and common sense, Keynes's insight, despite the passage of time, still holds today. In the global power structure, Canada is an insider, a nation founding and joining important global clubs. This book is a chronology of the public policies, the political environment, and the political players in Canada since the end of the Second World War. Each generation faces new challenges, but in the next fifty years Canada is remarkably well positioned to address a very different, globalized, interconnected world as an insider.

Pundits, politicians, and the media make much of the changed world order and a rules-based system, especially when a mercantilist, *dirigiste* president was in the White House, heading an administration bent on an ideological fetish to "make America great again." Each week of the Trump presidency produced more books and articles either defending U.S. policy as the ultimate *realpolitik* in a world of big powers or excoriating tactics of withdrawing from international military and trade agreements, weakening global institutions like the United Nations, the World Bank, and the World Trade Organization, and imposing a U.S.-based view of military and economic order on countries as diverse as Brazil, China, Iran, North Korea, and Venezuela.

Starting in the 1970s, but accelerating in the 1980s, the post-1945 world order was breaking apart, away from the Cold War's American–Soviet division, with allies on both sides. These shifts account for a new "Age of Consequence," as Canada struggled to find its way, away from an Atlantic-centred view of the world, just as Canada's provinces were adjusting to new demographics and new spending on health care and education, and showing less interest in an Ottawa-centric view of economic development. In all Western countries, including Canada, politicians were forced to deal with new social issues, the rights and responsibilities of individual citizens, and contentious issues of abortion, capital punishment, voting rights, marriage and divorce, race relations and social diversity, women in the workplace and politics, advances in medical science, and unparalleled threats to the environment, from dirty air and water to climate change.

Indeed, Canadians often take their international reputational clout for granted, consumed by internal political matters, and sometimes put forth proposals that might actually diminish the very qualities and strengths that other countries admire in Canadian society. For instance, as a parliamentary democracy that separates the head of state from partisan politics, and protects law-enforcement agencies and the judiciary, including the Supreme Court, from political bias, electioneering, and partisan interference, Canada stands at the forefront in providing equality before the law and protection of minority rights. In this sense, it contrasts with the practices of the Great Republic to the south, where the head of state, the elected president, is also head of a political party, serves as commander-in-chief of the armed forces, and appoints cabinet members, Supreme Court justices, and heads of the armed services, increasingly on strictly partisan lines. In the years ahead, national decisions taken today will impact future generations, in areas like climate change, the Arctic, medical technologies, corporate innovation, data flows and privacy, food production, and the retention and betterment of democratic values and institutions. *The Age of Consequence* addresses Canada's political environment in the post-1945 period and the new policy thrusts in the 1980s that have produced policy outcomes that are the envy of the world.

All governments face the urgency of the event cycle, knowing that many of their programs are pressing, expensive, and long term, while many issues are less costly but time- consuming, like dealing with apartheid in South Africa, raising the voice of the science community within the public service, and improving the gender balance in Canadian society. The arc of history may point to the future, but often at a huge cost of political capital. The narrative in this book is set out in three parts, starting in chapter 1 with Canada in the global system and the policies and institutions that set the context for major policy and institutional reforms. Chapters 2–5 set out the transformations in four areas: economic competitiveness, social policy, institutional alignments and constitutional reforms, and new and novel reordering of Canadian foreign and diplomatic policy. The third part focuses on the future, assessing Canada's Aboriginal policies, trade policy, and successful governments and prime ministers.

Since 1968 and the election of the Liberal Pierre Trudeau (serving 1968–79 and 1980-84), followed by the Conservative Brian Mulroney (1984–93), Canada has had nine prime ministers, some for only a short term, a series of minority governments, and 16 leaders of the Opposition, and, in the provinces, a turnover of party leaders. This rotation shows the vibrant nature of the political system that combines a measure of continuity and stability with change, turnover, and policy innovation. By any standards, these policy outcomes are impressive, even by international comparisons with other advanced democratic countries, including with the United States. This book is written for the general public, interested in the "sausage machine" of how law and public policy are actually made, the cleavages and conflicts facing senior members of the government, and the unique burdens placed on the prime minister. Only a few prime ministers rank near the top. The book is also aimed at the general public interested in these transformations, as well as the specialist policy analysts, showing the reality of policy change in a changing world, the institutional constraints, and the role of personalities that advance change, or hold it back.

This book starts from a point of view: a deep admiration for Canada's political system, federally and provincially, and the key players who fight nominations, contest elections, serve as MPs, and cabinet members. As a democracy, Canada has inherited ideas and models from other countries, especially the Mother of Parliaments, at Westminster. Each decade since Confederation, politicians have adapted a political model to Canadian circumstances. In fact, few people appreciate how flexible the Canadian system is next to other democratic systems, including Britain, France, and the United States, from which Canada learned much but also rejected much, in part to avoid the extreme polarization of political views, by geography, age, and income.

Toronto, June 2020

Acknowledgments

As an author, bystander, political and policy activist, and insider participant, I have had the advantage of living outside Canada for a number of years, in Britain, France, and Japan, spending considerable time as well in countries as diverse as Kyrgyzstan, Poland, Sweden, and the United States. I have also had the good fortune to live in Canada outside my home province of Prince Edward Island, in Edmonton, Quebec City, and Toronto, plus four years in Ottawa, the last sojourn as much an accident as a planned stay. I was active in Brian Mulroney's 1976 campaign for the Progressive Conservative leadership, and, in this losing cause, I assumed my political activity was confined to giving free political and policy advice to friends in provincial and federal campaigns, including Peter Lougheed when I was at the University of Alberta, Bob Stanfield, when he became PC leader in 1967, and various riding campaigns such as those of Heath Macquarrie in Charlottetown, Don MacDougal in London North, and Duff Roblin in Peterborough, Ontario.

My involvement in the federal Conservative leadership race in 1983 started over a cup of coffee in Toronto, when Brian Mulroney and Michael Cogger, his real campaign manager, asked me to do some delegate tracking and policy advice, proving again that there is nothing so permanent as a temporary assignment. That convention was one of the most eventful in Canadian history, not only for the leadership issues, but for the preparation of a new government and a dramatic change in economic direction – literally a new, outward, forward-looking, competitive agenda to replace Sir John A. Macdonald's 19th-century National Policy.

Given my family responsibilities, academic life, and consulting, I originally offered my services to lead the policy unit in the Office of the Leader of the Opposition, starting in June 1983, intending to stay only until the end of the forthcoming national election, win, lose, or draw. After the election, I agreed to stay for two years, offering my letter of resignation exactly two years later on 4 September 1986. Coincidentally it was the same day my assistant, confidant, and close friend Nigel Wright also resigned, when he returned to the Law School at the University of Toronto. It took me another nine months to plan my exit, leaving on Thursday, 11 June 1987, four years after Brian Mulroney won the party leadership.

During both my formal tenure in Ottawa and the years following, I was asked to advise on a range of files as diverse as the free-trade negotiations, regional development, science and technology, relations with Japan and South Korea, the Churchill Falls electricity project, privatization, Canada's relationship with former Soviet republics, and the Meech Lake Accord. I wrote detailed memorandums on government policy, machinery, election planning, and party organization; my "personal and confidential" memos to Brian Mulroney fill a full six binders!

I have had the good fortune to make many lifelong friends, and too many, unfortunately, have passed away, but now enjoy well-deserved patronage assignments in the hereafter. I won't name them all, but I single out five premiers, Alan Blakeney, Richard Hatfield, Ralph Klein, Peter Lougheed, and Duff Roblin, plus three political operatives, Keith Davey, Fred Dickson, and Jean Pigott, who combined strategy, wit, and a love of the game.

I happily acknowledge insights, personal experiences, private memos, and clear thinking from a range of Canadians, including Tom Axworthy, Stephen Azzi, Lucien Bouchard, Premier Alex B. Campbell, Jean Charest, Michael Coates, Michael Cogger, David Crane, John Crosbie, James Crossland, Premier Bill Davis, Michael Decter, David Dodge, Mike Duffy, Governor Michael Dukakis, Wayne Easter, David Emerson, Dan Gagnier, Jeff Gandz, Martin Goldfarb, Jerry Grafstein, Peter Harder, Premier Mike Harris, David Johnston, Monte Kwinter, Jacques Lamarre, Premier Peter Lougheed, Greg Lyle, Ian MacDonald, Peter MacKinnon, David MacLaughlin, Wade MacLaughlin, Barbara McDougall, Roy McMurtry, Mary McQuaid, Vic Murry, Nik Nanos, David Naylor, Harry Near, Peter C. Newman, Peter Nicholson, Sedeeki Numata, Premier David Peterson, Louise Pinard, Premier Bob Rae, Lee Richardson, Louise Simard, Jeffrey Simpson, George Stalk, Andrew Stark, Janice Stein, Paul Tellier, Richard Thibeault, Bernard Valcourt, Lisa Van Dusen, Wilf Wakely, Ben West, and Nigel Wright.

I want to thank particularly the Rt Hon. Brian Mulroney, whom I first met as a member of Peter Lougheed's Alberta delegation at the Niagara

Falls Conservative policy convention in 1969, hosted by the Hon. Robert Stanfield and chaired by Professor Tom Symons. We struck up a friendship well beyond the political realm, in part helped by our Maritimes university education. Like both of my parents, who first met on a ferry from Charlottetown to Pictou, Nova Scotia, and whose studies at St Francis Xavier University in Antigonish had a profound influence on them, the same happened for this young student from Baie-Comeau. When I introduced my mother to Brian Mulroney in Charlottetown after he became party leader, they both largely ignored other people in the room and talked about their "X" experiences, teachers, and friendships, ranging from Danny Gallivan, the CBC English-language broadcaster for the Montreal Canadiens, to Sr Frankie Kirwin, another "X" alumna and member of the Grey Nuns, who built a huge and successful high school in Japan.

Many friends ask me if it was challenging to write memos and provide advice to the prime minister, who wanted the hard truth. I had a reputation in Ottawa circles for writing short, terse memos. In fact, at a barbecue hosted by a prominent Liberal premier, I was taken aside in his living room and asked directly if I was intimidated against giving the real goods to the prime minister. He felt his own staff wasn't being straight and wondered if he was short-changed. I responded simply: never. The prime minister preferred frank and candid memos for his nightly reading, and he would reflect on the contents, usually making phone calls to his network of outside advisers, and often discussing the contents with me a day or two later over coffee, breakfast, or lunch. I knew that any advice offered might be accepted only in part, but a third is a very good batting average, even in baseball.

I am profoundly grateful to the following friends and relatives who have read drafts of one or more chapters, and offered their own insights and nuances on topics in the chapters, as well as offering corrections, challenging my conclusions, and questioning dates and timing: Tom Axworthy, Stephen Azzi, Sandy Borins, Mel Cappe, David Crombie, Tom Creary, Bill Fox, Tom Hockin, Lowell Murray, and Geoff Norquay, as well as my brother, Colin McMillan, and my daughter, Aya McMillan. I offer in advance apologies for errors of omission or commission, but also my profound appreciation and thanks.

Abbreviations

ACOA	Atlantic Canada Opportunities Agency
ARDA	Agricultural and Rehabilitation and Development Act
BRIC	Brazil, Russia, India, China
CBA	Canadian Bankers Association
CCB	Canadian Commercial Bank
CCF	Co-operative Commonwealth Federation
CDIC	Canadian Deposit Insurance Corporation
CETA	Comprehensive Economic and Trade Agreement
CHST	Canada Health and Social Transfer
CHOGM	Commonwealth Heads of Government
CMA	Canadian Medical Association
CN	Canadian National, formerly CNR, a crown corporation railway
CRTC	Canadian Radio and Television Commission
DFAIT	Department of Foreign Affairs and International Trade
DRIE	Department of Regional and Industrial Expansion
EPF	Established Program Financing
Eurozone	EU members using the euro as their currency
FBDB	Federal Business Development Bank
FPI	Fisheries Products International
FPRO	Federal–Provincial Relations Office
GATT	General Agreement on Tariffs and Trade
GDP	Gross domestic product – total market value produced domestically
GNP	Gross national product – total value of all final products including net exports
GST	Goods and Services Tax

IMF	International Monetary Fund
NAFTA	North America Free Trade Agreement
NAJC	National Association of Japanese Canadians
NATO	North Atlantic Treaty Organization
NGO	Non-government organization
NORAD	North American Aerospace Defense Command
NDP	New Democratic Party
OAS	Organization of American States
OECD	Organization for Economic Co-operation and Development
OSFI	Office of the Superintendent of Financial Institutions
PAFTAD	Pacific Trade and Development
PAG	Policy Analysis Group
PECC	Pacific Economic Cooperation Council
PMO	Prime Minister's Office
PCO	Privy Council Office
QP	Question Period
RCMP	Royal Canadian Mounted Police
SDI	Strategic Defense Initiative
SNC	Montreal engineering firm founded in 1911
TPP	Trans-Pacific Partnership
USSR	Union of Soviet Socialist Republics
USTR	United States Trade Representative
VAT	Value-added tax

The author with the Right Honourable M. Brian Mulroney in Ottawa. October, 1984.
*All photos are courtesy of the author.

Two St. F.X alumni in action: My mother, D. Eileen McMillan, and the Right Honourable M. Brian Mulroney in Charlottetown. April, 1987.

Ottawa – Before the final vote, Leadership Convention, June 11, 1983; Author with Roger Nantel – Comparing private Mulroney polls, actual voting by candidate, and delegate tracking by candidates.

Travelling from Windsor to Barrie on the 1984 Election Campaign Bus. August, 1983. Seated: Brian Armstrong, Patrick MacAdam, Bonnie Brownlee Standing: The Right Honourable M. Brian Mulroney, the author, Bill Fox.

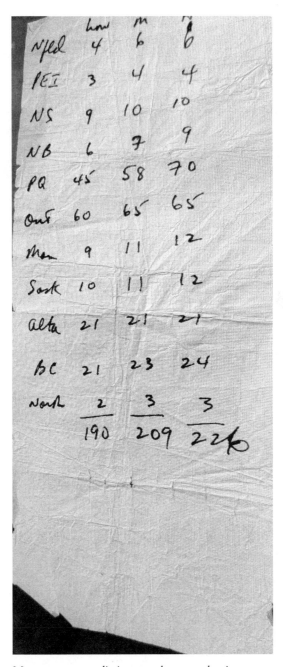

My seat count predictions, made on an aluminum cigarette wrapper, for the September 4, 1984 Federal Election, made mid-August in Quebec City with Bonnie Brownlee, Bill Fox, and Lisa VanDusen.

My then-assistant Nigel Wright, recruited as a student from the University of Toronto Law School, who became a member of the PMO Policy Unit, and after two years, graduated, did a Harvard degree and joined Onex Corporation, and then served as Chief of Staff for the Right Honourable Stephen Harper.

Briefing the Toronto Press with Jon Johnston (left) and Bill Fox on Campaign Promises and Costing Analysis, August 30, 1984.

A post-Cabinet Meeting assessment with Gordon Osbaldeston, Clerk of the Privy Council, November, 1984.

Planning the Federal Budget in the Cabinet Committee Room. April, 1985.
Right to Left: The Right Honourable M. Brian Mulroney, the author, Mickey Cohen, Deputy Minister of Department of Finance; Michael Wilson, Minister of Finance, Paul Tellier, Clerk of the Privy Council, and Stanley Hartt, Chief of Staff and a secretary taking notes.

Speaking to the Right Honourable M. Brian Mulroney with Gordon Smith, Under-Secretary in Department of Foreign Affairs at the Caribbean Commonwealth Summit in Kingston, Jamaica, February, 1985.

My daughters, Aya and Mari, presenting flowers to Her Majesty Queen Elizabeth, the Queen Mother in Ottawa with my wife, Kazuyo, overseeing the proceedings. The photo is autographed by the Queen Mother, thanks to the ingenuity of Roy McMurtry, Canadian High Commissioner of Canada to the United Kingdom. June, 1985.

At a reception in Ottawa with Yasuhiro Nakasone, Prime Minister of Japan. My wife Kazuyo, who attended the same high school in Shizouka as the Prime Minister, looks on. January 6, 1986.

A note from Noburo Takeshita, Prime Minister of Japan, on his visit to Canada. January 15, 1988.

With Mikhail Gorbachev, General Secretary of the Soviet Union, and his interpreter, Pavel Palazhchenko, in Toronto. May 29, 1993.

Author, PM Mulroney, President Reagan in the Rose Garden after lunch at White House, September 25, 1984.

PRIME MINISTER · PREMIER MINISTRE

June 29, 1987

Dear Charley

This is a special word of gratitude from an old friend who is deeply aware of the significance of your contribution to the party and the Government.

From the outset, you have been dynamic and devoted and I shall always be thankful for the skill and enthusiasm you brought to the resolution of challenging national issues.

On a more personal level, you have been a loyal and valued counsellor and friend and I shall never forget your important contribution to our goals — and the good fun we had in achieving them!

With love to Kazuyo and the girls

Sincerely
Brian Mulroney

A handwritten letter from the Prime Minister. June, 1987.

PART ONE

Canada in the Global System

1

From Colony to G7 Partner: Canada in a Global World

*Building the Post-1945 Order – The End of Bretton Woods –
The Golden Age of U.S. Corporate Domination –
International Financial Policy Coordination – An Ode to Politicians –
Canada's Post-1945 Economic Agenda – The Age of Conseuqnce –
Managing the New Challenges of the Global Economy*

In the long run every Government is the exact symbol of its People, with their wisdom and unwisdom; we have to say, Like People like Government.

Thomas Carlyle

INTRODUCTION

With the ninth-largest economy in the democratic world, and the tenth overall in the 2010s, Canada is a testimony to the carefully contrived policy outcomes of a smallish population in such a huge country. In each generation after Confederation, the political elites faced unique challenges, beginning in the age of Sir John A. Macdonald, to build a national economy of former British colonies, with constant threats from the imperious sentiments of American manifest destiny. Both in Ottawa and in the provincial capitals, there was accepted wisdom to follow a continental North American practice, namely, to reject the European system of vast land ownership for a few (nobles, the monarchy, and the church) and serfdom for the majority. Unlike the revolutionary sentiments of the Great Republic to its south, Canada was more cautious, circumspect, less revolutionary as the norms of equality and material well-being became widespread, accentuated in selected cities – Halifax, Montreal, Toronto, and in recent years, Calgary. Where the United States took the lead – in the arts, commerce, education, finance, and science – Canada usually followed, with a time lag, often decades.

Wilfrid Laurier, inheriting national leadership after Canada's first prime minister, Sir John A. Macdonald, of a small, fragmented, and underpopulated nation so closely bound to Britain, was a lawyer by profession, a French Canadian by birth, and a politician with vision. Laurier was an optimist, and he deeply admired his archrival, and he also shared Macdonald's vision of Canada and the Confederation bargain as a nation-building dream of a great country located in North America. Like all Canadians, he witnessed the expansion of the Great Republic and accepted Canada as a country endowed with British institutions and parliamentary government and with economic links to London. Laurier followed Sir John A.'s inheritance, a Canadian-based tradition of provincial autonomy, mass immigration, and nation-building, reflecting the heritage of anglophone and francophone duality. The age of Macdonald had left the Conservative party fractured and unsure after he died in office in 1891. Laurier had every intention to complete the Confederation bargain with his Liberals becoming Canada's nation-building party of record.

Those who succeeded Laurier followed similar paths, starting with Robert Bordon, the third Nova Scotian to hold the top job. William Lyon Mackenzie King, R.B. Bennett, and then King again faced a new reality, a mass depression, a political culture where many citizens openly doubted the merits of the capitalist system and searched for other models, as diverse as the Soviet Union, fascist Europe, and socialism with a human face, starting in Britain. Unlike the United States, with two parties now entrenched, Laurier knew his own Liberals needed nourishment, party discipline, and experience in government. Historically, Canadians were less ideological, devoid of what Richard Hofstadter called the "paranoid style in American politics," and accepting of a belief that Canada evolved with the best of three worlds – British parliamentary government, American economic prowess, and French culture. Such assurances would be tested more than once.

Some countries understand the seismic transformations now under way in the global economy. But many do not. Curiously, the one country that should have been the most aware, the United States, has a political system that seems to outsiders to be in a state of denial. The United States can still lead, but not unilaterally. For example, the establishment of the G7 club, with regular meetings of national leaders and finance and foreign ministers of the richest economies, initiated new policy coordination in the developed world in the 1970s. It also dealt with the rise of the Organization of Petroleum Exporting Countries (OPEC), Third World debt, fluctuating currency movements, inflation, and the end of the Breton Woods system of fixed exchange rates. This "capitalist club" became the G8 to include Russia as the biggest republic in the former Soviet Union, but that club morphed into the G20, an initiative led by Canada's Liberal Prime Minister Paul Martin, which included the BRIC countries – Brazil, Russia, India, and China – and now meets annually to coordinate a range of global issues. The days are numbered for a U.S.-centred global order, with the U.S. dollar as the main global currency. Despite many forms of imperial overreach, the United States pursued domestic policies of high consumption, low taxes, and rising consumer and public debt – the hallmarks of a credit-card economy. It wasn't "guns or butter" but "guns and butter."

What has changed profoundly in the past decade is the entry of new players. China, of course, is the outstanding example, which introduced the market system in 1972, and accelerating with the policies of one key person, Deng Xiaoping, a committed communist but enormously pragmatic and with a penchant for poignant humour, pushing industrial growth beyond urban areas towards the hinterland. In 1977, Deng's overseas visits, including to Japan, taught him directly the technological gap between China and Western countries, and his speeches extolled the virtues of learning from Western nations, much like Japan's experience after the Meiji Restoration in 1868. Chinese policies have slowly but steadily shifted the investment balance away from heavy industry to internal consumption and services. In an amazingly short period, the country has transformed itself, technologically, materially, and intellectually, in two generations, reaching almost parity in gross national product (GNP) with the United States. More technically, the latter still leads, with GNP of $20.4 trillion in 2018, compared to China at $14.1 trillion, a gap that is likely to close by 2023, with projections of $24.5 trillion to $21.6 trillion.

Within a decade or so, six emerging economies, the so-called BRIC – plus Indonesia and South Korea – will collectively account for about one-half of economic growth in the global economy. The old paradigm and its three anchors – first, the international institutions flowing from Bretton Woods: the International Monetary Fund (IMF), the World Trade Organization (WTO), and the World Bank; second, a steady flow of capital via foreign investment, foreign aid, and government lending; and, third, the centrality of a dominant currency, the U.S. "greenback" – face new challenges, including headwinds in the American political system. By definition, emerging countries normally lack corporate debt ratios on a par with developed countries because they're not as profitable, wealthy, or credit worthy. They also tend to default first, as shown with Mexico in the 1980s, followed by Russia, where the ruble's value, despite IMF support, dropped almost to zero against Western currencies. Despite many forms of imperial overreach, the United States pursued domestic policies of high consumption, low taxes, and rising consumer and public debt – the hallmarks of a credit-card economy.

For comparison, Japan has a GNP of $5.1 trillion, projected to reach $8.9 trillion by 2023, with Canada at $1.8 trillion, heading for $4.43 trillion in 2023. However, when adjusted for purchasing power parity (PPP), China is now the largest economy, with GNP of $25.2 trillion, overtaking the Americans in 2014, and projected to reach $37.0 trillion in 2023, compared to $24.4 trillion in the United States, reaching $25.2 trillion in 2023, and this economic strength accounts for the country's forward-looking initiatives in foreign policy. Three general factors make economic projections tentative at best: countries' annual growth rates, different population levels (China has four times as many people as the United States, ten times as many as Japan, and about forty times as many as Canada), and internal demographics. All advanced economics have rapidly ageing populations, but China now faces real demographic challenges, especially in urban areas. Reforms in economic policies of the 1970s, more *perestroika* than *glasnost*, lay groundwork that is self-reinforcing: a state-led industrial strategy to match top Western firms in ten growth sectors, the Global Belt and Road initiative to capture long-term sources of raw materials (e.g., importing $65 billion in iron ore for its steel mills) and future markets in central Asia, Africa, and Latin America, and an infrastructure plan that builds state-of-the-art facilities (highways, passenger trains, ports) that link the diverse regions of China like Beijing and Shanghai and stretching from Vladivostok to Istanbul and Rotterdam, and from southern Egypt to the Arctic. Steady economic growth has brought rising education and health standards, and steep declines in poverty, from about 77 per cent at the start of the 1980s to under 15 per cent today, as measured in per capita income below $3,000. China also shows the capacity to think big.

The Chinese government is now run by a highly educated "mandarin" civil service despite the pretensions of Communist party rulers, with many alumni from top foreign universities. The system is committed to markets and micro-economic reforms, including channeling high Chinese savings, as high as 50 per cent of GNP or more in rural areas, into productive entrepreneurship in the private economy. Contrary to foreign perceptions, China's central government spends scarcely more than 11 per cent of total

CORRUPTION, 2017	GDP/CAPITA ($, PPP), 2017	INCOME INEQUALITY (FAMILY) GINI INDEX, LATEST YEAR	HUMAN DEVELOPMENT INDEX, 2018
1. New Zealand	$38,900	36.2	16
2. Denmark	49,900	29.0	11
3. Finland	44,100	27.3	15
4. Norway	71,800	26.8	1
5. Switzerland	61,400	29.5	2
6. Singapore	99,400	45.9	9
7. Sweden	51,500	24.9	7
8. Canada	48,300	32.1	12
9. Netherlands	53,600	30.3	10
10. UK	44,100	32.4	14
16. US	59,500	45.0	13
172. Equatorial Guinea	9.850	39.4	175
173. Guinea-Bissau	1,800	35.5	177
174. North Korea	1,700	n/a	n/a
175. Libya	8,000	n/a	108
176. Sudan	9,900	35.3	167
177. Yemen	1,300	37.7	152
178. Afghanistan	2,000	27.8	168
179. Syria	2,900	35.8	155
180. South Sudan	1,500	46.0	187
181. Somalia	n/a	n/a	n/a

Source: Adapted from Transparency International, CIA Factbook

Figure 1.1 International Comparison of Countries: Corruption and Well-Being

outlays and employs only four per cent of all public servants. Further, despite its controversial aims – as variously a Chinese Marshall Plan, a twenty-five-year imperial extension of the country's political and financial influence, or a forward-looking plan to link the vast nation to the global economy – the Belt and Road initiative offers powerful testimony to its capacity to think globally in the 21st century. Further, these narratives have proven remarkably successful at uniting diverse sides and illustrate the future steps Canada must take to remain globally competitive.

I

Both before the Second World War, and ten years after hostilities ended in 1945, Canada's federal government and prime minister were guided by royal commissions, useful tools to provide independent advice, such as the Rowell–Sirois Commission, set up in August 1937 as a result of the pending bankruptcy of Saskatchewan and Manitoba. Newton Rowell, a former Liberal leader of the Opposition in Ontario who joined Bordon's Union Government in 1917 and took over the running of the war effort, was chosen as chair, but he had a serious stroke and was replaced by Joseph Sirois, a noted constitutional lawyer from Laval University. Their report, issued in May 1940, comprehensively outlined powers within Canada's federal system, including the constitutional implications of federal and provincial spending and taxation, especially in areas like health and education, and laid the groundwork for the post-war welfare state. This approach was followed by the Green Book spending measures in 1945 that framed federal welfare policies and spending for a generation. Some premiers were resentful – Ontario's George Drew, a Conservative, called it "a dictatorial federal bureaucracy." More specifically, the concept of provincial autonomy – a core theme in the Rowell–Sirois Report – was largely ignored in the Green Book proposals, submitted by the federal government at the Dominion–Provincial Conference on Reconstruction in August 1945.

In June 1955, Liberal Prime Minister Louis St Laurent appointed another royal commission, chaired by Walter Lockhart Gordon from Toronto, a rich, brilliant, and highly capable heir to the accounting firm Clarkson and Gordon, under the auspicious title, Canada's Economic Prospects. Gordon had first gone to work in Ottawa in 1939, one of Liberal "Minister of Everything" C.D. Howe's "dollar-a-year men." The order-in-council, signed by Robert Bryce, clerk of the Privy Council, charged the five commissioners to "inquire into and report upon ... the probable economic development of Canada and the problems to which such developments appear like to give rise." A preliminary version of their report was presented in December 1956 to key civil servants, and the final version was published in 1957. The document confirmed the regional nature of the Canadian economy, the existence of a wide range of interprovincial trade barriers, and the reality of multinational firms investing directly in Canada as a substitute for export trade, setting up operations, usually in Ontario, with output directed to the small domestic market. The report's timing also coincided with the choice of a fiery new pro-British leader of the Conservative Opposition, John Diefenbaker. Public opinion polls showed that many Canadians were angered by the American stance on the Suez invasion, a disastrous folly led by British Prime Minister Anthony Eden that received support from but then enraged recently retired Conservative Prime Minister Winston Churchill ("I would never have dared, and I if I had dared, I would have never dared stop" and "One thing is certain, I wouldn't have done anything without consulting the Americans.") Both the British and the Canadian governments were soon to learn yet again that. while it might be difficult to live with U.S. policy, it was also impossible to go forward without the Americans.

The Canadian federal election of June 1957 put the Liberals out of power after more than two decades of rule. The new Progressive Conservative minority government of John Diefenbaker basically shelved the Gordon Report, and selectively borrowed only certain recommendations in areas such as regional development, expansion of international trade, especially wheat sales to the Soviet Union and China, and policies to implement Diefenbaker's northern vision, Roads to Resources. Gordon himself returned to Toronto and, personally enriched by the intellectual work of the commission, devoted his efforts and money to what he viewed as the central problem – too much foreign (i.e., American) investment in Canadian industry. Lester ("Mike") Pearson had become Liberal leader but knew little about the messiness and brutality of political warfare, only to face the rhetorical scorn of Diefenbaker's ire, who called another election and won a sweeping majority. The Liberals were reduced to forty seats. Gordon admired Pearson, assumed he would become prime minister, and invited his wealthy friends to invest in Pearson's future under the rubric of the Algoma Fishing and Conservation Club, of which Pearson jokingly called himself the janitor (he was MP for Algoma East, in northern Ontario). Gordon's Canadian nationalist vision took hold in the Liberal party. Despite warnings by friends like John Deutsch, Grant Dexter, and the new editor of the *Winnipeg Free Press,* Tom Kent, a British immigrant who had worked at the *Economist*, and saw the views of Walter Gordon and Bob Fowler as "errant nonsense," this "defensive nationalism" would guide Canadian economic policy for another generation.

The United States, of course, retained its global geopolitical responsibilities. Despite past policies by American officials, who played the U.S. hand often nobly, shrewdly against adversaries, and effectively with allies around the world, four years of Donald Trump might not be edifying, but the foundations go beyond the destructive powers of a one-term president. At home, the United States has cultivated its first-class universities to train the best doctors, engineers, scientists, and entrepreneurs at home and around the world. Its immensely rich market of 330 million consumers is a tradeoff when other countries accept the unique role of the U.S. dollar as a store of value, and a security haven for money fleeing from political turbulence. The *Economist* summarizes and underscores this central role: "The world depends on America's currency, and hence an access to dollar payment systems and the banks America has effective control over. Greenbacks fuel trade everywhere. On average, countries' dollar imports are worth five times what they buy from America. More than half of all global cross-border debt is dollar-denominated. Dollars make up nearly two-thirds of central bank reserves." Indeed, trade partners and allies take comfort in the Americans' military and nuclear umbrella, tacitly acquiesced in their unique prerogatives as possessor of a reserve currency, what French President Valéry Giscard d'Estaing called an "exorbitant privilege." For the United States, this means seigniorage gains from financial arbitrage, national macroeconomic (fiscal and monetary) autonomy, and balance-of-payments flexibility against leading currencies like the yen, the Euro, and now the Chinese renminbi or yuan.

The European Union (EU) had hoped the euro, introduced in 2002, would become a rival to the U.S. dollar, with its over $14 trillion in dollar-denominated marketable debt supported by the U.S. government, three times more than marketable euro-denominated debt. In fact, while about 350 million people in nineteen countries belong to the Eurozone, few countries beyond them and former French colonies in Africa use the currency for foreign-exchange transactions, at about 35 per cent, and less than the combined share of the Japanese yen and pound sterling. New York is at the centre of a hub-and-spoke system for global currency exchange, or, to quote Jared Blanc of the Carnegie Endowment, "The global financial system is like a sewer and all of the pipes run through New York."

II

In the late 1970s and early 1980s, as central bankers, governments, and global firms struggled with the new rules and jargon of international finance, most political leaders accepted that this arcane field was beyond their brief, implicitly endorsing the motto of the Bank of England, "Never explain, never apologize." To cite a dramatic example, in the United States, the federal government increased the national debt under presidents from Gerald Ford, who assumed office in 1974, to Ronald Reagan, departing in 1989, by more than the debt amassed by all previous presidents from George Washington in 1789 to Gerald Ford. Canada entered the 1980s as a relatively wealthy country, next door to the United States, with a population smaller than many metropolitan regions in the world, and with its largest province, Ontario, having fewer people than each of the world's top 20 cities. Canada was experiencing growing nationalism in Quebec, four western provinces keen for a bigger say in national policy, and a federal public service heavily imbued with the traditional nostrums of the only two departments that counted, External Affairs and Finance. Canada's geography is almost unmatched by size – at almost ten million square kilometres, the second biggest, crossing five and a half time zones – it faces onto three oceans, and it has the world's longest undefended border with the world's largest economy, a military and scientific colossus.

When Pierre Trudeau returned to power in 1980, knowing his legacy left a thin policy gruel after he resigned as leader in November 1979, not expecting his Lazarus-like transformation with a new mandate, his personal priority was the Quebec referendum, and measures to repatriate the constitution with a bill of rights. Faced with global energy issues, not only the rising price of imported oil, but new wealth for the energy-producing provinces like Alberta and Saskatchewan, his Liberal government introduced the National Energy Program (NEP). It was a program conceived in sin, by a limited number of civil servants and cabinet ministers, and imposed a policy framework that strengthened Ottawa's control over energy policy across the board, with priorities for exploration on crown lands and the high Arctic, a tax regime where revenues would flow to Ottawa, not the producing provinces, and a new crown corporation, PetroCanada, to be Ottawa's window on the energy sector.

Thomas Axworthy calls Trudeau's approach a "strategic prime ministership," where "a prime minister has the time to concentrate extensively on four or five issues at most ... to work intensively on four or five problems (that) requires saying no to hundreds of other requests." In many respects, this advice giving is misplaced. New governments have to deal with campaign promises, some big, some small, some policy outcomes, some involved in policy processes. Few have come to power without a number of election promises, including, for the Tories in 1984, very big items like repeal of the Liberals' National Energy Program and Foreign Investment Review Act and enactment of the Atlantic Energy Accord. The Trudeau government 1980–84 was dedicated largely to the very things that took its leader to Ottawa in 1965 – repatriation of the Canadian constitution from Westminster, enshrining of a Bill of Rights in this constitution, and an open attack on the separatist threat in Quebec. John Turner replaced him in June 1984 and had a chance to govern for at least a year. But a short-term rise in the polls allowed the party hawks to persuade him to call a quick election, which led to a 58-day campaign and the worst electoral defeat in the party's history.

III

Since Confederation, Canada has looked outward, not just exploiting its geography and trade routes and its proximity to the United States but fostering close contacts and historic ties to Britain and France and other countries in Europe. In this sense, Canada has developed an amazing soft-power advantage, a governance notion of *shared sovereignty* arising from the country's federal political structure and unwritten (until 1982) constitution. Canadian politics is a relentless, unending debate between Ottawa and the provinces, exacerbated by the rise of cities with populations bigger than some provinces. Through this maze of perpetual bargaining, political infighting, and policy debate, Canada has emerged as a country admired globally, a bilingual, multicultural society that stands as a model for pragmatic problem-solving, political accommodation, and social inclusion, admired as a parliamentary democracy, and envied by outsiders and begrudged by some for its vast natural resources, and sometimes disparaged for its achievements. While Canadians might afford to be a little smug, knowing voices who say the world needs more of Canada, they also, in a stereotypically self-effacing way, never tire of downplaying national accomplishments. The unsung heroes of much of Canada's national success are found in the political system. The popular phrase "peace, order, and good government" (from the British North America [Constitution] Act, 1867, sec. 91) is taken seriously, and, despite occasional, disastrous failures, Canada has evolved with a competitive party system that provides stability and continuity, accumulated experience, and time to remedy faulty judgment.

Politicians provide a magnet for discontent, anger, the disheartened, and the alienated, but also a wholesome sponge, a channel of communication to listen, to absorb, to meet and confront citizens who feel they won't get a hearing, but want to be heard. If ice hockey is the nation's most popular sport, politics follows as a close second. There is nothing quite like an election – federal, provincial, municipal – to focus the collective mind on issues, personalities, and who is in and who is out. And contrary to accepted belief, Canada's political structure lives for disruption and novelty – the names of the ten premiers and their political affiliations change far more regularly than most people assume. This unpredictability, added to geographical and cultural realities, and a constitutional division of powers, enable provincial governments to act as a check on federal intrusion, and often as a spur to national policy innovation. Similarly, the political culture changes as well, and such old shibboleths that wintertime elections offend the voters – one of the most famous was in the 19th century, when John A. Macdonald lost to Alexander Mackenzie in 1874. In more recent times, Pierre Trudeau returned from political death in biblical-style reincarnation on 23 February 1980 with the whimsical battle cry, "Welcome to the 1980s!," while Liberal Paul Martin lost the January 2006 general election to Stephen Harper's newly christened Conservative Party.

Joseph Howe, the articulate Nova Scotian, offered advice to elected politicians: "You are representatives of the people, and I put it to you, as you are greatly honoured, should you not greatly dare? You are sent to do your duty to your constituents, whether your acts always give satisfaction or not." But who can challenge the wisdom of Sir Winston Churchill on the duties of members of Parliament? Speaking only a few days before he tendered his resignation as prime minister for the last time on 26 March 1955, the veteran statesman and still-sitting parliamentarian opined:

> The first duty of a member of Parliament is to do what he thinks in his faithful and disinterested judgement is right and necessary for the honour and safety (of Great Britain). His second duty is to his constituents, of whom he is the representative but not the delegate. Burke's famous declaration on this subject is well known. It is only in the third task that his duty to the party organization or program takes rank. All three of these loyalties should be observed, but there is no doubt of the order in which they stand under healthy manifestations of democracy.

At their best, members of Parliament are constituency politicians, serving as unheralded ambassadors to show Canada as an advanced, uncorrupted democracy, as well as to help deliver government services for their often very diverse constituents. Across the country, constituencies vary widely by population, from less than twenty thousand because of constitutional agreement, to as high as ten times that number. They also vary by geography – compare those vast tracts in the Arctic with the small, compact density of Hillsborough, encompassing the provincial capital,

Charlottetown, a contrast with the constituencies in Montreal, Toronto, Calgary, or Vancouver. How different it was when the British House of Commons was a gathering that included rank amateurs whose seats were sold to the highest bidder, and Edmund Burke attempted, a bit naïvely, to lead a campaign for parliamentary changes, with the slogan "Economic Reform." Dilettante status remained a presence for a century and a half, where members of the Commons and the House of Lords may have had a sense of *noblesse oblige*, where duty, not ambition, was a prized value. The 20th century brought notable changes, with professional political status, not neophytes like Prime Minister Ramsay MacDonald (a founder of the Labour party in 1900) leaving 10 Downing Street to attend a meeting by hailing a cab while more serious politicians like David Lloyd George and Winston Churchill took their parliamentary duties as their main occupation. This point was not lost on another future prime minister, Edward Heath, a skilled musician, yachtsmen, and the only bachelor to hold the highest office since William Pitt the Younger in 1783. When asked by his tutor at Balliol College, Oxford, "Now that you have taken your degree, what do you intend to do in life?" Heath replied, "Become a professional politician."

Today, Canada's parliamentarians, albeit better paid and offered housing and travel allowances, focus primarily on constituency affairs. Despite disproportionate media attention on Question Period, most MPs spend the vast majority of their time on committee work, scrutinizing legislation, attending debates, and meeting expert witnesses and civil servants during committee meetings. This work by individual members is the key to how Parliament really operates, along with policies to promote jobs and public welfare. Often too boring for the media, too tedious for academics, and too inquiring for some ministers, parliamentary committees review departments' performance against agreed outcomes and budgets. To a degree the public may not appreciate, successful members develop rapport with ministers and MPs in other parties. As a general rule, MPs from Atlantic Canada have earned a reputation as very good constituency workers, in part because they're unlikely to serve in cabinet. One MP who won ten elections under four prime ministers before his appointment to the Senate was Heath Macquarrie from Charlottetown. His regular media appearances, personal letters, and speeches were seen as a model to emulate, and his constituency staff scanned the newspapers for a winning hockey team, a silver or golden anniversary, or a new appointment – chances to send a letter of congratulations. Singer and CBC performer Nancy White, when asked if she was surprised at receiving the good news from her obstetrician that she was pregnant, responded – "I already knew – I've already had my congratulatory letter from Heath Macquarrie"!

Committee participation in clause-by-clause study of draft legislation and its possible unintended consequences may seem tedious. The Standing Committee on Finance has resources for pre-budget, cross-Canada hearings wherein interest groups and individuals can provide direct testimony or prepare briefs on policy and budget matters. Whether these events are held in Ottawa or elsewhere, committees listen to outside experts, who help members wrestle with crucial national issues as they scrutinize draft legislation and provide input to the final report. In short, the committee endeavours of MPs parallel Arthur Conan Doyle's comment about the work of Sherlock Holmes: "It has long been an axiom of mine that the little things are infinitely more important."

Incumbency, of course, starts with election. In the past, many MPs were lawyers, who work in a profession with more flexibility to leave and return than most, excepting perhaps academe. The trends are clearly to elect more women and younger MPs among all parties, although Canada lags many countries outside North America or Asia in gender equality. The oldest sitting member was William Anderson Black, a founder of the Maritime Life Assurance Co. and Conservative MP from Halifax, first chosen in a by-election at seventy-six, who died in office at eighty-six years, ten months, and twenty-two days. The youngest, Pierre-Luc Dusseault, first elected in 2011 in Sherbrooke, was only a month short of twenty years, and he succeeded Claude-André Lachance, a Liberal, first elected in 1974 at twenty. Carole Jacques, the youngest woman elected in the Mulroney sweep in 1984, was only twenty-four, but a younger woman was chosen at twenty for Rivière-des-Mille-Îles in 2011. That election was a watershed, when several younger women under twenty-four years were elected, including Charmaine Borg, in Terrebonne-Blainville, Ève Péclet, twenty-one, and Mylène Freeman, twenty-two.

Effective MPs tend to cultivate curiosity, good listening skills, and an understanding of the dynamics of cross-party dialogue. Like the prime minister's role as chair of the cabinet, House committee chairs hold a position of prominence, judiciously granting the talkers, the decided, and the righteous their say without imposing command and control on the collective task, but also allowing the prepared, the experienced, the prudent, and those who want to make a decision to actually come to a decision. Committee chairs operate in a decidedly partisan environment and must cultivate a set of capacities and skills to reduce conflict and find common cause, often by focusing on sorting through options, in the search for acceptable outcomes. Through such committee work, Parliament and parliamentarians make Canadian democracy work.

IV

Canadians, like members of any electorate, have varying views about their political system, often disdaining flawed leaders and broken promises and displaying bouts of anger and even outrage. Political scientists reflect on such matters but perhaps overstate the case, where two scholars remark: "If Canadians have traditionally been Burkeans, inclined to invest power and responsibility in their elected representatives, they appear now to be becoming Jeffersonians, constitutionally distrustful of government and insistent that their representatives respond more sensitively and directly to the voice of the people." Because most MPs belong to a political party, they carry the banner of party loyalty and decorum, but lack the ideological identification found in the United States and Europe. In Canada and other parliamentary democracies, the caucus offers members a special place, a chance to air grievances, challenge party policy, and at times criticize, sometimes in withering fashion, ministers (including the chief minister) in a no-holds-barred internal debate.

Those members unattached to parties, though not completely unheard of in the 19th century, have certainly been a rare breed in modern Canadian parliaments. Recent examples stand out mostly because they show the flexibility of the electoral system. Chuck Cadman, a former Reform-party member, ran as an independent in Surrey North, BC. André Arthur won Port-Neuf–Jacques Cartier in 2006, and was re-elected as an independent two years later. Nova Scotia's Bill Casey, a prominent Progressive Conservative, saw himself expelled from the new Conservative party, and ran and won in 2008 as an independent. Party affiliation, of course, does bring a measure of principled thinking often disguised as party philosophy. New Democratic Party (NDP) members tend to place prime value on the welfare state and believe government is the best instrument to redistribute income and supply basic services, like health care and education, to those less fortunate. Conservative principles (if not ideology) have a bias towards individual action, smaller, less intrusive government, lower taxes, and the role of the market.

In the period of over 150 years since Confederation, Canada has held forty-two national elections, and by 2015 the voters produced thirty majority and twelve minority governments. The four largest majorities were in 1896, with Laurier's Liberals; in 1958, with John Diefenbaker's win; in 1984, with Brian Mulroney's sweep, the largest ever; and in 2015, with Justin Trudeau's victory. Canada is truly unique among Commonwealth countries, as only two national parties dominate the political system, fielding candidates in every district, but third parties win a sizable share of the votes. Despite the rise of minority parties like the Co-operative Commonwealth Federation (CCF), which became the NDP, and the Bloc Québécois, or the special case of a national, Unionist government during the First World War, under Robert Borden, only the Liberals and the (Progressive) Conservatives have served in government in Ottawa. Only once, in 2011, did the Liberals fail to win enough seats even to form the official Opposition.

In the 19th century, there were seven federal elections (1867, 1872, 1874, 1882, 1887, 1891, and 1896). It was the "age of John A. Macdonald," who so dominated the political landscape until 1891 that he won six elections (including one with a minority, in 1872). Laurier's victory in 1896 was a game-changer for the Liberals and for Canada, as the election anchored two national parties; two successive Liberal leaders, Laurier (headed the party 1887–1919) and William Lyon Mackenzie King (1919–48), governed the country for thirty-seven of the next fifty-two years. The Liberals became what some observers saw as a "natural governing party," developing clever ploys like alternating a francophone and anglophone as leader and building a strong electoral base not just in Quebec but in francophone ridings in Ontario and New Brunswick. Before the Second World War ended, the 20th century saw eleven elections (1900, 1904, 1908, 1911, 1917, 1921, 1925, 1926, 1930, 1935, 1940), and the Liberals gained power in six and formed minority governments in 1921 and 1926. When King became the leader in 1919, assuming the mantle from Laurier, Canada's political landscape became the "age of King," until he resigned in 1948.

By tradition, every prime minister has three central, unending tasks. The first is dealing with issues for Canada's two founding cultures, French and English, and now more direct attention to Aboriginal issues. The second is the governance challenge of Ottawa's relations with the provinces and territories, even more so with overlapping jurisdictions and aggressive premiers wanting more control, including tax points. And the third is the judicious and sustained diplomacy with the United States, including the White House, but also the multiple contacts, agencies, institutions, and the 50 state governments and governors. Starting in 1976, as Canada became an active member of the G7, with regular bilateral and international meetings, now including the wider G20, new demands are placed on the prime minister's schedule. The prime minister, of course, is not head of state, only a trustee, where the exercise of power is held in check. To quote a constitutional historian, Frank MacKinnon, "The people and their parliament can control the head of government because he cannot identify himself with the state or confuse loyalty to himself with allegiance to the state and criticism with treason." The timelines of Canada's prime ministers are shown in Table 1.1.

After 1945, the Liberals still dominated the political terrain, not only in Ottawa but in several provinces, including British Columbia and Saskatchewan, as well as in their base in eastern Canada and in francophone ridings. National elections were held in 1945, 1949, 1953, 1957, 1958, 1962, 1963, 1965, 1968, 1972, 1974, 1979, 1980, 1984, 1988, 1993, 1997, 2000, 2004, 2006, 2011, and 2015. Of the twenty-two elections in 1945 or later, the Liberals won 13, and there were nine minority governments (King in 1945, Diefenbaker in 1957 and 1962, Pearson in 1963 and 1965, Trudeau in 1972, Joe Clark in 1979, Martin in 2004, Harper in 2006). The Liberals' national base, its support in provincial governments, and its general governing principle – campaign from the left, govern from the right – have made it enormously successful, and in minority status, it has even staged its own defeat on a confidence motion and openly stolen the policies of other parties. Only twice, after Diefenbaker's minority government following the 1957 election, and Stephen Harper's after 2006, have the Conservatives gone forward to win another election. In theory, governments had up to five years in office before fixed mandates were enacted, but only two since 1945 – Pierre Trudeau's beginning in 1974, and Brian Mulroney's in 1988 – have lasted five years.

The Liberals have developed the myth of being a "natural governing party" and have won the majority of elections, quietly borrowing from opponents when necessary and running elections from the left and governing from the right, thereby upsetting the red Tory tradition wherein the NDP and Conservatives prefer each other over the "unprincipled" but astute Liberals. But perhaps Robert Borden, quoting the Marquis of Salisbury, was closer to the mark about Canadian politicians: "If you believe the doctors, nothing is wholesome; if you believe the theologians, nothing is innocent; if you believe the soldiers, nothing is safe. They all require to have their strong wine diluted by a very large admixture of insipid common sense."

Table 1.1
Timelines of Canadian Prime Ministers

19th century	20th century	21st century
John A. Macdonald – C*	Wilfrid Laurier – L	Jean Chrétien – L
Alexander Mackenzie – L	Robert Borden – C	Paul Martin – L
John Abbott – C	Arthur Meighen – C	Stephen Harper – C
John Thompson – C	W.L. Mackenzie King – L	Justin Trudeau - L
Mackenzie Bowell – C	R.B. Bennett – C	
Charles Tupper – C	Louis St Laurent – L	
Wilfrid Laurier – L	John Diefenbaker – PC	
	Lester Pearson – L	
	Pierre Trudeau – L	
	Joe Clark – PC	
	John Turner – L	
	Brian Mulroney – PC	
	Kim Campbell – PC	
	Jean Chrétien – L	

*C = Conservative, L = Liberal; PC = Progressive Conservative.
Source: *Parliamentary Guide*

Not everyone makes a good politician, sporting a temperament for constant scrutiny from the media, the voters, or both. Businesspeople in particular rarely do well, because of their incapacity to make compromises, often because the goals are unclear, the means to meet them are vague and experimental, and the feedback can't be expressed in dollars or the bottom line. But there are exceptions. Not everyone holds on to principled earnestness or has the patience for pragmatic outcomes. Any member of Parliament will concede that the legislative "sausage machine," with its demands for party discipline, loyalty, and policy tameness, can breed disenchantment and disappointment. One notable Conservative MP and adviser to Joe Clark, James Gillies, notes this frustration: "Cicero and Demosthenes together would not change a vote in the Canadian Parliament ... Few speeches are even listened to."

In his celebrated novel *The Prime Minister*, Anthony Trollope has one of his characters observe: "One wants in a Prime Minister a good many things, but not very many things. He should be clever but not need not be a genius; he should be conscientious but by no means strait-laced; he should be cautious but never timid; bold but never venturesome; he should have a good digestion and genial manners, and, above all, a thick skin. These are the gifts we want, but we can't always get them, and we have to do without them," In reality, political leaders vary widely in their empathy, warmth, sense of humour, sang-froid, boldness, and feel for the moment. These personal factors have influenced the role and power of political strategists and made all parties more open to democratic processes for leadership. The stylized roles of a political leader and a prime minister are depicted in Figure 1.2.

Leaders of the Opposition face different circumstances, such as when they assumed party leadership and their party was out of power (Diefenbaker in 1956, Pearson in 1958, Stanfield in 1967, Clark in 1976, Mulroney in 1983, Chrétien in 1993, Harper in 2003, Ignatieff in 2008, and Justin Trudeau in 2015; see Appendix A and Appendix B re contested leadership conventions. Since the Second World War, many new party leaders, whether Conservative or Liberal, have had little background in the national party, as distinct from party work in their own province or their own district. Louis St Laurent (succeeded King in 1948) was a lawyer, Pearson was a bureaucrat and foreign minister, Pierre Trudeau (succeeded Pearson in 1968) and Michael Ignatieff were academics, Stephen Harper headed the National Citizen's Coalition, a small-c conservative advocacy group, and his limited electoral experience was offset by his political advisers, personal friends, and (soon) key cabinet ministers.

By contrast, Diefenbaker was a party fixture and a popular speaker well before he won the leadership in 1956. Stanfield had been premier of Nova Scotia since 1956, and regularly attended federal party events, conventions, and policy conferences. Joe Clark was a party activist for the Young Progressive Conservatives before he became an organizer for Peter Lougheed, ran unsuccessfully in Calgary South in the provincial election in 1967, and worked for Lougheed's Progressive Conservatives who gained power in 1971. He ran federally in Rocky Mountain near his home in High River, and won eight times in federal elections.

Before leading it, Brian Mulroney had every conceivable other role in the national party. During his university days at St Francis Xavier (Antigonish, NS) and Laval (Quebec City), he started building a network of contacts that crossed party lines, and in the party, he played multiple roles – raising funds, recruiting candidates, and advising leaders. He also worked as an assistant to Alvin Hamilton, agriculture minister in John Diefenbaker's government. Justin Trudeau was raised as a child of a prime minister at 24 Sussex Drive, travelled with his father on foreign trips, lived in Vancouver after his studies at McGill University in Montreal, and, when courted to run for the party leadership, became a keen student of every prime minister since Pearson, knowing their strengths and weaknesses, including those of his father.

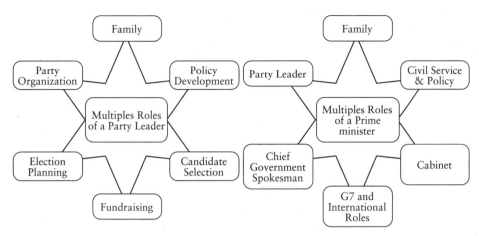

Figure 1.2 Two Role Sets: Party Leader and Prime Minister

Michael McMillan and Alison Loat's *Tragedy of the House of Commons*, based on interviews with former MPs from all parties, further illustrates members' tendency to put party ideology and political advantage ahead of public-policy initiatives, and warns young Canadians considering a political career: "We should not be surprised that so few young people consider the political arena a worthwhile place to invest time or an effective way to make a difference." These conclusions are only reinforced by lower turnout of young voters across the country in recent elections. The Samara Centre for Democracy, which tracks such matters over time, gives Canada a lowly B- (up from C in 2015) for its democratic health, based on participation in government, representative engagement, and diversity in politics and the legislature, which suggests that democratic government is a work in progress, not an end game, requiring constant vigilance and improvement.

History and tradition, of course, have a teaching role in the Canadian system, including civil-service norms of non-partisanship and impartiality. And so do the pressures for political patronage and party affiliation. These lessons aren't new. W.L. Mackenzie King, when asked to join Robert Borden's Unionist government in 1917, agreed to do so, so Newton Rowell took the message to Borden. But King reneged, and later denied he had ever agreed, because what he really wanted was to replace Laurier as Liberal leader. When Laurier won his first election in 1896, he introduced a deputy minister, in charge of the Great Seal, at the swearing in of the new cabinet – Joseph Pope, John A. Macdonald's private secretary and first biographer. That evening, Laurier hosted a dinner party, on the day the Toronto *Globe* editorial called for a wholesale cleaning out of "Tory Deputy Ministers." Pope's wife, Minette, uttered a few words to the new prime minister: "*Ave Caesar Imperator, morituri te salutant* (Hail, Caesar. Those about to die salute you)" – the famous Latin phrase of Roman gladiators about to die. Laurier, showing his usual magnanimity, a scarce resource in Ottawa, gave short shrift to her concerns: "Why *morituri?*" and added, after a pause, "The *Globe*'s rubbish."

V

If politics is defined as the "science and art of government," professions other than medicine are both a science and an art, and good politicians learn by experience that you need both. It takes a certain ego to run for election, and it takes a colossal ego, burning ambition, and tuition paid by experience to succeed, while avoiding the challenging onslaught of hubris. In democratic societies, politicians serve as magnets, for the hopes and dreams not just of the high and the mighty and of the underprivileged, but of the militantly innocent, the sanctimoniously self-righteous, and the evangelical fanatics. Politics, in its highest form, is a calling, a forum to advance issues and policies, and a tool to promote change in society. It can be a messy business, a battle of competing ideas, but it can also be a noble calling, with a sense that a defeat can bring about a sense of humility when the other side may have a better case. Members of Parliament are on the frontline, the foot soldiers in this battle, and often must endure personal ridicule and invective to achieve better results. Politics also needs happy warriors, with an appreciation of an imperfect world and the untidiness of policy and the legislative cycle, and the judgment to understand the folly of certain politicians, like U.S. President Gerald Ford's admitting, well after the fact, "'Sometimes I wish I had never pardoned that son of a bitch [Richard Nixon]."

Political life, in short, requires special skills and the discipline to balance constituency needs, parliamentary work in Ottawa, and personal and family obligations. And on some occasions, it demands that parliamentarians address truly national issues that have long-term effects and consequences, like votes on great moral issues, constitutional change, or agreements with foreign governments. On such occasions, party loyalties must be set aside, in favour of individual conscience or, even more rarely, selfless service, in a partisan, fast-moving, and competitive world where putting the welfare of the whole over the party or the individual at times is essential. Winston Churchill, a parliamentarian for over sixty years, under six sovereigns, put it well: "Courage is rightly esteemed the first of all human qualities ... because it is the quality which guarantees all others."

Politicians and parliamentary committees have a role to play in this political-innovation game, first, by adding to their reactive roles of legislative scrutiny a proactive, forward-looking approach, and, second, by grasping what is important today and needs attention, and what will be important tomorrow but is not well understood. To quote Frank Mackinnon again, "Political long-sightedness is developed in part by rear vision or a sense of history. Those who have practiced the art of viewing the affairs of men over long periods of time are better able to assess the significance of contemporary events than those whose only concern is for the immediate. They appreciate, not just actions, but the consequence of actions ... People flatter themselves unduly if they think the future is based on only the contemporary." Both in government and in opposition, leaders need stamina, good health, a good memory, and a political instinct and a temper that nurtures reflection and judgment as well as humour and even a sense of the absurd. Winston Churchill, with decades in Parliament and two stints as prime minister, offered this advice to Louis St Laurent – "Never walk when you can ride, never stand when you can sit, never sit when you can lie down, and never avoid a washroom when one may not become available."

This book chronicles the policy process in Canada's political system, the cycle of success and failure in governments since 1945, with a focus on the nine years of the two Mulroney governments (1984–93) in the context of its predecessors and its successors. To a degree not fully appreciated or understood, policy initiatives have a very long life cycle, often overlapping governments representing different parties, or separate mandates of the same party. For instance, during the post-1945 era of Louis St Laurent, Parliament discussed issues like repatriating the British North America Act, a new Canadian flag and Canadian constitution, and introducing a bill of rights, first proposed by John Diefenbaker when he was an MP. But as John A. Macdonald knew only too well, political ideas are like fruit – "The fruit is green and not fit to pluck" – and premature picking means getting ahead of the people, a costly political error.

In Canada's political landscape, MPs are the backbone of political parties, the caucus, and the cabinet, and better people make better governments, and better outcomes. Starting in the 1980s with television, then computers and the internet, governments and political leaders faced unprecedented policy challenges. Political leaders had no roadmaps or guidelines to deal with these massive disruptions. All governments face the urgency of the event cycle, knowing that many of their programs are pressing, expensive, and for the long term, while many are less costly but time-consuming, like the apartheid nightmare in South Africa, raising the science voice within the public service, and improving the gender balance in Canadian society. The arc of history may point to the future, but often at a huge cost of political capital. The storyline of Canada's success is really a story of the parliamentary foot soldiers, often unrecognized and unappreciated, who made cabinet ministers better cabinet ministers, and prime ministers better prime ministers, with a measure of praise, well beyond the odd headline in a local newspaper or a clever quip in a political speech. Politicians deserve an ode to political class: in the electoral bear pit of winning – grace, nimbleness, and humility; in the parliamentary chamber of debate – homework, judgment, and assiduity; in constituency representation – selfless restraint, patience, and serenity; in the public square – dignity, imagination, and magnanimity.

VI

The new prime minister, Brian Mulroney, assumed office on 17 September 1984, after the Tories' election sweep on 4 September. The civil service and the public at large hoped the priority for the new government was from the main campaign slogan, "Jobs, jobs, jobs." In Opposition in 1983, and then in their first mandate in 1984, the Conservatives struggled with a series of competing topics but faced a serious constraint: the rising rate of inflation and thus corresponding high interest rates were growing faster each year than the growth rate of the economy. This vicious spiral meant interest-rate payments were taking a larger portion of the federal budget, leading to less money for social programs, and a debt spiral also threatening the exchange rate for the Canadian dollar.

It is not an overstatement that when he won the leadership on 11 June 1983, Brian Mulroney was the best-informed candidate on all matters political, well attuned to the personalities and machinations in his own party and the Liberals and NDP. Unusual for most leaders, he had personal friends in other parties, and many were Liberals, including Jim Coutts, who, at Pierre Trudeau's urgings, had tried to recruit him to run as a Liberal. Both Coutts and Trudeau knew the growth potential of this future leader and prime minister and his powerful Rolodex of people to contact. Alas, Mulroney also knew the problems Canada was facing, and appreciated that strong cabinets, at least in terms of individuals' résumés – Pearson's in 1963, Trudeau's in 1968, and Jean Lesage's in Quebec City in 1960 – all soon faced political troubles. See Appendix C about the size and structure of federal cabinets since 1948.

During his months in Opposition, starting with the two by-elections at the end of August 1983, when he won a seat in Central Nova (where former and future Tory cabinet minister Elmer MacKay graciously stepped down to open the seat, and returned to it when Mulroney won in Manicouagan, in Quebec, in September 1984), Mulroney focused aggressively on developing policy, knowing an election would be called within a year. Some elements for that process were already in place, starting with the Conservative party's Research Office, led by Geoff Norquay (who expected to be fired). There were six other staff members: Emile Franco, Anne Harris, Michael Hatfield, William Hinz, Lynn Richardson, and David Wegenast. By the end of September 1983, the renamed Policy Analysis Group (PAG) included Peter Burn, Jocelyne Côté-O'Hara, Jim Crossland, Lorna Higdon, Jon Johnston, Jim MacEachern, Geoff Norquay, and Ian Shugart, and I was formally in charge, reporting directly to the party leader. From the beginning, the entire effort of the PAG – all draft speeches, policy ideas, working papers, semi-annual think pieces on progress and forward-looking agenda prepared for the Christmas break or summer holidays, and, after September 1984, cabinet notes – were a team effort, often enhanced by Wednesday dinners of good wine and lobster in summer, beer and spaghetti in winter, thanks to Jim Crossland's fountain of creative accounting and hospitality.

The PAG soon became the party's core "civil service," charged with developing policies before the election campaign with such key caucus members as Donald Mazankowski on Western issues, Pat Carney on energy, Michael Wilson and Sinclair Stevens on competitiveness and economic growth, Flora MacDonald on population and labour-market policies, Jake Epp on health care, and John Crosbie on trade and regional development. The PAG worked closely with the press office, the leader's tour group under Lee Richardson, and the election-campaign team. With few members from Quebec in the caucus, a small group of policy advisers, academics, and consultants, led by Jean Bazin and Pierre-Claude Nowlan, worked closely on future policies for the province and the campaign platform. Further, a Policy Advisory Board was established to give ideas for the Government Planning Group, the PAG, and the leader. It included Frank Stronach, from Magna Corp., and Darcy McKeough, from Union Gas and formerly Ontario's treasurer. Another advisory group, focusing in economic issues, growth, and jobs, included Robert de Cotret and met monthly, often with caucus members like John Crosbie, Donald Mazankowski, and Michael Wilson.

With the party in Opposition before the 1984 election, the PAG had three basic functions: first, to work with the party's parliamentary critics – a sort of shadow cabinet, to use the British term – to formulate sector policies, not only for the 1984 campaign but for a future government to enact; second, to be the locus of speech writing, policy briefings, and background papers, such as the campaign debates in 1984, where the PAG drafted working documents and compiled briefing notes; and third, to coordinate background papers prepared by caucus members, external groups, think tanks, academics, and party members. The PAG's seven members had excellent contacts within the party, with the campaign organization and the Conservative premiers, and with domestic and international think tanks and other organizations – investment banks, law firms, and consulting organizations, all serving as sounding boards for policy formulation. The PAG, caucus members, and many parliamentary critics consulted widely with academic experts, legal and consulting firms, think tanks, advisers such as Alan Waters from British Prime Minister Margaret Thatcher's Policy Unit, former provincial and federal cabinet ministers, Liberal and Conservative union leaders like Louis Laberge, Dennis McDermott, and Bob White, and retired deputy ministers, including Simon Reisman, were especially helpful, on substance, process, and occasionally civil-service personalities.

An indication of the advice given to the PAG is provided by a thirty-five-page memorandum from Dr Sy Friedland, a business economist at the *Financial Post* and professor of economics at York University:

> Economic growth will be reduced, and unemployment increased if the inflation rate in Canada exceeds the inflation rate of its tradition competitors. The reaction of Canadians to this unfortunate turn of events typically has been directed at the symptoms of the problems rather than the causes.
> - Tax incentives are adopted to encourage investment.
> - Training programs are introduced to help the unemployed.
> - Failure to adopt new technology is viewed as a problem of ignorant Canadian managers, rather than a reflection of high interest rate, so money is spent on conscious-raising activities as productivity centers.
> - Fears that Canada will be left behind in the high-technology world encourages the government to convert troubled high-tech companies into crown corporations.

In September 1983, Brian Mulroney set out the potential policy traps expected to be created by the Liberals in the House of Commons, by divisions within the Conservative party, or by disagreements between the federal party and the Conservative premiers, such as the energy file during Joe Clark's brief government in 1979, with Ontario Premier Bill Davis preferring policies for low energy prices for consumers and PetroCanada as a window to the global energy industry. He also set out a detailed workplan to be undertaken for the next twelve months, with the parliamentary critics developing policy in such areas as economic competitiveness, energy, foreign investment, health care, immigration, language policy, and transportation.

The three-day caucus in September 1983 of all members at Mont Ste Marie, a ski resort in Quebec an hour's drive north of Ottawa, was a watershed event, a signal of the big-tent approach where personal animosities, leadership rivalries, and candidates' ambitions from three months past melted like snow on a spring day, and, galvanized by a party atmosphere, caucus members who hadn't spoken to colleagues in years struck up new friendships. At this "Mont Ste Marie I," Brian Mulroney outlined the main policy themes, which became the Four Pillars framework – economic renewal, national conciliation, social justice, and constructive internationalism. His speech was a quasi-history of the party, its successes and failures, particularly after 1945, with the Liberals still dominating politics, not, he claimed, because they offered good government, but because the Conservatives lost their bearings as a national party, appealing to narrow interests and failing to focus on the 110 federal constituencies where francophones had a plurality of the votes.

Throughout the autumn and winter of 1983, policy development proceeded under the leader's watchful eye, allowing the caucus team to consult, listen, and prepare draft working papers. Most of the policy plans were presented at Mont Ste Marie II in April 1984 (see Figure 1.3) and later served as the basis for training new candidates, campaign materials and speeches, and the three policy conferences during the campaign, one in Prince Albert, one in Sherbrooke, and one in Halifax.

In early April 1984, to the immense annoyance of several parliamentary critics, the PAG, the campaign organization, and Mulroney's chief of staff, Peter Harder, Deputy Leader Erik Nielsen took it upon himself to cancel Mont Ste Marie II and advised Mulroney accordingly. Somewhat shocked, surprised, and then extremely agitated, I confronted Nielsen in his office, with Peter Harder standing beside me. Nielsen immediately backed down. What was especially disconcerting was how many parliamentary critics openly expressed their disdain for Nielsen's political judgment, weakness

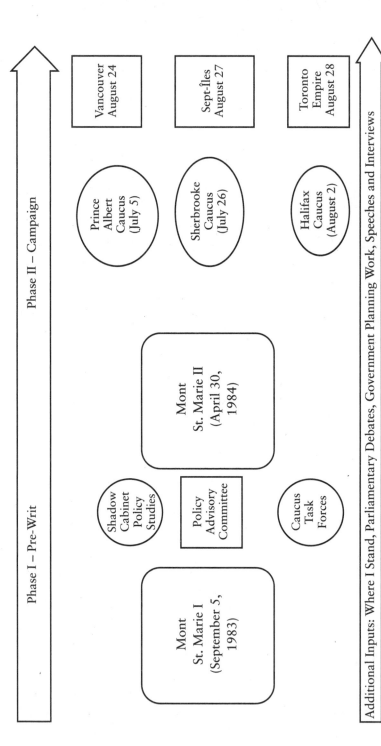

Figure 1.3 The Mulroney Policy Process: (14 June 1983–4 September 1984)

in policy substance, and command-and-control approach with colleagues. At Mont Ste Marie II, attended by all caucus members, most of the central campaign team, and personnel who were planning for government, Nielsen was largely mute.

The Conservatives went into the summer 1984 election campaign comforted by three factors: a well-oiled campaign organization, tried and tested by numerous rallies, riding visits, candidate selections, and major events; a training school for all new candidates, held mostly in Ottawa, but also in Quebec, where the party had to recruit an entirely new slate of candidates through the efforts of Jean Bazin, Michael Cogger, and their seasoned and aggressive campaign team; and a well-thought-out policy platform, with each candidate having a *Pocket Politics* summary and a detailed platform for government. This policy process began in the summer of 1983, helped by caucus members like Doug Lewis, who reflected on his time in Parliament and Joe Clark's short government in 1979. It started in earnest at Mont Ste Marie I.

During the last half of 1983 and early 1984, behind the scenes, Brian Mulroney travelled regularly, even weekly, visiting every province except Newfoundland (to the annoyance of campaign manager Norman Atkins, who was not terribly interested in policy) because he was waiting to finalize the Atlantic Energy Accord. After Mulroney finally did go to Newfoundland, spending three days there in June 1984, John Crosbie and his campaign workers expected to win all of its seven seats. On his weekly tours, Mulroney spent time with MPs and their riding executives, met privately with new candidates and ridings' campaign teams, and gave local media interviews as well as speaking at radio and TV stations. The result was wide local coverage outside the media outlets of Ottawa and Toronto, and a trial run for the campaign team, which would be on the plane, led by wagon-master Ross Reid, the affable and capable Newfoundlander and key backer in John Crosbie's leadership campaign. Ross was helped by his two assistants, Camilla Guilbault and Perry Miele, who served as babysitters for the travelling press court. The press team – Bill Fox, Michael Gratton, and Lisa Van Dusen – in addition to the people in media and press relations, worked closely with the campaign's best two logistics organizers, Bob Chant and Stuart Murray. This whole approach was nicknamed the "boonie strategy" by the Ottawa campaign organization and was largely the work of press aides Bill Fox and Michael Gratton, who were compiling an evolving list of issues, local policy questions, and even notes on the quality of the advance team for regular review and feedback later in Ottawa. Before the election, especially during the campaign, Pat MacAdam, an early riser, photocopied national and regional media stories to distribute to journalists, while his son Lane became the ideal all-purpose assistant to coordinate tasks among campaign groups.

Only days before the election, getting a haircut at the Ritz-Carlton Hotel in downtown Montreal before a rally for eight local candidates, Mulroney was surprised when the barber mentioned that former Prime Minister Pierre Trudeau had been there only an hour earlier. When asked what Trudeau thought of the campaign so far, he gave a short answer: "*Ça va bien.*"

The electoral victory meant it was time to start implementing bold new policies, starting with a Throne Speech six weeks later and an economic statement on 5 November. The policy reforms would undo many accepted assumptions of the pollical class on U.S.–Canadian relations, industrial competitiveness, tax policy, constitutional reform, and Canada's position in the world's major forums.

PART TWO

Policy Outcomes: The Four Pillars of Government

2

Setting a Policy Agenda: New National Policy Challenges

Reformulating Canada's National Policy – A Global Competitiveness Agenda (The Policy Unit) – The Angst of Policy Development – Financial-Services Reform – The Four Pillars – Big Bang in London – Western Canadian Bank Failures – Energy Policy – Science and Technology Policy – Pensions and Venture Capital – The Policy Fallout for the Competitiveness Agenda

Aim at prosperity and employment will follow. Aim at employment and you will get anything but prosperity.

C. Northcote Parkinson

INTRODUCTION

The unsettling events of the 1970s – two oil embargoes and the rise of the Organization of Petroleum Exporting Countries (OPEC), civil-rights unrest in the United States and protests against the Vietnam War, growing inflation pressures, and currency imbalances – left a bad omen a decade later. Think tanks, academe, the leading consulting firms, and public intellectuals such as Daniel Bell, Peter Drucker, Herman Kahn, Irving Kristol, and Daniel Patrick Monahan published weighty tomes on the need for more flexible systems, such as floating exchange rates, market-opening measures to allow foreign competition, and a shift from physical capital to intellectual capital and corporate innovation.

Even John Kenneth Galbraith, the Canadian-born liberal economist at Harvard, who was no slouch when it came to supporting government spending on liberal causes, recognized the strait-jacket of Keynesian pump-priming, the postwar legacy of civil-service thinking in Ottawa's mandarinate. Galbraith set out the policy mix: "If expenditures can be increased but cannot be reduced and taxes can be reduced but cannot be increased, fiscal policy becomes obviously a one-way street. It will work wonderfully against deflation and depression but not very well against inflation."

Old habits die hard, and corporate Canada, the civil service, the political class, and the public at large had only limited appreciation of a high-inflation environment, with interest rates reaching 22 per cent, as huge increases in oil prices had the same effect as a massive tax increase on Western domestic economies, quickly lowering aggregate demand and thus increasing unemployment. For these macroeconomic reasons, global competitiveness became the mantra of the Mulroney government in 1984. It was a paradigm shift in core economic assumptions, open to political perils. The prime minister's experience as CEO of the Iron Ore Company, plus his background as a labour lawyer knowing the deep-seated antagonisms between management and trade unions, was an insider's view of the competitive challenge. After the 1984 election, the general mood in Ottawa, and widely shared by the public service, was a can-do mindset, with a government openly pushing a competitive agenda, sector by sector, region by region. Relative to other advanced countries, Canada was in a catch-up mode across a range of competitive challenges.

As depicted in Figure 2.1, many sectors were concentrated in low-value-added products. To cite an example, pulp and paper, the largest export sector, was shipping logs, newspaper, or cut timber and leaving the making of high-grade paper or furniture to other countries, including Japan. Was Canada to be a low value-added economy, from hogs to logs, or a country with the skills and ingenuity to build companies that could compete in the global marketplace? While the party was in Opposition, its Policy Analysis Group (PAG) had three basic functions: first, to work with parliamentary critics to formulate sector policies, not only for the 1984 election campaign but for possible legislation; second, to be the locus of speech writing, policy briefings, and background papers, as with the campaign debates in 1984, when it drafted working documents and compiled briefing notes, guessing (correctly) the potential questions and proposed answers; and third, to coordinate background papers prepared by caucus members, external groups, think tanks, academics, and party members.

Prime Minister Mulroney, recognizing the policy work his party had done in Opposition, wanted bold action to be a central legacy of his government. Indeed, he often said privately that the ensuing election (in 1988, as it turned out) would be won on policy and organization (i.e.,

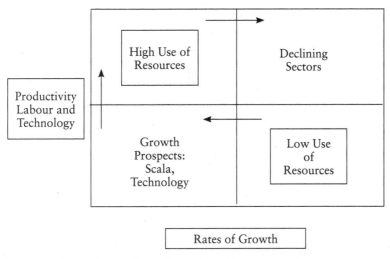

Figure 2.1 Industries and Dynamic Model of Competitive Advantage

bold policies forming the core ideas of election promises to enact during the first mandate) and on a superior campaign organization. Unknown to most people, Mulroney, at the urging of Norman Atkins, Michel Cogger, Bill Fox, Janis Johnstone, and a select few in the Prime Minister's Office (PMO), made a decision immediately after the 1984 election to maintain a strong team at party headquarters and to keep campaign issues totally divorced from the PMO. In fact, a meeting of the full cabinet in October 1984 asked ministers with unspent campaign funds to donate these to the national organization. Sinclair Stevens, sitting on $400,000, immediately offered $100,000.

Starting in September 1984, members of the renamed Policy Unit were Jocelyne Côté-O'Hara, Anne Harris, Jim MacEachern, Pierre-Claude Nolin, Geoff Norquay, and Nigel Wright (in August 1985, Dalton Camp joined), with me as "coordinator" and each member encouraged to have close relations and daily sessions with the press office, led by Bill Fox, and the communications group, led by Ian Anderson. The prime minister's chief translator, Gerard Godbout, was a forceful policy advocate, and knew that any document or speech, if ineptly translated, could lead to ambiguous meanings and outcomes. The Policy Unit coordinated the policy work originating from campaign promises with the lead ministers and their chiefs of staff. Speech writers like Ian Macdonald had a double role, coordinating inputs to the text from various sources and drafting the text for the prime minister's approval. Mulroney, however, often used speech drafts as part of his briefing on complex subjects, and, between direct calls to staffers and outsiders, any speech often had numerous drafts based on his additions and subtractions.

As depicted in Figure 2.2, the Policy Unit also provided briefing notes on issues before cabinet, often coordinated with those drafted by the Privy Council Office (PCO). Depending on the issue, it also worked collaboratively with other PMO staffers and the PCO on materials for Question Period. The work of the Policy Unit was greatly aided by strong policy experts in the exempt staff of the cabinet ministers, often the chief of staff, like Tom Trbovich in Finance, Sal Badali in Defence, Jim Good in Transport, Effie Triantafilopoulus in Industry, and Jodi White at External Affairs. When the cabinet was sworn in on 17 September 1984, media speculation and some disgruntled deputies thought the chiefs-of-staff approach distorted the traditional deputy-minister relationships with both the minister and the clerk of the Privy Council. In fact, the exempt-staff structure, with its own policy advisers and chief of staff, was welcomed by most deputy ministers, in part because it freed them up to formulate and execute policy.

When the government took office, the civil service had an appreciation of the Mulroney policy agenda. Given the emphasis on constitutional issues in Ottawa from 1980 to 1984, with many economic issues put on hold, the public service welcomed the new emphasis on competitiveness policy. There was no shortage of work: in the first six months of government, aside from a Throne Speech, work on an economic statement, visits of the Queen and Pope John Paul II, and a visit to the White House, priority items included the replacement of the Foreign Investment Review Act, implementation of the Atlantic Energy Accord, and measures to deal with national competitiveness. Figure 2.3 illustrates only some aspects of the economic-policy agenda, and doesn't include a range of issues in defence, the Nielsen Task Force on Program Review, social policy, and smaller issues bearing on federal–provincial relations or related to local initiatives in members' ridings or pleas from premiers for their "fair" share of federal funding. Even on its own, each policy issue required immense study and substantial consultations, but most also affected other policies, directly or indirectly, which used up more time for a prime minister sorely lacking in that priceless commodity.

Contrary to media speculation, and commentary in academic circles, there was little worry over civil-service loyalty, a contrast to 1957, after twenty-two years of Liberal rule, or Joe Clark's public firing of the clerk of the Privy Council in 1979. The fact that Mulroney asked Gordon Osbaldeston to stay on in that top job was a signal of future close

Setting a Policy Agenda: New National Policy Challenges 37

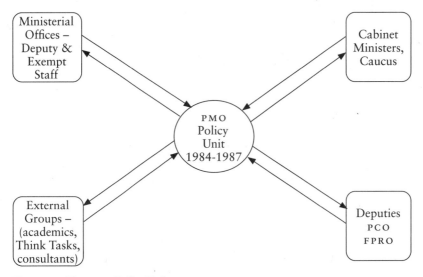

Figure 2.2 The PMO Policy Unit

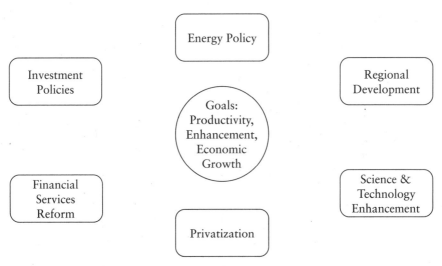

Figure 2.3 The Mulroney Competitive Agenda

collaboration between the political side and the public-service side of government. In the PMO, whether in policy development, on regional files, or in sector competitiveness, senior civil servants such as Fred Gorbet in Finance, Gerry Shannon in External, Ian Clark and Harry Swain in the PCO, Gérard Veilleux in the Federal–Provincial Relations Office (FPRO), and Bob Brown and Paul L'Abbé in Industry became part of the policy "ecosystem," commenting on draft papers and memos, helping to find specific policy expertise in the federal bureaucracy or elsewhere, and advising on the speed and sequencing of policy initiatives.

The Conservative party's policy agenda in 1984, which it intended to implement over two mandates, was aggressively reformist. The powerful contingent of cabinet ministers from western Canada – many with long experience in Parliament dating from the Diefenbaker and Stanfield era – meant that a new approach was attuned to the region's crucial industries – energy, minerals, oil and gas, potash, pulp and paper, and wheat and other agriculture of all kinds – including the markets they served, such as Japan and the broader Pacific Rim, and transportation by airlines, highways, key ports, pipelines, rail, and roads. Led by Joe Clark as secretary of state for external affairs, whose first overseas visit was to Japan, the cabinet ministers from the west – such as Harvie Andre, Pat Carney (born in Shanghai), Ray Hnatyshyn, Charlie Mayer, Don Mazankowski, Bill McKnight, and Tom Sidden – had grown sick of party infighting under Diefenbaker, Stanfield, and Clark. Their priority was clear: they wanted to get on with governing, and executing policies for western Canada.

Unlike Quebec, where many policy issues are viewed through a constitutional prism, western Canadians saw the Mulroney government as a new partner with the four provinces. Two had Conservative premiers, Peter Lougheed, elected in 1971, and Grant Devine in Saskatchewan, with an MBA from the University of Alberta. Both wanted to strengthen and diversify their economies, and, like the federal caucus, western Canadian ministers, and their exempt staff, knew only too well the harsh warnings to Pierre Trudeau at the Western Economic Opportunities Conference in Calgary in June 1973:

> The Western Provinces wish to extend their frontiers and broaden and diversify their industrial base in order to increase job opportunities for their citizens today and in the future. Essential to this undertaking is an adequate availability of financial resources at competitive rates through institutions which are responsive to the particular needs of the Western Provinces. The branch banking system, characterized by the five major Canadian chartered banks ... and head offices in Central Canada, has not been adequately responsive to Western needs. ... The oligopolistic position of the Canadian chartered banks results in higher interest rates than are justified, a more conservative lending attitude, and less flexibility

in their lending policy ... The chartered banks' stimulation of development of Central Canada appears to have been done at the expense of the other regions of Canada.

From the first announcements when the cabinet was sworn in, policy initiatives invited intense scrutiny, not only from the opposition parties, now reduced to a rump, but the *Ottawa Citizen* announcing editorially that "we are the opposition now." The Liberal Opposition's "Rat Pack," a weak imitation of the so-called Four Members of the Apocalypse in the Pearson era, took the lead in Question Period (QP). Over time, this news cycle took a toll when the House was in session, casting a narrative independent of substance. While in office, Prime Minister Pierre Trudeau had sometimes taken inspiration from an inscription pasted inside his daily briefing book: "O Lord, help my words to be gracious and tender today – tomorrow I may have to eat them." But John Crosbie, a vastly underestimated policy wonk with a Newfoundlander's way with words, was closer to the mark on using sarcasm, humour, and invective to deal with the Rat Pack: "Pass the tequila, Sheila [Copps], lay down and love me again."

|

Isaiah Berlin once noted that "what philosophers do in the privacy of their studies can change the course of history." This fact represented a challenge for the proposed policy agenda in 1984, which addressed a hundred years of a protected, cosseted business community with a domestic mindset comfortable with the regulatory system approved by Ottawa mandarins and sanctioned by the political class. Intellectually, it took time to overcome dramatic reforms by the major initiatives of the competitive agenda. Indeed, I kept a card on my desk with the slogan, "When you are up to your neck in alligators, it is easy to forget you are there to clean out the swamp."

In this sense, the aspirational idea that the new government, even with a massive parliamentary majority, could overturn quickly a century-old economic framework was unrealistic. The prime minister, the cabinet, and most of the caucus had a clear picture of the policy priorities, thanks to the parliamentary critics' work in Opposition. It also helped that Jack Manion, then deputy minister at the Treasury Board, in the final days of the 1984 election, had a chance meeting with Geoff Norquay, a member of the Policy Analysis Group, who passed on the party's policy briefing books. As a result, the civil service was unusually well prepared, and assured that the new government was finally addressing the fiscal and competitive challenges facing Canada. The PCO had compiled a list of all the Conservatives' election promises, and Finance had prepared a four-part agenda consisting of the campaign promises around the coherent four-pillar package. For the new government, there was only one choice: proceed, one step at a time. Despite party members' desire to expedite policy results, the process of consultation, at times in an aura of secrecy, became as important as the policy package.

II

The Department of Finance is seen within the federal bureaucracy as "imperial finance" and shudders at the thought it is equal with External Affairs, Industry, or Health, or even Treasury Board. But it is the most important department, with a deep bench strength of competent mandarins, setting the financial and budget rules for the government and crown corporations and affecting Canada's standing in the world through its involvement in international financial gatherings. These issues brought the national government, the Bank of Canada, and the minister of finance into sustained and highly public controversy in the Diefenbaker government and again in the Pearson years. The minister of finance, working closely with the prime minister, sets the budget framework for annual spending, often in great secrecy. No two roles in the cabinet are so crucial. In the last sixty years, three finance ministers have resigned – Donald Fleming from Diefenbaker's cabinet, Walter Gordon from Pearson's, and John Turner from Pierre Trudeau's – all expressing displeasure with government policy and unhappy with the leader, his style of governing, and his (to them) unnerving approach to formulating policy. Michael Wilson was the parliamentary critic for international trade during his time in Opposition, even though John Crosbie had been finance minister in the Clark government, but there was little question that Mulroney would name him to Finance.

The Finance Department and the minister's tasks have changed over several decades (Figure 2.4). Budget timing varied over the years, but Michael Wilson initiated a policy with his first budget in 1985, presenting it in February, thus allowing the provinces and the private sector time to prepare their budgets shortly afterwards, in time for spring meetings of the World Bank, the IMF, and global finance ministers held in Washington. Changes initiated by the McGrath Report, named after

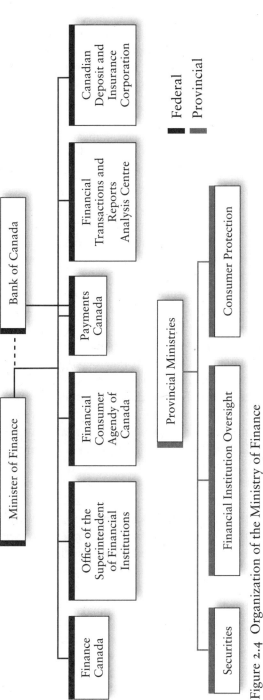

Figure 2.4 Organization of the Ministry of Finance

Conservative MP James McGrath, in December 1984 allowed the House of Commons's Finance Committee, representing all parties, to receive briefs and prepare its "wish list" for future budgets. The conventional rules of intense budget secrecy have become a thing of the past, and today most of the key provisions are leaked to the press, a game of managing expectations and a signal to the financial markets that affects the exchange rate of the dollar.

In Britain, the role of the chancellor of the exchequer is often the accepted path to becoming prime minister. Sir Robert Walpole was the only person to hold both positions simultaneously (1721–42). Starting notably with William Ewart Gladstone, the classic "Little Englander," who allegedly read 20,000 books while in office, kept taxes low, and relished in balanced budgets, who was four times prime minister and chancellor between 1868 and 1894, more recent times had witnessed several chancellors reaching the top job: David Lloyd George, Winston Churchill, James Callaghan, John Major, and Gordon Brown. The finance job in Canada, by contrast, can be a graveyard for aspiring politicians; only three, all Liberals, have become prime minister, two for a short time – John Turner and Paul Martin – while Jean Chrétien won three majority elections, with Paul Martin serving as his finance minister.

The Finance ministry has a wide reach over other departments, now assisted by the Treasury Board, introduced in 1966. Finance's international role has increased steadily, starting in the 1980s as Western governments struggled to address capital movements and coordinate international policy. The organizational architecture of Canada's financial services is the preserve of Finance, while the Bank of Canada focuses on monetary policy and its effects on banking and investment banking. The regulators of financial services – the Office of the Superintendent of Financial Institutions (OSFI) and the Canadian Deposit Insurance Corporation (CDIC), established in the 1960s to insure deposits up to $60,000 in the case of a bank run – for a while supervised performance indicators, with mixed results. Government-insured mortgages and deposit insurance changed the risk premium and offered greater opportunities for moral hazard for the lenders, while some provinces supervised locally incorporated financial firms, including co-ops. Fareed Zakaria, writing in *Newsweek* in 2009, sums up the Canadian approach to banking: "Canadian banks are typically leveraged at 18 to 1, compared with US banks at 26 to 1 and European banks at a frightening 61 to 1. Partly this reflects Canada's more risk averse business culture, but it is also a product of old-fashioned rules on banking."

For much of the 20th century, Canada's "Big 5" banks were ranked among the top fifty financial institutions in the world in profitability and investment returns. Their success was due in part to a protective regulatory regime that set the rules for bank ownership, for entry barriers, and for cross-ownership in other sectors, such as insurance. Historically, Canadian public policy was generally pro-merger, resulting in a concentrated domestic banking industry. Today, while Canadian banks are unassailable in the domestic market (despite the presence of foreign players), only Scotiabank has a global footprint. The combination of a centralized banking system and decentralized capital markets – a route to success for Canadian banks in the 20th century – is now coming into question among public policy-makers and corporate strategists who recognize that financial institutions need to cultivate global financial markets to finance domestic growth. What will best serve the Canadian public – a framework based on capital markets, where ownership of particular institutions is secondary, or one that fosters a Canadian-owned financial industry? What are the policy tradeoffs?

These were the issues confronting the Mulroney government in 1984. As part of the policy consultation exercise, in June 1985 Barbara McDougall, minister of state (finance), released a green paper, *The Regulation of Canadian Financial Institutions, Proposals for Discussions*, which set out the changing global environment of financial services, reforms in areas of provincial jurisdiction (e.g., co-ops, investment banks, and trust companies), and a provision to allow financial holding companies as a one-stop-shopping universal banking model. As in many aspects of public policy, the event cycle took over, as Britain undertook audacious reforms.

III

On 27 October 1986, in a move nicknamed the "Big Bang," the British government transformed the City of London financial district and forever changed the world of global finance, although the world little realized what was happening. It was a rare instance where the United States dithered while Britain acted quickly. This eventually massive change stemmed from a relatively minor issue, fixed commissions on brokered transactions, when the Office of Fair Trading (OFT) began the case in 1979. A change of government – the Labour party lost to the Conservatives led by Margaret Thatcher in 1979 – allowed a settlement that came into effect on 13 March 1984 through the Restrictive Practices (Stock

Exchange) Act. Brokerage firms, or investment banks, could become up to 29.9 per cent owned by foreign interests, a figure later increased to 100 per cent. Additional members would be allowed onto the London Stock Exchange, including foreigners. Unlike the United States, where the Glass–Steagall Act of 1933 separated retail or commercial banking (or clearing banks, the term used in the United Kingdom) and investment banks; cf. Canada's "four pillars" of banking: chartered banks, insurance, investment banks, and trust firms. In the old-boy, clubby network in London's Square Mile (the City of London), the four tier-1 banks were Barclays ($11,637 million), National Westminster ($10,453 million), Lloyds ($4,822 million), and Midland ($4,272 million). By assets, Barclays ($258,339 million) was the largest, followed by National Westminster ($229,272 million), Midland ($111,126 million), and Lloyds ($95,971 million). These regulatory changes were unleashing the City of London on the new world of global banking.

The United States, and New York in particular, viewed events in London with a mixture of shock and awe and worried about the competitive impact of the City's location, so close to the huge financial market of Europe, and its commercial links to Africa, India, and the Middle East, as well as the Soviet Union. The United States had a very different banking tradition, highly decentralized, including regional units of the Federal Reserve. Each major city has large global firms and small, supportive supplier firms (Coca-Cola in Atlanta, FedEx in Memphis, Boeing and Microsoft in Seattle). Canada, by contrast, operates with 13 separate provincial and territorial securities commissions. An open policy question remains: can Canada and other countries afford to have such decentralized regulation of capital markets, which require centralization for coordination and speed to enhance liquidity? If Britain was making it easy to allow both domestic and foreign firms to operate in London, what did this imply for countries like Canada that require foreign capital to finance growth, but using domestic institutions? Canada's five big banks knew the implications, and they sought to strengthen their hand in the reorganization, ideally locating headquarters near the Bay Street financial district in downtown Toronto.

As the Mulroney government set out bold reforms in financial services, the cabinet was fully aware of the regional tensions in the competitive position of several sectors – autos, energy, equalization, export financing, shipbuilding, small-business start-ups, support for small business, tourism, trust firms, and related issues of trade promotion. (Appendix D compares the performance of Canada's economy with those of several other North

Atlantic countries.) Regional interests, which historically took umbrage at and resented the centralizing desire of Bay Street, made new initiatives for changes to the federal Bank Act contentious. Despite attempts by Alberta, Vancouver, and Montreal to promote their stock exchanges, the perception was widespread that the federal Finance Department and the banks preferred the centralizing role of Toronto, especially when 90 per cent of investments by law had to be in domestic securities, which meant investing in publicly traded firms on the Toronto Stock Exchange. For 120 years after Confederation, financial institutions located in central Canada dominated, despite smaller, undercapitalized banks, co-ops, and trust firms established in the 1970s and 1980s in western Canada.

The co-evolution of the chartered banks continued with the creation of the Bank of Canada in 1934, recommended by the Royal Commission on Banking and Currency (Macmillan Commission), largely on the advice of Deputy Minister of Finance Clifford Clark. Unlike many other countries, Canada had had no central bank, as the Bank of Montreal had served that role. Thirty years later, following the recommendations of the Royal Commission on Banking and Finance (Porter Commission) of 1964, the Bank Act of 1967 covered a wider range of domestic institutions. When innovation and competition occurred, the Department of Finance ensured that the chartered banks enjoyed a level playing field, but the new act encouraged new domestic entrants:

> The failure of the Home Bank and a series of mergers in the early 1920s had reduced the number of banks active in Canada from 18 at the outset of the decade to 11 by the end of 1925. In the succeeding four decades, only the formation of the Mercantile Bank of Canada in 1953 altered the measured decline in the number of Canadian banks to a 1961 low of eight institutions. In the late 1960s, however, interest in the formation of new banks revived. The Bank of British Columbia was established in 1967 along with the Bank of Western Canada, which never came into operation. The Unity Bank of Canada was established in 1972 ... The Canadian Commercial Bank (initially the Canadian Commercial and Industrial Bank) and the Northland Bank were created in 1975 ... The Continental Bank of Canada came into existence in 1977 ... Two more small western banks were granted letters patent in 1983 and 1984.

Accordingly, the Bank Act of 1980 created a new class of closely held foreign institutions: Schedule "B" banks. Their operations and market share were restricted, as the act placed foreign banks under federal rules. These changes reflected a desire to exert federal policy in the banking sector: "Approximately 60 Schedule B banks came into existence between 1980 and 1984, frequently through the transformation of foreign-owned subsidiaries which had previously been operated in Canada on the basis of provincial incorporation."

While the entry of foreign banks did not indicate a fundamental change in direction, the emergence of new Canadian banks did. Western premiers knew that their key industries – agriculture and seafood, energy, mining, potash, pulp and paper, wheat – had a Pacific Rim dimension, provinces were selling their bonds in Tokyo, and executives from Japanese security firms and the massive trading firms (Marubeni, Mitsui, Mitsubishi) were trolling western Canada in search of new opportunities. Closer analysis showed that the Liberal federal government was still advised only by Ottawa mandarins, among whom only one of the top thirty-three deputy ministers came from west of Winnipeg, and Otto Lang was the only minister with any political standing in the west. Their memories also extended to the lame response by Finance Minister John Turner, with a promise to amend the Bank Act, and he did introduce a new bill, B-13, four months before the 1974 election, only to see it die on the order paper. When the Liberals regained a majority government, the banking lobby went into a full-court press, arguing that provincial involvement in banking and financial services would weaken Ottawa's control over monetary policy.

Pierre Trudeau and his Quebec lieutenants, but especially Marc Lalonde, knew that a powerful influence in Quebec's financial and business circles was Jacques Parizeau, a former top civil servant in Ottawa, who had been Quebec's finance minister *and* minister of financial institutions and cooperatives. He had big designs for building a powerful financial-services sector around Quebec's own four pillars: the province's pension plan, the Caisse de depot; the Provincial Bank (later the Banque Nationale); investment brokers like Lévesque Beaubien and the Montreal and District Savings Bank; and the large co-op movement and firms like Mouvement Desjardins, with its headquarters in Montreal, at Place Desjardins, and its modernist sculpture, with the inscription: "*La société de demain appartiendra toute entière à ceux qui savent s'unir*" (The future belongs to those who unite!).

Another Montreal-located financial institution was the Federal Business Development Bank (FBDB), a Schedule-D crown corporation, established on 2 October 1975. The FBDB was formerly the Industrial Development

Bank, created by Parliament in 1944 to finance small manufactures, but expanded in peacetime to offer equity financing and advisory services. But unlike western Canada, Quebec had built up a cadre of young, sophisticated, well-educated, and bilingual talents, many with MBAs from Montreal's Haute Études Commericales (HEC), Canada's most underrated (and superb) business school, led by Pierre Laurin, the brother of provincial Education Minister Camille Laurin. HEC had mentors like Parizeau, Claude Béland, Michel Bélanger, Claude Castonquay, Marcel Dutil, Yves Pratte, and Guy St-Germain, who all helped move younger Québécois away from the traditional professions of doctor, lawyer, and priest towards banker, business consultant, engineer, entrepreneur, and investment banker.

IV

In the week of 19–25 March 1985, Prime Minister Mulroney and his cabinet had a packed schedule, including a televised consultation exercise at Ottawa's Congress Centre related to the Nielsen Program Review. Voluntary advisers were reviewing twenty major topics to find ways of improving government service and saving money, it was hoped in the range of $1 billion annually. The prime minister had returned two weeks before from Moscow, attending the funeral of Soviet General Secretary Konstantin Chernenko. That week followed the highly successful Shamrock Summit in Quebec City on 15–17 March, another opportunity to probe the U.S. appetite for a new trade deal with President Ronald Reagan and his team.

Nothing eventful was expected. But unknown to the cabinet or the PMO, trouble was indeed brewing – a bank failure in Alberta. (Table 2.1 depicts the evolution of Canadian banking and financial services.) The Canadian Commercial Bank (CCB) was established in Edmonton in 1976, by the founder and CEO Howard Eaton, but in 1983 he was displaced by Gerald McLaughlan, who soon started to build a network of branches – a very costly exercise.

By 1984, retail deposits accounted for 20 per cent of the CCB's deposit base, a significant jump from zero, but low by the standards of Canada's big banks. The Northlands Bank in Calgary faced identical lending problems. It was a strategy to buy time, hoping the general economic improvement would lessen the firm's risk. Alas, the CCB's true state was not disclosed, precisely the same problem as plagued earlier failures like the Home Bank in 1923. The CCB's shareholders, sponsors, and other supporters (the public at large, and the customers), with moral support from provincial

Table 2.1
The Evolution of Canadian Banking 1867-1967

Era	Regional Issues	National Issues	Policy Issues	Bank Impacts
Limited Expansion of Canadian Banks (1792-1867)	Need for a Stable Currency for To Facilitate Local Trade	Bank of Montreal Serves as quasi-central bank to assure a stable currency	Centralized national branch banking, high entry barriers	Control restricted to British subjects; HQ of banks with branch strategy & limited international reach
Post-Confederation Centralization: (1867-1900)	Strong branch networks per province	Financial Diversification by Public Trust in System	Depositor Safety: Statutes on Capital & Reserves, shareholder liability, high entry barriers	1891 – CBA established by Act of Parliament, Goals of stability and bank branches
Mergers and Internationalization (1900-1934)	Bank Failures	Central Bank Created, 1934	New Rules for Mergers, Bank Failures lead to national oligopoly	27 Banks absorbed by big banks, CBA Serves as price setter
New Era in Banking – international flows of money (1934-1967)	Quiet Revolution in Quebec – threats to four pillars model	Citibank acquires Mercantile Bank in 1963	1954 Bank Act allows personal lending	Banks add mortgage and chattel loans, more international activities
Rise of Global Finance (1967+)	Rise of provincial financial institutions	Political Fears of non-Canadian Control, New Financial Groups	Understanding Tradeoffs in Domestic Banking and International trade & growth	Threats to four pillars of banking, insurance, trust, and investment banks

governments in western Canada, appreciated its early success, as increased oil prices allowed an optimistic growth culture to flourish, which meant extending loans to customers. In the early 1980s, the business environment had shifted dramatically, with a steep decline of house prices, commercial firms facing insolvency, and interest rates climbing steadily because of U.S. Federal Reserve Chair Paul Volcker's anti-inflation campaign.

Ottawa seemed blind to the plight of western Canada, as a series of negative events happened simultaneously. The Liberal government's National Energy Program favoured exploration on Crown lands, especially in the Arctic. Declining world wheat prices put pressure on western farmers, just as the Crow's Nest Pass railway rates were being revised, and rail lines were being abandoned or closed. And population pressures were affecting Saskatchewan. Higher energy costs hit Alberta's gas-based petrochemical sector, affecting especially by-products like plastics. These combined factors created a perfect storm for the western provinces, but other regions faced similar challenges.

However, a recession plays havoc with the asset (loan) side of a bank's accounts, as unpaid loans lead to dynamic repricing, from write-offs, discounting, or new terms for loan payments. Ontario and Quebec were more diversified, but the Western provinces relied on fewer high-growth sectors. The CCB's loan strategy was fundamentally flawed: the bank concentrated on wholesale deposits, inherently more volatile and, even worse, not covered by the Federal Deposit Insurance Corporation (CDIC).

The core dilemma facing the CCB beginning in 1982 was its false hope for new infusions of capital. Significant write-downs would have led to further public recognition of the deterioration of its capital base, a perverse case of the American subsidiary dragging the Canadian parent to insolvency. The house of cards was about to collapse. In Ottawa, the actions of the American regulator, the Federal Reserve Board (FRB), forced William Kennett, the inspector general in Canada, to recognize the CCB's precarious state. In response, the bank's CEO, McLaughlan, assured Kennett that the U.S. regulators were overreacting, as they often had! None the less, despite his promise to do so, McLaughlan did not forward the FRB's report to Kennett, who unfortunately accepted the bank's version of events, to be sorted out at the meeting scheduled in Ottawa for 14 March. Kennett then went on holidays until 20 March, a baffling move. But the event cycle kicked in, with its own momentum. By 8 March, officials at the Bank of Canada were fully apprised, and at the 14 March conclave, the idea of a rescue package resurfaced, and Kennett, in order to buy time, arranged liquidity support from the Bank of Canada.

The next day, on 15 March, the assistant inspector general and André Brossard, the director of compliance for the OIGB, met with Secretary of State (Finance) Barbara McDougall, and on the same day, at the suggestion of Gerald Bouey, governor of the Bank of Canada, the board of the CDIC was convened, with also present Deputy Minister of Finance Marshall Cohen; Don McPherson, the assistant inspector general; and Serge Vachon, chair of the Canadian Payments Association. On their own, Bouey and McPherson decided to invite the CEOs of the big five chartered banks to assess the impact of closing the CCB. Bouey was the leading advocate to save the bank, a decision he would later regret. On 14 May, Michael Wilson and Barbara McDougall, with Marshall Cohen and Governor Bouey, plus the inspector general, decided "tentatively" to save the bank by implementing the plan originated by McLaughlan, based on a memorandum from McPherson. Under this plan, the CDIC would purchase all the bank's loan-loss provisions ($244 million), to be repaid by its granting the CDIC 50 per cent of future profits for fifteen years. In Calgary, the Northland Bank was in a similar position, what Robert MacIntosh, the head of the Canadian Bankers' Association, called a "perceptual contamination" facing unsustainable loans in the oil sector, and he feared all financial institutions in western Canada would face liquidity crises, and then bankruptcy.

At a meeting on 22 March – a Friday, a fateful day in a busy week – the rescue plan was presented, and Governor Bouey made it clear that the issue was solvency, not liquidity, and a clear decision had to be taken before markets opened on Monday. Alan Taylor, CEO of the Royal Bank, indicated little interest in a merger, forced or otherwise, concluding that the CCB's strategy was fundamentally flawed. The crux of the issue was whether the $244 million would be adequate. It was not clear that the rescue initiative needed the backing of the government or of the prime minister, but the governor knew that the ministers had to be warned in advance. The prime minister and many powerful ministers – Pat Carney, Ray Hnatyshyn, Charles Mayer, Don Mazankowski, Bill McKnight – were attending the consultation at the Congress Centre, with Stanley Hartt presiding over the televised discussions.

A message went out to the Congress Centre – in a pre-digital era, Ottawa had a huge convoy of messengers delivering notes, memorandums, and confidential papers – and late Friday afternoon, Michael Wilson and I were summoned to the Bank of Canada and informed about the proposed rescue package. I asked that the prime minister be informed immediately, returned quickly to my office in the Langevin Building, across the street from the Parliament Buildings, drafted a memo on the events at the Bank of Canada, and added that the key question was two-fold: should the government be involved in a bailout, and is the proposed figure, $244 million, sufficient to placate depositors? I arrived about 9:30 p.m. at 24 Sussex Drive, the prime minister's residence, and briefed him with the memo and the two key questions. He requested a meeting at 24 Sussex at 8 a.m. on Saturday to address the larger issues. Since Barbara McDougall was not in Ottawa, he asked me to arrange a government plane be sent to bring her for the breakfast meeting. I then left to join a very late dinner with Nigel Wright and my brother to discuss his tourism consultations paper.

While the bailout was the context of the breakfast meeting, the larger issue was deciding between the government's competitive agenda, an unpalatable tradeoff to solve an immediate problem by a thrust of government subsidies and accepting perverse incentives, the moral hazard, or staying the course. Even in jittery markets, it is difficult to believe that the CCB's failure would jeopardize the entire sector, as both the policy advisers and the banks knew too well. Attending the breakfast with the prime minister at 24 Sussex Drive were the following:

- Gerald Bouey, governor of the Bank of Canada
- Marshall ("Mickey") Cohen, deputy minister of finance
- William Kennett, inspector general of banks
- Barbara McDougall, secretary of state (Finance)
- Charles McMillan, senior policy adviser to the prime minister
- Bernard Roy, principal secretary to the prime minister
- Michael Wilson, minister of finance

The participants recognized these challenges, and the prime minister set out the question at the start: should the government consider a bailout, and was the amount sufficient? Curiously, the $244 million was an estimate from bank CEO McLaughlan, not the Finance Department, and a decision was needed before the bank's opening on Monday in Edmonton and before the stock market began operations at 9:30 a.m. in Toronto, plus press releases and possible briefings, and advance warning to the Toronto Stock Exchange, and preparation for Question Period on Monday.

When asked by the prime minister what the government's position should be, the three central officials – Bouey, Kennett, and Cohen – recommended the rescue package. All participants from the political side advised against it. The prime minister reluctantly, and decisively, sided with the officials, perhaps reminding himself of the earlier conflicts in 1962 between Governor James Coyne and John Diefenbaker. Besides, the government's new budget was to be presented to Parliament within sixty days.

The resultant press release on Monday 25 March, drafted by Finance, reassured the public that the bank was solvent and would continue to be supported by the four Western provinces. It provided the details: the CDIC, funded by its member deposit-taking institutions, would provide $75 million, and the remaining $180 million would come equally from the province of Alberta, the banking group, and the government of Canada, $60 million each. In a separate arrangement, the governments of Alberta, British Columbia, and Canada would purchase up to $39 million of the subordinated debt. When the two banks opened on Monday, the news of the bailout started a contagion run, with over $1.5 billion withdrawn, including the holdings of the big Toronto banks hoping to limit their losses.

By July 1985, only four months later, Michael Wilson learned that the bank would have to be liquidated, and in September the inspector general advised him to appoint a curator. The Continental Bank was eventually acquired by Lloyd's Bank in Britain, which later sold it to HSBC in 1990. The other two small western banks, the Western & Pacific Bank of Canada (1983) and the Bank of Alberta (1984), amalgamated as the Canadian Western Bank ("Think Western"), which survives to this day.

In the end, the bailout package failed. In retrospect, its supporters had badly underestimated the extent of the problem loans at the CCB, reflecting the long history in banking circles – and hence the required level of equity capital, which affects leverage levels for loans and the risk level for both lender and borrower. Yet the Canadian government agreed, as much to appease the bureaucrats as to settle the real solvency problem.

The decision to attempt a bailout was costly, almost $2 billion, but, as John Turner, the Liberal leader, discovered, the political fallout was serious, because the government had unwittingly assured the public and the depositors that all was well. The government was consequently liable for all deposits, not just the insured amount. It wasn't the first instance where the civil service took the lead in making policy against the political instincts of the cabinet. For ministers, it was a case study of damned if you do, damned if you don't.

V

Financial-services reforms, like other policy initiatives, put two forces on a collision course. The first was an ideological test, i.e., free-market purity and price setting, against the practical world of politics and personality. An indication of the multiple goals and challenges was the enhancement of Canada's small-business sector. Industry Minister Sinclair Stevens had three ministers of state reporting to him: André Bissonnette for small business, Tom McMillan in Tourism, and Frank Oberle in Science and Technology. The deputy minister, Bill Tsechie, and the associate deputy, Gordon Ritchie, who would later be seconded to the free-trade negotiating team, provided a masterful briefing to the ministers and some of their exempt staffers, led by Chief of Staff Effie Triantafilopoulos. This briefing later led to a memo to the prime minister, stating that Canada was one of the few advanced countries where industrial policy was divorced from trade promotion and development, which were later transferred to External Affairs. It singled out Japan's mighty Ministry of International Trade a8nd Investment (MITI) and France's Ministère du Commerce Extérieur, which worked closely with le Centre Français du Commerce Extérieur (CFCE). Sinclair Stevens had developed a reputation in the media as a cost-cutter while Treasury Board minister in the short-lived Clark government, and he and many MPs wanted a vigorous campaign to privatize crown corporations. On that list was the Federal Business Development Bank. But in the time before the 1984 election, pursuant to his own private business interests, he had travelled to places like Silicon Valley and Boston, and he became an apostle of a free-wheeling startup culture and a critic of Canada's banking oligopoly.

Shortly after taking office in 1984, Stevens visited Cape Breton, Liberal Allan J. MacEachen's political fiefdom, and saw for himself the reckless financial waste and subsidies to obsolete industrial projects, such as SYSCO, the aged steel mill in Sydney, and nearby, DEVCO, the crown corporation that operated the coal mines, often extending to three miles under the Atlantic seabed. Near Port Hawkesbury was one of Atomic Energy of Canada Limited (AECL's) two heavy-water plants, constructed to supply the Canadian Deuterium Uranium (CANDU) reactors, with the other in Glace Bay, and they employed fewer than 600 workers, who were trapped in a declining product line in a declining industry, but unable to find work elsewhere while unemployment was running at 20 per cent. The entrepreneurs he met, like Joe Shannon, had an optimistic bent, but complained about financing problems with "Toronto's" banks. Paradoxically, when AECL announced that its two plants would cease operations, the FBDB provided advisory services for the laid-off workers.

The FBDB had a prominent role in the plans of former Liberal ministers like Ed Lumley, who wanted to locate two officials from the Department of Regional Industrial Expansion (DRIE) near the FBDB, the first to do due diligence, the second to approve loans. Within the federal Conservative caucus, Don Blenkarn, the MP for Mississauga, who aspired to be minister of finance, given his role as finance critic in Opposition, now chaired the House of Commons's Finance Committee. Blenkarn was a tyrannical and at times quite abusive critic of the FBDB, ostensibly for its financial losses, about $65 million annually. Behind the scenes, he saw the bank as a "Quebec institution" and wanted it privatized, closed, or merged. CEO Guy Lavigueur, expecting the worst, met Small Business Minister André Bissonnette, who suggested a meeting with members of the Conservative caucus, which was quickly arranged. Lavigueur, not a neophyte in the ways of Ottawa, brought senior managers and presented a vigorous defence of the FBDB's operations, including business advisory services and loans to small businesses – over 100,000 cases. Blenkarn didn't attend, so a meeting was set up soon afterwards, when he was domineering and uncompromising, and even offered Lavigueur another job in government when the bank closed.

Blenkarn felt self-assured, in part because he saw the Nielsen Program Review as the perfect vehicle to terminate the FBDB. The Industry Department had a new task force called Services and Subsidies to Business under Harry Swain, assistant deputy minister for plans, and Jack Walsh, a vice president at DuPont Canada, representing the private sector. It had a big agenda, and, like Heinz, the department had fifty-seven subsidies, costing over $4.5 billion a year in grants, $7.7 billion in federal revenues, and directly employing 11,440 person-years of staff, with another 155 programs providing business services to small firms. This review exercise, followed by others in areas as diverse as agriculture and real-estate holdings, focused on the mandate for program review and offering cogent advice to the ministry's task force.

As the Nielsen Task Force proceeded, DRIE officials continued with their own work, including an internal study on the financial gaps for small business, initially confirming Conservative doctrine that private firms were addressing the gap. DRIE's program, the Small Business Loans Act, with an annual payment of $23 million, turned out on closer examination to be a subsidy to the big banks. The FBDB did the market analysis for small business, and banks made the safe loans. Meanwhile, the Nielsen Task Force completed its work in the autumn of 1986, including its review of the FBDB. It recommended that the government consider restricting planning services to twenty branch offices, increasing the price for these services to recover costs, and setting up one-stop shopping for small businesses, at least for a two-year trial period. The bank's CASE counselling program, first thought to be redundant in the private sector, received endorsement from the Canadian Federation of Independent Business (CFIB) and the Canadian Organization for Small Business (COSB). In the end, the Industry Department's task force had two proposals about the FBDB – either termination or expansion, with the FBDB as the lending unit not only for small businesses, but for other programs in agriculture (Farm Credit Corporation), in the Department of Communications for film production, in fisheries, and in Student Business Loans. In the Industry task force, despite these two conflicting views, the private-sector co-leader, Jack Walsh, preferred termination.

To give advance warning, Peter Harder, Erik Nielsen's chief of staff, visited the Langevin Building to meet Bernard Roy, other members of the Policy Unit, and me, who were working on two related programs, the Atlantic Canada Opportunities Agency, to be announced in the forthcoming Throne Speech, and Western Diversification, ironically using policy advice from the FBDB! Peter Meyboom, the deputy minister of the Nielsen Task Force, contacted the FBDB's CEO, Guy Lavigueur, to update him on the decision to terminate FBDB. On his own, Lavigueur contacted Bernard Roy, who also kept a close eye on all things related to Quebec. It was well known that the Canadian Bankers Association was running a lobbying campaign to terminate the FBDB and having other business lobbies – the CFIB and the Chamber of Commerce – declare it a money-losing, subsidized institution that was now redundant.

The timing of the Industry task force's work couldn't have been worse, as another file was getting attention, the plight of the "rustbelt" economy of eastern Montreal, with factories closing, unemployment rising – over 30 per cent in certain neighbourhoods – and labour unions and municipal officials calling for action. Montreal had set up a planning exercise, the Picard Report, to identify economic priorities. The prime minister had asked me to focus on some investment possibilities there, and in my memo, I suggested attracting international agencies, on the model of the International Air Transport Association, originally established in Havana in 1945, now located at Place Victoria in Montreal. Harry Swain, now in the economics section of the PCO, and secretary to the Cabinet Committee on Economic Development, added an idea about developing an information-technology (IT) centre for small business. (The final Picard Report emphasized attracting headquarters of large UN-related international organizations, in sectors such as aeronautics, biotechnology, and communication technology.)

A meeting in the PMO's boardroom was short and sweet, and Bernard Roy then set up a meeting at 24 Sussex with the prime minister, and that too was brief, with a decision to overturn any recommendations to terminate the FBDB. Roy made a call to Erik Nielsen to tell him to delete this recommendation. A few weeks later, at a meeting in the PMO's boardroom, Jack Walsh openly admitted that he and his task-force members had focused on internal FBDB operations, not on the larger, national landscape and the frustration and discontent outside the "Golden Triangle" about the absence of venture capital. As it turned out, when he returned to DuPont, Walsh played an activist role in another Mulroney initiative, the development of the Montreal Protocol of 1987 banning chlorofluorocarbons (CFCs). Clearly, the CBA, representing the big banks, had overplayed its hand. Some cabinet ministers were deeply annoyed. And Ray Hnatyshyn, not one to speak out in cabinet on issues outside his own department, spoke for many – with a finger pointing at Michael Wilson – deploring Finance's subservience, even obeisance, to the banks, which sought to control the four pillars, including insurance, and stated that this stance was creating a political backlash. Addressing his ministerial colleagues, he said that if it was a choice between supporting the few bank managers in his province, with a mandate from Toronto, there was an easy choice – keep the banks at bay. No one in cabinet demurred.

VI

The bank failures in western Canada affected the politics of competitiveness and illustrated the political reality that the success or failure of one industry, such as energy, had a widespread collateral effect on other sectors, like real estate and financial services. After Mr Justice William Estey submitted his report on the bank failures in 1986, and suggested various regulatory changes, such as increasing CDIC premiums, the big five banks essentially agreed with Allan Taylor, the CEO of the Royal Bank, that no significant changes in the federal government's regulatory and supervisory role were necessary. Other views were more guarded, including that of CBA head Robert MacIntosh, who felt the bank collapse weakened the role of the smaller financial firms in the secondary market, including loans for small firms. MacIntosh was a protégé of Cedric Ritchie, chair of Scotiabank, who worried that commercial banking was an exercise in protecting depositors, while investment banking was high risk–high payoff casino capitalism. The latter, Ritchie felt, involved too much MBA-school shenanigans, not enough Sunday-school caution.

In June 1985, the swearing in of David Peterson's Liberal government ended 42 years of Progressive Conservative rule in Ontario. The next year, the new government, faced with massive lobbying, ended ownership policies for securities firms, which had in effect "captured" the Ontario Securities Commission (OSC). Security firms like Burns Fry, Wood Gundy, and Yorkton were also watching events unfold in Quebec, knowing the federal government had plans to promote Vancouver and Montreal as financial centres. Scotiabank wanted to establish a brokerage house in Montreal. OSC Chair Stanley Beck, a Toronto lawyer and former dean at Osgoode Law School, lobbied the Peterson government and minister Monte Kwinter to allow the banks to own securities firms.

Various meetings with Kwinter were held in secret, and the bank CEOs pushed for the removal of regulatory barriers, including ownership, to instigate a Toronto-based "mini-bang" to match London's Big Bang, and at the same time protect the province's strengths in financial services. It would also allow the securities firms' shareholders and executives a financial windfall through takeovers by Canadian banks. Ontario then asked Ottawa to announce amendments to the federal Bank Act. Finance Minister Michael Wilson had met with Canada's five bank CEOs at Château Montebello, a resort in Quebec outside of Ottawa, on 19 October 1986. Only the deputy minister, Marshall Cohen, and CBA head Robert MacIntosh were invited to discuss the way forward. The banks realized their vulnerability, given reforms in London, the potential entry of large American investment banks like Goldman Sachs or Lehman's or of financial conglomerates like American Express or GE Capital to compete in Canada, and the stirrings of change in Quebec, led by the Caisse de dépôt.

By December 1986, Ontario wanted to go even further, with a "steadily bigger bang," while the new federal minister, Tom Hockin, who had replaced Barbara McDougall, who moved to a new ministry, Privatization, preferred a go-slow approach, arguing the federal supervision of banking. A measure of the tiny, clubby world of Canadian finance was the fact that Tom Hockin, as well as David Dodge and Fred Gorbet in the Finance Ministry, knew many of the players in the investment community – like Tony Fell and Ted Medlin – from their school days at St Andrew's College in Aurora, north of Toronto. But the cycle of events was moving fast, settled temporarily by a truce between the two governments in April 1987, whereby Ottawa would supervise the regulation of banks and their in-house security firms while Ontario supervised the independent brokers. The federal Office of the Superintendent of Financial Institutions would be the watchdog for the entire industry.

Tom Hockin released a revised green paper, *New Directions for Financial Services*, a discussion paper setting out proposals and options for legislative changes. He argued that the "philosophy underpinning financial services integration will be to build, not buy." "To protect against harmful concentration, acquisition of financial services companies will require the approval of the Minister of Finance. As a rule, large financial institutions will not be allowed to acquire other large financial institutions." Within weeks, the reform package was hijacked, first by Ontario's moves to protect Toronto's banking turf, and then by Quebec's strengthening of financial services in Montreal. The cosy and secretive world of Bay Street had quietly decided its next moves, a massive round of mergers. CIBC bought Wood Gundy, Montreal (BMO) took over Nesbitt Thompson, National acquired Lévesque Beaubien, the Royal Bank purchased Dominion Securities, and Scotiabank bought McLeod, Young and Weir. Foreign banks like Germany's Deutsche Bank, Japan's Sanwa Bank, and Citibank from New York acquired smaller dealers. In Ottawa, various civil servants worried about future outcomes for the sector. No one doubted the powerful role of the Canadian banks, but also the meekness and limited power of securities regulators, especially the biggest, the Ontario Securities Commission, with its dual functions as both an investigator of corporate missteps and an enforcer, with a pathetic record. This view was also shared by money managers, pension-fund analysts, and investment advisers like Stephen Jarislowsky, a prominent Montreal critic of the cosy smugness of Bay Street.

In short order, billions of dollars changed hands, and Toronto's brokerage firms and their executives made out like bandits, selling not only at a high premium but at double book value. The minister, Tom Hockin, and senior bureaucrats like David Dodge called for more independent directors, and were not initially greeted with enthusiasm – BMO's Bill Mulholland asked if a few "nuns and social workers" would meet this test. In the end, the five Canadian banks were the big winners, and now controlled two of the four pillars. They, with their various subsidiaries, over 130 in all, became financial conglomerates.

These policy matters formed a series of complicated issues facing Ottawa, and they remain a challenge today. Cedric Ritchie, the shrewd and thoughtful chair of Scotiabank, rarely left little doubt to his listeners that he worried about the mix of retail banking, the need to protect depositors, and Canada's failure to develop a second tier of strong financial institutions, a contrast to the United States, Britain, and Japan. In Canada, public policy towards financial services destroyed any semblance of balance between "global competitiveness" and significant "domestic competition," especially in the personal or retail sector. In 1986, the revised proposals announced by Tom Hockin effectively gave 80 per cent of the Canadian financial sector to the five chartered banks.

In the space of fifteen years, Canada's banks came to dominate three of the four pillars – banking, investment banks, and trust firms – and were well established in the fourth pillar: insurance. Canada is the only major country that allows such high levels of concentration. In terms of governing jurisdiction, while the banks were federally regulated, the securities dealers were provincially regulated, and the remaining two pillars were regulated according to province of incorporation. In truth, both provincially and federally, this institutionally driven policy also shows that personalities do matter. Moreover, Ottawa's constitutional lack of sole jurisdiction over capital markets did little to increase the policy interest by federal politicians and the Department of Finance. It was all an echo of Sir Josiah Stamp, a director of the Bank of England: "Banking was conceived in iniquity and was born in sin. The Bankers own the earth."

VII

The reforms of financial services, like those the Tories had already enacted in energy, foreign investment, privatization of crown corporations, and trade promotion, and like others by then under way, from broadcasting to science and technology, illustrated to the prime minister and the cabinet how reform had a federal–provincial dimension and often international implications. Bold reforms also reduce the stock of political capital. These issues were at front of mind for the Finance Department, the prime minister (who had served as a director at CIBC), and some CEOs like Cedric Ritchie and Paul Desmarais at Power Corporation, and offered an early sign that the Canadian market players had to sort out a competitive-policy package. However, reform of financial services was facing a headwind based on self-interest on Bay Street. Subsequent events would show how the banks and their lobby association had alienated huge sections of the corporate community, including small business, and created fear that the banks would take over the coveted insurance sector.

Four big firms dominated an extremely diversified and segment insurance industry: London Life, Manulife, and Sunlife in Ontario and Great-West Life in Winnipeg. Federal regulation of life insurance had fostered, as with the banks, a goal of stability. New reforms proposed in 1987 limited 30 per cent common shares of any one company. Insurance policies were protected by regulations that ensured policy reserves met certain investment standards, such as low risk and conservative capital adequacy. For instance, investments in mortgages of commercial buildings or a portfolio of housing could total only 75 per cent of a property's real value. The insurance companies went from a relatively passive stance to a more aggressive approach once they fully appreciated the banks' hardball stance about entering the insurance sector.

When Finance proposed new regulations requiring trust companies to reduce their equity ownership from 100 per cent to 65 per cent of a single entity, a move that meant Power Corporation had to reduce its ownership holdings in Montreal Trust, the traditional four-pillar framework was about to collapse, which helps explain why Power Corporation later sold its holdings in Montreal Trust to Scotiabank at their peak price. The insurance companies lobbied heavily to allow demutualization, a policy reform to allow public companies listed on the stock exchange to be owned by shareholders.

The next round of financial-insurance reform started in 1999 when five firms demutualized, issuing eligible policy-holders shares in the new firms: the Canada Life Insurance Company, Industrial-Alliance Life Insurance Company, the Manufacturers Life Insurance Company, Mutual Life Assurance Company of Canada, and Sun Life Assurance Company of Canada. Clearly, there was a distinct difference between life-insurance companies, where Canada excelled, and property and insurance firms, which were mostly foreign. To give an example of Canadian firms' aggressive foreign strategies, Manulife acquired large holdings in China, Japan, and Vietnam, while Sun Like did the same in India and Indonesia. Except for Scotiabank, which aimed to become global, the four other banks expanded operations abroad, but lost heavily outside North America. TD, acquiring the Commerce Bank in New England after the Wall Street bank crisis of 2008, has become effectively a mid-sized North American bank.

Previous governments had made changes to the Bank Act, enacting strict ownership rules for Canadian banks: no single shareholder could own more than 10 per cent of a bank's stock (the reason why Hong Kong's Li Kai Shing was restricted in share-holding at CIBC, for instance), and foreign ownership was restricted to 25 per cent of any one institution. In effect, the ownership rules mandated that banks had to be widely held by Canadians, and that remains a cornerstone of banking policy today. However, collaterally, this policy means in reality that Canadian banks and their executive management teams cannot be acquired by foreigners or by other Canadian concerns, a policy with perverse incentives. It prevents the commingling of industrial and financial institutions, which was a concern when so much industrial activity was dominated by large conglomerates like Argus Corporation, Brascan, Canadian Pacific, and the Irvings, and Pierre Trudeau's government established the Royal Commission on Corporate Concentration in 1976, after Power Corporation attempted to buy Argus Corporation. The Bank Act of 1967 also granted the banks protection from any real social control: Parliament restricted takeovers, the stock market discounted foreign takeovers, and government regulations freed bank management from direct challenges by Canadian entrepreneurs. If controlling blocks of stock are not in play, how easily can CEOs and the senior management be changed?

All such corporate moves remained a concern in Ottawa, and the ongoing aim to create a national securities regulator, dating back to 1935, when the Royal Commission on Price Spreads recommended one, has always met fierce provincial opposition. By the 1980s, as global finance changed dramatically, Ottawa advanced the case for a national regulator as a federal responsibility under the trade-and-commerce section (91.2) of the constitution. Stephen Harper's Conservative government appealed to the Supreme Court, which in 2011's *Securities Reference* held that a draft Canadian Securities Act was outside of federal jurisdiction. Jim Flaherty, the finance minister, the third successive incumbent to strengthen Canada's image in global finance, following Michael Wilson and Paul Martin, responded with a new Memorandum of Agreement (MOA), a voluntary measure entered into by provinces and territories, to set out a passport scheme where each jurisdiction would pass parallel legislation. Six provinces and one territory accepted this compromise, but not Alberta, and Quebec went further – the province sought a reference to the Quebec Court of Appeal. Even Doug Hyndman, head of the BC Securities Board, admitted the complexity of onerous filings – over 1,600 firms worth under $10 million forced to submit documents.

The majority on the Quebec court agreed that the MOA may constitute illegal delegation, but also argued that the court did not have jurisdiction to review the MOA, an intergovernmental arrangement, not a piece of legislation. The minority opinion was far less equivocal: Justice Mark Schrager, disagreeing with the majority opinion, argued that both the federal and provincial laws were *intra vires,* but agreed with the majority that the MOA may constitute illegal delegation, but there was no breach of provincial sovereignty, if the legislature chose to amend or repeal the act at any time. He also argued that Parliament itself has the power to delegate, as long as it also retains the sovereignty to rescind the delegated authority. Yet another act in the drama had failed on constitutional grounds, with no clear picture of future steps.

The various reforms to financial services took place in response to changes in the global financial environment. For Ottawa, starting with the Mulroney government, the reform packages for national competitiveness required substantive consultations, just as the media and the opposition focused on everything from patronage appointments to issues like the tuna scandal in September 1985 and the resignation of Fisheries Minister John Fraser. These two narratives – competitive reforms and political scandals – became a preoccupation of the prime minister and the cabinet, as they recognized the slow but steady shift of Canadians' mindset towards global forces, despite their falling support in national polls. The free-trade negotiations were a symptom of the larger forces reshaping the global economy, and financial services were only one example. A watershed moment came in 1998, when two banks, the Royal and Montreal, announced on 23 January their plans for a merger, followed by another, proposed in April between TD and CIBC. The first merger came from a conversation between the two CEOs, without any foreknowledge or a warning to Finance Minister Paul Martin. The bank mergers set off a frenzy on Bay Street, where the four banks hired law firms and lobbyists with contacts in Ottawa to support the banking narrative that size and scale are the vital ingredients for global success. Prime Minister Jean Chrétien, first elected an MP as a unilingual lawyer in 1963, now with 35 years' experience in federal politics and serving as minister of finance, privately admitted that the bank merger was the hottest topic ever in caucus, and almost all MPs were opposed.

During the 1990s, as global inflation eased, the profits of Canadian banks soared, from a total of $4 billion in 1994 to $7 billion in 1997 (about one-eighth of all the corporate profits in Canada) and to almost $10 billion in 2000, up almost 270 per cent in the decade. When Finance Minister Paul Martin refused to sanction the mergers, he left no doubt about the policy dilemma for Canada – either go with the flow to keep the country's financial system a player, or retreat even further, like the banks themselves, to a domestic focus only. No one doubted that the five banks enjoyed privileged "benefits status": the Bank Act placed restrictive barriers against foreign banks, the CDIC socializes default risk for depositors, and the doctrine "too big to fail" requires federal support. Two examples illustrate the banks' privileged role: Pierre Trudeau's government's "rescue" of CIBC from its loans to Dome Petroleum, or the Chrétien government's policy, announced in January 2002, to forgive more than $100 million in bad student loans to CIBC, Royal, and Scotiabank. Despite maintaining these privileged but exceptional rules, the Department of Finance could release a document in 1997 and say straightforwardly, "In our society, it is accepted that ownership of a regulated financial institution is a privilege, not a right."

The two proposed bank mergers were a political non-starter. Almost a year of work by the federal Competition Bureau disclosed the obvious market power and the absence of direct competition or any advantages of scale and product scope, despite the stated rationale for the mergers. The bureau assessed the effects through the prism of branch banking, geographical markets (125 urban communities and 99 rural markets), market concentration, and competitive performance with high entry barriers, and other institutions came to similar conclusions.

More concentration followed in other sectors, such as the dominant role of the Toronto Stock Exchange (TSX), when it took over the services of the Vancouver and Alberta Stock Exchanges, growing from about 15 per cent total market capitalization at the start of the 1990s to one-third a decade later. The competitive threat for Canada in financial services and most sectors is global, not domestic.

All three groups – international financial markets, global financial institutions, and stock exchanges – are pushing for rapid democratization of finance and significant financial innovation. As global finance has evolved, with the rise of two new financial powerhouses – pension funds and private equity firms – vast pools or aggregations of capital have emerged: hedge funds, sovereign wealth funds, union funds, venture funds, even social-investment funds. Further reforms cultivated a wide range of public and private pension funds, which invest assets in Canadian equities, government bonds, infrastructure firms, and wealth management. Fortunately, as recommended by the National Advisory Board on Science and Technology, some pension funds have set up venture-capital funds to invest in Canadian small-business start-ups.

As financial services become truly global, and more like knowledge companies to survive, they need to heed the wisdom and warnings of Adam Smith: "This free competition too obliges all bankers to be more liberal in their dealings with their customers, lest their rivals should carry them away. In general, if any branch of trade, or any division of labour, be disadvantaged to the public, the freer and more general the competition, it will always be the more so."

VIII

The Liberals' National Energy Program (NEP) of 1980 was more than a tax-and-control grab – it was an approach that combined energy policy with addressing the needs of Liberal voters, especially in the high-energy consuming provinces of Ontario and Quebec. To many people in western Canada, or the bars and restaurants of Calgary, the NEP seemed akin to Vladimir Lenin's NEP, new economic policy, a five-year plan with a rigid bureaucracy. It was no accident that when Ottawa announced the NEP, it included establishing a new, Canadian-owned oil company, PetroCanada, where the headquarters in Calgary was known as Red Square. But, as soon became clear, the Liberals paid a heavy political price for the NEP and the resulting constitutional fights. By 1984, a succession of key Liberal ministers had resigned, including John Turner as finance minister.

For the new Mulroney government, energy policy represented a good example of the party's work in policy formulation during its last year in Opposition. Pat Carney was not only the energy critic, appointed in September 1983, but minister of energy in the new government.

Energy policy had numerous political and economic dimensions – global v. domestic, federal v. provincial, public-policy needs v. private-sector preferences, western Canada v. Ottawa – and illustrated how process – who is consulted and when, whose advice is being accepted or rejected – was as important as the substantive outcomes. Trudeau's NEP, enacted in the wake of major events in the Middle East, started originally with the Royal Commission on Taxation (Carter Commission, 1962–66) and disputes over royalty schemes. But the price of energy remained low, so energy was less controversial as a national political topic. The 1973 world oil crisis, followed by the 1979 oil embargo, tipped the global balance away from what Anthony Sampson dubbed the "Seven Sisters," the giant, vertically integrated oil companies, towards the countries holding the oil reserves in the Middle East, but especially Saudi Arabia.

The federal department responsible for the sector – Energy, Mines, and Resources – like many others, had a functional role, implementing policies often originating elsewhere – in the Finance Department, for example, where tax policy and "tax expenditures" became a tool to favour energy and mining projects. The department had a fabulous depository of statistics on oil and gas reserves and on mining deposits – everything from copper and gold to palladium and zinc – not only in Canada but around the world. The "Seven Sisters" controlled about 85 per cent of the world's petroleum reserves, with a global reach and diplomatic connections to governments around the world, and often served as a private conduit for initiatives of their own governments. The seven firms were the following: BP (formerly Anglo-Iranian Oil), Exxon, Gulf, Royal Dutch Shell, SOCAL (Standard Oil of California [now Chevron]), Standard Oil of New York (SOCONY [which became Mobil, then merged with Exxon to become Exxon Mobil]), and Texaco. In the 1970s, an era of national-liberation movements, Libya and other oil-producing countries set up the Organization of Petroleum Exporting Countries (OPEC), a Middle East cartel to manage oil reserves and design policies on ownership and pricing, while the more radical members wanted to use their financial assets as leverage for political action, including energy embargoes.

The resulting dispute was stark: oil-producing nations and their massive windfall financial wealth, deposited largely in banks in London and New York, against the consuming nations like India, Japan, the United States, and Third World countries. Oil was a point of leverage against the United States and its close ally, Israel. For Canada, the same issues were equally stark: the rising wealth of the oil-producing provinces such as Alberta and Saskatchewan against the large consuming provinces like Ontario and Quebec.

In Canada, with an abundance of crude and refined oil in the west, but a shortage in the east, Ottawa intervened, and the National Energy Board imposed an export tax, calculated on the domestic price and export prices. A series of Liberal budgets in Ottawa attempted to equalize prices across the country, but the net effect was to reduce royalties to the producing provinces and lower the price of energy – fuel oil, gas, and so on – for the consuming provinces. For companies and the oil industry, new rules and regulations and tax policies of the producing provinces and Ottawa became bewilderingly complex, and difficult to understand, confounding efforts to forecast future energy prices.

To encourage energy conservation, Ottawa offered new incentives, such as a two-year write-off for certain energy-conserving capital expenditures incurred after 1980, removal of federal sales tax on certain non-fossil-fuel energy generators like heat pumps, solar furnaces, and wind-powered generators, with special excise taxes on high-energy-consuming motor vehicles and motor-vehicle air-conditioners. In the three years from June 1976 to June 1979, all Canadian taxpayers were allowed to deduct 100 per cent of their resource-exploration expenditures against other income, in the years just before Joe Clark's government took office in May 1979. In Clark's Ottawa, personalities, departmental in-fighting, a minister of energy with little knowledge of the sector, domestically or globally, and mixed signals to the provinces on what to do with PetroCanada left the Clark government reeling, Alberta fuming, and the Liberals laughing about a sector where they assumed the Conservatives would show some competence.

In 1983, still in Opposition, the Conservative party was crafting two main initiatives in energy policy: the Western Accord and negotiations with Alberta; and the Atlantic Accord, essentially the energy agreement with Newfoundland and Labrador, with overtones for Nova Scotia. As the parliamentary critic for energy, Pat Carney took the lead. She was an accomplished business consultant, with experience in the Arctic and her home province and well connected in the smaller Canadian energy companies, often declaring, "Energy could be the Canadian engine of growth." She was, despite her Irish temper, popular in the Tory caucus, with a habit of borrowing cigarettes from colleagues, often standing, puffing, and sorting through her considerable and weighty thought processes. In Opposition, when Allan MacEachen presented his 1981 budget, her speech in the House of Commons eviscerated its premises, a bad omen for the Trudeau Liberals, and Carney's clear, forceful explanations to the media made her a future minister to watch.

Mulroney's celebrated "Red Barn speech" of 8 July 1984, delivered at a campaign rally in Edmonton, had set out the premises for the Western Accord, including scrapping the much-hated petroleum gas revenue tax (PGRT), a multi-billion-dollar tax grab by Ottawa. Premier Peter Lougheed introduced him to the large, overflow audience. Just before his introduction, he read an advance copy of Mulroney's remarks, and his endorsement of the federal Conservatives was both glowing and heartfelt. The Atlantic Accord was a policy priority laid out in the summer of 1983, during Brian Mulroney's by-election campaign in Central Nova.

During the leadership race, Mulroney never visited Newfoundland, leaving all the province's leadership delegates to John Crosbie, and when Crosbie dropped out before the final ballot, he and his delegates wanted an iron-clad agreement that the province's offshore oil reserves would be a priority. Only the Mulroney campaign, before the final ballot, offered that promise, and most of the Crosbie delegates supported Mulroney. The province was deeply rattled by the very disadvantageous deal for Churchill Falls in Labrador signed in 1969 by Liberal Premier Joey Smallwood with Hydro-Québec, to last until 2041. Its MPs and senators were equally upset with the Supreme Court's ruling of March 1984 in favour of Ottawa against its own claim to jurisdiction over the Hibernia oilfields, while Nova Scotia's premier, John Buchanan, was also putting pressure on

Mulroney for policies to develop the Atlantic offshore. Mulroney had spent time touring all parts of Newfoundland and Labrador as president of the Iron Ore Company and knew that another big energy project at Churchill Falls also offered more huge potential for job creation and energy security.

As energy critic, Pat Carney led the negotiation team and established close relations with Newfoundland's energy minister, William Marshall, knowing that the prying eyes of John Crosbie would be looking over her shoulders. Mulroney invited Conservative Premier Brian Peckford to Ottawa in October 1983 for private discussions, and both agreed that, with good faith, a deal could be negotiated. All those involved in the negotiations knew the national implications, including Pat Carney, remembering that British Columbia's appeal to the Supreme Court on mineral rights in 1967 had failed, just as Newfoundland's had in 1984.

For the next six months in late 1983, as the negotiations set out the elements of a deal in the east, Mulroney travelled the country, selecting new candidates with local appeal, and giving his four-pillar speech tailored to local circumstances. The one province he didn't visit was Newfoundland, because, in the absence of an energy agreement, the reaction to him would be entirely negative. By early June 1984, the deal was in place: a six-page, single-spaced letter of agreement to be signed in St John's on 14 June, a Thursday. This letter became the basis of Mulroney's speech to the Chamber of Commerce at noon, and I cheekily added to the penultimate paragraph a phrase, "I am not afraid to inflict prosperity on the people of Newfoundland," a play on words of the front-page editorial in the St John's *Telegram* when the province lost the Supreme Court challenge. The line, like the speech, received a standing ovation. Behind the scenes, as a measure of his preparations, Mulroney read the text to the caucus before his departure to St John's, and then spent most of Wednesday night on the phone conferring with Tory Premiers Peter Lougheed (Alberta), Bill Davis (Ontario), and John Buchanan (Nova Scotia) on the terms of the Newfoundland Accord, lest any feature would raise provincial ire. Once he was in government, the Atlantic Accord was approved by cabinet as a record of decision (ROD), repeating his speech almost word for word, and it was formally signed in Newfoundland on 11 February 1985.

Pat Carney was also working closely with Alberta's energy minister, John Zaozirny, who was receiving mixed signals from within the provincial bureaucracy. An internal memo, based on discussions with a senior federal civil servant, suggested that Ottawa's Finance Department, not Pat Carney, was really in charge of the Alberta–Ottawa energy negotiations, a viewpoint not shared in the premier's office or by the premier. In fact, after a Question Period in January that year, the prime minister chaired a meeting in the small cabinet room and laid out the precise sequencing of the negotiations: Newfoundland first, and then Alberta, a process that was followed to the letter. Pat Carney, Marshall Cohen, Paul Tellier, and Michael Wilson were present, with Harry Near and me taking notes. However, it didn't help the mood in Pat Carney's office or the PMO that Cohen phoned me the following week, to tell me that Finance had prepared its own document setting out its approach to energy negotiations. I expressed my shock and demanded that the paper be sent immediately to Pat Carney. This episode left a very bad taste among the participants and replayed a case earlier in January on the health accord, with Michael Wilson and Jake Epp in total agreement, according to Finance, when in fact Jake Epp hadn't agreed. Pat Carney often spoke openly about Cohen's poor judgment and Finance's limited sense of cabinet solidarity.

The signed deal between Alberta and Ottawa was a major accomplishment and showed that in a federal system the process issue of consultations is a central component of substantive policy outcomes. It helped that, in 1984, there were seven Conservative premiers, but the same issues applied to other governments, like the Socreds in British Columbia, the NDP in Manitoba, and the Liberals in Quebec. It also helped that many private-sector CEOs, like Bob Blair at Nova, Jim Gray at Canadian Hunter, Bernard Isautier at Canterra, and Cedric Ritchie at Scotiabank, all thought Canada had to become a more aggressive player, not only in energy but in science and technology, in trade access with the United States, and in the Pacific Rim. It was also noticed that labour leaders like Louis Laberge (Fédération des travailleurs du Québec), Dennis McDermott (Canadian Labour Congress), and Bob White (United Auto Workers) were quietly supportive, not on every policy initiative and certainly not on any wholesale neoconservative agenda, but on the need to invest in new technologies, equipment, and state-of-the-art work methods.

IX

From its first days in office, the Mulroney government knew that continuous deficits and rising national debt would put a squeeze on spending plans. Despite calls for draconian cost-cutting, most government programs were merely limited to non-discretionary financing, including joint programs with the provinces. Both in private briefings and in cabinet presentations, Michael Wilson recognized that initial savings would range from zero to as high as $15 billion. The recession of the early 1980s meant that all governments were spending more than they were taking in in tax receipts, and the expected $37.5-billion deficit forecast for the 1984-85 fiscal year, plus the forecast deficits of the provincial governments and their agencies (hospitals, universities, and utilities), amounted to $100 billion per year for the two levels of government, adding to the dangerously high debt ceiling as a percentage of GNP for Canada. This amount of debt affected bond ratings and the interest to finance the debt. The pending free-trade talks with the United States had made industrial subsidies a sensitive subject, in part because most subsidies and non-repayable loans were at the federal level, while in the United States, subsidies occurred at the state level. Ottawa had over 600 crown corporations, many operating within a corporate umbrella like CN, only one of the Department of Transport's many holdings.

In 1935, a plan for a national airline was considered by Prime Minister R.B. Bennett's government. However, an autumn election returned William Lyon Mackenzie King to power, and the Transport portfolio was entrusted to C.D. Howe. He introduced the Transport Act of 1936, with a new Department of Transport, which consolidated three departments: Civil Aviation, Marine, and Railways and Canals. At a stroke, he ended the era of the railway as the driver of transportation policy, and for the next fifty years the policy focus was on domestic issues and a domestic mindset. Two ministers in Pierre Trudeau's government sought some changes, in part because of growing dissatisfaction about rail and air service and inquiries on several accidents. Jean-Luc Pépin and Lloyd Axworthy – and two high-profile patronage appointments to cabinet, Edgar Benson and Jean Marchand – struggled to make changes, including in response to the impact of the U.S. Staggers Rail Act of 1980, which opened up railways from their highly regulated, cartel features.

In 1984, Don Mazankowski was an ideal choice for Transport: as the parliamentary critic and as minister in the Clark government, he knew the transportation files, given deregulation in the United States and globally. As an MP from western Canada, and frustrated with his short time as minister under Clark, like all his colleagues he wanted results. He had backed Joe Clark in the leadership convention in 1983, and that summer he probably felt his political future was in doubt, with a new leader from central Canada, where transportation always seemed to be a secondary priority. But Mulroney worked his charm, and by early autumn he and Mazankowski struck up a close working relationship that would become a lasting friendship. Mazankowski had a free hand, and, as in many other policy initiatives, changes would be radical. The study that Lloyd Axworthy had commissioned on multi-mode transportation found that, comparing the United States and Canada, "the rail regulatory systems of the two countries are no longer compatible." This report and others became the framework for a fundamentally new approach, announced in July 1985, one of 18 radical policy-position papers from the new cabinet. *Freedom to Move – A Framework for Transportation Reform* called for less government control, measures to open markets, and a new regulatory agency.

Within a year, on 26 June 1986, Mazankowski brought forward Bill C-18, the new National Transportation Act, a framework approach that has guided policy reforms ever since. It was, in short, one of several items in the Mulroney competitive agenda to remove Macdonald's hundred-year-old National Policy and push towards an international and global perspective, a frontal attack on the established order, where command and control in Ottawa gave way to market-based performance measures. The past accumulation of agencies, assets, and bureaucratic games, often fuelled by inexperience, patronage, and shuffling the chairs, went up in smoke. Not everyone agreed, including the media, the opposition, and some civil servants. When John Crosbie replaced Mazankowski at Transport, both men strong supporters of free trade, in the summer shuffle of 1986, the reform agenda was supercharged.

Mazankowski became deputy prime minister, which also included chairing the cabinet's new Operations Committee, with Glen Shortliffe as his deputy and exempt staffers including Sharen Andrews, Jamie Burns, Phil Evershed, Rob Parker, and Tom Van Dusen. Mazankowski and this new committee had a mandate to manage short-term implementation and coordination of all policy, appointments, and communications. This position also gave Mazankowski, perhaps the most popular minister in the cabinet and the caucus, a window on all government operations, and close access to the prime minister to advance new measures for western Canada, including economic diversification and trade promotion in the Pacific Rim.

The economic subcommittee of cabinet was now well briefed on a range of reforms: the removal of entry barriers, ownership restrictions, and regulatory measures, starting in the airlines and trucking industry. New start-ups in the United States like FedEx and UPS and Toyota's just-in-time philosophy, with a new plant in Ontario, were spreading quickly. The Transport Department had numerous programs governing safety, inspections, and a wide range of assets – airports, ferries, highways, ports, and a behemoth in CN. CN was a corporate empire, with holdings in hotels, trucking firms, terminals, a luxury boutique hotel in Paris, vast lands, and a wholly owned subsidiary, Air Canada, itself a conglomerate structure facing more demands for new aircraft, better runways for jumbo jets, and new cargo planes for long-distance flights, to cite examples. To add to its complexity, Transport also included the Canadian Coast Guard, in charge of marine safety, including implementing transportation policy, regulations, navigation, and safety inspections. The range of files facing a minister in departments like Energy, Industry, or Transport added to the sheer information complexity, often requiring ministers to delegate to senior bureaucrats but acquiescing to norms of ministerial responsibility. To take the complexity to an extreme, it was up to the transport minister to decide which taxi companies could pick up passengers at an airport terminal!

In Canada, the initiatives to start privatization came pragmatically (see Table 2.2). While the party was in Opposition, Mulroney spoke widely about a new approach to the private sector, ranging from less regulation to selling crown corporations like PetroCanada. His personal manifesto, published just before he was elected party leader in June 1983, stated, "There is something wrong about the existence of some 600 Crown corporations" in this country. Thus, it is not surprising that Canada has a different history than other nations in the march to privatization. The concept of privatization is often associated with the legacy of Margaret Thatcher, who actually hated the word – "a dreadful bit of jargon to inflict on the language of Shakespeare" – even though it was first given popular meaning in an article in the *Economist* describing the changes in Germany under Nazi rule. To some degree, all advanced countries have a measure of public ownership, including the United States and Japan (e.g., highways, hospitals, national parks, ports, universities, and utilities). In many cases, this arrangement was a matter of political ideology, especially in Britain and France, with a view that public ownership would foster greater social justice, weaken class differences and inequalities, and provide greater security.

Both the federal and provincial governments in Canada accepted public ownership, especially in sectors that had monopoly characteristics – broadcasting, electric utilities, transport (e.g., ferries), with both private and public ownership in airlines, hotels, and railways. The Conservative Bennett government had set up the Canadian Radio Broadcasting Commission (CRBC) in 1932 less for ideological reasons than to allow Canadians to acquire ownership in this new sector. Trans-Canada Air Lines (much later Air Canada) followed in 1937. Over time, such crown

Table 2.2
Selected Privatization Initiatives, 1985–1988

Firm	Sector	Date*	Buyer	Proceeds
Northern Transportation	Marine shipping	1985	Inuvialuit / Nunsai	$53 m
Canada Development Corporation	Conglomerate	1985	Two public offerings	$377m
Canadian Arsenals	Munitions	1985	SNC	$92m
Teleglobe	Telecommunications	1986	Memotec Data	$488m
Canadair	Aerospace	1985	Bombardier	$143m
FPI	Fish-processing	1987	Public offering	$104m
deHavilland	Aerospace	1986	Boeing	$99m
Pêcheries Canada	Fish-processing	1986	La Coopérative Agro-Alimentaine Purdel	$5m
CN Hotels	Hospitality	1988	CP Hotels	$265m
Northern Canada Power	Electricity	1987	Yukon Power	$76m

* Privatizations are listed in the chronological order in which they were finalized.

corporations came to number more than 600, and many were subsidiaries of other entities. Air Canada, for instance, was a wholly owned subsidiary of CN, itself operated within the federal Department of Transport. Multiple goals interacted in the Mulroney policy agenda: reducing government spending in the face of rising deficits and strengthening the private sector, while recognizing that competitiveness required more sectors to create wealth via trade, valued-added production, and an international mindset.

It took experience and external advice to establish a privatization agenda, including a new Ministry of Privatization. The PCO-drafted mandate letters for Industry Minister Sinclair Stevens and Treasury Board Minister Robert de Cotret made both men responsible for privatization, requiring a greater clarity of purpose and accountability. The biggest crown asset in the Industry Department was the conglomerate Canada Development Corporation (CDC), set up in 1971, which included Polysar Energy and Chemical Corporation. On the strength of advice from investment advisers, CDC's top management and the civil service decided to sell the firm as a single unit, rather than each firm individually. This privatization sale reflected a range of issues of primary concern to the cabinet: the fear of underpricing the assets, the degree of competition in each industry, the potential of job losses, and the worry that many crown corporations might offer no real value to potential investors.

The Mulroney government privatized case by case, not using a neoconservative approach to allow unfettered control for the business community. Canada, like most countries, had sectors relatively "closed" to outside ownership that traded goods internationally. For instance, most national governments owned and operated an airline, such as Air Canada, Air India, or Japan Airlines. A large conglomerate like Canadian Pacific, operating as a private firm since 1881, differed little in performance with Canadian National, each operating a bewildering number of corporate entities – airlines, ferries, hotels, railway lines, trucking firms, and the like – while co-owning the national telegraph service, CNCP. Stock-market analysts preferred shares in focused companies and gave a discount to purchase conglomerates. "Corporate Canada" was an economy with an overweight of conglomerate firms, such as Argus, Bell Canada, Brascan, Canadian Pacific, and Molson's in the private sector, and CDC and CN in the public sector.

The government's step-by-step learning approach seemed to work, and when Barbara McDougall became minister of state (privatization), she issued a policy framework in 1987 that set out the rationale for privatization: a) the changing competitive economic environment; b) the test of efficiency and profitability; c) self-sustaining or future subsidies required; d) quality of management, and e) fairness and equity in the marketplace. Nonetheless, other factors were at play, and many civil servants thought privatization had gone too far. Ian Clark, associate deputy of plans in the PCO, told the operations committee early in 1987 about a view, which he shared, that the government was no longer cutting the fat but was going beyond the muscle and cutting the bone. I disagreed, and gave my own list for privatization, including the Post Office, the Royal Canadian Mint, some airports, and even certain ocean ports. And that was before the cabinet had plans to deal with two big privatizations, the sale of CN and all its vast holdings, including Air Canada, eventually sold in two public offerings in 1988 and 1989, and PetroCanada, in four tranches, starting in 1991.

Privatization required a high degree of secrecy to be well managed, but few people outside the inner circle of cabinet, the PMO, the PCO, and Finance appreciated how the veil of secrecy led to media speculation and allowed vested interests to attack the process. As well, privatization for many crown corporations required a legislative mandate, which effectively announced intentions in advance. The case of Air Canada is instructive because, as President Claude Taylor kept reminding Ottawa, the airline faced the challenge of an ageing fleet of aircraft, with competitors acquiring new, fuel-efficient planes for long-distance flights, like the Boeing 747, or short-distance, like the Airbus 320 series. He also reminded anyone who cared that these planes cost up to $200 million each, and each required an order booking in advance. The choice for the government as owner was either to add these costs to the government deficit or let the airline raise the money in capital markets as a privatized entity. The minister's chief of staff, Elizabeth Roscoe, in a note dated 28 May 1987 to the Policy Unit, neatly summarized the issues:

> The timing of the Air Canada announcement involves a lengthy process ... The legislative process will be the lengthiest component of the privatization and must be completed before preliminary prospectuses can be issued ... There are at least four important reasons to consider proceeding ... before the House rises this summer ... First, the financial community and the media are expecting the Government to make an announcement ... Second the process for competition of privatization will be at least five to six months ... Third, the outlook for the airline equity market is projected to be stable for the next six months; Fourth, Air Canada is facing a period where its major competitor, CIAL, is rationalizing from its recent merger ... By deferring action ... Air Canada's financial performance and value to potential investors may deteriorate.

In all, the Mulroney government's privatization program – twenty-seven crown corporations, including several within CN's diversified conglomerate portfolio – was intended to strengthen Canada's competitive edge, with each firm forced to assess risk, future spending and investments, and international opportunities. A separate, secondary advantage allowed privatization measures to increase the role of public markets as a tool to raise capital for existing businesses, lessen the need for bank financing, and encourage pools of capital to provide venture funding for start-ups. Three of the privatized forms – Air Canada in Montreal, Cameco in Saskatchewan, and CN, the top carrier railway in North America – are rated "best in class" by international investors, operating global supply chains for small Canadian-owned small-business suppliers. This approach illustrates the longer-term advantages for domestic firms in extremely competitive international conditions. Curiously, few subsequent governments followed the privatization approach, and Conservative supporters, policy analysts, and the business community expected that Stephen Harper, with a four-year mandate and a majority government in 2011, would have a checklist for a focused, competitive policy agenda. It never happened.

Reducing government spending is never easy, because each spending allotment has a constituency, but the Chrétien–Martin cuts of the 1990s, however painful, including fiscal arrangements with the provinces, left the Harper government in a surplus position. That's why expectations were high that it would launch a privatization agenda, starting perhaps with the Post Office, following the practice of the Labour government in Britain, plus the Royal Mint and the Wheat Board, plus dramatic changes in the funding of the CBC, such as the licence system used in Britain. Its minority status for five years required it to be largely reactive, and many policies and much spending were a reaction to the Wall Street crash of 2008 and the deep recession that followed. The government also had the advantage of the five-year pact signed by Paul Martin with the provinces, funding education, equalization, and health care. Short-term economic challenges and associated job creation, depicted in the much-hyped Economic Action Plan, could be sustained by government procurement, infrastructure improvements, job-ready stimulus measures, and lowering the Goods and Services Tax (GST). Ensuring long-term competitiveness is far more challenging, requiring a vision based on a clear understanding of how Canada's exchange rate is affected by trade, federal and provincial debt levels, and a bias towards investment over consumption.

Given the sheer scale and potential of privatization offerings – measured in the hundreds of billions of dollars – academic research now provides abundant evidence that such schemes, in whole or in part, strengthen over time the economic performance of former state-owned firms, offering better value for shareholders and better service and choice for customers. For instance, in the *Journal of Economic Literature*, William Megginson and Jeffry Netter analysed privatization initiatives around the world, including Canada, to understand both the short-term effects, such as revenue flow to governments, and, in the longer run, firms' actual performance, in areas such as employment, growth, and returns to shareholders. Contrary to received historical wisdom, there was far less ideological thinking than opponents believed were at play.

X

Daring, bold, exciting – such adjectives describe the myth and reality of the technology sector and powerful firms like Alibaba, Amazon, Apple, Facebook, Google, and Samsung, as countries seek to create global winners and job creators (see Figure 2.5). Unfortunately, Canada has no institutional agency, centre, or department that can undertake long-term science policy and research. The Science Council of Canada, set up in the 1970s, served as a public-sector think-tank, but its influence rarely matched its promise, and it was abolished in 1992. The United States has a world-class system of engineering and technical schools (so does India) like MIT, a research university that attracts students, offers teaching programs, receives research grants, and fosters business–academic alliances that spawn new start-ups and cultivate emerging technologies, plus it has the highly influential American Office of Technology. France develops new technologies through its state-owned firms and its national-champions strategy. Japan has its Science and Technology Agency and has launched a new initiative, the National Institute of Science and Technology Policy.

The Mulroney government in 1984 faced shifting choices in science and technology, such as basic research and applied research (development). The U.S. government was allocating huge spending to the natural sciences and engineering programs that feed (via scientific papers and patients) new technology start-ups. Japan spends vastly more in the corporate sector than in government or university programs, while Europe increasingly invests in projects for artificial intelligence, climate change, medicine, and space. In Ottawa, the new government recognized that international comparisons exposed Canada's weak position in science and technology measured by a range of indicators, including actual expenditures on science and technology. For instance, in terms of domestic patents granted to residents per 100,000 population, patents filed within the country, and scientists and engineers per 1,000 people in the labour force, Canada had one of the lowest ratings among advanced nations.

More tellingly, Canada's ongoing weak performance in research and development (R & D) directly relates to its future trade patterns. Compared to global competitors, Canadian private firms rank last in company-funded R & D, and only a tiny fraction undertakes any R & D. In the 1980s, of the leading industrialized countries, Canada's position was least favourable, especially compared with the United States and Japan, then Canada's biggest trading partners. The competitive challenge was that Canada would be caught in the middle, between the growth sectors represented

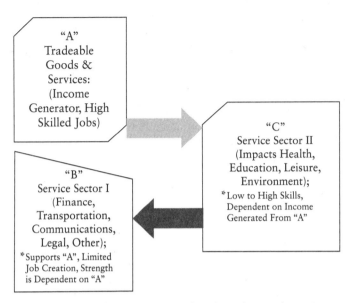

Source: Adapted from Canadian Institute for Advanced Research

Figure 2.5 The Components of a Wealth-Creating Economy.

by high-technology trade fostered by the United States and Japan, and the low-cost sectors, increasingly dominated by Asia. During the first months of office in 1984, Industry Minister Sinclair Stevens and the minister of state for science, Frank Oberle, were looking for precise data on federal expenditures on science and technology, department by department. No one had ever compiled the actual amounts, and the trend lines. By December 1984, the department had a complete document, not only by department but including certain agencies like the National Research Council. Unfortunately, the paper went to the PCO, which turned it into a cabinet document, thus a secret paper and not available to the public. At a luncheon in the minister's boardroom in the C.D. Howe Building (235 Queen Street), I was asked what should happen to the paper and suggested to Frank Oberle that he leak it, i.e., forward it to David Crane, economics columnist at the *Toronto Star*. Such excessive secrecy on such a crucial component of competitiveness was an example of the crippling mindset in Ottawa.

The question for Canada is simple: what master instruments does it possess to reshape its organization of science and technology to meet the needs identified? R&D, the major driver of the knowledge economies, is based on the ratio of R&D spending to GNP spending for countries (1.5 per cent in Canada, 2.74 per cent in the United States, 3.14 per cent in Japan, 4.3 per cent in Israel), and on the ratio of R&D spending to total sales for corporations. For Canadian firms, whether measured by domestic patents, by scientists and engineers in the labour force, or by sectors with a positive trade balance, science-based innovation has remained weak. The balance between publicly funded research, mainly in universities and government labs, and the private sector affects the efficiency of dollars spent. Such spending gives credence to the slogan popular at 3M, a leading American knowledge company: "Research is the transformation of money into knowledge. Innovation is the transformation of knowledge into money." That idea goes to the heart of science-based innovation. In recent years, the biggest shift has been in the availability of equity capital to finance new start-ups.

For decades, Canada has struggled to make science and technology policy a priority on the national agenda. However, geography and domestic politics play an invidious role here. True, federal and provincial governments have taken steps to overcome political parochialism, but corporate spending on R&D trails international rankings, including in, until recently, high-speed broadband and 5G technology, which affects sectors like agriculture, education, finance, and hospitals, and the creation of the Canada Space Agency. As well, Canadian corporate R&D suffers from the low level of absolute amounts per firm, the limited number of Canadians participating in research alliances across the world, and the low expenditures relative to annual sales. Not many Canadian firms have research budgets like OpenText, with annual revenues of almost a billion dollars in 2009 and an R&D budget of $133.3 million, or 14 per cent of sales.

Both the policy issues and the government machinery for innovation, such as advisory councils, were laid out in the pioneering Lamontagne Report tabled in 1973, but the recommendations never received traction. Initial thinking in the Mulroney government, where Frank Oberle was minister of state (science), was to appoint a chief science adviser reporting to the prime minister. As laid out in the 1986 Throne Speech, a new approach allowed the prime minister to evaluate science and technology policy as a national agenda by appointing the National Advisory Board of Science and Technology, which he chaired, including the industry and finance ministers and a distinguished blue-ribbon group of scientists like Nobel laureate John C. Polanyi and Dr Fraser Mustard, three university presidents, private-sector scientists, labour leaders like Nancy Riche, and CEOs from across the country. In Michael Wilson's first budget, presented in 1985, a small item was inserted that received little attention, a $50-million investment in the new Fonds de solidarité FTQ, to help finance business start-ups and firms having trouble raising capital from traditional bank financing. Today, that fund exceeds $1 billion. The Centres of Excellence began with $500 million matched by the private sector, with each of the 15 projects recruiting leading research scientists and engineers from universities, government labs, and private firms – a lesson for universities, even in the same city, which rarely collaborate to gain critical mass.

The National Advisory Board of Science and Technology, chaired by the prime minister, following a similar model in Japan, was a tool to elevate science and technology as a national policy priority and recruited leaders like Jim Gray, chair of Canadian Hunter; Doug Wright, president of the University of Waterloo; Regis Duffy, a former science dean at the University of Prince Edward Island (UPEI) and founder of a new pharmaceutical start-up; and Pierre Lortie, prominent lawyer and future president of the Montreal Stock Exchange. Many senior bureaucrats were lukewarm to this initiative, including Arthur May, president of the National Science and Engineering Research Council, but when the prime minister elaborated these issues in a speech at the University of Waterloo, calling one unsuccessful tax measure a "boondoggle," there was no turning back.

The board members, with help from the civil service, the PMO's Policy Unit, and consultants, undertook a fresh look at all science policies, including through seven sector studies, on cooperation with provincial bodies, the National Research Council (NRC), scholarships, social and cultural impacts of science and technology strategies, including a scholarship program for gifted students, strategic technologies in the resource sector, technology-transfer strategies to encourage commercialization from universities and government labs, and venture capital. Canada's NRC has earned one Nobel Prize in two generations; Germany's network of Max Planck Institutes has won twenty-four. Marjorie Nichols, an Ottawa journalist always skeptical of the Mulroney competitiveness agenda, suggested that, on the science front, while "the words were low key, its actions have not been. The effort to address the country-wide poverty in scientific research and development is one of the most ambitious since the rallying of national support a decade ago to deal with out-of-control wages and prices."

Board members and the cabinet understood that a new science and technology culture would take time, given past policies in corporate technological innovation and worker training, a labour-management climate that pays only lip service to technological change, and a university system too often disdainful of commercial and private-sector links, precisely at a time when public spending in Canada on university education is well below comparable U.S. levels. Federal policy remains mixed, in part because of past embarrassments from the 1980s, such as the fiasco surrounding the scientific research tax credit (SRTC), and a tax regime more accommodating to the real-estate industry than to knowledge-based research and innovative small companies. However, R&D spending is an ongoing process and can't be cut or interrupted if it is to remain a force for innovation, and political action, like the cutbacks by the Harper government, weakens Canada's competitiveness over time.

Despite some exceptions, particularly in western Canada, where the desire to diversify the economy through new strategic industries and market outlets is strongest, Canada has a political culture that has failed to grasp the full implications of the knowledge economy — particularly the need for critical mass and world standards of evaluation. Prime Ministers Mulroney, Chrétien, and Martin were strong champions of research and innovation and set the stage for Justin Trudeau's government to increase funding, starting in 2015, with a five-year commitment of almost $10 billion. However, other relative weaknesses remain, and can be succinctly summarized: the ratio of business start-ups to failures is too low. Too few start-ups are spin-offs from universities, large firms, or research centres.

XI

The century-old dominance of Canada's banks in the financial-services sector has been a sore spot among politicians of all parties and was a priority for the Mulroney government in 1984. The issues went beyond the five powerful banks headquartered in Toronto but extended to novel forms of financing initiated in other countries. The rise of Japan as a creditor country was a wakeup call, as powerful companies there had access to corporate funding through related bank groups, and the large trading firms themselves provided financial services. In Silicon Valley, new innovations to fund start-ups ranged from venture capital to new listings on the junior stock exchange called NASDAQ – established in 1971 as the world's first electronic trading market. The rise of the National Venture Capital Association in the United States, associated with new-technology start-ups in computers, semi-conductors, and software, was matched by a speed of decision-making and understanding of fast growth that traditional banking firms not only didn't understand but wanted to avoid. Venture capital was an American invention, but easy to replicate in other countries, with a mandate to combine risk capital with entrepreneurial management. A *Wall Street Journal* article in 1983 conveys a sense of the risk profiles:

> More and more ... venture capitalists are financing the birth of new companies. The typical venture-capital concerns used to provide money only after a few hundred thousand dollars or more had been put into a business by relatives and principals, and only after the company had a product well along in development. But now the values of young companies are rising so rapidly that venture capitalists who invest at the traditional stage often can't make the five to tenfold profit they typically require.

Canada's National Advisory Board of Science and Technology became a strong advocate for new forms of venture capital, including allowing Canadian pension funds to invest in new start-ups and making it easy for small firms to go public on a stock exchange. In the 1980s, the Alberta Stock Exchange and the Vancouver Stock Exchange shifted their focus from mining and oil and gas to include new technology start-ups, using an innovative financing mechanism to take a listed corporate shell and vend in a new start-up with growth potential. Both exchanges were merged into the Canadian Venture Exchange (CDNX), together with the Bourse de Montréal (MSE), with headquarters in Calgary. Canada has a mixed record in venture capital, smallish by American standards and minuscule by Silicon Valley benchmarks. "Angel" investors are still found in knowledge clusters in Waterloo, Ottawa, or Calgary, and some companies have start-up venture-capital funds. RIM, in Waterloo, with Blackberry Partners Fund, is one example. Two decades ago, in the absence of funds devoted to venture capital by Canada's financial sector, the federal government and some provinces created labour-sponsored venture-capital funds, allowing lucrative tax breaks for individuals and labour unions who invested. Despite a few successful start-ups, this innovative initiative, while well intentioned, was a blowout. Funding inadequacies cannot be blamed on inadequate R&D tax incentives. It is widely believed, especially in the Department of Finance, that, by all measures of tax credits, Canada is second to none in the world. Recent studies show that the issues are more complex, including the capacity to direct capital towards growth enterprises with science-based innovations and provide tools to foster fast growth through scale-up strategies.

However, while initial public offerings (IPOs) are a sign of dynamic innovation, they give a warning signal that research clusters need constant renewal to be successful. Fortunately, the debate starting in the Mulroney era has moved beyond pointing fingers at past failures. Recent reports by the Conference Board of Canada, the E-Business Roundtable, Industry Canada, and Canada's provincial science advisory boards and industry associations have provided new impetus, and federal programs have changed the policy mix and improved the climate for science and technology. New federal initiatives building on the Mulroney government's framework, such as Jean Chrétien's creating 2,000 university chairs, new approaches to intellectual property (an updated patent policy, plant breeder's rights, and software and publishing copyright), expanded Centres of Excellence programs (now called "superclusters"), a national program for science and engineering scholarships, and tax incentives for business–university linkages, all add up to a very new approach to science policy.

For Canada, the familiar obstacles remain – limited managerial appreciation of the issues, interprovincial trade barriers, and private-sector inertia, with many family-owned firms unwilling to invest in long-term technology research – in the resource sector and in manufacturing and financial services. Even the industrial base of Canada's heartland – automobiles and steel – is severely challenged, as new global competition, especially from Japan and the rest of Asia, alters these capital- and technology-intensive sectors. What real lessons have been learned? Has the knowledge mindset really changed? Canada is one of the few advanced countries where the top three business associations – the Canadian Chamber of Commerce, the Canadian Federation of Independent Businesses, and the Council of Chief Executives – have not made science and technology a corporate priority. Tom Jenkins, CEO of OpenText and chair of the board at the University of Ottawa, has his own views on this competitive challenge:

> If there is one single economic lesson about the most effective way to create wealth from the past century, it is that open market competition is the most effective and efficient basis for the economy of a nation. We would be wise to remember this lesson. With the globalization of finance and investment, Canada removed all restrictions of domestic set-asides by the country's largest pension funds. This should have motivated all Canadian firms to achieve the same relative productivity as their counterparts throughout the world, as they are all competing for the same investment dollar, and therefore must achieve competitive returns on investment. This did

not happen. Part of the reason is that domestic firms can still return a competitive return on investment by raising prices in relatively less competitive markets and thus increase revenues. The sector regime firms have no incentive to be as cost competitive or productive as other firms exposed to global competition since they can still achieve competitive return on investment (ROI) by raising prices.

Almost a generation ago, the 1989 conference of Canada's science advisory committees produced an important document, *The Halifax Declaration: A Call to Action*. It then expressed the sense of urgency and the need for action this way:

No one seriously doubts the essential message. Canada is not maintaining its position. Canada is, in fact, slipping. No political rhetoric can disguise this fundamental reality. The strong consensus of the Halifax Forum was to adopt a real target, to accept a figure as a national goal, where all Canadian partners can and must play. A 2.5 per cent of GNP expenditure, achievable by the end of the century, would not be a federal target, a provincial wish or an industry approach. It would be a national target, involving real commitment, applicable to public and private sectors as well as to the Federal Government and to each Province.

Clearly, this target of 2.5 per cent of GNP for R&D was not met by the start of the 21st century, and the figure now rests at 1.56 per cent, one of the lowest among all advanced countries, with the OECD average being 2.4 per cent. Canada still lacks the kind of national commitment to R&D called for in the *Halifax Declaration*. A national commitment is more than a political promise or a campaign slogan: it must be embraced nationally, by the leading corporations, including the banking sector, to push relentlessly in the right direction, for both knowledge jobs and long-term wealth creation.

XII

Two decades later, while the same challenges prevail, there is good and bad news on Canada's science infrastructure and ecosystem. The good news is that a blue-ribbon panel, headed by Dr David Naylor, president emeritus of the University of Toronto, has completed a comprehensive and far-reaching analysis. *Investing in Canada's Future: Strengthening the Foundations of Canadian Research*, a refreshing update on changes taking place globally, and what they imply for Canada, compares benchmarks with peer countries, including those with smaller populations like Canada. The bad news and core conclusion is stark: the national research ecosystem, despite many strengths, is now weakly coordinated, inconsistently evaluated, and lacks consistent oversight.

What does Canada's science ecosystem look like? Over time, successive governments have added funding to new agencies and programs, yet there is wide variation in the level of annual funding, in regional or national coverage, and in the range of disciplines. As the Naylor Report notes,

> It is hard to imagine another developed nation that would allow more than 40 years to pass before undertaking an integrated and integrative review of functions that have such clear-cut national importance and involve billions of dollars each year. This unfortunate vacuum may explain why the landscape we have been exploring embodies and supports tremendous professionalism and accomplishment, but also features a proliferation of small agencies and one-off investments in research facilities and programs. Moreover, notwithstanding some fine collaboration on varied fronts, many examples of inconsistencies and poor coordination are clearly visible across the four pillar agencies.

After widespread consultations, including with the business community, the panel made numerous recommendations. The current external advisory body, the Science, Technology and Innovation Council, has no independent reporting authority and a constrained disciplinary mandate, unlike the board chaired by Prime Minister Mulroney. The statutory appointment of a new chief science adviser, which formed a central part of a related bundle of the Naylor Report's recommendations, would give voice for "an independent National Advisory Council on Research and Innovation," which would "advise on evaluations for all programming in both the research and innovation spheres, including proposals for new agreements with external entities and renewals of extant agreements."

To bring funding back to a competitive level, the panel envisaged "a four-year phase-in involving base increases averaging 9 per cent each year ... New spending would be balanced across investigator-led research operating grants (the highest priority); enhanced personnel supports for researchers and trainees at different career stages; targeted spending on infrastructure-related start-up (small equipment) and operating costs (Big

Science facilities); and enhancement of the environment for science and scholarship by improved coverage of the institutional costs of research."

The cumulative base increase would move annual spending on science from approximately $3.5 billion to $4.8 billion. The steady-state increase in base funding by the end of four years, however, is small, amounting to 0.4 per cent of the federal budget, and by comparison with peer countries, with targets exceeding 3.5 per cent of GNP, the Naylor Report's recommendations keep Canada in the global game. The panel urged more emphasis on support for "independent, investigator-led research by front-line scientists and scholars" while sustaining current levels of priority-driven and partnership-oriented research. In all, and more vitally, the panel correctly believes that these commitments produce "the very highest-yield investments in Canada's future."

Of the leading Canadian firms in Fortune 500's top 100 companies, seven of the eleven largest are in the financial sector. To be fair, firms like IBM Canada, OpenText, RIM, SNC, and Spotify have mobilized a cluster of knowledge workers, but for a country so well endowed with natural resources, Canada has few global leaders in agribusiness, dairy, or food production. Firms like Clearwater, McCain, and Saputo are large domestically but relatively small globally. Ironically, Canada's record in scientific research by engineers and scientists stands up well by international criteria, and the recommendations of the Naylor Report could reinforce that standing. In science-based sectors like advanced materials, information technology and electronics, and medicine and biotechnology, progress requires long-term horizons, a critical mass of researchers, and the desire to move the technological frontier forward.

According to Statistics Canada's first-ever Survey of Intellectual Property Commercialization, Canada's 12 largest universities account for 77 per cent of invention reports, 68 per cent of new patent applications, and 74 per cent of active licences. However, Canada needs to improve the two sides of the innovation game – strong linkages between publicly funded support for science-based research, as outlined in the Naylor Report, and business–university linkages to commercialize ideas. In this game, to quote again from a corporate technology leader, 3M, "Research is the transformation of money into knowledge, while innovation is the transformation of ideas/knowledge into money." Canada's private sector faces the paradox of long life-cycles to meet the research side of R&D but very little time to develop products. Getting the two frameworks right is central to national success. The recommendations of the Naylor Report, *Investing in Canada's Future,* accepted and approved by Justin Trudeau's government in 2018, put the country's independent research program on a greatly improved footing, which in turn offers long-term payoffs for industry and civil society.

The second framework now needs to be stepped up – the corporate–university nexus to focus on the development side of R & D, where discoveries and ideas are transformed into products and services. This entails vastly increasing the rate of creation of new start-up firms, improving access to early and later-stage venture capital, and changing protocols that govern university intellectual property.

In this sense, science-based innovation has become a never-ending match of wits, much like a game of contract bridge, with three identifiable variables. The first, akin to classical economics, is the lay of the cards. The players can play only the cards in their hands – i.e., governments and firms are at the mercy of uncontrolled market forces and national resource endowments. The second variable is how players play their cards. Here, strategy, cunning, and guile all play a role (surrogates for international trade policy, political pressure groups, and management competences and capabilities). But that relates to the third: how the competitors play the game, and their desire to win, often with a ruthlessness rarely seen in Canada. The international benchmarks in the Naylor Report show the opportunity to win is also Canada's to lose.

3

Social Justice and Defining Individual Rights and Responsibilities

Three Eras of Social Reform – Immigration –
The Criminal Code: The Just Society – Bilingualism – The Supreme Court –
Medicare and the Universality Debate – The GST – Environmental Policy –
Climate Change – Aboriginal Rights – Japanese-Canadian Redress –
Social Policy as Wedge Politics – Lobbying and the Transparency Game –
The Enabling Society

No society can surely be flourishing and happy, of which the far greater part of the members are poor and miserable.

Adam Smith

INTRODUCTION

Canada, with its legacy of Judaeo-Christian traditions, has a history of enacting social policies that support the less well-off in society. In the decades following the end of the Second World War, public spending on social welfare increased in most advanced countries, where total expenditure on social security in OECD countries averaged 8 per cent of gross national product (GNP) per annum. In the 1970s and 1980s, the OECD average was about 22.1 per cent, higher in Scandinavian countries, lower in Australia and Japan, with Canada and the United States in the middle, spending 19.2 per cent. However, private spending on social programs – 5.1 per cent of GNP in Canada, 10.6 per cent in the United States – was a stark contrast to the OECD average of 2.5 per cent. Further, while all advanced countries expanded their welfare systems, or the social safety net, there remain many differences within each country, including Canada, with differences by province.

Since 1945, Canada's welfare system owes much to the Green Book, unveiled at a Dominion–Provincial Conference on Reconstruction on 6 August 1945, a series of forward-looking proposals prepared for the Liberal government. Prime Minister W.L. Mackenzie King, who considered himself a social reformer, nearing the end of his tenure in the top job, could turn to the civil service, especially the Department of Finance, to focus on new programs and the ways to finance them. Written largely by policy activists like Colin Clark and Robert Bryce, the Green Book followed and refined Britain's Beveridge Report, and its proposals were implemented by King, St Laurent, Diefenbaker, Pearson, and Pierre Trudeau. King was many things, but he was anything but a Keynesian. However, like many prime ministers before or since, he was not strong on economics, and the conventional wisdom was that the postwar economy might see slow growth. Even the wunderkind of the American economics profession, Paul Samuelson, writing in 1943, could warn of over-optimism: "There is a serious danger of underestimating the magnitude of the problem ... in the postwar period. Those who complacently predict a boom are likely to find their expectations fulfilled, but not with respect to employment and real-income aspects usually associated with a prosperity period."

Canada's social-policy priorities have evolved over the years. Demographics, immigration, and the knowledge economy, with the resulting demands for education and talent, now affect social policy in unprecedented ways. In thought and action, John Diefenbaker, despite his pro-Britain sentiments, was closer to American thinking, not only to the New Deal of Franklin Roosevelt, a Democrat, but to other presidents who stressed individual action and social support. The Conservative leader was advised by two Saskatchewan intellectual mavens, Roy Faibish and Merrill Menzies, who saw an arrogance in the Liberal approach and recognized in their own province a need for focused assistance. Faibish was part intellectual, part policy activist, and, coming from the home of agrarian socialism, he knew and accepted the need for strong government, yet he wanted protection of individual liberty and the role of the market. With Allister Grosart, a Toronto advertising executive, Faibish received a good hearing from Diefenbaker, who rebranded traditional welfare as "social justice." Tom Van Dusen, in his biography, *The Chief*, spells out the leader's thought processes: "Diefenbaker's thinking stemmed from his background on the prairies. His social thinking was radical. He didn't conceal it, nor did it ever change. It derived from his experience of the helpfulness of the individual in the face of giant catastrophes – depression, drought, dust storms. He felt that in organized societies, the individual should be able to count on help from the state."

These changes were not fully understood by the political class. As a general proposition, the main postwar programs funded by Ottawa were family allowances, health insurance, pension programs like the Canada Assistance Plan, unemployment insurance, and a package of transfer payments to the provinces – Established Program Financing (EPF), to support health care, education, and cultural programs. Other measures included funding support for Aboriginal Canadians, the environment, fitness and amateur sport (including such initiatives introduced in 1967 for the summer and winter Canada Games, with associated infrastructure), and labour-market training. Ottawa wanted to take the policy initiative, but also to assure that the federal presence was visible through advertising, federal ministers attending events, and public awareness that federal support was more than a window for provincial initiatives. Federal social programs had another feature supported by all parties: they were redistributive, using federal tax dollars for programs universally applied to all citizens, rich or poor. Clearly public opinion and social values often marched in advance of the political class (see Table 3.1).

Legislators in Canada, federal and provincial, have removed government scrutiny over private life, using direct legislative measures, from no-fault divorce to gay marriage, and the recent decriminalization of marijuana illustrates more dissimilarities with the United States. Ironically, in the Great Republic, it is the court system (specifically the U.S. Supreme Court) that forced change on many social issues – desegregation of schools (*Brown* v. *Board of Education*, 1954), narrowing the definition of legally proscribed obscenity (*Roth* v. *United States*, 1957), abortion (*Roe* v. *Wade*, 1965), birth control (*Griswold* v. *Connecticut*, 1965), homosexual sex (*Lawrence* v. *Texas*, 2003), and gay marriage (*Obergefell* v. *Hodges*, 2015). In Canada, the Charter of Rights, introduced in 1982, has played a significant role, but so has a succession of federal justice ministers, who have balanced the positions of conservatives and progressives on moral issues. The Department of Justice is the only federal department that has had the same structure since it was set up, in May 1868, with a dual mandate – political, with a minister reporting to cabinet, and legal, in the office of the attorney general (the same person). Overall, the department both makes policy and appoints judicial officers, and has boasted a series of cabinet stars, such as Pierre Trudeau, John Turner, Marc Lalonde, John Crosbie, Ray Hnatyshyn, Kim Campbell, Anne McLellan, Irwin Cotler, and Peter MacKay. Justin Trudeau's appointment of Jody Wilson-Raybould

Table 3.1
Three Eras of Social Policy in Canada

	Expansion era (1945–70)	Rise of distribution rights (1970s–80s)	Consolidation and reformulation (21st c.)
Economic growth	Sustained economic expansion, social policy as fiscal dividend	Stagflation and rising unemployment	Regional tensions on slow growth and fiscal restraint
The political environment	Rise of interest groups, new tradeoffs	New tradeoffs between individual responsibility and equity	Federal–provincial tensions on shared-cost programs
Social values	Widespread political support for social safety net	New alignments with social and economic policy	New acceptance of targeting and selectivity in ageing society
The policy environment	Ottawa-centric, green-paper legacy	Growing conflicts between government and markets	Balancing universality (e.g., healthcare) + targeted programs

as the first Aboriginal to hold the post was a path-breaking initiative, but her resignation from cabinet in 2019 after being moved to Veterans Affairs is the only example of a justice minister leaving on a point of disagreement with the prime minister.

All political parties realized that postwar reconstruction would place strains on government finances. They were well aware of the comprehensive proposals advanced in Britain by William Henry Beveridge, who in 1942 presented his report to Winston Churchill's government and had made sure it was widely distributed, including through briefings to parliamentarians and key journalists. Beveridge, not a shy man, an early practitioner of social propaganda, proposed universal social insurance, including a national health service, workplace accident insurance, family assistance, and, to maintain high and stable employment, unemployment insurance. The election of Clement Attlee's Labour government in June 1945, a month after victory in Europe, ensured that Beveridge's proposals shaped postwar social policy, financed mainly from the state budget and uniform, lump-sum contributions. In short, the Beveridge framework is a redistribution model, and the path adopted by Canada.

|

There were other options. One, known in some circles in Ottawa, but generally not to the public at large, was the Bismarck system, dating back to German Chancellor Otto von Bismarck, who introduced statutory health insurance in 1883. In effect, it was a comprehensive system of social insurance, and a political lesson in how to thwart social unrest and cries for socialism from trade-union leaders and church-run labour federations. The German system insured gainfully employed people, with financing via contributions, graduated according to income and paid from wages or salaries. In an ideal world, an optimal version leads to no redistribution between income groups. However, both approaches – British and German – have an inherent flaw, namely a static view of the demographics of society at large. Increases in life expectancy, extension of periods of non-employment, and dependence and changes in fertility rates alter the age structure of the population. Clearly, the biggest shift in a society's demographic profile comes from immigration, and greatly affects the dependency ratio – the proportion of the population over sixty-five plus the young cohort divided by the number of working age. Unlike most areas of economic and social policy, where data and their interpretation are an inexact science, demographics offers a certain, unambiguous "exactness" – what is aged ten today becomes aged twenty ten years hence.

Until recently, population ageing rarely received much public attention, but now the demographic makeup of a nation affects such crucial areas as education and health care and the tax revenues of the country at large. Further, in Canada and other countries, regional variations, including differences between urban and rural areas, longstanding patterns of low fertility, and significant reductions in adult mortality, affect health care and hospital payments, labour-market policies, social security, and unemployment insurance. Demographics also plays a huge role. As shown in Figure 3.1, Canada has experienced a steady aging effect, with a decline in the ratio of youth to the total population, and a similar rise in the number of seniors. Politically, the harsh rhetoric between those who prefer universal programs available for everyone, independent of age, income, race, or sex, and those who would target programs for specific groups, especially those most in need, traditionally follows a simplified left–right political dichotomy.

When Lester Pearson's Liberal government introduced the guaranteed income supplement (GIS) for the elderly in 1967, it proved a very successful target program to help a particular age group but was an exception to the universal approach. To cite another example from the Macdonald Commission in 1985, much heralded in some quarters for recommending free trade, it also proposed a guaranteed annual income: a transfer by Ottawa of roughly $9,000 for a family of four, taxed at a rate of 20 per cent, a policy not unlike a measure advocated by Robert Stanfield when

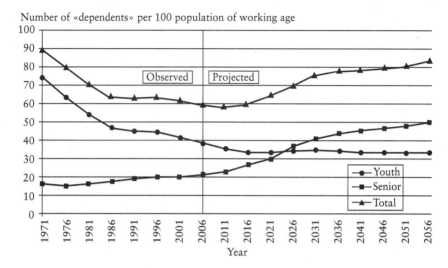

Source: Adapted from CANSIM

Figure 3.1 Observed and Projected Youth, Senior, and Total Demographic Dependency Ratios, Canada 1971–2056.

he was Tory leader. Such a proposal should be a political winner, but in the messy world of policy, it might mean replacing existing measures – children's tax credit, family allowances, federal housing support, the GIS, and personal and married allowances. Political reality can be an intrusive force, a brutal awakening inside the policy jungle.

Starting in the 1960s, especially with John Diefenbaker's "One Canada" mantra – an appeal to include citizens who were of neither anglophone nor francophone heritage – governments and political leaders of all parties, federally and provincially, began to accept the politics of inclusion. From women's rights to opportunities for new immigrants, Canada slowly, reluctantly, but at times heroically – as in the Joe Clark government's acceptance of 60,000 Vietnamese boat people in 1979 – bent, changed, or reformed the rules to reduce barriers – social, economic, and constitutional. Some initiatives were immensely symbolic – Prime Minister Brian Mulroney appointing Ray Hnatyshyn as the first governor general of Ukrainian heritage and the charismatic Lincoln Alexander, Canada's first Black viceroy, as lieutenant-governor of Ontario – or Jean Chrétien appointing Adrienne Clarkson the first woman of Chinese heritage to be governor general – or Prime Minister Paul Martin's legislation for same-sex marriage, which was defended by a Conservative, Peter MacKay, in the parliamentary debates. Together, they illustrated a growing societal maturity. Individual acts of altruism and heroism are rightly celebrated, but less well-known actions come from Parliament in the expanding committee structures, such as the Senate Special Committee on the Charitable Sector, or the Special Parliamentary Committee on the Disabled and Handicapped, that allow members to travel, hear witnesses, study measures in other countries.

If, to quote Edward Kennedy, speaking in 2007 on a new immigration bill before the U.S. Senate – "Today is the day, now is the time, this is the place." – he could have been referring to Canadian Minister of Justice Pierre Trudeau. Timing and chance are indeed everything in politics, and unlike his predecessor, Trudeau combined luck, timing, and the event cycle and used them to great political advantage. When he became justice minister in the Pearson government in 1967, Canada was celebrating the centennial of Confederation and the tourist magnet of Expo 67 (the Montreal World's Fair), swept along with the changing values of a younger generation less tied to traditional, even prudish values of the churches, the WASP and Québécois establishments, and the sort of religious conformity sometimes found in small communities.

Trudeau's initial priorities as justice minister focused on the Criminal Code, an outdated relic from an earlier age reflecting elite values on abortion, marriage and divorce, and sexuality, often mirroring practices in Britain, with its embedded social hypocrisy on homosexuality, gay marriage, and Church of England protocols. As an academic working with trade unions, young lawyers, and social activists in the 1950s fighting tradition-bound justice practices in Quebec's right-wing, authoritarian Union Nationale government of Maurice Duplessis, Trudeau had close contacts with leaders in the CCF (soon to be NDP), writers like Frank Scott and Frank Underhill, and organizers like David Lewis, a Rhodes scholar and future CCF national leader.

Trudeau shared their interest in advancing political change for greater social liberties – challenging the infamous padlock law in Quebec, antilabour measures in Ontario – but the CCF showed little interest in joining Quebec labour activists to fight Duplessis. Clearly, Trudeau was fully aware of the CCF's famous Winnipeg Declaration of 1956 and its call for "Social Planning for a Just Society" – an ideal slogan for his reformist work as justice minister in the Pearson government. His celebrated remark of 1967 – "The state has no business in the bedrooms of the nation" – was perfectly timed and set him apart, as he defended reforms on homosexuality, birth control, and abortion. As a made-for-TV personality, visually kinetic, athletic, single, effortlessly bilingual, a politician with a quick wit and an aura of insouciance, Trudeau represented young peoples' view of themselves, far more attuned to the values of openness, acceptance of social differences and diversity, and the significance of minority rights.

In the new TV age, Trudeau was a novelty in Canadian politics, a wealthy intellectual who had the wherewithal to travel, study, debate, and learn from celebrated professors, without worrying much about grades, social approval, or conforming to accepted wisdom. He viewed the Canadian constitution – the British North America Act – as a clever and flexible document. As a young man in the postwar period, he saw for himself the constant yearning to break away from faceless, impersonal, (in Quebec) authoritarian rule. His treatise on federalism and later his address in 1967 to the Canadian Bar Association brought into focus three central elements. The first was the political system with political rights in a real democracy, not an entitled bureaucracy or a one-party state. In his view, Canada was exceptionally fortunate in bringing two civilizations, cultures, and languages into a unique federal system, the first country in the British Empire to become independent from London's rule. Second, he sought a judicial system backed by constitutionally protected human rights, which would have the flexible advantages of the parliamentary system but the legal responsibilities to protect individual liberties, outside the whims of Parliament. And Canada needed a third attribute, a continuity in constitutional order where individual politicians or parties could not upset the social order, based on temporary circumstances or ideological zealotry – what he called "brutal circumstance or blind disorder."

Trudeau foresaw the dangers inherent in democracies, when a bloc of voters can impair or unsettle an elected Parliament, or majority rule overturns the rights of minorities. He wasn't alone in his calls for a multicultural society, but he was the most articulate, and, like many others, he was aware of famous tracts like Mabel Timlin's *Does Canada Need More People?* (1951) – her answer is a resounding "Yes" – as well as calls for immigration reform by the Gordon Report in 1957.

II

In creating the modern welfare state after 1945, the Liberals took the lead, as the main governing party from the mid-1930s to the beginning of the 21st century, and its model was Britain. When Pierre Trudeau campaigned in the 1968 federal election, on a resonant, amorphous slogan, "The Just Society," his timing coincided with television exposing the gross injustices of poor people in Third World countries and the U.S. civil-rights movement openly challenging whomever was occupying the White House, as well as the inner sanctums of political parties, corporate boardrooms, and university campuses. As an immigrant-based country, Canada has always accepted the general principle of bringing in newcomers, but often selectively. Wilfrid Laurier followed Macdonald's strategy for settling western Canada, ramped up by Minister of the Interior Clifford Sifton. Sifton, a lawyer by profession, born in Ontario but living in Manitoba from a young age, was imbued with the political bug as a teenager, working on his father's provincial campaign and then winning provincial office himself in 1888. He became attorney general in the Liberal government of Thomas Greenway, beginning in 1891. His other post, provincial land commissioner, gave him deep insight into the settlement business in the vast North-West Territories, a troublesome burden for the federal government and a political liability for the prime minister. This politically delicate mix included Aboriginal reserves after the British government relinquished administration of them, at a cost of a million dollars a year. Other grievances in Manitoba became the "Declaration of Rights." The Manitoba and North-West Farmers Union blamed Ottawa for steep freight rates, high costs of administering public lands, the monopolistic practices of the grain-elevator operators, and the monopoly.

Almost a decade earlier, in 1885, Sir John A. Macdonald pulled off another political miracle, quieting his 40 Quebec MPs who threatened to bolt, and he refused to accept the resignation of Minister of Inland Revenue John Costigan, a popular Irish Roman Catholic member from New Brunswick, where the Irish vote was vital to the party's standing. The prime minister confronted injurious press comments in London and across Britain, while pushing his MPs to pass the Pacific Railway Loan Act and a doubling of the subsidy for the CPR. All these efforts were trouble enough, and a far cry from his optimism in 1883. In Parliament, he attacked Liberal leader Edward Blake's pessimism, "darkness rather than light, shadow rather than sunshine, Rembrandt rather than Turner," while Wilfrid Laurier sat across the aisle, absorbing the master's rhetorical skills in action. In 1891, Macdonald passed away, the Conservatives were in disarray, and the vexing Manitoba schools question was opening old party wounds between the ferociously Protestant Orange Order and French-Canadian nationalism.

In 1896, Laurier won the national election. Clifford Sifton, now a federal MP, became minister of the interior, pledging a new, vigorous, and aggressive immigration policy to settle and populate Manitoba and the north-west. His targets had an ecumenical flavour, with aims to attract British and American immigrants, and what he called "stalwart peasants in sheep-skin coats" from Ukraine, the Austro-Hungarian Empire, Scandinavia, and even the Doukhobors from Russia, pacifists and religious dissenters who disdained secular government as well as the Russian Orthodox church, and were assisted by the celebrated novelist Leo Tolstoy. With Sifton in charge, Canada had lenient immigration measures, and clever would-be newcomers learned new ways around the three restricted categories – the sick and diseased, the criminal or vicious, and those judged likely to become public dissenters and a burden to taxpayers – while the ports of entry – Halifax, Quebec City, and Montreal – had inspectors for landed immigrants, who then travelled by railway to destinations in the west.

In British Columbia, immigration started on a different track, as a result of the gold rush in the Fraser Canyon in 1858, and, over the decades, immigrants arrived from China, Japan, and India. In 1907, U.S. President Theodore Roosevelt signed a "Gentlemen's Agreement" with the Empire of Japan, whereby that country would no longer permit emigration to the United States by its subjects, many of whom had been doing so via the new American territory of Hawaii, and up to 7,000 of them entered British Columbia instead. An organized group of 500 Vancouver workers formed the Asiatic Exclusion League. On 7 September 1907, some five thousand people marched on Vancouver City Hall, supported by an estimated crowd of twenty-five thousand, and there followed riots, marches, and mayhem in Chinatown and then in Japantown and Little Tokyo. As a result, the League and other activist groups lobbied for measures practised in the United States, and in the Hayashi–Lemieux "Gentlemen's Agreement" of 1908 Canada limited passports to only 400 male immigrants and domestic servants per year from Japan.

Any complaints from the Department of Justice or local municipalities might interrupt new arrivals' acceptance at entry, but restrictions were minimal under Sifton's watch. When he left Ottawa in 1905, the process became more bureaucratic, and the Immigration Act of 1910 imposed many entry barriers. The act's real goal was to spur economic development, and the new policies were racist, setting out "preferred" countries of origin, whose inhabitants encountered fairly easy entry requirements. Historians have documented many case studies, including two incidents that marred Canada's reputation as a home for immigrants. The first took place in 1914, when the Japanese charter ship the SS *Komagata Maru* arrived in Vancouver after a long ocean voyage via Hong Kong and

Yokohama, carrying 376 people from Punjab, mostly Sikhs, but also twenty-four Muslims and twelve Hindus. Only twenty-four passengers were allowed to leave the vessel. After months of officials' prevaricating, the ship was forced to return to India, only to face more violence in Calcutta (now Kolkata). This incident, with widespread media coverage, portrayed Canada, like Britain, as "a white man's country."

The second incident reinforced the first. The Depression years dramatically changed Canadian immigration policy, as Prime Minister Bennett all but eliminated immigration from Europe. Just before hostilities broke out in 1939, when asked about accepting German Jews, a civil servant responded coldly, "None is too many." Thus it was no surprise to bureaucrats in Ottawa when the King government in 1939 turned away 907 Jewish passengers travelling aboard the German MS St *Louis,* which departed Hamburg on 13 May on route to Havana. Barred from entry both in Cuba and in the United States, they then sought refuge in Canada but to no avail, so the ship returned to Antwerp, the passengers were dispersed, and 254 ended up in the death camps, yet more victims of the Holocaust, memorialized in the movie *Voyage of the Damned* (1976) and in *None Is Too Many: Canada and the Jews of Europe, 1933–1948*, the classic 1983 study by Irving Abella and Harold Troper.

Almost sixty years passed before changes were made to Canada's racist Immigration Act. The huge reforms to immigration policy initiated by the Diefenbaker government, and improvements under Pearson and Pierre Trudeau, set the stage for a new branding of Canada as an unusual country openly soliciting immigration. But attitudes change slowly. Canada made serious improvements with a novel points system, where applications had to score well on such factors as age, education, language skills, occupational skills, and work experience. The path was now opened to a superior model of intergenerational mobility. About two-thirds of newcomers were economic migrants, chosen for their special skills, while about a quarter arrived under family sponsorship, and about 10 per cent were refugees. Successive changes welcomed Federal Skilled Workers, Quebec Skilled Workers, Provincial Nominees, Canadian Experience, Live-in Caregiver, and Business Immigration (Investor, Entrepreneur, and Self–Employed Persons) and immediate family members. Unlike many countries, and notably more recently in the United States or even in Britain during the Brexit saga, there was little fear that immigration was a drain on Canada's welfare system, or many immigrants were coming illegally, or the entry system was rigged. Moreover, as more provinces have a direct say on immigration policy, perversely a legacy of the failed Meech Lake constitutional accord of 1987–90, there is little sense that provincial social priorities are distorted or imposed by the Ottawa bureaucracy.

While the Pierre Trudeau government's immigration reforms became part of a plan to make Canada a diverse, multicultural society, they also helped the Liberal party to attract the "ethnic vote." Clever advertising, using the Liberal red colour to associate with the Canadian flag, nationalist initiatives like PetroCanada, and shrewd narratives stressing ethnic engagement and paths of inclusion forced two responses. The first, by the Mulroney government, was to copy and improve it. Immigration levels dropped to only 80,000 in 1983. When the new government was sworn in in the autumn of 1984, with its emphasis on the competitive agenda, social policies favoured increased immigration and recruitment of skilled workers. The new caucus reflected the shifting profile of Canadian society. To cite a small but symbolic example, when the government sent a delegation to Ukraine in 1992, to celebrate Canada's being the first country to recognize that country's independence after the collapse of the Soviet Union, the entire team, including Governor General Ray Hnatyshyn and Deputy Prime Minister Don Mazankowski, spoke Ukrainian, although their hosts in Kiev spoke Russian.

Global migration was a big issue in the 1980s. The Mulroney government debated the merits of raising immigration levels as high as 350,000 per year, but settled on 250,000. At cabinet and in caucus, the cabinet, led by forceful arguments from Flora MacDonald, recognized the Canada was the only G7 country without ready access to a market of at least 100 million people. Earlier calls to have immigration levels approach one per cent of the population were no longer seen as outlandish. By combining the Immigration Department with Labour and Employment, the Mulroney government aligned immigration policy with labour-market and training needs, with an emphasis on attracting skilled workers. Today, all parties accept the reality of these population trends, and new obligations for the leaders and party spokespeople to reflect the realities of a bilingual, multicultural society. The media extensively covered the anti-immigration sentiments and indiscretions of Reform party or Canadian Alliance members like BC writer and journalist Doug Collins, briefly a Reform candidate for Parliament in 1988; Bob Ringma, a Reform MP from Vancouver 1993–97; and Betty Granger, briefly an Alliance candidate in Vancouver, who called foreign students an "Asian invasion." These instances revealed a pattern that the party was slow to learn, leaving a perception of xenophobia as a legacy that marred the future Reform–Alliance merger and the revamped Conservative party and the Harper years in government.

III

The expansion of the welfare state in the Western world after 1945 created a political backlash in many countries, and a political challenge to find the optimum balance between collective choice via parliamentary government, with a degree of social coercion, compared to the ideals of laissez-faire, which embraced individual choice and unfettered markets and accepted market failures. Perhaps no jurisdiction spells out more clearly a social-justice framework than the European Union, with annual reports, and benchmarks by individual countries based on outcomes and a key indicator – can children born into poorer and less well-educated families climb the social ladder to middle-class incomes? Denmark scores at the top, with other European countries like Britain, Germany, and Sweden showing a child's educational attainment is completely independent of their parents' education (see Figure 3.2). Elsewhere, Japan ranks near the top, and so does Canada, far ahead of France and Italy. American society defies the myth and illusion of the American dream, showing among the lowest levels of intergenerational mobility among the wealthier, advanced countries.

In Canada, the evolution of health insurance, Medicare, and what eventually became the Canada Heath Act contrast dramatically with the American experience. It may be an overstatement to cite European influences, but health care is an instance: Canada borrowed substantially from Britain's National Health Service, an initiative of Clement Attlee's Labour government in the late 1940s, but developed its own health-insurance system slowly. The Canadian Medical Association (CMA), unlike its American counterpart, approved the idea of public insurance, in 1923. Immediately after 1945, Prime Minister King floated the idea of a national system of hospital insurance but backed off when the premiers thought it too expensive. When Prime Minister Louis St Laurent chaired another federal–provincial meeting on 2 October 1955 to discuss fiscal arrangements, the idea was resurrected, in part because Ontario's Tory premier, Leslie Frost, had publicly endorsed the concept in September and secretly provided background papers to the prime minister and his chief policy adviser, Maurice Lamontagne.

By this time, the political narrative had changed. In Atlantic Canada, a group of doctors led by my father, working with Catholic bishops (as in Quebec and Ontario, many hospitals were operated by the Catholic church), introduced Blue Cross prepaid plans, and Newfoundland soon joined after entering Confederation in 1949. In 1948 in Alberta, Ernest

Poverty (triple weight)	Education (double weight)	Labour Market Access	Social Cohesion & Non-Discrimination	Health Policy	Inter-Generational Mobility
At Risk of Poverty or social Exclusion:	(Qualitative)	Employment Rate: Older Employment, Foreign-born To Native Employment,	Inclusion Policy (Qualitative) Gini Coefficient	Health Indications (Qualitative) Self-reported	Family Policy (Qualitative)
Total Population (Total Population/ Children/Seniors), Population Living in Quasi-Jobless Households, Severe Material Deprivation (Total/ Children/Seniors)	Socioeconomic Background and Student Performance, Pre-primary Education, Early School Leavers	Employment Rates: Women/Men Unemployment: Long-term Unemployment – Youth, Low-skilled, Temporary Contracts, In-work Poverty Low Pay Incidence	Non-discrimination Policy (Qualitative) Seats in Parliament held by Women/ Men Integration Policy (Qualitative NEET Rate – Young People, 20-24, not employed or in training)	Unmet Needs for Medical Help. Healthy Life Expectancy Health Systems' Outcomes Acessibility and Range	Pension Policy (Qualitative) Environmental Policy Qualitative): GHG Emissions. Renewable Energy-R&D Spending. Government Debt Level. Old Age Dependency Ratio.

Source: Author's adaptation of Daniel Schraad-Tischler and Christian Knoll, "Social Justice in the EU: A Cross-National Comparison," 2014

Figure 3.2 The European Union: Social Justice Framework.

Manning's Social Credit government had introduced catastrophic insurance for all families, ensuring that no family would go bankrupt due to health bills. Rejecting the universal approach of Saskatchewan, it applied a means test and subsidized hospital care in municipalities, covering 650,000 residents, with another 118,000 receiving hospital coverage through Alberta Blue Cross and 86,000 buying prepaid plans, through Medical Services Inc., directly from the Alberta Medical Association. Another 33,000 people, unable to pay themselves, were covered for medical care, hospital care, and drugs.

In Saskatchewan, in 1944, Tommy Douglas and the CCF campaigned on a platform that promised free access to health care for all citizens. Scots-born Douglas was a mesmerizing Baptist preacher, and as a youth he was stricken with severe osteomyelitis, a rare but debilitating bone disease, but treated pro bono by a family doctor in a profession where such *noblesse oblige* was widespread. Campaigning in 1944, Douglas promised free health care, using his own afflictions as a rallying cry: "No boy should have to depend either for his leg or his life upon the ability of his parents to raise enough money to bring a first-class surgeon to his bedside." He was elected to power with a sweeping majority – the first of his four winning provincial campaigns. He accepted the advice of Henry E. Sigerist from Johns Hopkins University to set up government-funded programs for hospital, medical, nursing, and physiotherapy care; more and improved clinical facilities; a medical school; and salaries for doctors (instead of the traditional fee-for-service model), and he introduced a provincial scheme of hospital insurance in 1947. Other provinces followed, and by 1956, almost all Canadians had some form of health insurance, either non-profit or private insurance, compared to only 50 per cent in 1950, so the idea of government involvement was generally accepted by all parties.

Prime Minister John Diefenbaker, recognizing a political opportunity, knew that hospital insurance alone would not address the changing world of health care. In 1961 he willingly appointed Mr Justice Emmett Hall, his close friend and former classmate at University of Saskatchewan Law School, to chair the Royal Commission on Health Services (Hall Commission). The CMA was fully supportive. Hall was of conservative persuasion and an unlikely advocate for a national system, initially publicly funded, but his country-wide consultations and the lessons from a then largely unknown American economist, changed his thinking. Kenneth Arrow, a future Nobel laureate, in 1963 wrote a path-breaking article in the *American Economic Review*, comparing the market for medical care to other industries, where traditional markets, the price system, and competition bring optimum outcomes, such as lower prices and better quality for consumers. Medical care, he proposed, was a special case, where

> the failure of the market to insure against uncertainties has created many social institutions in which the usual assumptions of the market are to some extent contradicted. The medical profession is only one example ... The economic importance of personal and especially family relationships, though declining, is by no means trivial in the most advanced economies; it is based on non-market relations that create guarantees of behavior which would otherwise be afflicted with excessive uncertainty ... The logic and limitations of ideal competitive behavior under uncertainty force us to recognize the incomplete description of reality supplied by the impersonal price system.

Three years later, Hall's report, in seven massive volumes, including one on medical education, recommended a comprehensive national system that excluded the patient from the payment system and reimbursed doctors and hospitals through a single payer. A national debate ensued, with one side including a loose coalition of conservative-minded stakeholders – the medical profession, Conservative premiers, and senior civil servants, who preferred a mixed, public –private insurance system, and the second, smaller, more vocal, with a command of the media – social activists, the NDP, the trade unions, and the governments in the poorer provinces.

This debate followed a federal election in 1963, in which the Liberals under Lester Pearson won a minority government. The new prime minister knew that health care left no room for political retreat. He accepted this challenge, building on the measure Louis St Laurent had introduced in the dying days of his government in 1957: the Hospital Insurance and Diagnostics Services Act, which would have Ottawa pay half the costs of medical services, a form of first-dollar coverage in an area of provincial jurisdiction, and the start of a hospital-oriented health model. Pearson, receiving private backing from Tory Premier John Robarts in Ontario, introduced in 1966 the Canadian Medical Care Act. Parliament passed the bill almost unanimously, with a shift to medical, not hospital insurance, and a bias to curative rather than preventive medicine.

In 1984, in Pierre Trudeau's last year in office, Parliament passed his Canada Health Act, with its five traditional but rigid principles: complete reimbursement direct to hospitals (i.e., no co-payments or "extra billing"), comprehensive coverage, interprovincial portability, public funding, and universality. The premiers saw all five points as intruding in areas of provincial responsibility but lacked the tax points to fund the programs. They viewed this retreat from shared-cost funding as a sore point, while Ottawa was using the carrot-and-stick approach, largely by providing initial financial transfers to force the provinces to accept social initiatives, but then insisting they accept federal demands on coverage, mobility, and fees for the medical profession. However, all premiers knew the widespread popularity of health-care coverage and accepted the recommendations for hospital and medical services as a universal system.

However, the event cycle was in play. Pierre Trudeau's government intended the 1984 act to clarify general principles, and the bill had received unanimous support in the House of Commons, although a few Conservative dissenters deliberately missed the vote. To the utter dismay of the Liberals, who had planned a press campaign against the Conservatives' new, untested leader and his party, the Conservative caucus had discussed this issue at its policy retreat at Mont Ste Marie in September 1983. Health critic Jake Epp had laid out the pros and cons of supporting the measure and backed his arguments with opinion research on the popularity of Canadian health care and the views of provincial medical associations and the CMA. Caucus support came from all parts of the political spectrum, despite misgivings about the bill's rigidities. (Figure 3.3 sets out a three-dimensional framework for health-care spending in Canada – coverage, benefits, and payments.)

Under Mulroney's watchful eye, the caucus had consulted with numerous health experts and health ministers, including the former Ontario minister Larry Grossman and his former deputy, Graham Scott. Grossman, by this time the province's treasurer, knew the tradeoffs – the high and increasing costs of health care and declining federal payments – but also the social need for a very popular program. Health care was the largest item in provincial budgets, and eight provinces had medical schools, the most expensive professional schools in the university system. Ontario, for example, covered 80 per cent of the negotiated fees for doctors, allowing them to bill patients privately for the rest. To remain eligible for the federal transfers, Ontario eliminated "full billing," which the media and the NDP called "extra billing," a pejorative term that weakened the credibility of the medical community.

To control total spending, allow more flexibility vis-à-vis provincial priorities, and reduce federal outlays, the Mulroney government

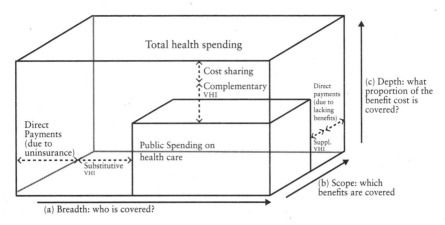

Source: Adapted from The Commonwealth Fund

Figure 3.3 Health-care Spending: Coverage, Benefits, and Payments.

introduced new formulas, based on population and the growth rates of the economy. Like other OECD countries, Canada's evolved into a mixed system, 70 per cent publicly funded, 30 per cent private, with the felicitous term "out-of- pocket spending." In the two generations after 1945, Ottawa won the argument for a national health system, using its powers of persuasion and funding to bring the provinces in line, but creating a system with inherent cost inflation, despite numerous warnings by the provinces, health experts, and the medical profession (see Figure 3.4). Further, the system soon became an insiders' game known only by experts, because of acronyms like CHST – the Canada Health and Social Transfer – increasing federal budget restraints, and little political appetite to rethink the basic system. Health care politically had a new credo, echoing Mackenzie King on conscription, "Funding of health care where necessary, but not necessarily federal funding."

In truth, as more experience with this fairly rigid funding system collected, the political dilemma remained. Any hint of a move away from the universal model, favoured by the NDP and many progressives in other parties, to an improved, flexible funding system smacked of a move towards the unwieldy, disjointed, breathtakingly costly, multi-payer American model. In Canada, a series of measures, combining federal spending restraints, more flexibility for the provinces, and long-term funding commitments, without any real change to the Canada Health Act, became the new norm for what is now a mixed system, with public

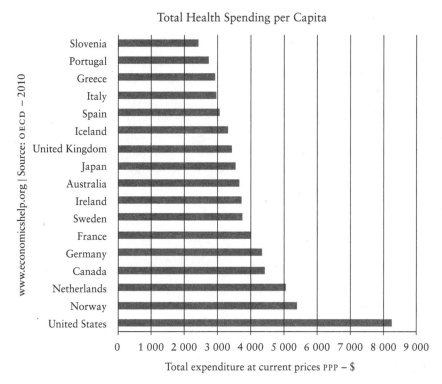

Source: Adapted from The Commonwealth Fund

Figure 3.4 Health-Care Cost (1970–2016).

money skewed to medical payments and hospital services, with outcomes superior to the American model, although, on balance, the French, Swiss, and Japanese models achieve more while spending less.

In 2004, Paul Martin's government introduced a Health Accord (see Table 3.2), a ten-year funding package to allow long-term and predictable planning, as recommended by the Royal Commission on the Future of Health Care in Canada (Romanow Commission) of 2001, which also led to the Health Council of Canada (HCC), which was disbanded in 2014. This advisory body, consisting of medical and health professionals, was a forum to promote best practices and procedures, and set benchmarks for shorter waiting times, reform of primary health care, improved access to home care, electronic health records, Aboriginal health, catastrophic drug coverage, and prevention and health promotion. While Ottawa kept its funding commitments, the HCC hoped to foster and facilitate pan-Canadian approaches to digital innovation and creation of the Innovation Portal, but progress was slow, incremental, and limited. Three years before the Health Accord of 2004 expired, Finance Minister Jim Flaherty unilaterally announced that the 6 per cent funding would be replaced in 2017 by an escalator tied to GDP, with a floor of 3 per cent, not population need, a move that angered provincial finance ministers.

Seventy-five years after the Second World War ended, Canadian health care has retained the essential principle of universality, with Ottawa still taking the lead in policy and funding, but time and circumstances have moved to a system of province-based, hospital-centred delivery. Health experts know that money alone won't solve the difficult tradeoffs, such as the pressures of waiting times, the need for more innovation, and use of private clinics and extra billing within the rigid framework of the Canada Health Act, now an untouchable political edifice. Further, as federal direct initiatives decline, the provinces are taking the political heat, and being blamed for slow adoption of technology and inadequate drug plans, mental-health programs, home-care coverage for post-acute medical care, and palliative home care. More recently, Quebec passed a bill unanimously that allowed assisted dying, a measure eventually approved by Parliament as well in 2017.

IV

On the premise that big problems need big ideas, a surprising mix of economists, political figures, and social thinkers return to a bold idea advanced two generations ago: a guaranteed annual income. As a general rule, social policy evolves incrementally. Examples include minimum-wage laws, rent subsidies, and tax credits; the Harper government initiated a range of tax measures such as the Children's Fitness Tax Credit, the Home Renovation Tax Credit, the Public Transit Credit, and the tax credit for first-time home-buyers, plus income-splitting for seniors – a social-engineering approach that reduces tax revenues, perhaps by over $40 billion per year, a figure almost one-third greater than the annual cost of Old Age Security.

Deciding tax policy and taxation levels is a burden for any minister of finance, where failure can ruin a career, where the chance of success is, at best, politically risky. At Finance, the minister faces another, unique hurdle – designing and changing tax policy, and advising the prime minister and the cabinet on all the political implications. Few observers noted what Finance Minister Michael Wilson said in his 1986 budget speech,

Table 3.2
Funding the 2004 Health Accord to Date

Canada Health Transfer (CHT) and top-ups	2004 Health Accord	Harper gov't plan (2011)	J. Trudeau gov't ultimatum (Dec. 2016)	J. Trudeau gov't bilateral deals (winter 2016–17)	Needed to maintain existing services
CHT escalator	Annual increase of 6% for 10 years	Annual increase: nominal GDP growth (est. 3.5–4%) for 10 years, with a floor of 3%	Annual increase: 3.5% with no fluctuation for growth for 10 years	Annual increase: nominal GDP growth rate (est. 3.5–4%) for 10 years with a floor of 3%	5.2% CHT increase per year for 10 years
Additional funds for national priorities	$4.5b waiting-time reduction targeting cancer care, cataracts, cardiac care, hip and knee replacements, MRI & CTs. $16b for primary care, home care, and drug coverage	None	$11.5b over 10 years for mental health, home care, prescription drugs innovation – 2.4% over 10 years in addition to the 3.5% base escalator	Approx. $11.5b home care and mental health over 10 years: NFLD 160m PEI $45.1m NB 229.4m NS 287.8m QC $2.5b ON $4.2b MB $1.1b SK $348.8m AB $1.3b BC $1.4b + $10m opioid crisis Territories $36.1m	Plus: Additional funds would be required to establish new or enhanced programs.
Total	6% per year for 10 years + $21.5b over 10 years	Est. 4% per year for 10 years	3.5% per year + $11.5b in "target" funds	Est. 4% per year less than 1/10 of 1% in target over 10 years	5.2% per year for 10 years plus unspecified amounts for any new programs/ enhancement

while announcing the social-reform measures that "must reduce the after-tax value of benefits going to the higher income Canadians who do not need assistance." In short, Canada was moving from a universal to a mixed system, where programs may have an income threshold. Family Allowances and Old Age Security didn't require income tests, which were already enacted by the Liberals, but other existing programs (e.g., the Guaranteed Income Supplement and the refundable tax credit) and any new programs, such as a potential national daycare or drug program, could have an income test, calibrated through the tax system.

Tax policy is a central feature of national competitiveness, affecting key indicators such as corporate investment, employment creation, and take-home pay. In one sense, Canada has a tradition of comprehensive studies of taxation through royal commissions, which allow arm's-length, non-partisan considerations of optimal tax measures. The Royal Commission on Taxation (Carter Commission, 1962–66), announced by John Diefenbaker during the 1962 election campaign, operated with the slogan "A buck is a buck," or, more eloquently, "Taxation should be equitable," i.e., every dollar acquired, no matter how, should be taxed. It took the commission six massive volumes and numerous background reports to explain why. Tax policy, in short, is complicated, involving personal or corporate tax, and direct and indirect taxes.

While many people might agree with the general sentiments of Justice Oliver Wendell Holmes, Jr, "Taxes are the price we pay for civilization," or those of Albert Einstein: "The hardest thing in the world to understand is income taxes," their voting instincts clearly are for lower taxes. In the 1980s in Canada tax policy became a central political issue independent of how taxes affect the economy, economic growth, and international competitiveness. Leading economists such as the Americans Milton Friedman and Paul McCracken joined a chorus of political tacticians to press such mantras as a flat tax, a minimum tax, the supply-side Laffer curve (if the tax rate is zero, total tax receipts are zero; if tax rates are very high, tax revenues border on zero). Other measures being discussed included tax simplification, on the premise that, to starve the (government) beast, inflict massive tax relief to assure cuts in program spending, ignoring the possibility of high deficits, higher interest rates, and potential currency devaluation.

When Friedman proposed a negative income tax – an income floor, below which there would be no tax – he sought to simplify the administrative state, such as the more than a hundred programs U.S. President Lyndon Johnson proposed in the mid-1960s for his Great Society. Robert

Stanfield, after he took over Canada's Progressive Conservatives in 1967, spent enormous amounts of time with leading thinkers, top economists, and ex-civil servants who understood the maze of social programs in Ottawa. As a former premier, he also knew that many provinces didn't have the fiscal capacity to fund new programs, and Friedman's proposal of a negative income tax therefore had special appeal.

Many people in Canada, not immune to this debate, saw this measure as a tax issue. In the 1980s, John Bullock of the Canadian Federation of Independent Business (CFIB), joined tax experts, the Institute of Charter Accountants, and big accounting firms to call for massive reforms to the income tax. In the tax world, the leading spokesman was J. Lyman MacInnis, a senior partner at Touche Ross (accounting and professional services) in Toronto. Calling the Income Tax Act "an unmitigated mess," in 1983 he expressed his anger publicly and became a media star:

> Our entire Income Tax was re-vamped back in 1972. That's really not that long ago, and that so-called 'reform' of the Act was supposed to give us a well-thought-out, simpler tax system. Well, since 1972 there have been more than thirty major amending acts. There were 350 changes in 1980-81 alone. Two months ago, Finance Minister Marc Lalonde introduced the last amending act – it had 133 amendments in it. Most of them were more incomprehensible than what's in the existing Act ... All Revenue Canada has to do is assess us and it's up to you and me to prove they are wrong ... And we have that hanging over us in an Act that even tax professionals admit they have difficulty understanding.

In the closing weeks in Parliament before the summer election campaign of 1984, Perrin Beatty led a carefully orchestrated team in the Conservative caucus that clashed with the policies of Revenue Canada, its minister, and the treatment of taxpayers. The arena was Question Period. The topic turned out to be a political gold mine. When Prime Minister Trudeau was about to travel to a Commonwealth meeting in Australia, the Conservatives held a meeting on a Thursday afternoon, to plan the next day's Question Period. During the discussion, Joe Clark suggested waiting until Trudeau had departed on the weekend, leaving it to his ministers to respond. On Monday, the carefully orchestrated week of attacks began. Brian Mulroney (representing Central Nova in the House) led the charge, asking the first questions in French to the government benches, answered by former finance minister Allan MacEachen in English. Not only did the government's responses look weak and amateurish, the Conservative caucus became emboldened for a two-week stretch of media coverage about the callous treatment of taxpayers, the onerous complexity of the tax system, and the incompetence of the minister, the hapless Pierre Bussières. Here were the Liberals, the promoters of bilingualism, answering French questions in English, while the Conservatives asked questions in French. In the end, the government was saved by the shrewd Marc Lalonde, deflecting the questions but knowing the political damage was real. This proved a case study where a government front bench was tired, indolent, and smug, and an energetic opposition pounced.

The Conservatives' extended work on tax policy during the 12 months before the election and the attacks at Question Period offered two lessons: policy does matter, and, cleverly played, it has political consequences. In Opposition, the Conservatives had studied various aspects of tax policy. Don Blenkarn chaired a committee on tax simplification, which submitted its report to the leader and the caucus in April 1984; the document was a collective effort and received input from the caucus, which included several MPs who were farmers, fishermen, and small-business owners, as well as from others like Perrin Beatty, Ron Huntington, Chris Speyer, Sinclair Stevens, and Michael Wilson. Caucus members, the Policy Analysis Group, and invited outsiders offered ideas, discussion papers, and recommendations on numerous tax measures: capital-cost allowances, capital-gains exemptions, the dividend-distribution tax, integrating federal and provincial tax systems, mortgage-interest deductibility, small-business tax rates, and tax expenditures.

Tax policy, in short, was an unavoidable issue for the new Conservative government, despite warnings by senior mandarins like Simon Reisman, now retired but an active policy-watcher in Ottawa. The new cabinet needed little advice on tax reform – the media provided ample coverage of the Reagan tax cuts in the United States. However, the problems of high and rising deficits in other Western governments had a special salience for Canada, in part because of the massive increases in imported energy from the OPEC countries of the Middle East and the downturn in the North American economy in 1981. Ottawa had now become home to a succession of tax lobbyists, led by the Business Council on National Issues, the CFIB, and the Canadian Manufacturers' Association, as well as many new non-governmental organization (NGOs), such as the National Anti-Poverty Association, the National Council on Welfare, and the Public Advocacy Centre, all interested in tax policy and in tax avoidance as a social-justice issue. Their original target was the Liberal government and a series of budgets that created a tax jungle with staggering inefficiencies. Tax credits for research and development had become a corporate boondoggle and a stark example of how perverse tax incentives encouraged tax avoidance and gaming the system.

Starting with his Economic Statement in November 1984, Finance Minister Michael Wilson stressed the stark choices on the country's fiscal problem:

> In each of the past ten years the expenditures of the federal government have exceeded its revenues. These continuing deficits have led to an enormous growth in the burden of debt and the costs of servicing that debt ... We are on a very dangerous treadmill ... If our debts and our interest payments continue, year after year, to grow faster than our incomes ... we reach the point where we must start borrowing money just to pay the interest on our debts This year almost 50 per cent of government borrowing is required just to cover interest costs and, if we do not take action, this will rise to more than 76 per cent by 1990.

It took almost seven years, from November 1984 to 1 January 1991, to launch the goods and services tax, despite years of internal ministerial debate and massive consultations with the provinces and stakeholders in the business and tax community. The proposed tax went through various names, such as "business transfer tax," "consumption tax," and "value-added tax."

Three issues complicated its introduction, aside from the need to clarify the tax confusion inherited from the Liberals in 1984 and to find a steady stream of tax revenues. The first was simplifying the Income Tax Act by removing many giveaways to special interests. A report published in the *Globe and Mail* in April 1984, to the effect that hundreds of well-off Canadians were paying zero income tax, was raised by NDP Leader Ed Broadbent in the first televised leaders' debate in the summer campaign and left the impression that both opposition parties favoured a minimum tax. Second, various interest groups, but especially the manufacturing and export community, made presentations on the inequities of the manufacturers sales tax (MST), which was implemented in 1924, at a rate of 6 per cent on sales by manufacturers, reaching 8 per cent in 1936, and accounted for about 30 per cent of total federal revenue receipts. The Carter Report in 1966 focused on income tax but suggested an integrated "national" retail sales tax. A little-noticed Department of Finance discussion paper of 1983 outlined three options to replace the MST – a consumption tax, a federal sales tax, or an integrated retail sales tax involving the provinces.

The third issue facing the cabinet was how to retain social programs in a time of budget restraint. The prime minister's famous phrase, "Medicare is a sacred trust," was code for the Conservatives' acceptance of universality as a core principle of social programs. But many in the cabinet, including red Tories like Joe Clark, David Crombie, Marcel Masse, Don Mazankowski, and Lowell Murray, were not against targeting programs for the less well-off and knew about the legacy of Robert Stanfield's promise of a guaranteed annual income. Ministers were aware of an appetite to experiment with smaller programs to test income-support measures, following such trials in Manitoba in the 1970s to address the enduring challenges of extreme poverty. A national plan would be a big-ticket item, a clear social-policy branding for the Conservative party.

It was also a tool to align incentives for work, rationalizing existing programs, as well as a supplement to the Canadian Pension Plan, Old Age Security, and unemployment insurance. Ironically, while the Conservatives supported the Canada Heath Act in unambiguous terms in the autumn of 1983, despite internal debate and policy anguish, the Mulroney cabinet had some room to consider targeting on some social programs, like measures for the Aboriginal community, disabled citizens, and youth programs (see Table 3.3). These plans could be achieved by direct funding and changes to the tax system. Michael Wilson's Economic Statement of November 1984 and his first budget in May 1985 set out the general plan for economic growth, through job creation and rising wages, as well as by lowering the deficit, restraining expenditures, and shifting incentives to corporate investment, start-ups, and tax changes.

Wilson's budget of May 1985 laid out a new tax-measure option:

> Every year the deficit remains near $30 billion another $3 billion of interest charges is added to the next year's spending. These tax increases help us hold the line. But they are only part of a comprehensive debt control program, 70 per cent of which will be achieved through expenditure reduction ... Like the debate on pensions, discussions on a better sales tax system have been going on for a long time. Canada is now the only industrialized country in the world that still imposes a sales tax at the manufacturers' level. It is time to act on this issue, to bring our sales tax system into line with today's realities ... My officials have for some months been examining the value-added tax ... at alternative systems, including

Table 3.3
Social Justice: Evolution of Canadian Social Programs by Type

Universal Programs
Old Age Security
Canada Heath Act
Family Allowances

Targeted Programs
Spousal Allowance
Unemployment Insurance
Veterans' Disability Pensions
War Veterans' Allowances
Special Allowance for Workers in the North

Tax Measures – Deductions and Exemptions
Seniors Exemptions
Pension Income Deduction
Child Credit Exemption
Disability Deductions
Training and Tuition Deduction
Moving Allowances

a business transfer tax, which involve less administrative complexity and paper burden ... Our intention is to move to a new system that will encourage growth, improve equity, and yield revenues sufficient to replace the federal sales tax, to end the surtaxes. I have announced today ... adequate offsets for low-income Canadians.

The first six months of 1986 set the tone for the legacy of the Mulroney government, where specific, comprehensive, and all-encompassing policy measures in most departments brought internal cabinet confidence to the government's overall direction. The caucus needed weekly assurance to accept policy reforms, and the prime minister's task was part sermon, part policy discourse, part exhortation to avoid the insidious, self-fulfilling Tory syndrome of defeatism and internal dissension. The press gallery focused on patronage appointments, scandals, and the impact of changes in the political landscape – the defeat of the Conservatives in Ontario, the re-emergence of the Liberal Robert Bourassa in Quebec, the pending departure of close supporters like Premiers Peter Lougheed in Alberta and Richard Hatfield in New Brunswick. Rising employment and the lowering of annual inflation, but also the effects of necessary but painful budget cuts to discretionary programs and overall spending restraints, brought mood swings for the cabinet and caucus, as the prime minister emphasized in private meetings, only too aware the government was running against political headwinds, like Diefenbaker's government in 1962, Pearson's in 1965, Pierre Trudeau's in 1972, and as would buffet Paul Martin's in 2006 and Stephen Harper's in 2015.

Within the caucus, and the party at large, the debates were as much about political direction as particular measures, because of the difficult tradeoffs and the regional implications. Certain issues were politically unassailable, such as defence commitments, the new energy accords, east and west, including the petroleum gas revenue tax (PGRT) in the Western Accord, and Medicare and social programs. In the government's first two years, the combination of program spending and budget restraints had a bias towards institutional gains – the provinces, the business community – and costs to individuals, who are actual voters. Deindexing proved a political case study, where Finance introduced the measure, with huge political implications, but the cabinet didn't have much say. The May 1985 budget had an anti-inflation theme and contained a measure to deindex Old Age Security cheques – but only after pensioners received the first 3 per cent of the inflation increase. Few recognized the immediate political implications until a 63-year-old Ottawa resident, Solange Denis, addressed the prime minister near the entrance to the Parliament Buildings' Centre Block, as she shouted in French, with TV cameras in tow, "*Touche pas à nos pensions, ou c'est 'Goodbye, Charlie Brown'*" (Don't touch our pensions, or 'Goodbye, Charlie Brown'). The measure was dropped a month later, a somber finance minister conceding defeat.

The move to design a new sales tax, whatever its name or format, left many ministers wary and uneasy about the Finance officials, but not about the minister, Michael Wilson. Jake Epp and many ministers on the Social Affairs Sub-Committee knew about the run-in with Finance over consultations, the deindexation mess, and the clash with Finance over the "Little Egypt Bump," a little-known enriched write-off for Paul Reichmann's acquiring Gulf Oil. At a late-evening meeting in Pat Carney's Centre Block office, attended by Perrin Beatty from Revenue Canada, Robert de Cotret from Treasury Board, Industry Minister Sinclair Stevens, Michael Wilson, Harry Near, chief of staff to the energy minister, and me, this contentious issue was being thrashed out, with Pat Carney knowing the Reichmanns had received an advance ruling from Revenue Canada that their proposal was permissible in current law. At Finance, Wilson had already decided to discontinue this measure, but he asked to see a copy of the ruling. I wasn't sure that he was allowed to see it, thinking that such rulings for complex mergers were a private matter between the client and Revenue

Canada only. When I expressed my reservations, the other ministers agreed. I called the prime minister at home, and he immediately asked the clerk of the Privy Council, Gordon Osbaldeston, to join the meeting at this late hour, almost 11 p.m. The clerk gave us the gist of the ruling but warned that no outsiders could read it. What wasn't known by the ministers was that the original measure was the work of Marshall Cohen, former deputy in Energy and now deputy in Finance, and the real author of the Liberals' National Energy Program, not Ed Clark, who left the government shortly after the 1984 election.

When Stanley Hartt replaced Cohen as deputy minister at Finance, a welcome and quiet relief was noticeable in the cabinet. On 24 April, in preparation for a cabinet meeting in Prince Albert, Saskatchewan, before the summer recess, when the cabinet actually made the final decision to approve the goods and services tax (GST), even if the precise terms required consultations with the provinces and tax experts, as did the timing to announce the measure, I wrote a memo to the prime minister:

> Canadians may well feel that social programs are too complex, too expensive, and are misdirected, so that changes are needed. The Guaranteed Income scheme may have growing appeal, much like tax equity and tax reform. Within Cabinet, the key concern is the degree to which reform is Finance-driven or driven by social policy. Many Ministers do not trust Finance's blunt instruments ... Another concern is the timetable determined by Finance, where the Budget is the determining factor for the schedule. Ministerial and inter-departmental collaboration are fundamental to the success of this process – no games, no end runs, no turf wars ...
>
> There should be no attempt to underestimate the political and policy sensitivity of this (BTT) reform. Tax reform has a terrible history in this country, nowhere so evident as in the area of small business. The merits of this reform, from a fiscal position, must be weighed against potential opposition – the provinces, small business, the very tight timetable, the need for more Revenue Canada personnel, and the impact on the middle class.

By this time, the free-trade talks were under way, and various business groups, accounting firms, and leading tax experts knew the manufacturers sales tax had to be revised, even if the trade negotiations might fail. The prime minister's travels in Europe and Japan kept him abreast of tax measures, such as the consumption tax, where the value-added tax (VAT) is collected from producers according to the value at each stage along the production chain, so is almost impossible to avoid. The VAT differs from a sales tax, which is calculated on the final sales price, but is seen as regressive, hurting people with lower incomes. To maintain overall progressivity, other measures are needed, such as excluding it on certain items like food, but thereby adding to the complexity of calculating the tax.

When the GST was finally enacted on 1 January 1991, at a rate of 7 per cent, it met the twin objectives, namely a steady and reliable source of federal revenue and removing the disincentives of the antiquated MST. The arguments for applying a 5 per cent tax with no exemptions, as a measure for administrative simplicity, and stating it explicitly, unlike Europe and Japan, which include (hide) the tax in the total price of goods, were politically audacious, and allowed the Liberals to campaign in the 1993 election with a promise to eliminate the tax. It remains a political curiosity that the Harper government, elected in a minority in 2006, and inheriting a huge budget surplus, chose to reduce the GST to 5 per cent, with each tax point costing $5.5 billion in federal revenues each year, and not lowering personal income tax instead. By this time, Canada, like the United States, had a tax bias in favour of personal consumption, not investment by corporations and infrastructure spending, so the result was a decade of rising and high personal debt.

V

The 20th century in Canada saw a series of social issues – abortion, capital punishment, gun control, and language rights – that became hotly debated, much as, in the 21st century, measures like assisted-dying legislation, decriminalization of marijuana use, and stem-cell research have done. Unlike many countries, Canada has managed to avoid the divisive and polarizing impact that typically surrounds issues of conscience and religious belief, which serve as wedge incidents to force politicians to make binary choices, supporting either their party or the policy. Such policies place governments in invidious positions, where they must design legislation to define clear sets of rules for the people affected. Canada's abortion debate illustrates the complications, political, legislative, and legal. Both Pierre Trudeau's government in the 1970s and Brian Mulroney's in the 1980s had to confront these headwinds from divided public opinion, Supreme Court rulings, and caucus views. In the United States, the landmark abortion decision of the Supreme Court, *Roe v. Wade* in 1965, became a benchmark for other countries, including Canada.

Abortions, of course, have been performed for millennia, and many people accepted this medical procedure. For governments, especially in provinces with a large Catholic population, it was easy to adopt the position of the Catholic church, with its clear, unambiguous "pro-life" stance. When Pierre Trudeau was appointed justice minister in 1967, he began a wholesale review of a series of social policies, including abortion, divorce, and homosexuality, and when he won election as leader in 1968, with John Turner replacing him at Justice, both were determined to bring their country in line with 20th-century norms. Both men were Catholic. The government knew that such medical procedures were widespread – much more than the public realized – but few were performed by doctors or in proper facilities, such as medical clinics or hospitals. The new legislation, which also decriminalized contraception, was a means to clarify abortion policies, especially making them legal where the mother's life was in danger, broadly interpreted, such as when the mother's health (including mental health) was at risk, allowing hospitals with a therapeutic-abortion committee to make the decisions.

The fact that these two practising Catholics advanced this bill, despite the agonizing role of personal conscience, indicates the difficult tradeoffs made in government. Two extreme partisans on the matter, each of whom received enormous media attention, illustrated the compelling politics of the issue. Dr Henry Morgentaler travelled across Canada, openly defying the existing law, and wanted to allow six to seven thousand abortions a year, and his supporters had rallies on Parliament Hill, flashing a petition that had attracted allegedly a million signatures. Manitoba cabinet minister Joe Borowski, perhaps the leading anti-abortion activist, openly attacked the Charter of Rights and Freedoms, which he argued failed to protect the rights of a fetus and started a hunger strike. On four occasions, he was sent to jail because he refused to pay income tax. In 1988, almost twenty years after the abortion law was passed, and just as most advanced countries also liberalized their laws on the matter (two exceptions were Ireland and Poland), Canada's Supreme Court brought down a landmark decision. In the *Morgentaler* case, Chief Justice Brian Dickson argued that requiring approval from a hospital committee violated a woman's rights to "life, liberty, and security of the person."

The same issues now faced the Mulroney government. The prime minister set up a cabinet committee, headed by Lowell Murray, a practising Catholic, to draft changes to the extant legislation. Privately, most leaders hate dealing with such issues of conscience, because the public is split. In general, Canadians favoured abortion, provided the law gave clear medical criteria – the very stipulation put forward by the Supreme Court. To their credit, well-informed former cabinet ministers supported the government, including Opposition Leader John Turner and Liberal Senate Leader Allan MacEachen, who had agonized with the same issues in cabinet, as now did Joe Clark, also a Catholic, and Prime Minister Mulroney. Led by the bishops, the Catholic church came out in support of the bill, then changed position because the legal sanctions were too limited. Eventually, the bill was approved in the House of Commons, but lost in the Senate by a tie vote, an especially odd circumstance when a group of "pro-life" lobbyists, wanting a complete ban on abortions, converged with a group of strong "pro-choice" senators, who wanted no law at all. Curiously, rejection of the bill left Canada with no legislation on abortion, with two effects: it puts the onus on the medical profession to decide various cases, and there are wide variations across the country, about 23,000 abortions per year, with only about 600 occurring after twenty weeks of pregnancy, and those only under the most serious medical conditions.

The Reform party, and members from the Canadian Alliance coalition, also struggled with abortion policy, but as part of a wide set of social policies, starting with women's rights generally and extending to capital punishment, gay rights, gun control, and same-sex marriage. The Trudeau and Mulroney governments had both taken a middle road. For example, capital punishment, like abortion, was for some people a delicate and vexing matter of conscience. The last execution in Canada occurred in 1962, at the Don Jail in Toronto. Afterwards Prime Minister John Diefenbaker commuted capital verdicts – about sixty per year – to life sentences. A few years later, under the Pearson government, House Leader George McIlraith introduced a bill to abolish the death penalty, which failed. Finally, Solicitor General Warren Almond introduced an abolition bill, Bill C-84, excluding offences under the National Defence Act, which passed narrowly on an open vote, 130–124, even though public opinion favoured capital punishment by about two to one.

In 1979, the Clark government was under enormous pressure to reintroduce the death penalty. Lobby groups representing prison guards, police chiefs, and police associations devoted time and money to the cause. The government fell before it could address this divisive issue, but in 1984 the lobby groups hoped the Mulroney government would revive it. Contrary to many of the "right-wing" caucus members who supported him in the leadership bid, Mulroney was against capital punishment, partly because of the proselytizing efforts of Arthur Maloney, the silver-tongued Irish lawyer from Ottawa, an intensely committed abolitionist. In 1987, the Mulroney government had to confront this wrenching issue. A man from Edmonton, Gary Rosenfeldt, the father of a sixteen-year-old boy, Daryn Johnsrude, murdered by Clifford Olson, who was sitting in a jail in Kingston, Ontario, started a campaign to restore the death penalty, and found a willing public audience, including Conservative MP Bill Domm, from Peterborough. The sheer wickedness of Clifford Olson created a media storm, even as many church groups opposed the death penalty. The two sides were forceful and uncompromising: "Justice derived from death, an eye for an eye, a tooth for a tooth" vied against calls for mercy, "How can you balance the scales of justice with another broken body?"

Public opinion preferred the return to the death penalty – a Gallup poll in October 1983 showed 68 per cent in favour, and only 20 per cent opposed. A cover story in *Maclean's* on 16 March 1987, "The Death Vote," attempted to get a reading among sitting MPs. The cabinet debated the issue, knowing that statistics on crime, deterrence, and murder rates can be distorted to serve either side. Some ministers cited the case of Donald Marshall, serving eleven years in prison for a murder he did not commit. In February 1987, Deputy Prime Minister Don Mazankowski introduced a motion to support "in principle" the restoration of the death penalty, with an all-party committee of MPs to determine whom the state should kill and how, with a "free vote."

Free votes in Canada are rare and occurred during the debate about creating the Canadian flag (in 1964), about capital punishment (in 1966, 1969, 1973, 1976, and 1987), and about abortion (in 1969, 1988, and 1989). Later, they were allowed in the debates on constitutional amendments (in 1996 and 1997), on same-sex marriage (in 2006), and on medical assistance in dying (in 2006). When the death-penalty vote came on the last day of June 1987, MPs voted against, by 148 to 127. Prime Minister Mulroney, like John Diefenbaker a firm abolitionist, spoke, perhaps swaying some MPs, but afterwards gave a CBC-TV broadcast, saying that the debate was an excellent day for parliamentary democracy. The leading MP for restoration, Bill Domm, spoke for many: "I don't intend to ever give up representing 70 per cent of my constituents."

Two years later, the government faced another controversial issue, human reproductive biology. The march of science in medical technology had unknown effects and implications, both medical and ethical, and widespread media coverage of the healthy birth of the first "test-tube" baby, created by in-vitro fertilization, in Britain in July 1978, offered hope for millions of couples hoping to have children. The prime minister summoned a group of experts and, given his experience as a board member of a hospital in Montreal, spoke with many friends in the medical community, including doctors within the caucus. In October 1989, he appointed a Royal Commission on New Reproductive Technologies, with Dr Patricia Baird as chair. She was a paediatrician and medical geneticist, former president of the University of British Columbia, and a member of his National Advisory Board on Science and Technology. The prime minister also knew the endeavour would receive worldwide attention in legal circles, as well as from women's groups. The complex issues facing this group included the causes, prevention, and treatment of male and female infertility; embryo experimentation and fetal-tissue transplants; judicial interventions during gestation and birth; the legal, medical, and social procedures in cases of surrogate parenting; "ownership" of ova, sperm, embryos, and fetal tissue; and sex-selection techniques. Not surprising, no consensus emerged, and four commissioners, including Maureen McTeer and Louis Vandelaw, were fired and then filed a lawsuit, an unpreceded occurrence for such a body. In November 1993, the Baird Report, *Proceed with Care,* made 293 recommendations.

Alan Rock, the minister of health in the new Chrétien government, called for a moratorium on certain medical procedures, an action that pleased no one, so the government took time to study the recommendations and tried four times to pass legislation. Finally, in March 2004, Bill C-13 received parliamentary approval; the Assisted Human Reproduction Act banned many practices, such as combining human and animal DNA, human cloning, "rent-a-womb" contracts, the sale of human ova and sperm, and sex selection. It allowed donation of reproductive material, surrogacy, use of embryos, sperm, and ova to assist conception, and use of human embryos and stem cells in research. The act set up the Assisted Human Reproduction Agency of Canada (AHRAC), with headquarters in Vancouver, to administer the regulatory framework of reproductive technologies.

VI

Few politicians start their careers as environmentalists, in part because most of them are lawyers, with little formal education in science. For the most part, successful politicians are those who create jobs, so they avoid anything that impedes that. In the recent past, environment was thought to do just that. In Ottawa, the Department of the Environment, established by Parliament in 1971, was attached to the Ministry of Fisheries, which was of immense importance to rural voters on all coasts, but also one that incorporates such programs as the National Parks and scientists in the weather bureau, plus the Environmental Protection Review, which conducts compliance orders for legislative initiatives like the Antarctic Environmental Protection Act, the Canada Wildlife Act, the Canadian Environmental Protection Act, 1999, the International River Improvements Act, and the Migratory Birds Convention Act, 1994.

Despite sundry warnings about how massive consumption of resources was not sustainable, politicians and the public, and even many experts, took it for granted that new technologies and innovation would find solutions via substitutes or new sources of supply. However, environmental tragedies, such as Japan's crisis with the crippling Minamata disease (methylmercury poisoning) that arose in the 1950s and 1960s from mercury contaminants released into Minamata Bay, created a wake-up call to the corporate community. Shin-Nippon Chisso Hiryo KK, a firm rechristened "Chisso Corporation," was forced to pay over $3 billion in compensation, leading to strict new regulations in Japan on the use of mercury and the international Minamata Convention on Mercury (signed 2013, effective 2017), now ratified by 50 countries. Over the years, the media began investigative stories on pollution damage and oil-spills, and huge bestsellers such as Rachel Carson's *Silent Spring* (1962), Paul Ehrlich and Anne Ehrlich's *The Population Bomb* (1968), and Edward Goldsmith and Robert Allen's *A Blueprint for Survival* (1972) received global coverage and raised consciousness on university campuses and elsewhere, focusing minds on the idea of a pending ecological crisis.

Earth Day was celebrated for the first time on 22 April 1970, and the green movement became a political force, starting in West Germany, and environmental non-government organizations (ENGOs), like Greenpeace in Vancouver, and Friends of the Earth, became forceful lobby groups. Their media-savvy spokespeople were soon difficult to ignore, even as they became more action-oriented, outspoken, radical, and self-righteous. Private-sector entities like the oil companies tended to soft-pedal massive oil-spills, such as the *Exxon Valdez* in Alaska in March 1989, which was eventually settled for over a billion dollars.

But big changes had started in the 1960s, a time of radical protest and demands for new policies. Events encouraged activism. Various NGOs sprang up, some not on radical university campuses, but from middle-class voters, including many women, and groups, such as the Audubon Society and the Sierra Club, which could organize the mainstream media, as well as from prestigious publications like *National Geographic*. And a relatively new force, celebrity activism, elevated environmental causes to the public eye.

The central role that environmental issues now play both in public policy and in corporate strategy represents a radical departure from the attitudes, the science, and the mindsets of the 1970s and 1980s. From heroic action to tragedy can be a small step, and Rachel Carson's *Silent Spring* opened the floodgates of heightened awareness on college campuses, and 20 million people marched on the first Earth Day, 22 April 1970. An example of the growing change in public awareness came with the UN conference held in Stockholm in June 1972, to launch environmental issues worldwide and highlight their impact on health, economic, and development policies. As a sizable mining and natural-resource economy, Canada played a major role at Stockholm, and scientists and highly respected economists like Anthony Scott from UBC wrote landmark background papers. The resulting Declaration of the United Nations Conference on the Human Environment (Stockholm Declaration) included Principle 21: "States have, in accordance with the Charter of the United Nations and the principles of international law, the sovereign right to exploit their own resources pursuant to their own environmental policies, and the responsibility to ensure that activities within their jurisdiction or control do not cause damage to the environment of other States or of areas beyond the limits of national jurisdiction."

The Canada–United States Air Quality Agreement (1991) was a major achievement for the Mulroney government (see chapter 5), but few outside Ottawa knew it would help launch the global campaign on climate change. This debate is a political forced choice, between deniers of climate change who question the science, such as most of the U.S. Republican party and former president Donald Trump, and powerful voices on the other side, such as the U.S. military, leading global-insurance firms, the medical community in advanced countries, and the 174 countries that signed the Paris Agreement (2015), including two of the biggest polluters, China and India. Munich Re (Munich Reinsurance Company), for instance, documents global weather-related disasters, such as Typhoon Haiyan in the Philippines, when 7,500 people died or were lost and 4 million made homeless, and flooding in the state of Uttarakhand, India, which killed 6,000 and cost the insurance sector $65 billion in 2012 and $45 billion in 2013. Rising temperatures affect agriculture and fishing and increase the prospects that huge areas of farming land will be lost for food production, which will hurt the poor the most. David Miliband, the former foreign secretary in Tony Blair's Labour government in Britain and now CEO of the International Rescue Committee – a major NGO for refugees – told the political editor of the *Guardian* newspaper in December 2006: "Climate change is about social justice ... If you are not serious about social justice you cannot tackle the climate change problem."

One of the top officers in the U.S. military, Admiral Samuel J. Locklear III, cites climate change as the biggest threat to American security in the Pacific theatre, from Hawaii to India. The science arguments are straightforward: the levels of greenhouse gases in the atmosphere are at record levels, and global temperatures are projected to climb by 5.8 C° by the end of this century, unless steps are taken to limit the temperature increases to 2 C° (see Figure 3.5). Canada became an international leader in climate change with the signing of the Montreal Protocol, an initiative of the Mulroney government in 1987. Within the public service and the Conservative caucus, and in some provincial governments, including Tory premiers in Alberta and Nova Scotia, there were dissident voices, with strong lobbying by the oil industry.

The prime minister wanted to be assured of the science issues on climate change, and mobilized the strong scientific community in the public service, in academe, and in the medical community. Tom McMillan, the new environment minister, hosted a major conference in Toronto, which laid out the policy issues. Mulroney was fully aware of both the economic and the climate issues – drought on the prairies, soil erosion and rising sea levels, ice melting in the Arctic, predictions for colder winters and hotter summers – with implications for the health-care sector because of possible infectious diseases. He led a strong delegation to the Rio Summit in Brazil in June 1992 and there signed the Convention on Climate Change, knowing that what happened in legal and social programs in each country would really determine the long-term success of climate policy.

The Chrétien government continued this approach by signing the Kyoto Protocol of 1997, accepted by 187 countries. As with most international agreements, there were three components: an aspirational goal to change the public mindset; an educational role to help poorer countries build capacity; and a framework, about process as much as policy, to design tools and benchmarks to achieve a goal (here, reduce carbon emissions). Because the United States didn't sign the protocol, the Harper government, elected in 2006, decided to reduce its commitments. But its real goal was to take advantage of the booming commodity market in China, and a voracious demand there for aluminum, coal, copper, iron ore, but especially oil and gas. However, most of Canada's exportable oil is in land-locked Alberta, so the policy imperative was to build four new pipelines:

- Energy East, across Canada to the Irving refinery in Saint John, New Brunswick
- Keystone XL (Phase 4), through Saskatchewan, Montana, South Dakota, and Nebraska, to connect to Texas refineries
- Northern Gateway, across Alberta and British Columbia to Kitimat, on the Pacific coast
- Trans Mountain, from Edmonton to Burnaby, on the Pacific coast

Each pipeline faced delays for environmental approval, court challenges, and intense disapproval from the Aboriginal community and environmentalists, and the Trans Mountain was purchased by Justin Trudeau's government in May 2018 for $4.5 billion.

The effects of climate change are more serious for developing countries than for the industrialized West, with its superior technologies and capacity to bear financial costs. Estimates by economist like William Cline found that a rise of 2.5 per cent in global temperatures would cut agricultural productivity by 6 per cent in the United States but by 38 per cent in India. Similar studies show the same effects on maize production in the United States and in China, which is the world's largest emitter of greenhouse gases (over 50 per cent of its energy comes from coal) and contributes about a quarter of the global total. India accounts for 83 per cent of the global increase in carbon emissions in 2000–11. Alas, both China and India have made a Faustian bargain: in return for high growth and jobs for rural people, they also sanction increases in dirty-fuel consumption, thus leading to pollution and rising emissions. If they stick to the same levels of fuel consumption as Western economies had, rising by 200 per cent, this means a zero-sum tradeoff and one seen as politically unacceptable to the Western democracies, hence the political stalemate. In 2018, energy-related emissions increased 2.2 per cent in China, and 3.1 per cent in the United States, but declined in Europe and Japan. The evidence of the earlier warnings about climate change now shows the impact of human infectious diseases.

Various proposals have been made for a tax on carbon emissions, such as a suggested $16-per-ton charge on carbon dioxide, to rise by 4 per cent annually. Some countries have implemented a carbon tax, and three Canadian provinces – Alberta and Quebec in 2007, and British Columbia in 2008. California has recently initiated a cap-and-trade system, which auctions carbon permits to companies. Globally, government and corporate strategies now converge, often led by youth activists. Justin Trudeau's government's plan for a national policy on climate change, involving all the provinces and territories and including a carbon tax, by OECD

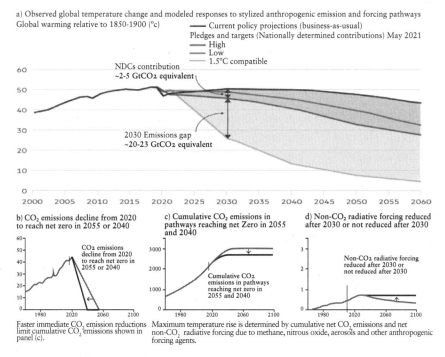

Source: Adapted from *Financial Times*

Figure 3.5 The yawning gap between pledged and required near-term reductions in emissions

standards dwarfs that of European countries, or even that of Britain or Japan. This initiative thus faces the same reality as the GST introduced by the Mulroney government, with many parallels: lengthy, disputed, and disputatious negotiations with the provinces, inter-regional tensions, and even political infighting within provinces between the urban and metropolitan cities that see the ill-effects directly in terms of polluted air and water (see Figure 3.6).

VII

On the last day of Parliament before prorogation, 28 June 1984, only days before the start of a national election campaign, Opposition Leader Brian Mulroney asked the government to apologize formally for the internment of Japanese Canadians during the Second World War. The question caught the government by surprise, leaving cabinet members reeling, since there was no good answer to justify that action. In a country with a new Charter of Rights setting out constitutional rights for individual

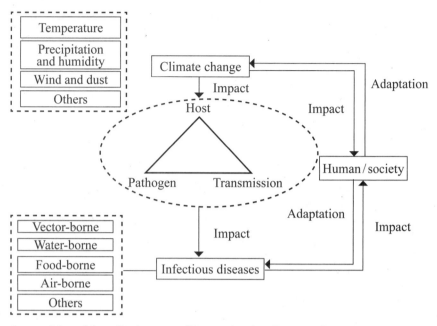

Source: Adapted from *Environmental International* 26 (Jan. 2016)

Figure 3.6 A General Framework Illustrating Climate Change, Infections Diseases, and Society.

citizens, how could a government tolerate and justify such serious past wrongs? The numbers weren't small, more than 21,000 men, women, and children were evacuated, and their property was seized and sold.

The background of this historic injustice is now well known. King's government used the Defence of Canada Regulations to authorize the internment of anyone who was acting in a manner "prejudicial to the public safety or the safety of the state," a policy directed at Canadian and foreign citizens considered sympathetic to Germany, Italy, or Japan. Ottawa ordered the evacuation of all Japanese Canadians living on the BC coast, even though the military and the Royal Canadian Mounted Police advised against the move. Beginning on 8 December 1941, the day after the Japanese attack on Pearl Harbor, Ottawa impounded 1,200 Japanese-Canadian fishing vessels as a "defence measure." For seven years and four months, from 8 December 1941 to 31 March 1949, Japanese Canadians suffered a massive infringement of their civil liberties: they were forcibly uprooted, were relocated to internment camps in the BC interior, and had their goods and properties stolen. Many families moved to sugar-beet farms in southern Alberta and Manitoba. Any resistance by them meant internment in prisoner-of-war camps in Ontario, even though most were civilians, and the Nisei, i.e., Canadian-born, were British subjects.

Even worse, as federal authorities confiscated their private property and sold it without consent, Japanese Canadians were confronted with a choice – staying east of the Rockies or being deported to Japan. Scots-born BC Liberal MP Tom Reid, at a meeting of Liberal associations, left no doubt on his position: "Take them back to Japan, they do not belong here and there is only one solution to the problem. They cannot be assimilated as Canadians for no matter how long the Japanese remain in Canada, they will always be Japanese." Reid represented New Westminster 1930-49 and then sat in the Senate until 1967. Ian Mackenzie, the bilious former minister of defence, who once identified social-security policies with socialism, was now the Liberal minister of pensions and health, and, hoping to ensure that Japanese Canadians never returned, introduced measures to dispose of their farms and property as cheaply and as quickly as possible. He asked his cabinet colleague Thomas A. Crerar, the minister of mines and resources, to investigate. Crerar, a 19th century-style laissez-faire fanatic, asked his deputy, Gordon Murchison, to execute the policy, surveying the properties using data from the 1930s when values were low, and discounted building costs by 70 per cent. The cabinet then passed Order in Council PC 5523, authorizing Crerar to seize 572 farms without consulting the owners. Any letters of appeal were sent to the Department of the Secretary of State, Japanese Evacuation Section, headed in Vancouver by F.G. Shears, and received a standard, bureaucratic reply: "We are carrying out an overall policy applicable to all Japanese properties in this area. As you are aware, your own land was included in a group sale, which was made to the Director, the Veterans' Land Act. Your remarks have been carefully read and we note your reference to what you consider may be the present value of this property. The sale to the Veterans' Land was based on current independent appraised values and the sale was completed on that basis."

In Ottawa, on 8 January 1942, Mackenzie chaired a Conference on Japanese Problems. He invited a BC delegation, which included the provincial minister of labour, George S. Pearson; and Commander T.W.S. Parsons of the Provincial Police, both publicly supporting suspension of all Japanese-Canadian fishing licences, forced sale of fishing vessels to non-Japanese people, and internment of all male Japanese Canadians of military age. Also attending were Norman Robertson, under-secretary for external affairs; Dr Hugh Keenleyside, head of the American and Far Eastern Divisions at External Affairs, and two of his assistants, H.F. Angus and Escott Reid; Colonel S.T. Wood, commissioner of the RCMP, and Assistant Commissioner F.J. Mead; Lieutenant-General Maurice A. Pope, vice-chief of general staff; Commodore H.E. Reid, deputy chief of naval staff; representatives of the Departments of Labour and Fisheries; and a representative of the Office of the Press Censor, concerned about the wider implications, including Canadian prisoners in Japanese POW camps, who argued against these measures. The provincial delegation remained adamant on proceeding.

In public statements, the government cited "national security," yet admitted there was no evidence of espionage or sabotage ever committed. Despite the stereotype that community members were quiet, even passive, some launched protests, starting in mid-1942 with the Nisei Mass Evacuation Group. The deportation orders were challenged in the courts, and many letters were sent to local politicians and Ottawa. Other groups were very sympathetic, such as the Cooperative Committee on Japanese Canadians, a Toronto group of Nisei fighting the deportation orders, despite court cases approving the government's power under the War Measures Act and strong public support in favour of King's actions.

After the war, the Royal Commission on Japanese Claims (Bird Commission, 1947–51) produced a deeply flawed report that left few people happy, but it launched a twenty-year process seeking redress, which the community called "Twenty Years of Silence." While Japanese Americans returned to their homes on the U.S. west coast in 1946, their counterparts in Canada could not move back to the BC coastal area until 1 April 1949.

But two later events changed the process for redress. In 1977, the 100th anniversary of the first Japanese immigration to Canada brought support from government grants and financial aid from the community and generated numerous conferences, re-enactments, and oral- and photo-history recordings in several provinces, and young members focused on their new Sansei (third-generation) youth organization. In Hamilton, a conference on the War Measures Act, featuring Walter Tarnopolsky, a prominent legal scholar on civil liberties, addressed the broader implications and the need to change the act. Now better organized, the National Association of Japanese Canadians (NAJC) initiated projects about redress and six years later made appeals for a formal government apology, individual compensation, and the abolition of the War Measures Act. It also, in 1986, hired accounting firm Price Waterhouse to determine economic losses to victims using historical documents.

Meanwhile, various books, theses, and anthologies had documented the actions of ministers in the King government, especially the role of Ian

Mackenzie. During the run-up to the 1984 federal election, various Conservative candidates, party members, and the Policy Analysis Group in the leader's office met with members of the community. There was never any doubt about the case at hand, and the party adopted a three-part campaign promise – a formal apology, financial support of $10 million for a centre on human rights in western Canada, possibly at the University of Lethbridge, and steps to abolish the War Measures Act. During the election campaign, numerous Japanese Canadians expressed their appreciation, and no interest was ever expressed in full financial redress. Yet when Manitoba's Jack Murta, MP, was appointed minister of state (multiculturalism), the Japanese redress agenda became a top priority.

Recently retired Prime Minister Pierre Trudeau was not a fan of offering apologies for actions of past governments. He outlined his views in the House of Commons, and cited examples in Canadian history, such as the British expulsion of Acadians from the Maritimes (1755–64) and the treatment of Chinese labourers employed in the 1880s to build the transcontinental railway. Perhaps he was aware of suspicions about W.L. Mackenzie King's personal views, often expressed in his private diaries, such as his anti-semitic desire to limit Jewish refugees or his entry on 6 August 1945, with the news of the atomic bomb on Hiroshima: "It is fortunate that the use of the bomb should have been upon the Japanese rather than upon the white races of Europe."

By coincidence, on the Friday after election day in September 1984, I ran into Pierre Trudeau in the Langevin Building. Being the shy type, I went over to him, introduced myself, and said hello. The former prime minister said, in an amazingly cordial way, "I know who you are, and you guys have a big job ahead of you. Try to have some fun in Ottawa." That afternoon, I was at 24 Sussex, where the prime minister-elect hosted Trudeau and offered him a government plane to pick up an award in New York. Trudeau, with a zillion topics to discuss, took time to suggest the Conservative government drop Japanese-Canadian redress. Whether he resented comments made by the NAJC on how the new Charter of Rights gave incomplete human-rights protection, or any demands by the Redress Committee in Canada, is a matter future historians can decide.

Several new ministers, including Harvie Andre, David Crombie, and Jack Murta, joined an internal group to focus on that election promise, including Geoff Norquay, Nigel Wright from the PMO's policy staff, and me, to start an implementation plan. Background memos from the PMO's Policy Unit and the PCO noted that, starting in the late 1950s, Ottawa had abolished or changed many legislative measures displaying racial or religious discrimination, often as a result of judges' rulings. It didn't take long for us, after consultations in Toronto and Winnipeg, to realize that Japanese Canadians were split between two views. One group, headed by Jack Oki in Toronto, wanted a formal apology, and a centre on race relations, to include a library and archives as the basis for teaching materials for Canadian schools, costing in the order of $25 million. Privately, many conservative-minded members of the community warned that some groups sought full compensation, even though many of the families had moved or passed away, and some leaders would use the media to hold the government to ransom.

As it turned out, the media later picked up on the Price Waterhouse study of 1986, which found that in the period 1941–49, community members lost about $110 million in seized property, including rich. fertile Fraser Valley farmland, amounting to $49.3 million, as well as lost income and other damages worth about $330 million, for a total of an estimated $443,139,000. In a policy environment of scarce resources, including demands for additional funding for war veterans, Japanese redress took a lot of time, consultations, and sorting out of funding options on the part of the PMO and the prime minister. Mulroney raised the issue several times in caucus and in cabinet, as a case study of how Canada must protect minority rights, fight the scourge of racism, and fulfil its potential to be a global, multicultural country.

In the fullness of time, Defence Minister Perrin Beatty introduced legislation to repeal the War Measures Act and tabled Bill C-77, eventually passed as the new, omnibus Emergencies Act. This law groups emergencies into four categories:

- a Public Welfare Emergency, for a serious natural disaster, disease, accident, or pollution;
- a Public Order Emergency, for "threats to the security of Canada," as defined in the Canadian Security Intelligence Service Act;
- an International Emergency, when Canada is subject to intimidation, coercion, or the real or imminent use of serious force or violence; and
- a War Emergency, when war or other armed conflict involves Canada or any of its allies.

Finally, on 22 September 1988, the prime minister offered a public apology and a compensation package through a Japanese Canadian Redress Agreement, signed jointly by him and Art Miki, head of the NAJC. This accord set up a Japanese Canadian Redress Foundation to ascertain and issue redress payments for internment victims, and a program with

$8 million for building homes and service centres for Issei (first-generation) senior citizens.

The official acknowledgment stated:

> The acknowledgement of these injustices serves notice to all Canadians that the Excesses of the past are condemned and that the principles of justice and equality in Canada are reaffirmed. Therefore, the Government of Canada, on behalf of all Canadians, does hereby:
> 1) acknowledge that the treatment of Japanese Canadians during and after World War II was unjust and violated principles of human rights as they are understood today;
> 2) pledge to ensure, to the full extent that its powers allow, that such events will not happen again; and
> 3) recognize, with great respect, the fortitude and determination of Japanese Canadians who, despite great stress and hardship, retain their commitment and loyalty to Canada and contribute so richly to the development of the Canadian nation.
>
> Brian Mulroney

Despite the settlement of this wartime atrocity, many Japanese Canadians were embittered at the final result, not by the government's actions but by the political games played by a number of their own leaders, some of whom leaked documents to the media about the negotiations, and others of whom were only too willing to play partisan politics. Art Miki described the settlement as "a historic day for Canadians of Japanese ancestry who have been struggling so long to resolve the injustices of the 1940s." He ran as a star candidate for Jean Chrétien's Liberals in Winnipeg-Transcona in the 1993 federal election, losing by 203 votes to the NDP incumbent, Bill Blaikie, and provincially in Radisson in 1995, losing again. In 1998, he accepted a job as a citizenship judge. In politics, often gratitude is next year's patronage appointment.

VIII

Lobbying, a political process aiming to influence government policy, is as old as democracy, combining a delicate task while perched between two competing claims, the identification approach of political parties, with its emphasis on loyalty, tradition, and internal cohesion, and the more prosaic and demeaning call of vested interests, which often thwart reforms intended for the public good. After Confederation in 1867, Sir John A. Macdonald played the lobbying game in Washington, where British interests might take priority over Canadian needs, and he retained a professional lobbyist, George W. Brega, for $21,500 to advise him on trade reciprocity and other issues, including the Atlantic fisheries. The United States, of course, has a distinctive system, where every member of Congress is a lobbyist for his or her district and state, often financed by lobby groups and sundry industry associations.

In Ottawa the lobby industry started in earnest during Pierre Trudeau's tenure in the 1970s, and steadily grew, with practitioners playing a direct role in leadership races and election campaigns. In 1981, the Economic Council of Canada estimated there were over 300 lobbying firms in Ottawa, spending upwards of $125 million per year to promote their cause.

During the summer of 1985, the Mulroney government saw the first signs that its political honeymoon was coming to an end, after less than a year in office. Both public and party polling showed its favourabilty rating below 40 per cent. The spring budget was a big factor, as the government wrestled with spending cuts, tax measures that increased the costs of government services, and the relentless and increasingly nasty charges of the Liberal Rat Pack, consisting of Don Boudria, Sheila Copps, John Nunziata, and Brian Tobin. But what had really stirred the political pot in Ottawa was appointments at Air Canada, a prime candidate for privatization, together with its "owner," Canadian National, both headquartered in Montreal. The wholesale additions to the board included David Angus, head of the PC Canada Fund, and Frank Moores, former Newfoundland premier and CEO of Government Consultants International (GCI), which had such foreign clients as MMB (Messerschmitt-Bölkow-Blohm), a German aerospace firm, and Airbus. The gossip columnists, the scandal-mongers in the media, and the Liberal Rat Pack went into overdrive. In August 1985, when the inner cabinet, Priorities and Planning (P&P), met in Vancouver, the national media confronted the prime minister, in the light of his game-changing statement in the 1984 election debate about John Turner's implementing Trudeau's patronage appointments: "You had an option, sir." Both the PCO and the PMO offered memos with similar themes – the government had to act. In fact, the issues were more complicated, because the focus was on the PMO itself.

When Brian Mulroney sought the Conservative leadership for the second time in 1983, Fred Doucet was working in the Alumni Office at Mulroney's alma mater, St Francis Xavier University, in Antigonish, NS. His older brother, Gerry, had been minister of education in Nova Scotia's Buchanan government but, after the 1984 election victory in Ottawa, joined Frank Moores's lobbying firm, GCI. Fred became chief of staff when Mulroney was leader of the Opposition, and then moved to the PMO as a special assistant. He brought two things to both roles, and he did not hide them. The first was his access to Brian Mulroney. The second was his ability to state, "The prime minister wants..." without ever explaining why. Cabinet ministers fumed in private but said nothing too publicly. Both in Opposition and in the PMO, Fred Doucet antagonized the exempt staff, fought with Norman Atkins and the campaign organization, and insisted that everyone call him "Dr Doucet" and that his name be given in full: "J. Alfred Doucet."

In Ottawa, Fred made himself available 24/7 to the prime minister. In government, he quickly took control over the logistics planning when Mulroney visited his riding, attended federal–provincial meetings, and travelled abroad, including to Washington. Unlike in Opposition, in the PMO he had ready access to the civil service, and frequently called meetings, including ambassadors from their posts overseas, to plan international trips. At federal–provincial gatherings, often televised, he insisted that he sit just behind the boss. Shortly after the 1984 election, he chaired a meeting in Ottawa of officials planning the federal–provincial conference to be held in Regina. Deep frustration became the order of the day, all logistics and no substance. At the day's lunch, provincial representatives vented their frustrations about possible new policy thinking, on anything from Senate reform to equalization payments. The most outspoken was Henry Philips, representing Jim Lee from Prince Edward Island, one of seven Conservative premiers: "Fred, where are the new ideas on federal–provincial relations? What can we work on together? Senate reform? Equalization? What do you want us to do? Fred, we all wish to make this new era work, even Michael [Decter] who represents an NDP government is ready to help." Fred's response was chilling: "Henry, that is not how it is going to work. We are not going to hand down the ideas and proposals from on high in Ottawa. The ideas will spring up in the gardens of the provinces." Philips's response was one for the ages: "That's rich, Fred. You drive, and I'll spread."

Doucet's thirty-two months in the PMO were publicly uncontroversial, including his work on the Mulroney–Reagan Quebec Summit in March 1985. Behind the scenes, the seeds of discord in the party, the Ottawa gossip circuit, and the civil service were widely known, including in the PMO. Fred wanted to be seen as close to Mulroney and have everyone know that was the case. A phone call from him was equal to hearing from his boss, with the opening words, "The prime minister asks ... " – a phrase that infuriated many cabinet ministers. His favourite tactic was to interrupt a call, saying the prime minister was on the other line. When John Crosbie, speaking to a radio reporter in his riding in St John's, was asked if the PMO was staffed by dolts, he responded: "I wouldn't say it is staffed by dolts, but perhaps you could say they aren't as astute politically or as politically intuitive as they should be." All offices have internal political manoeuvres, but in this case, Fred's brother, Gerry, was a lobbyist for several corporations whose business was influenced by federal funding decisions – and for three provinces.

Media coverage on the lobbying industry started to focus on the role played by GCI and the work of Frank Moores and Gerry Doucet. At cabinet, Sinclair Stevens complained openly to his colleagues, and to the ministers belonging to the Economic Sub-committee. His beef was with the lobbying by certain people, especially Gerry Doucet, whom he gave as an example one day. He cited a breakfast meeting with PEI officials at the Château Laurier Hotel next door, on the electricity package, with Gerry sitting at the table as that province's lobbyist. At noon, he met an industry group from Manitoba, with Gerry Doucet attending as its lobbyist. That night, as he descended from a government jet in Sydney to meet an auto-parts company investing in Cape Breton, Gerry Doucet was waiting for him on the tarmac.

Unknown to most people outside the inner circle, before joining the Mulroney leadership campaign, Fred Doucet had been CEO of East Coast Energy, a company with plans to develop Atlantic Canada's offshore oil and gas reserves, to which John Buchanan's government had committed significant time and resources. The Atlantic Accord, which the Conservative party reached with Brian Peckford's government in Newfoundland on 14 June 1983, was a signal of a sea change in energy policy, and East Coast Energy was one of several new start-ups intending to begin exploring. Two investors in the firm were Brian Mulroney and Walter Wolf. Wolf was a peripatetic entrepreneur, born in Austria, who came to Canada when he was fourteen. His first wife, Barbara Stewart, was the daughter of Charlottetown mayor David Stewart, a prominent Conservative and adviser on all things that mattered in the province, including federal funding from the Diefenbaker government for the Fathers of Confederation Centre, opened by the Queen in October 1964.

Wolf was an accomplished athlete, a downhill skier, who hosted Pierre Trudeau on one of his skiing trips in the Austrian Alps. He won contracts for underwater construction and security (including protecting the Royal Yacht *Britannia* moored in the port of Montreal during the Queen's visit to Expo 67), as well as underwater cable drilling for Canadian newspaper baron Lord Thomson of Fleet in his North Sea oil operations. Wolf's Formula 1 experience, with the Wolf–Ford team winning five races from Monaco to Argentina, brought him international fame, added to his considerable fortune, and made him an obvious contact to bring Formula 1 racing to Montreal for Labatt Brewers, headed by CEO Don MacDougall and legal adviser Michael Cogger. Like many entrepreneurs, Wolf made and spent money with abandon, on everything from helicopters to private jets. He owned five properties, in London, near Nice, in Acapulco, in Graz, his birthplace in Austria, and a 4,000-acre ranch near Kamloops, BC.

In late 1986, he brought a lawsuit against East Coast Energy and Fred Doucet. He provided documents to *Maclean's* magazine and the Toronto *Star*, and his TV interviews singled out Doucet for passing misleading information to shareholders and investors. This publicity did not come as a surprise to senior members of the PMO or the prime minister, but what many others didn't know was that Wolf was also financing Quebec delegates to the annual Conservative convention in Winnipeg in January 1983 that voted en masse against Joe Clark in its leadership review. He also was close to Frank Moores, who had his own personal financial difficulties at that time. Wolf purchased the former premier's fishing camp in Labrador to lessen his debt burdens, buying him time to finance his new lobbying firm, GCI, with Gerry Doucet as his partner.

In the lobbying game, appearances are as important as substance. Many lobbyists are former campaign workers, both for leadership races and for elections, but some are often unduly lax in telling the public at large, the media, and policy insiders their real purpose – selling access. In January 1987, a cover story in *Maclean's* exposed the details of the lawsuit facing Fred and Gerry Doucet and their former employer, East Coast Energy. Whether Wolf hoped ever to recoup any money was another story, but his clear intention was to embarrass the brothers and reveal his disdain for their probity and judgment. It didn't help that another scandal facing the government – the Oerlikon (Aerospace) affair in January 1987 led to the resignation of André Bissonnette, the fourth minister to quit – coincided with the prime minister's trip to meet Pope John Paul II at the Vatican and to Africa for meetings on apartheid in South Africa.

Just before his return, a story broke that Fred Doucet had promised a deal with France to allow French trawlers from St Pierre and Miquelon access to Canadian waters, just when Newfoundland was facing the crisis of depleted cod stocks on the Grand Banks. The media coverage was extensive. On the day Mulroney returned to Ottawa, 2 February, with a pending resignation of ministers Bernard Roy and John Crosbie, the prime minister, exhausted from his eleven-hour flight and a case of flu, asked Bill Fox and me to sort out the problems – "Do whatever it takes."

The next week, at a morning meeting in the PMO, the Wolf lawsuit came up, as a story that might embarrass the prime minister and waste time for many PMO staffers already working long hours. I didn't say much there, in part because I knew a lot more than I was letting on – the prime minister had asked me to suggest a reorganization of the office, a plan he largely accepted at the end of February. However, with Bernard Roy in the chair, I did suggest, almost off-handedly, that Fred should take a few months off and clear his name.

That night, returning to Toronto and walking in the front door, I was asked by my wife to take a call from Mulroney, who was waiting on the phone. He was rather angry, or, more accurately, he was furious. He singled out my remark that morning. He added, "There is no difference between Fred and Gerry Doucet, and you and your brother, personal friends and advisers." I quietly responded: "There is a difference – a huge difference. Tom and I are sworn to cabinet secrecy. Gerry is a paid lobbyist, and even Frank Moores admits Gerry and Fred speak almost hourly." The long silence, perhaps only 30 seconds, made me think the phone went dead, or Mulroney hung up, or walked away. After a pause, he said, quietly, "You're right. See you Monday."

Within two weeks, Derek Burney took over as the new chief of staff. Fred Doucet left the PMO, accepting the title of ambassador to manage the G7 summit in Toronto in June 1988. Shortly afterwards, he became a lobbyist, subject to a registration system for paid lobbyists. Michel Côté, minister of consumer and corporate affairs, had issued a discussion paper, "Lobbying and the Registration of Paid Lobbyists." Alas, one of the clients for Fred Doucet's lobbying firm, Karlheinz Schreiber, banned by Premier Peter Lougheed of Alberta from meeting anyone in his caucus, was an Ottawa lobbyist for Airbus, now a supplier to Air Canada. Despite numerous warnings, Mulroney kept up his personal contacts with the Doucet brothers, and shadow money payments led to the Oliphant Inquiry in 2009-10, itself a case study of friends with access to high office themselves benefiting more than those they were meant to serve.

4

National Reconciliation: Institutional Alignments

Canada's Two Systems of Government – The Nature of Federal–Provincial Relations – Equalization – Constitutional Redistribution – Regional Development: ACOA and Western Diversification – The Arctic and Two New Territories – The Saga of Meech Lake – A New Voice: Aboriginal Peoples – The Council of the Federation – The Fixed Link

One of these days, all the persons in Canada will be Canadians.
                                                    Chief Dan George

INTRODUCTION

As a highly urbanized country, Canada, with over 80 per cent of its population living in cities, and the largest, Toronto and the greater Toronto area (GTA), with roughly seven million people, larger than seven provinces, illustrates trend lines based on demographics, shifting industrial sectors, and employment prospects that open a new divide between urban growth and rural areas facing rustbelt economics, outward migration of young people, and families facing retirement. This bifurcation, with 18th-century British poet William Cowper noting that "God made the country, and man made the town," is a global challenge, with cities' growth spiral of rising employment and knowledge industries. In rural areas, there is a cruel, vicious cycle, a shift away from traditional sectors like agriculture, fisheries, and mining, leading to shortages of skilled workers and community activities that create a self-reinforcing spiral of economic decline. Canada's north, of course, typifies these challenges, where the land mass of Yukon and Northwest Territories is greater than that of Germany, France, and Spain combined, or greater than Texas and California. with a total population – about 120,000 – smaller than that of Prince Edward Island.

Clearly, both history and geography help explain Canada's concentration of economic and industrial activity, now encompassing a growing city–rural divide within provinces. Historically, Atlantic Canada and Quebec had easy access to rivers, lakes, and waterways, natural resources of all descriptions, and a location near the Atlantic seaboard. That provided proximity to markets in New England and Britain and generated a legacy of extractive production, where the vicissitudes of life involve a game against nature, outsiders, and strangers.

But more than geography accounts for the tensions between Ottawa and the provinces, or between the centre and the periphery, a pairing invoked by economists and political scientists to explain the differences in density of firms, economic activity, and population. At the Charlottetown Conference in September 1864, Inspector General Alexander Galt of Canada outlined his considered and cogent views, and the twenty delegates attending accepted them, as did the thirty-seven who met a month later in Quebec City, formalizing the Quebec Resolutions to be presented to the British government. With most government revenues coming from tariffs and customs, representatives of the colonies debated the role of centrifugal forces against the preferred decentralization for provincial powers, knowing the national government would collect the money and then transfer payments to the provinces, which would be limited to levying direct taxes and royalties from national resources.

Gone are the days when provincial and federal legislatures had politicians designing policies and programs for rural areas, even though by numbers these regions dominated the population. In 1901, two-thirds of Canadians lived in rural ridings, and politicians worked with an operating assumption, following poets and philosophers, that an agrarian economy was good for democracy. Socrates felt agriculture was the "mother and nurse of all the other arts." In 1910, Wilfrid Laurier accepted a brief from Canadian farmers extolling rural virtues: "The greatest problem which presents itself to the Canadian people today is the problem of retaining our people on the soil, we come doubly assured of the justice of our position."

|

Confederation in 1867 accelerated the migration of economic and industrial activity in the Maritimes away from Halifax, for instance, to Montreal, and much later to Toronto. Local and regional banks proliferated in each Maritimes province, but banking became concentrated a generation later in Montreal and then in Toronto. Today, about 175 of the country's top 200 firms, domestic and foreign, have their headquarters in Toronto. This gap between the centres of urban, service activities is associated with knowledge organizations like hospitals, universities, and cultural and sports institutions, while the periphery, with a low-density population, focuses on primary sectors, often in one-industry communities.

The contrasts between Canada and the United States in regional economic activity are telling, but other countries use similar terms – regional disparity, devolution, and decentralization. The vastly more decentralized American economy exploited its advantages, in part by transportation and infrastructure programs, like building the Erie Canal that linked eastern port cities on the Atlantic to the industrial heartland, and, beginning in 1956, under President Eisenhower, the construction of the national, interstate highway network. The political system also helped. The congressional budget system of appropriations and earmarks allows such special budget measures as the highway system to be included in bills supporting, for instance, defence procurement, and the well-tested system of "logrolling" that creates political leverage for members of Congress. The highly political budget process, in fact, is a unique tool in the American industrial arsenal of regional-development policy.

The British North America Act passed by Westminster in 1867 gave the main economic powers to Ottawa, including banking, defence, and international trade. Provincial powers were limited and included property rights, which were assigned in 1930. For some 100 years, as a general proposition, planning for national economic development flowed from dominion (federal) commercial, fiscal, and monetary policy. Because the population was concentrated mainly in Ontario and Quebec, there was a strong political incentive to favour central Canada, so a common theme in development was the centre's bias against the periphery, especially when the Liberal party's base was concentrated in the two largest provinces.

Starting in the late 1960s but more aggressively in the 1970s, economic development in the west shifted dramatically away from direction by Ottawa. In a succession of provincial elections, after long party tenure extending over decades – for example, W.A.C. Bennett was Social Credit premier of British Columbia for 20 years (1952–72) – new leaders campaigned for change. In 1971 in Alberta, Conservative Peter Lougheed defeated Social Credit after it had governed there for 36 years, led 1943–68 by Ernest Manning. Lougheed studied for a Harvard MBA, just when the curriculum there was revised to become more global. In his years in opposition, when he increased his party to ten seats, he cultivated a network of advisers in areas as diverse as the arts, education, energy, and medicine, and he had a special interest in the Pacific Rim and countries like Japan. Political changes in Saskatchewan and British Columbia added to the political momentum for new approaches to modernize the western economy, especially by adding value to products in vital industries – agriculture, mining, oil and gas, potash, pulp and paper, uranium – and the related "complementarities," such as education, finance, immigration, and transportation, and through tax incentives for highly skilled jobs and service industries.

Lougheed's travels and meetings with stakeholders in academe, agriculture, and energy and with private-sector consultants and economists helped change the mindset of the electorate in Alberta and throughout the west. Cleverly, once in office, he rekindled and updated John Diefenbaker's Roads to Resources policies and sales of wheat to Japan, China, and other Asian nations and of other commodities, ranging from coal to potash. He developed close political cooperation with the other western premiers, who provided new ideas and approaches, helped by research studies from the universities and senior civil servants. Senior advisers and friends like Jim Gray, Ralph Hedlin, Peter Meekison, and Lee Richardson made his caucus aware of the debates and options about the role of an Ottawa-directed, centralized approach and a province-building model, which he himself never thought were in contradiction. The lessons he drew from his studies in Boston, and from the United States generally, were that a strong national economy comes from strong state / provincial and regional economies, and both require serious expertise and strong administrative skills within government and the private sector.

Like other Conservative premiers, including John Buchanan in Nova Scotia, Bill Davis in Ontario, Grant Devine in Saskatchewan, and Richard Hatfield in New Brunswick, Lougheed wanted Brian Mulroney's government to enact its 1984 election promises, but he appreciated it would need time to learn the policy ropes – he grasped that, because of the complicated relationships within the federation, a policy helping one province could be seen as a slight to another. This was especially true on the economic-competitiveness agenda. Industrial policy, whether an implicit, market-driven approach with enabling policies to let market forces determine winners or losers, or government intervention, where the power and resources of government determine policy outcomes, reflects both national circumstance and political realities.

Personally, Lougheed had big dreams for Alberta. They were immensely practical, such as turning Calgary into a great centre for energy law, as new producers in Asia, Latin America, or Africa might want advice independent of American practices. He became an early advocate of tourism promotion and hoped to turn Banff into a great cultural and artistic centre, and the University of Alberta in Edmonton into a centre for medical research. The western provinces were well aware of the new economic muscle of Quebec, the initiatives of Jean Lesage's Liberal government (1960–66), and the fact that that province was now a big player in the energy sector with Hydro-Québec. Lougheed saw parallel possibilities for Alberta in energy policies, and a very large initiative, the oilsands in Fort McMurray.

With the steady increase in global oil prices, and thus a rising income from its royalty regime, the Lougheed government established the Alberta Heritage Fund, an investment to save for a rainy day, a model used by many oil producers, such as Kuwait, Norway, and Saudi Arabia and now called sovereign wealth funds. Alas, successive Alberta governments raided the piggy bank, so the fund's value now amounts to about $18 billion, compared to Norway's $1 trillion. Norway puts all its oil revenue in its wealth fund, matched by a high, 51 per cent corporate tax and 27 per cent income tax. Alberta's complex royalty regime, varying for conventional and non-conventional oil and gas, and its policy of using its royalties income for current spending in health care and education (including the university sector and two technical colleges), explain the difference. The contrast between present spending and long-term savings for these two jurisdictions with the same population is a telling commentary on differing political time horizons.

II

The philosophical contrast between Canada and the United States in regional development is enlightening in terms of building local capacity in smaller regions. With some exceptions, the American federal system, with Washington at the core, operates with a distributive model in federal spending. Congressional-committee structure and appropriation measures, including earmarks, locate economic initiatives like infrastructure, military bases, and even federal offices more evenly among the regions and states. This spending pattern is especially noticeable where the strength of small states in Congress (each state, regardless of population, has two senators) produces national policies that are attentive to regions, and committees allow members to foster "pork-barreling" that gives a measure of equality and adjustment between regions of differing economic capacity. Starting in the Depression of the 1930s and Franklin Roosevelt's New Deal, regional programs such as the Public Works Administration and the Natural Resources Policy Board emphasized regional planning – for instance, the legendary Tennessee Valley Authority (TVA) built hydro dams and waterways and improved transportation, mining, and energy production. The stated rationale for such programs was often national security or defence, and public investments in libraries, flood control, workforce training, and sports and recreation projects provided additional support for industries like agriculture, coal, and steel. Little thinking about the purity of the market or an ideological preference for private enterprise prevented conservative members of Congress from endorsing federal funding for projects like "farm payments" ranging from southern Texas to the northern plains and the states of the Rockies.

In Canada, regional ministers traditionally played a powerful role as pork-barrelers and dispensers of patronage. In Liberal governments, Jack Pickersgill, elected in Newfoundland, Lloyd Axworthy in Manitoba, and Allan MacEachen in Nova Scotia, stand out. Ottawa differs from Washington's approach by applying a redistributive model via federal–provincial economic agreements and cabinet intercession on selected "big" projects like shipbuilding, the St Lawrence Seaway, and the Pacific Gateway investments under the Chrétien and Harper governments, and the special case of the cod fisheries in Newfoundland, negotiated by John Crosbie, Michael Wilson, and Brian Mulroney. Canadian senators play almost no significant role in regional development, although the Senate Banking Committee has been a powerful voice to protect the Toronto-headquartered banks from foreign competition, a classic case of regulatory capture. In Ontario and Quebec, usually one party controls the government in Ottawa, while voters often choose another to run the province. There are some temporary anomalies – Ontario premier Oliver Mowat serving briefly in Laurier's cabinet after the 1896 federal election, Ontario's Conservatives under James Whitney winning power in 1905, or Maurice Duplessis's Union Nationale in 1958 backing John Diefenbaker's Conservatives, who lost most of the seats four years later.

In more recent times, the Conservatives' forty-two-year reign in Ontario (1943–85), with a capacity to change their leader every ten years or so, contrasted with a Liberal reign in Ottawa (1935–57, 1963–79, 1980–84). The Ontario Liberals' victory under David Peterson in 1985 coincided with Conservative rule in Ottawa, and *René* Lévesque's success in Quebec (1976–85) during Pierre Trudeau's time in office (1968–79, 1980–84). These cases confirm a general rule of a balance of power in the federation, with one party ruling in the provinces, another in Ottawa, despite Atlantic Canadians' general preference to align parties provincially and in Ottawa. Such factors variously add to or detract from the political tensions between Ottawa and the provinces.

The 1982 constitutional guarantee (section 36.2) of fiscal equalization is now a strait-jacket for federal policy, guaranteeing expenditures for essential public services like education, health care, and unemployment insurance. Total equalization payments now amount to a large proportion of provincial revenues, and thus reduce incentives in Atlantic Canada for governments to pool resources and coordinate policies for the region. Despite studies recommending integration of regional policies on trade, tourism, and procurement, and removal of interprovincial barriers – a stark contrast to the approach in western Canada – progress has been minimal. However, the "rep by pop" model of Canada's first-past-the-post electoral system gives a huge advantage to Ontario and Quebec and incentives for the Liberal party to appreciate its electoral support, best illustrated by westerners angry with Trudeau's National Energy Program, when Ottawa sided with the energy-consuming provinces in central Canada against energy-producing Alberta and Saskatchewan.

The comfortable slogans of Lester Pearson's "cooperative federalism" or Robert Bourassa's "profitable federalism" helped shift the balance, so that federal spending is often based on new programs of conditional grants for health, post-secondary education, and welfare. These grants are calculated on a per-capita formula, such as the Canadian Health and Social Transfers (CHST) and science and technology measures like the Canadian Foundation for Innovation, Technology Partnerships Canada, and Canada Research Chairs, which favour the bigger universities in the four most populous provinces. Steady population changes, due mostly to immigration, and the resulting new seats in the House of Commons, give an added incentive for executive federalism – meetings dominated in fact by the four big provinces and Ottawa. For the smaller provinces, federal disparities are likely to widen, given the demographics of too few younger people and an ageing population, the declining competitive strength of traditional resource industries due to global forces, and the relentless migration of younger people westwards to greener pastures.

III

It remains a paradox that so few Canadians appreciate how a federal system brings huge advantages over time, as the benefits of each region or province can be pooled to help the disadvantaged, because today's advantages can turn quickly as external circumstances change. History records that the British North American colonies that refused to join the federation in 1867 – Newfoundland and Prince Edward Island – were enjoying an economic boom. A motion at the Charlottetown Debating Club in 1870, presented by the island's colonial secretary, gave a definitive view of the terms of union: "Not just and equitable to PEI, and should not be accepted." The island's slogan – "Better terms" – expressed well the ongoing reality of protracted and interminable negotiations between Ottawa and the provinces, as if each premier were taking a cue from Charles Dickens's Oliver Twist, "'Please, sir, I want some more."

Until 1957, Ottawa and the provinces had regular meetings to discuss federal–provincial issues relating to shared spending and priorities for particular matters (building the Trans-Canada Highway, economic links to Britain, or commercial ties with the Americans). Laurier's lament in 1911 in a campaign speech in Trois-Rivières has parallels for every prime minister since: "I am branded in Quebec as a traitor to the French and in Ontario as a traitor to the English. In Quebec I am attacked as an Imperialist and in Ontario as an anti-Imperialist ... I have had before me as a pillar of fire by night and a pillar of cloud by day a policy of true Canadianism, of moderation, of conciliation."

For almost 100 years, the operating assumption by all governments was that federal authorities took the lead in economic policy, stability, and a balance of monetary and fiscal policy to sustain economic growth, low unemployment, and low inflation. By extension, Confederation gave Ottawa wide taxing powers with few restrictions and limited the provinces to "direct taxation" within their borders. Ottawa retains powers to impose tariffs and export duties, withhold taxes on payments to non-residents, and impose sales or excise taxes on intermediate goods and services intended to be passed on to other consumers. The provinces are able to levy the most important taxes, as on incomes and sales, but municipalities, as their creatures, only taxes that the province authorizes, for instance, on land.

Two circumstances changed this equation after 1945. During wartime, reluctantly, the provinces surrendered their income- and estate-tax fields to Ottawa in lieu of intergovernmental transfers and debt relief, and

Ottawa assumed unemployment insurance as a constitutional responsibility. Immediately after the war and accelerating in the 1950s, the provinces wanted to regain their taxing powers, especially given the rising costs of education and hospitalization. At the Dominion–Provincial Conference on Reconstruction in August 1945, the federal delegation, led by Prime Minister King, Finance Minister Brooke Claxton, and his deputy, William Clark, and including other top officials like Robert Bryce, John Deutsch, and O.D. Skelton, hoped to continue the wartime arrangement. Despite King's accommodating tone, with the media expecting more than a war of words, Ontario's Conservative premier, George Drew, took a harsh, hard line, and was followed by Quebec's Maurice Duplessis. When the media learned that the two men were having lunch together, on the third day, the press gallery's rumour machine went into overdrive and speculated on a new Ontario–Quebec axis modelled on the (Mitchell) Hepburn–Duplessis alliance in the 1930s.

In the end, despite this conference's failure, other meetings produced a compromise, including provincial governments like Ontario and Quebec introducing a corporate income tax in the late 1940s, and Quebec a personal income tax. The other provinces signed tax-collection agreements (TCAs) on personal and corporate income taxes, a classic Canadian compromise, where Ottawa paid for collection costs, and the provinces agreed to accept federal policies, allowing some flexibility for determining rates and credits. Steadily, all governments and each prime minister took it as an axiom that Ottawa had a responsibility to help each province, usually by direct payments.

Indeed, when Justice Minister Louis St Laurent attended the Dominion–Provincial Conference in August 1945, he became Ottawa's spokesman, giving press interviews on the need for federal intervention to have the wealthier provinces help the poorer ones. But it was his successor as prime minister, John Diefenbaker, the prairie populist, who introduced a new system, now called "equalization," to ensure some minimal level of public assistance. The thinking behind this new approach came from a former university professor at Laval University, Maurice Lamontagne, assistant deputy minister in Ottawa to Liberal minister Jean Lesage at Northern Affairs and Natural Resources, and he continued for the new Diefenbaker government. His background paper on equalization for the federal–provincial meeting in November 1957 also included ideas for national hospital insurance and extension of supplementary benefits for unemployment insurance.

The immediate aim for the prime minister was to help the Atlantic provinces, in part because they provided crucial seats for the Conservative victory. Originally, the calculation to provide services to the two wealthiest provinces, British Columbia and Ontario, was based on three taxes (personal income, corporate, and inheritance), but it had been refined to include up to twenty-five specific tax measures. The original program had the goal of giving each province the same per-capita revenue as the wealthiest provinces calculated on three tax bases: on personal income, corporate income, and succession (inheritance taxes). Five years later, 50 per cent of natural-resource revenues were included as the fourth tax base. At the same time, however, the standard of the two wealthiest provinces was lowered to the national average. The Diefenbaker government greatly expanded cost-shared programs, with five major measures and fifteen smaller ones, and increased budget expenditures from $144 million a year to $606 million in 1962. It added an initiative to allow an abatement on personal income taxes to permit provinces to raise money, including for cost-sharing. In 1967 the system was redesigned to work with every government revenue scheme except energy.

As this system evolved, with new names and acronyms, governments refined the approach. In 1977, the cost-sharing funding for post-secondary education and health was redesigned as Established Programs Financing (EPF), which combined a transfer of tax points, which went to provinces permanently, and a cash transfer as block grants, starting in 2004 with the new Canada Health and Social Transfer, divided in 2015 into the Canada Health Transfer and the Canada Social Transfer. If Ottawa commits itself, for example, to reducing tax levels for individuals and corporations, or lowering the consumption tax, or reducing tax expenditures, how quickly do the provinces step in with higher taxation to satisfy their rising expenditures? This predicament was the situation facing Michael Wilson and the Mulroney government in 1986, and offers a lesson for every federal finance minister since.

Perhaps 100 people in Canada know the arcane details of calculating equalization payments, in what is now the most generous equalization system in any federation in the world. In 2018, the program amounted to about $19 billion, with the calculation formula now extended to 2024. Four provinces – British Columbia, Alberta, Saskatchewan, and Newfoundland and Labrador – provide the money from their above-average fiscal capacity, with Quebec receiving the largest amount, $11.7 billion, but making a stated commitment to become a "have province," revealing the permanent tension in federal–provincial relations. Welcome to the rhetorical world of "fiscal imbalance."

IV

In Ottawa since 1867, federal regional-development policy has, in theory, been subordinate to national commercial policy, despite special remedies in transportation like subsidies for isolated areas (see Table 4.1). Not without reason have premiers and the voting public in the west and the Atlantic region viewed Canada's east–west economy as, in fact, tilted towards central Canada. The celebrated Rowell–Sirois Report of 1940 exposed the fiscal incapacity of the poorer provinces, an early signal pointing towards later equalization grants for seven provinces – Quebec and the Atlantic provinces, plus Manitoba and Saskatchewan. In 1957, the Royal Commission on Canada's Economic Prospects (Gordon Commission), addressed the issue as follows: "One of the most striking features of the economy of the Atlantic Provinces is the disproportionately large number of people engaged in marginal activities, subsistence farming, fishing and logging ... What is needed we believe is a bold comprehensive and coordinated approach to the underlying problems of the region in order to make the best possible use of the underlying resources of the area and to improve transportation and other basic services." The report added an inopportune, politically insensitive comment: "If the pace of development, however, does not prove sufficient to facilitate such an adjustment easily, then those who may wish to re-establish themselves in other occupations elsewhere should, we suggest, be assisted in doing so."

When this report was released, the Diefenbaker government had been elected, and regional development became more focused. For much of the early mandate, the North American recession led to high unemployment. Opposition cries and public discontent led to new tax incentives in the 1960 budget for investment in areas with high unemployment and slow growth. The passage in June 1961 of the Agriculture Rehabilitation and Development Act (ARDA) for depressed rural areas was followed two years later by creation of the Atlan7tic Development Board. A succession of reforms followed, including by the new Pearson government first elected in 1963, such as changes to ARDA, renamed the Agricultural and Rural Development Act, and the new Fund for Rural Economic Development (FRED), which were combined in 1969 into the Department of Regional Economic Expansion (DREE), promoting two new programs, Special Areas (Growth Poles) and the Regional Industrial Incentives Act (RIIA) dedicated to Atlantic Canada and eastern Quebec. The 1968 Confederation

Table 4.1
Gross Domestic Product (GDP), by Province, Mid-2010s

Province or territory	Population (2017)	GDP (million 2007$) (2017)	GDP per capita (2007$) (2017)	Average total income ($) (2015)
Canada	36,712,658	1,751,898	55,405	41,129
British Columbia	4,945,559	228,195	53,267	40,196
Alberta	4,262,642	304,709	78,100	53,408
Saskatchewan	1,155,034	60,592	70,138	40,933
Manitoba	1,340,776	57,250	50,820	36,795
Ontario	14,153,806	651,932	55,322	42,643
Quebec	8,329,664	328,688	46,126	36,491
New Brunswick	768,212	27,363	43,818	34,164
Prince Edward Island	151,477	4,883	42,157	33,632
Nova Scotia	943,373	33,470	42,640	36,108
Newfoundland and Labrador	528,463	26,773	56,935	35,345

Source: Statistics Canada GNP (Taxation Statistics 2015)

of Tomorrow Conference introduced a new term to the federal–provincial vocabulary, "regional disparity."

Despite the time and resources devoted to these various approaches, the real gains were sparse. Money and initiatives like tax advantages, direct subsidies, and grants addressed only the symptoms of the pervasive problems of low income, high unemployment, and cyclical economic activity in Atlantic Canada. Even in areas like tourism, most visitors arrived in the summer, the short July–August season, so hotel owners and motel operators had to get returns for their investment, made doubly risky because certain areas, including all of Prince Edward Island, relied on the CN ferries for transportation, and a strike called in, for example, mid-August would remove any hope of profits for the calendar year. Such measures may sound arcane and bureaucratic, but lethargy, incompetence, or miscalculation can be politically explosive: in 1956 Ottawa overpaid the PEI government of Premier Alex Matheson by more than a million dollars, and it now wanted the money returned, so decided during the 1957 election campaign to compromise, by requesting payment in instalments. In the cunning hands of John Diefenbaker, already making political hay with the penurious sentiments of Walter Harris, the Liberal federal finance minister, running a healthy budget surplus but increasing old-age pensions by only six dollars a month, from $40 to $46, this was political manna in a campaign where the Tories won a minority government.

An abrupt shift took place in Pierre Trudeau's minority government in 1973. Each province would negotiate with Ottawa on a priority list of industrial projects, funded 50-50 – called General Development Agreements, and later Economic and Regional Development Agreements (ERDAS). Cabinet approved the arrangements for each province but allowed the minister discretion to negotiate special packages. In 1982, DREE was disbanded, and a new regional ministry was created: the Minister of State for Economic and Regional Development (MSERD) within the Department of Regional Industrial Expansion (DRIE). At this time, Ottawa was struggling to sort out the trade-offs – between spurring strong national industries that could compete internationally and easing regional disparities, including within the provinces. In the United States, for instance, the Department of Commerce shares industrial issues with the U.S. Trade Representative, the treasury secretary, the Council of Economic Advisors, and the State Department. France had a powerful lead ministry, Industrie et commerce extérieur, while Japan had the redoubtable Ministry of International Trade and Investment (MITI). Ottawa and the top civil servants, including Michael Pitfield and Gordon Osbaldeston, decided to combine the trade functions with the Department of External Affairs, while leaving commercial policy to the Department of Industry, located in the C.D. Howe Building at 235 Queen Street. Unfortunately, unlike other countries at this time, Canada paid little attention to data analysis and basing sound policy on the competitive position of domestic sectors and their relative cost advantages. This machinery was the inheritance of the new Mulroney government in 1984.

The Throne Speech of 1986 called for pushing regional development through an Atlantic Canada Opportunity Agency. In the leadership campaign, Brian Mulroney made several references to regional development, including forceful promises on specific topics such as energy (the Newfoundland Accord), high electricity prices in Prince Edward Island, transportation and shipbuilding, and policies beyond stabilization to help diversify the western economy. The Conservatives held three policy conferences during the 1984 campaign. The first, in Prince Albert on 5 July, explored western issues such as agriculture, energy, grain transport, mining and forestry, and entrepreneurship and small business. In Sherbrooke on 26 July, presentations about women's issues like pension rights, youth policy, and agriculture and textiles offered detailed promises, often drawing on the policy work of the parliamentary critics during the year in Opposition under Mulroney. Robert Stanfield chaired the conference on 2 August in Halifax, where strong commitments on regional development related to energy, ferry service and transportation, fisheries, shipbuilding, and tourism.

The Mulroney government placed the main responsibility for regional development in the Ministry of Industry, under Sinclair Stevens, and the Cabinet Committee on Economic Policy, which had an annual budget exceeding $2.1 billion. Atlantic Canada became a priority, as did Cape Breton. As minister and as chair of the powerful cabinet committee, Stevens had a special interest in regional development and felt that Ottawa's postwar policies unwittingly favoured central Canada. Unusual for a person with Bay Street experience, he thought outside the box, including an earlier initiative to be a founder of the Bank of Western Canada, with former Governor of the Bank of Canada James Coyne, which went into liquidation in 1972. One of his measures was to shut down the heavy-water plant in Cape Breton, a billion-dollar boondoggle initiated by Allan J. MacEachen, which even the workers knew was not a job creator. A series of initiatives, province by province, became the policy mainstay of this committee, in such areas as automotive suppliers, electricity pricing, highway construction, Japanese investment in auto plants, shipbuilding, small-business creation, technological upgrading for the pulp-and-paper sector, tourist promotion (including policies to extend the season), and transportation, with ideas to improve ferry service, from Boston to Nova Scotia (via Yarmouth), from Newfoundland to Cape Breton, and from the mainland to Prince Edward Island – from Cape Tormentine, NB, to Borden and from Pictou, NS, to Wood Islands.

V

In the aftermath of the 1984 election, the Mulroney cabinet's regional-development agenda was one of two-way cooperation with the provincial governments, fulfilling a campaign promise of national reconciliation after the bitter, often personalized battles of the Trudeau era. An air of optimism was evident about Ottawa's intentions, and an understanding that the Atlantic provinces now had a strong voice in Ottawa. The premiers had sent their top advisers for meetings with senior bureaucratic and political staffs, and the sense of a new approach was palpable. While John Crosbie and Elmer MacKay were seen as the regional powerbrokers, the fact that Brian Mulroney had spent so much time in Atlantic Canada, as a university student at St Francis Xavier University and in St Thomas, NB, and as a CEO in Newfoundland, where the Iron Ore Company had huge operations, were all testimony to his personal interest in the region. But the reality was obvious to policy-makers that the glories of the past, including the role of military bases at Chatham, Gander, Greenwood, or Summerside, were no guide to future prosperity. The relentless, relative decline of the region's economy – by some measures, the lowest productivity growth and per-capita income of the ten provinces and fifty U.S. states – stemmed from a small population, low adoption of technology, and reliance on seasonal industries. The result was a dependency trap – government-induced incentives for equalization payments from Ottawa. New England showed a capacity for flexibility and resilience missing in Atlantic Canada.

But two other factors were at play: lack of political cooperation within the region and the perils of demographic dislocation. The four Atlantic provinces operate as stand-alone political jurisdictions, despite a history of attempts to consolidate them. The Maritimes provinces were British colonies but before the Treaty of Utrecht in 1713 formed a single French territory called Acadie, or Acadia. In 1763 Cape Breton became a separate province, and Île Saint-Jean became Prince Edward Island, named after Queen Victoria's father, Edward, Duke of Kent, in 1798. The celebrated Charlottetown Conference in 1864 was in fact summoned to discuss Maritimes union. When Prime Minister W.L. Mackenzie King established in 1926 a Royal Commission on Maritime Claims (Duncan Commission), chaired by the British industrialist Sir Andrew Rae Duncan, who was also studying the coal industry in Nova Scotia, he knew there was deep unrest in the region, inflamed by the Maritime Rights Movement calling for better terms. Maritimers knew their representation in the House of Commons declined from forty-one MPs in 1883 to only thirty-one in 1921, yet saw that Ontario and Quebec gained huge geographical extensions to their northern boundaries and that three new provinces on the prairies were receiving special financial treatment and control of property rights, and the Maritimers quietly expected King to offer at least minimal concessions, now that the 1926 election was over. When Newfoundland joined the federation in 1949 and became part of the Council of Atlantic Premiers in 1992, much of the basic architecture of the centre–periphery or centripetal–centrifugal tensions remained in place.

Various political leaders have advanced arguments for greater regional cooperation. Liberal Premier Louis Robichaud of New Brunswick, for instance, at a centennial conference in Charlottetown in 1964, proposed a reassessment that led to the Maritime Union Study of 1970. Other reports and appeals for better coordination and integrated policies, led by Liberal Premier Frank McKenna of New Brunswick, gained little political traction with provincial governments or voters. Of the three main options, the status quo, greater Atlantic integration, and outright political union (of the four provinces, or the Maritimes only), the third had zero mainstream support, and the political elites and civil service paid only lip service to the second. Consultations with the provincial governments (all Conservative), cabinet ministers, caucus members, and local entrepreneurs suggested that the idea of a central, coordinating agency might work. It was mentioned in the federal Throne Speech in 1986: "An Atlantic Canada Opportunities Agency will be constituted to facilitate and coordinate all federal development initiatives in the area. This agency will make fuller use of the expertise available in the Atlantic region and invite the maximum participation of other governments and organizations in the area."

The genesis of this new agency started with three passengers on a flight from Sherbrooke to Ottawa in September 1985: the prime minister, senior Tory guru Dalton Camp, and me, as senior policy adviser, PEI-born and -raised. Camp, by trade an advertising executive, American-born but raised in New Brunswick, was a Liberal youth delegate at the 1948 convention when Louis St Laurent succeeded W.L. Mackenzie King. He spent a year at Columbia University, and another at the London School of Economics, but on the advice of a few friends, mostly lonely Tories in New Brunswick but one, a very rich Tory living in Britain, Camp switched party allegiance. While in England, he had an interview with Sir Max Aitken, Lord Beaverbrook. Aitken was born in Ontario but moved to Newcastle, New Brunswick, on the Miramichi, where he started a newspaper at thirteen. He used his contacts to great advantage, moved to London and built a newspaper empire, served in the British cabinet in both world wars, and was ennobled. He became Camp's interlocutor. Camp helped draft John Diefenbaker's election promises in 1957, where the "Atlantic Resolutions" proposed "measures which will help to overcome the historic disabilities which have limited and even denied opportunities in this area," one of them an Atlantic Development Board.

Camp's brother-in-law, Norman Atkins, another Maritimer and a graduate of Acadia University, was a constant critic of many of the personnel in Mulroney's PMO, so, to placate criticisms from Ontario's "Big Blue Machine," the prime minister recruited Dalton Camp, on paper at least, into the PMO, though technically an employee in the PCO. Mulroney had made major commitments to regional development, and in Halifax, when meeting Robert Stanfield, a strong backer of the Atlantic Resolutions in 1957, he took action. Despite his cool demeanour and a Harvard law degree, Stanfield had a long memory and knew the difference between empty promises and serious policy.

On flying out of Sherbrooke in September 1985, the prime minister asked Dalton and me to focus first on a new Atlantic agency, knowing the status quo was no longer acceptable, but with a mandate to build a competitive economy in the region. Dalton was a bellwether – while he lacked bureaucratic finesse, he knew at first hand the problems and challenges of Atlantic Canada. This "ACOA file" gave him a project where he could learn the ways of Ottawa, the bureaucratic infighting, and the complicated business of developing policy under fire and dealing with the Atlantic caucus, the Atlantic premiers, the media, and business interests throughout the region.

Planning for what became the Atlantic Canada Opportunities Agency (ACOA) focused on three issues – the mandate, the machinery, and the financial commitment – under the assumption that these issues would be similar to those for Western Diversification, to be located in Calgary. Numerous meetings were held within the relevant departments – DRIE, PCO, Finance, Trade – plus bilateral meetings with the Atlantic premiers and members of caucus. Despite sundry names suggested for the initiative, including the word "development," implying government assistance, the bias was clearly on private initiative, hence the word "opportunity." Fortunately, a new CEO might be available, Don MacPhail, former ambassador to West Germany, who was familiar with the powerful West German Länder (states), with their technology and export strengths. MacPhail hoped to work in Ottawa, not in Moncton, likely site for headquarters, with regional offices in each province. A few choice words from on high made him relent. Donald Savoie, a professor at the University of Moncton, was commissioned to write a short report on the machinery and mandate issues, but when he recommended that the new independent board and the CEO report directly to the prime minister, that approach was quickly rejected. The prime minister later put Lowell Murray in charge as the reporting minister for ACOA, a shrewd choice, given his former work as cabinet secretary for Premier Richard Hatfield, where he negotiated umbrella agreements with Ottawa for specific projects and spending in sectors such as fisheries, highways, small business, and tourism.

On 12 March 1987, I wrote a memo to Prime Minister Mulroney, summarizing the workplan for ACOA:

> At the outset, I couldn't agree more on the need for placing the highest priority on regional development: tensions are building up to a very serious level, expectations are running high both in Atlantic Canada and the West ... Three important issues are involved in all this ... for brevity, 1) management process, 2) policy, and 3) politics ... At DRIE, the direction of these initiatives has major implications for the central mandate of the department, i.e. creating in effect a Ministry of Industry, downgrading regional development, or even shifting it out of the department ... There are major linkages to be decided with other areas, e.g. small business, tourism, MOSST, and sector departments like Energy, Forestry, and even agriculture ...
>
> There are very fundamental policy issues attached to these initiatives, such as: Instruments – loans, loan guarantees, grants, tax measures; Machinery – FEDC offices, agency structure, etc.; delivery – via Ministers or depoliticized mechanisms; focus – regional emphasis vs. development and building on strengths; coherence – coordination of department initiatives in the region, as well as federal–provincial linkages.
>
> ... The Atlantic Agency, while operating in tandem with the Western initiative impacts on fundamentally different problems (i.e. politically motivated projects) – a very weak private sector, a very limited industrial base, and very stretched provincial treasuries. Moreover, procurement policies – whether small scale or big scale (e.g. defence contracts) are vital development tools. All of this is to point out the thrust of regional development is a vital link to the trade initiative – indeed, it is no less than the introduction of a new national 'industrial policy' for Canada.

A month later, the prime minister flew to Charlottetown and met the four Atlantic premiers – John Buchanan, Richard Hatfield, Jim Lee, and Brian Peckford – to finalize the ACOA arrangements, including the announcement, the funding model, and the machinery and headquarters in Moncton. It was a busy schedule – a breakfast roundtable with small-business owners, a tour of the waterfront, and, appropriately, a lunch at Province House, where the Fathers of Confederation met in 1864. The topics included the levels of funding (more than $1 billion over five years), the corporate structure, the reporting relationships, and the priority funding areas for the entire region. On 5 June 1987, the prime minister made the formal announcement in St John's, declaring to a standing-room-only audience: "We begin with new money, a new mission and a new opportunity. The agency will succeed where others have failed."

Despite sundry criticisms from the beginning, especially that ACOA and provincial governments were in the business of picking winners, it became the model for other regional agencies, starting with the Office of Western Diversification, which had headquarters in Edmonton, where Deputy Prime Minister Don Mazankowski was the minister in charge, with outside assistance from Jamie Burns, Phil Evershed, Jon Johnston, and Ross Raid. Later initiatives, modelled on these two, followed in Quebec and in northern Ontario. Curiously, Stephen Harper, as Reform party member, leader of the Opposition, and even prime minister, and no fan of government involvement in economic development, kept these agencies intact, and created another in southern Ontario, in 2009, called FedDev Ontario, with a billion-dollar budget.

Each agency started with the simple principle of helping local companies and industries develop a capacity for exports, acquire the best technology available, and become profitable within an agreed time frame. ACOA helped change the mindset of the Atlantic region, by cultivating local start-ups and improving infrastructure and education, including community colleges. Clearly, other factors were at play, including large investments, such as rebuilding the military with the frigate program in Saint John, construction of the fixed link between Prince Edward Island and New Brunswick, conversion of the airbase in Summerside, PEI, to an aerospace park, investments in offshore energy, and federal spending in defence and aerospace in Nova Scotia. It took time, but the pending free-trade deal with the United States looked to have predictable and favourable outcomes, even though the Conservatives lost ten Atlantic seats, including four ministers, in the 1988 election.

The optimism of the 1980s and 1990s in Atlantic Canada – over major investments in the Hibernia oil-fields and the offshore, the Confederation Bridge, the national program for building frigates, and new investments in post-secondary science and engineering – gave way to lethargy, as provincial governments thwarted regional cooperation and turned inward. A succession of premiers, instead of looking outward, returned to an ingrained culture of contentment, and applied a variation of (Roy) Amara's law for technology, overestimating the effect of temporary job-creating investments in the short run and underestimating technology and education investments in the long run. Numerous studies addressing this issue recommended a common regional approach, like past initiatives to establish the Council of Atlantic Premiers, mostly on the urging of Premiers Frank McKenna and John Buchanan, who knew their provinces were dependent on equalization payments. Liberal PEI Premier Joe Ghiz, ever grateful for Ottawa transfers, designed a system where his government would hire workers for ten weeks, then lay them off, entitling them to unemployment insurance, a federal responsibility, for forty-two weeks. Small size can have huge advantages, but the lack of policy coordination limits opportunities for employment creation and growth.

The region is singularly positioned to be the Atlantic gateway for the flow of commerce from Asia and Europe to all of North America. A closer look shows its unique advantages, while congestion in much of North America, where delays and traffic jams lower overall productivity. Numerous studies, including the American Society of Civil Engineer's "Report Card," show U.S. federal and state investments in port, rail, road, and airport capacity hamstrung by lack of money, social concerns about noise, wasted fuel, environmental challenges, traffic congestion, and partisan gridlock among stakeholders. Thus, Canada's Atlantic region faces an opportunity, but also a question of how governments and the private sector fit into global transportation-supply chains. Global trade and global logistics are now realities, and the renewal of the North American Free Trade Agreement in 2018, and Canada's recent trade agreement with the European Union, open new opportunities, but only if the region wants to be a player in international trade and puts in the time and money to design a transportation system that has global reach and impact.

Canada's Atlantic gateway dates from the time of the first European settlers over 400 years ago and now consists of the two main ports, Montreal and Halifax, and regional ports like Quebec, St John's, Sydney, and the fledgling port of Melford in Canso, Nova Scotia. As a result of limited cooperation and rivalry among provinces, and the lack of a gateway champion driving the necessary policy focus, the Atlantic gateway strategy, centring on Halifax and Montreal, is less developed than that for ports in western Canada, such as Vancouver and Prince George, the port closest to Shanghai. The prospect of very large container ships from major shipping firms like Maersk makes Halifax the natural entry point for goods from Europe or from south Asia transported through the Panama Canal. In the United States, new investment developments and new infrastructure – for instance, railway lines, terminals, and warehouses – indicate that Washington is not a bystander to changing global trade, where over 90 per cent of international trade is ocean-based shipping. The question remains: are local and regional ports in Atlantic Canada prepared to build a major ocean gateway extending to a national transportation corridor? For instance, how does Labrador deliver its iron ore to the steel mills of Hamilton and Pittsburgh? The answer: by train and bulk cargo on the St Lawrence River. Today, the markets of Asia are open to Newfoundland via inshore shipping and container vessels.

Transportation, port infrastructure, and global supply chains illustrate the new opportunities in Atlantic Canada. However, recent performance, with mediocre high schools (the OECD ranked New Brunswick second last, slightly ahead of Prince Edward Island), limited immigration and a population that is ageing fast, bloated and redundant hospital systems, a quadruplicated civil service, and limited investments in state-of-the-art IT, plus so few firms that export even to a neighbouring province, obscures a global viewpoint. The western provinces' Agreement on Internal Trade (AIT) of 1995 could be a model for Atlantic Canada, with the four of them cooperating on government procurement, trade enhancement, and tourism, despite the recent spat between Alberta and British Columbia on pipeline politics. Curiously, the Atlantic region hasn't learned the economic advantages of small size from Iceland, Ireland, or Norway. Such laments echo comments from John Risley, a leading Atlantic entrepreneur, venture capitalist, and chair of Clearwater Foods: "Canada and Newfoundland, Nova Scotia, and New Brunswick can each have their own set of rules, but those rules will be judged by others, not us, and it may well be that judgement is not so favourable to us."

VI

National reconciliation was one of the four pillars of the Conservative election platform in 1984, and many of the campaign promises had a federal–provincial dimension. Less attention was paid to interprovincial rivalries, and one big initiative was time-consuming and planned in secrecy. Sadly, it had so much promise, but ultimately failed. Mulroney, long before he became leader in 1983, wanted a new hydro-electricity package where Newfoundland could resolve lingering tensions with Quebec, after Liberal premier Joey Smallwood signed a long-term contract (to 2041) in 1969 with Hydro-Québec to sell electricity from Churchill Falls (in Labrador) to Quebec at $2 per megawatt hour, a fraction of the world price. Energy prices climbed steadily after the OPEC energy crises in 1973 and 1979, making electricity from the Upper Churchill a massively lucrative deal for Quebec. Even worse, Newfoundland invested more than $2 billion on the Lower Churchill and $600 million in the Come By Chance oil refinery, which went into bankruptcy, leaving a poor province even poorer after terrible misjudgments and a measure of political corruption.

However, new governments in Ottawa and in St John's offered a chance to turn the corner. The signing of the Atlantic Accord on 14 June 1984, prior to the national election, and formerly approved by cabinet ten months later, allowed a new, cooperative attitude, with the possibility that Quebec and Hydro-Québec, selling electricity to voracious New England, might reconsider Churchill Falls. The strategic question was simple: can new construction at Churchill Falls spur investment that would create jobs and generate revenue for northern Quebec and Labrador, despite the legal dispute between the two provinces? Could a new package for green, renewable power, modelled on the huge success of the massive hydroelectric projects Baie James and Baie James II, be feasible?

On the prime minister's instruction, the PMO's Policy Unit took the lead, but with an air of secrecy, given the file's sensitive nature. A small, informal group of civil servants, cabinet members such as Sinclair Stevens and John Crosbie, Senator Bill Doodie, PMO staffers, and policy advisers in Pat Carney's office worked on a plan to exploit the huge power resources of Churchill Falls, knowing that water from the five rivers flowing to the St Lawrence went through the prime minister's riding, Manicouagan. Instead of opening up the existing contract, the new deal would involve Ottawa, Newfoundland, and Quebec, with Hydro-Québec providing the land-based transmission routes to New England, Newfoundland receiving abundant power for domestic needs, and construction firms in both provinces gaining most of the contracts, but with a bias towards Newfoundland as partial compensation for the original deal. In all likelihood, Quebec-based construction firms would be successful bidders on the huge investments needed to carry offshore oil to the mainland for refining and subsequent shipment to export markets. However, a few very big global firms were quietly consulted to see their interest in executing feasibility studies – Bechtel from San Francisco, and Bouygues from France, for instance. Len Good, then an associate deputy in the Department of Energy, wrote a fact-based memo on the Churchill file.

In principle, there seemed readiness to move forward on a more formal basis, and the prime minister suggested he have a private discussion with the Quebec premier, René Lévesque. The premier had been the minister who nationalized the electricity sector to create Hydro-Québec and knew the file extremely well, including Indigenous land rights for transmission, the enormous potential of Churchill Falls, and the huge competitive advantages for the entire northern region of sustainable, renewable, and lucrative energy power. Lévesque had his own political agenda, but a package of electricity development in this northern region, which faced high unemployment, including in the Aboriginal community, was part of his *beau risque* strategy to deal with Ottawa. Quietly he gave a private nod to the ideas in the package – it was a big, bold plan, and he liked it, in principle. However, as in many policy initiatives, the event cycle took over, personalities changed, and new priorities took over. The Liberal Robert Bourassa became premier in the 1985 election, after Lévesque resigned and Pierre-Marc Johnson became his successor (the second of three premiers from his family, along with his father, Daniel, Sr, and his brother Daniel).

Issues like the possible U.S. free-trade agreement and Meech Lake constitutional reform topped the policy agenda, and complications around full funding for the offshore oil and gas reserves took priority. In May 1989, Clyde Wells became Liberal premier of Newfoundland, and his savage attacks on the signed Meech Lake constitutional package, not energy, exposed his partisan agenda. Political rhetoric in Newfoundland against the Churchill Falls contract of 1969 blamed the Quebec government and officials at Hydro-Québec. Newfoundland's numerous appeals, to the Supreme Court of Canada, the Quebec Superior Court, and the Quebec Court of Appeal (which ruled five to zero against it), left it no further grounds to appeal.

The Churchill Falls package of 1985 was originally conceived as a three-way project to develop hydroelectricity involving the entire northern region, including Labrador, but morphed over a decade into an ill-conceived megaproject called Muskrat Falls on the Lower Churchill. Political memories last forever in Newfoundland, and many residents recalled or knew that Ottawa's negotiating team when the province joined Confederation in 1949 was led by Justice Minister Louis St Laurent, who once suggested that Canada buy Labrador from this former dominion, which in 1949 was in receivership and administered under a commission of the British government. By this time Muskrat Falls, instead of being a power project in Labrador, with part of the low-cost power transmission being sent to the island of Newfoundland, to replace high-cost power from the oil-fired Holyrood power station, and the rest sent to New England through Hydro-Québec's existing transmission system, now excluded Quebec. In short, it was designed to bypass a huge and growing hydro producer like Quebec with an 824-megawatt dam on the Churchill expected to start operation in 2020. Delays and cost overruns pushed the total investment up from $5 billion to almost $13 billion, with accusations flying of political interference over environmental damage to the local ecosystem for fishing and caribou.

The new transmission system would bypass the shortest land route through Quebec, partly using existing power lines, and convey power through an underwater cable to the island of Newfoundland, then through another to Cape Breton, and then across Nova Scotia and New Brunswick to the U.S. border, for potential export to New England, which now obtains 15 per cent of its power from Hydro-Québec. Whatever the feasibility studies might have suggested, this convoluted route made little economic sense, and electricity experts in Quebec and Atlantic Canada and civil servants in the Atlantic provinces knew this approach was a reckless economic gamble.

But politics and personalities intruded. Heading a minority government entering the 2011 federal election campaign, Stephen Harper needed seats in the Atlantic region and Newfoundland in particular to gain a majority. In 2006 and later he had missed an opportunity to appoint Liberal MPs to other jobs and free up their ridings for new Conservative recruits. Eight ridings were potential targets. On urgings from Newfoundland's former Conservative premier Danny Williams, Harper promised in the 2011 campaign to guarantee huge federal loans, perhaps as high as $10 billion, and called Muskrat Falls "an unprecedented opportunity and a real game changer," with many Newfoundlanders, embittered by the bad Smallwood deal, keen to avoid the "geographic stranglehold" of Quebec's direct route to New England. This investment was conceived more in anger than in good judgment, political or financial, and typifies a short-term, partisan approach to economic development. It contrasts with the Atlantic Energy Accord, which looked forward and was acceptable to the region and neighbouring provinces. With Muskrat Falls, the Atlantic region, in addition to servicing the debt, will pay more for this high-cost electricity and probably have little to export, because the only buyer for surplus power could be Hydro-Québec.

VII

The history of the Canadian constitution is akin to the saga of the National Hockey League (NHL), a Canadian game played mostly with Canadians, but most of the teams are in American cities. The rules and protocols for the league are decided by owners living elsewhere. The Canadian constitution has parallels, where the custody was kept in Westminster in 1867, but the real Canadian loyalties and identities were often regional and provincial. As in hockey, where the game and NHL players are national symbols, constitutional matters also involve symbols and deep loyalties – witness the parliamentary battles in 1964 to choose a flag – even though Canadian politicians have a mixed record on political metaphysics.

While the hockey metaphor is not perfect, the Canadian constitution as a legislative measure passed by the British Parliament in 1867, after the Canadian delegation led by John A. Macdonald reviewed each clause for Lord Blackford, who was presiding for the British government, with members of each colony overseeing the proceedings in case of misunderstandings of what was agreed in Charlottetown and Quebec. In fact, there was no disagreement; it was a meeting of minds, not a clash of wills. The Fathers of Confederation were practical men, less philosophical than some Americans like Alexander Hamilton, Thomas Jefferson, and James Madison, but many were aware of European writers like Edmund Burke, John Locke, Jean-Jacques Rousseau, and Adam Smith, and they all understood and pondered the strengths and weaknesses of the American constitution, its checks and balances, which on paper are an expression of popular will.

While the British North America (BNA) Act of 1867, as amended, was the Canadian constitution until 1982 (it's now called the Constitution Act, 1867), Britain itself doesn't have a written constitution, proceeding by convention, precedent, and practice accompanying formal laws passed by Parliament. For Canada's first five decades, Parliament and parliamentarians proceeded carefully, shrewdly, and often boldly, adding the vast landholdings of the Hudson's Bay Company, creating new provinces beyond the original four in 1867 to nine by 1905, and new institutional developments, from the Supreme Court to the appointment of the first chief justice, Lou Davies from Prince Edward Island. Elite accommodation, today a belittled term, is a political process whereby the prime minister, premiers, senior cabinet ministers, and their advisers sort out the finer points of reform, refinement, and improvement, and the system was generally politically acceptable. Other labels for this model included "executive federalism." Despite some efforts, neither Ottawa nor the provinces saw constitutional change or reform as a political priority, and by 1967, the centennial year of Confederation, Canadians expressed little interest in such matters, preferring "pocketbook" issues of jobs and economic growth.

Yet disputes about the division of powers between Ottawa and the provinces couldn't be ignored, especially as the arbitrating Judicial

Committee of the Privy Council in London tended to side with the provinces. At the Imperial Conference in London in 1926, Britain had to address postwar reforms. This conference led to the Balfour Declaration of 1926, named after the astute Lord Balfour, the former prime minister and lord president of the council, who used the phrase "British Commonwealth of Nations" to describe the "group of self-governing communities composed of Great Britain and the Dominions," each "equal in status in no way subordinate one to another." However, while the declaration offered equality of status, it left open "equality of function," and another conference in 1930 removed the last legal vestiges, whereby the British government would not advise the crown on any matter within a dominion against the advice of the dominion, and Westminster would not pass any law affecting any dominion without its consent. However, it did not mention judicial appeals to the Privy Council in London or disallowance of dominion legislation encroaching on provincial rights. In the enabling Statute of Westminster, 1931, section 7 addressed the Canadian situation, with its binational character and constitutional guarantees of minority rights for French and Roman Catholics, which necessitated Britain's custodial role, and forbade the federal government to amend the constitution, mostly because French Canada, despite its limited sentimental attachment to Britain, preferred its Privy Council over English Canada or Ottawa, including judicial dependence on the Privy Council rather than on the Ottawa-appointed Supreme Court.

This ambiguity continued to plague policy-makers and the federal government, who saw the Privy Council taking a too narrow, legalistic view of Ottawa's authority. In 1935, for example, during the Depression, Prime Minister R.B. Bennett introduced, and Parliament passed, the Employment and Social Insurance Act, which conformed to an international convention approved by the International Labour Organization. The provinces disapproved and appealed to London. The two federal lawyers, C.P. Plaxton, from the Department of Justice, and a Quebec barrister, Louis St Laurent, based their case on article 132 of the BNA Act, which gave Ottawa "all powers necessary or proper for performing the obligations of Canada or any province thereof." The Privy Council disagreed, arguing that the treaty-making provision was not contemplatable in 1867, and using a nautical response: "While the ship of state now sails on larger ventures and into foreign waters, she still retains the watertight compartments which are an essential part of the original structure."

This judgment from London in effect restricted Canada's authority to make treaties, so a bill introduced in the Canadian House of Commons barred all appeals to the Privy Council, which, when it was referred to the Supreme Court of Canada, was declared *ultra vires*. An appeal was sent to the Privy Council, which in 1947 upheld that judgment. During the Second World War, the King cabinet had set up two advisory committees to plan for postwar reconstruction, one headed by F. Cyril James, which included Leonard Marsh, a British-trained economist at McGill University, and the other a thirty-four-member, all-party House of Commons committee. Wartime needs took priority, but sentiment was moving towards expanding unemployment insurance, health benefits, and financial help for the provinces. Premier Stuart Garson of Manitoba received widespread support for the view he expressed in a brief submitted in June 1943 that the array of uncoordinated provincial approaches needed a national solution, including forgoing provincial taxation in exchange for Ottawa paying rent to borrow that taxing power. Other measures, including proposed amendments to the BNA Act, would increase provincial funding for projects that the provinces simply couldn't afford.

After the war, a succession of proposals, some big, some less consequential, affected constitutional issues and desires for reform. For example, in 1947 there were changes to Canadian citizenship, an initiative led by Liberal Secretary of State Paul Martin. He was assisted by a young, erudite member of the PMO, Gordon Robertson. A Rhodes scholar, Robertson had studied at Oxford the nationality laws in various countries, including those in the Commonwealth, and he knew the wide variations on the simple issue – who is a citizen. At the time, Canadians were designated "British" on registrations of births, marriages, and deaths, and "British subjects" on their passports. The new Citizenship Bill set out changed procedures for Canadians born in Canada, those who acquired citizenship, those who wanted to do so, and those who were British subjects in other Commonwealth countries, including Britain. In the debates, John Diefenbaker spoke first, agreed with the general provisions proposed, but argued that this act should be followed by a related Bill of Rights and criticized the clauses on British subjects, setting off an uproar about Canadians remaining British subjects, a conviction too weak for arch-imperialists in the Conservative party, and too strong in the view of French Canadians in the Liberal caucus. An editorial in Montreal's *Le Devoir* noted "*la double allégeance que ça soit envers le Canada and l'Empire ... C'st la négation même de la citoyenneté canadianenne et encore plus du patriotism canadien.*"

Diefenbaker proposed an amendment to include certain rights in the bill, including freedom of religion, freedom of speech, and the rights to peaceable assembly, no compulsion to give evidence without counsel to any tribunal, and no suspension of habeas corpus, which item the Liberals opposed on constitutional grounds. However, as a Saskatchewan lawyer and MP from western Canada, Diefenbaker knew that many immigrants came to Canada to escape the dictatorial, strong arm of governments in central and eastern Europe and the Soviet Union, and his popularity soared as an advocate for freedom and personal liberty.

When Louis St Laurent succeeded King, his new government, successful in the 1949 federal election, proposed in the Speech from the Throne to abolish appeals to the Privy Council in London or, more accurately, to the Judicial Committee of the Privy Council and require only parliamentary approval to amend the constitution in federal areas of jurisdiction. The prime minister, a constitutional lawyer who appeared on numerous cases before the Privy Council in London, generally representing the federal government, defended these measures but conceded they were "a half loaf only." It was a realistic assessment. Premier Maurice Duplessis of Quebec had no intention of allowing the Canadian Supreme Court to become the final court of appeal, but opposition came also from George Drew, the leader of the Opposition, and Conservative MPs like Tommy Church, former mayor of Toronto, leading arch-imperialist, and a member of the Orange Order, who called such measures "a separatist movement" in concert with other proposals, such as choosing a "distinctive" flag for Canada. St Laurent, like his successors, would soon learn the wisdom of the advice offered centuries ago by Machiavelli: "It must be remembered that there is nothing more difficult to plan, more doubtful of success, nor more dangerous to manage than a new system. For the initiator has the enmity of all who would profit by the preservation of the old institution and merely lukewarm defenders in those who gain by the new ones.'

Under St Laurent, Diefenbaker, and Pearson, disputes over cost-sharing programs, tax measures, and welfare policies that intruded in provincial areas of competence made federal–provincial meetings a forum to placate regional tensions, provincial resentment, and personality clashes. But close observers witnessed something more basic than such haggling: the need for better health care, education, and pensions for an ageing population. John Diefenbaker, ever the wily campaigner, saw the measures offered by St Laurent and Pearson as too little – "the six-buck boys" – even though none of them grasped that growing intrusions in welfare policies were against the views of Quebec Premier Maurice Duplessis, whose support gave Diefenbaker fifty seats in the 1958 federal election. Diefenbaker never believed in a bilingual or bicultural Canada or in the position, now widely accepted in Quebec, that Confederation was a compact between French and English Canadians. Led by Duplessis, the Quebec government claimed special responsibilities for *la survivance*, hence its need for special powers, including a check on federal authority to redistribute Commons seats and on the use of English and French in Parliament and the courts, all consistent with the compact theory of Confederation.

When Lester Pearson became prime minister in 1963, having spent so much time in his diplomatic career outside Canada, even he was surprised to learn how little he knew about these constitutional issues, and how much the Ottawa civil service operated mostly in English. When he appointed the Royal Commission on Bilingualism and Biculturalism, headed by André Laurendeau, the editor of *Le Devoir*, and Davidson Dunton, president of Carleton University, he too was starting to learn that different groups and regions had widely varying interpretations of history and future direction. Quebec Premier Jean Lesage, a former federal minister and at one point a potential successor to Pearson, had introduced sweeping reforms in many areas in Quebec as part of the Quiet Revolution, which really wasn't so *tranquille,* vastly expanding the province's role in the economy, setting up new institutions, notably Hydro-Québec, and taking over funding and administration of hospitals, schools, and universities from the Catholic church, a process of secularization that continues to the present. In the judicious balancing of the powers between Ottawa and the provinces, even Louis St Laurent, who raised a firestorm by calling Quebec "a province like the others," agreed to new tax measures, to increase Quebec's tax "room," giving it 10 per cent of the taxes collected by Ottawa, and he did not consult the other provinces. As a result, a new term was added to the federal–provincial vocabulary, "special status."

Pearson's new style of federal–provincial relations, which he came to see as resembling international meetings and negotiations and called "cooperative federalism," was novel but naïve, based on an assumption that consultations, negotiations, and personal relations could settle intractable problems or non-negotiable provincial demands. Early successes, such as a conference of first ministers in mid-October 1963 on procedures to amend the constitution without resort to the British Parliament, and a federal–provincial agreement on measures to opt out of federal programs with compensation, while seemingly enlightening displays of flexibility, exposed the internal contradictions of cooperative federalism, expanded federal social programs, including health care, and decentralized the federation. Other assessments were less kind, seeing it as "more give, less take." Lesage now called for termination of all federal–provincial joint programs, with the provinces able to opt out on social measures, like the Canada Pension Plan negotiated in 1964 while Quebec set up its own pension plan through the powerful Caisse de dépôt. Daniel Johnson, the Opposition leader in Quebec, went further: "We have to see whether this freedom of action can be had within a Canadian federation, or whether we must turn to the solution offered by the movements for independence."

VIII

In the autumn of 1967, Ontario Premier John Robarts invited his fellow premiers to a Confederation of Tomorrow conference. To a degree that few Canadians fully appreciate, Ontario and Quebec are deeply integrated beyond economic issues, and that includes regular civil-service meetings among deputies and cabinet ministers and bilateral meetings with the premiers. Robarts's conference was a bold move, partly a timely meeting for the 100th anniversary of Confederation, but actually reflecting deep concern at Queen's Park, seat of Ontario's government, about the growing tension within the federation. Robarts, with his amazing political instincts, seeing on the Medicare file that, without Ontario's support, poorer provinces simply couldn't afford the health-care plan, also knew that Pearson was simply out of his depth on Ottawa–Quebec agreements. The 1964 federal–provincial conference in Quebec City had been jarring for Robarts, as he watched Premier Lesage, fresh from his election win in 1962, pushing for reforms to the division of taxing powers, such as 50 per cent of direct taxes, compared to 10 per cent offered earlier by St Laurent or 13 per cent by Diefenbaker. Quebec had rejected the Fulton–Favreau constitutional deal previously agreed by all the provinces. Privately, in the growing tensions between Ottawa and Quebec City, with voices in Quebec calling for outright independence, Robarts thought Ottawa ill-prepared and waffling, like a scene in *The Untouchables,* where one side brings a knife, the other a gun: "He sends one of you to the hospital, you send one of his to the morgue. That's the Chicago way."

John Robarts proposed the Confederation of Tomorrow Conference on 18 May 1967, and the legislature approved a resolution to that effect, voting seventy to one. Five theme papers were widely distributed at the conclave: on goals of Canadians, the role of the English and French languages, the forms of federalism, institutional improvements, and the machinery and structure of federal–provincial relations. The timing was auspicious – November 1967 – with 2,000 delegates attending a two-week Estates General in Quebec City hosted by the pro-separatist Société

Saint-Jean Baptiste, and the Laurendeau–Dunton Commission releasing the first volume of its report. So was the location: the top floor of Mies van der Rohe's sublime new TD Centre, siding onto Toronto's Bay Street. Unwilling and somewhat unsure how to deal with these complicated issues, Prime Minister Pearson reshuffled his cabinet, and appointed Pierre Trudeau minister of justice, in charge of the constitutional file, which he once described as a "can of worms."

For the next twenty-five years, the constitution and constitutional matters were often front and centre in Canada's political landscape. Directly and indirectly, they influenced provincial and federal elections, making and breaking political careers. Canadians endured three referendums (two in Quebec, one national), numerous federal–provincial meetings, discussion papers, and the creation of a new, uniquely Canadian industrial sector, constitutionalitis, which too many people thought was a life-threating viral disease, but it proved lucrative to many lawyers, constitutional scholars, former politicians, and civil servants. By design and circumstance, constitutional matters are often abstract, ephemeral, philosophical, symbolic – involving "Peace, Order and Good Government" in Canada, "Life, liberty and the pursuit of happiness" in the United States – but often migrate to in-your-face politics, exposing unstated political sentiments and legal and psychological views of identity and rights. In a television age, they may serve as a proxy forum for long-held regional grievances and institutional barriers to equality and national even-handedness. Less abstract are the roles and powers of the courts, Parliament, provincial control over indirect taxation, appointments to the Senate, Ottawa's control over trade, foreign affairs, and all matters international with other countries, and matters under provincial jurisdiction, such as education, health, and culture.

Political scientist Peter H. Russell, one of the great scholars of Canada's constitution, traces the five rounds of constitutional change (see Table 4.2) following the Pearson government and the Robarts conference in 1967. On so seemingly a simple question, why can't Canada have its own made-in-Canada constitution, governments of all stripes have made changes *seriatim*, one at a time, to the original BNA Act of 1867. Any changes, even a plan simply to repatriate, was caught up in a maelstrom of other issues. Elite accommodation was and is the nature of the Canadian political system, where elected politicians exercise judgment and face the consequences of electoral sanctions as they justify their actions.

The first two of Russell's five rounds – the Fulton–Favreau agreement in 1966, named after a Conservative and a Liberal minister of justice,

Table 4.2
Five Rounds of Constitutional Negotiations (1971–1992)

Round	Date	Prime minister	Core issues	Legacies
1	1971	Pierre Trudeau	Victoria Charter: Quebec nationalism and collective rights v. pan-nationalism, bill of rights, bilingualism	Primacy of federal authority, limited public particip-ation, failure
2	1979	Pierre Trudeau	New accommodations to Quebec following separatist PQ victory in 1976	Fundamental regional differences exposed, failure
3	1982	Pierre Trudeau	Constitution Act, 1982: repatriation, Charter of Rights, nine provinces sign deal	First time that powers of a province (Quebec) changed without consent
4	1987–90	Brian Mulroney	Meech Lake Accord, dealing with western discontent, distinct-society clause, three-year deadline after Quebec ratifies (June 1987)	All ten provinces agree, but not ratified by Newfoundland, reawakening of Aboriginal rights and sentiments
5	1991–92	Brian Mulroney	Charlottetown Accord, massive public consultations, and national referendum	Failure of referendum, likely end of executive federalism

Source: Author's analysis, based on Peter Russell

E. Davie Fulton and Guy Favreau, respectively, and the Victoria Charter in 1971 – both gained provincial consent, but were stopped by two Quebec premiers, Jean Lesage and Robert Bourassa, respectively. Pierre Trudeau, first as justice minister and adviser to Lester Pearson, and then as prime minister, always wanted to entrench a Bill of Rights in the constitution. Of course, he understood, as did many constitutional and legal experts, including Bora Laskin, whom he nominated to the Supreme Court, that such a document would infringe on provincial rights and limit the power of Parliament. When he left office after his defeat to Joe Clark's Conservatives in 1979, Trudeau had failed to convince two of his majority governments, in 1968 and 1974, to accept his theory of nation-building, based around the entrenched charter.

A year before Trudeau joined the Pearson team in 1965, as one of three new Quebec recruits (with Gérard Pelletier and Jean Marchand), he advanced his proposal in an article in *Maclean's*:

A constitutional entrenched bill of rights seems to be the best tool for breaking the ever-recurring deadlock between Quebec and the rest of Canada. If certain language and educational rights were written into the constitution, along with other basic liberties, in such a way that no government – federal or provincial – could legislate against them, French Canadians would cease to feel confined to their Quebec ghetto, and the Spirit of Separation would be laid forever.

His first speech as justice minister to the Canadian Bar Association in 1967 outlined his views in detail, and, now in charge of the constitutional file, he published discussion papers that were widely circulated and discussed in academe and legal circles and by the growing numbers of constitutional experts in Ottawa and provincial capitals. Over the years, numerous commentators noticed a startling consistency in his personal views. A small but telling example was a speech he gave at Toronto's Royal York Hotel in the dying days of the 1979 federal campaign. Introduced by Donald Macdonald, the former minister of numerous departments, including Energy and Finance, Trudeau spoke without notes for an hour, not even using a podium, and set out his constitutional views. He received from this business audience a standing ovation, even though voters would soon defeat his government.

There were alternative views about constitutional reform and a charter. A prominent example is Donald Smiley, a political scientist who advocated province-building à la Peter Lougheed and other western premiers. In his 1969 presidential address to the Canadian Political Science Association, "The Case against the Canadian Charter of Human Rights," he argued presciently that "there are manifold complexities in the delicate balancing of social priorities which is the essence of protecting human rights. Unfortunately, none of these yield to superficial sloganeering about the rights of individuals preceding those of governments." And any moves to patriate the BNA Act had to be enacted by the British Parliament, which didn't have an entrenched Bill of Rights on the American model.

When Trudeau returned to office in 1980, he had his last chance to introduce his Bill of Rights, knowing this initiative would be his immediate, all-consuming preoccupation and his legacy. As documented in numerous books and articles, he mobilized a team of political advisers, civil servants, and prominent legal minds like Toronto's J.J. Robinette to take a final plunge to achieve three objectives: to patriate the constitution as an act of the Canadian Parliament, to include a new Canadian-made Bill of Rights superimposed on a parliamentary system, and to enshrine a new amending formula. The 1982 constitutional package, where nine provinces and Ottawa agreed to entrench a Charter of Rights and Freedoms, with a "notwithstanding clause," was a response to the Quebec referendum of May 1980. Various biographies describe his laser-like focus on constitutional reform beginning in February 1980, showing how he mobilized the federal bureaucracy and the cabinet, including via appeals to London, to accept Ottawa's demands.

In many ways, the constitutional debates, personality clashes, and various interpretations of Canada's constitutional history were a proxy war between two combatants, two immensely popular political figures among French Canadians. Trudeau was a constitutional scholar, at times cerebral and intellectual, more at home in a university seminar with his love of rational discussion, Socratic debate, and rhetorical flourish, but often with a touch of *froideur*, even among friends. René Lévesque, too, could be happy in a university setting, but he preferred the late-night card-playing and camaraderie of the pubs and bars, reflecting his background from New Carlisle in the Gaspé, nursed in schooling with Quebec nationalist sentiments, and representing a riding that includes the Îles de la Madeleine, once part of the diocese of Charlottetown. Lévesque had a flare for words, with a poetic, emotional streak that disguised his strongly held views, including a touch of victimhood vis-à-vis the Anglo establishment in Montreal. He built his reputation on his wartime reporting for the CBC, travelling with the American army, before he become a host broadcaster on shows like *Point de Mire* (the first to cover the Anglo–French invasion of the Suez Canal in 1956), demonstrating his small-town upbringing with a warmth and likeability that charmed audiences and the political class. The two men knew each other well, and both grasped that the Quebec referendum was akin to sumo wrestling, with a winner and a loser. And Trudeau won.

Trudeau's 1982 constitutional package actually made few changes to the BNA Act itself, which had been amended fourteen times over the years, but it shifted the dynamics within the federation. Trudeau was prepared in 1980 to proceed unilaterally, without the agreement of the provinces, an approach set out in a memorandum from Michael Kirby, but allowing the provinces to have their say, mainly to appease Margaret Thatcher's government in London, which had to ask its Parliament to amend its BNA Act. Ottawa felt it was time to end the constitutional paralysis, ignoring the fact that the BNA Act had been amended fourteen times, that the Charter weakened the powers of the provinces, and that the process was an arbitrary measure of Ottawa knows best, with the federal government recently moving into areas of provincial jurisdiction. Committed to its approach, Ottawa imposed a deadline, Christmas 1980, before the prime minister would notify London.

However, the rebuffed Conservatives, smarting from their loss in the February election, rallied against Trudeau's unilateral approach. The constitution was an area where Joe Clark felt comfortable, and many of his former cabinet members actually detested Trudeau and his economic record as prime minister. Clark rallied his caucus to start a parliamentary filibuster, and they hosted televised public hearings with expert witnesses and briefs. Some of the provinces, with good connections in London, lobbied British MPs, to the consternation of the Thatcher government, which expected unanimous Canadian support. Eight provinces, excluding Ontario and New Brunswick, together launched court challenges in Manitoba, Quebec, and Newfoundland. The judgments from the first two, while favouring Ottawa, were not unanimous, so Trudeau and the cabinet proceeded according to plan. However, the case in Newfoundland provided a unanimous rule against Ottawa's unilateral approach, so the prime ninister now had no choice but to appeal to the Canadian Supreme Court, a process that created more time to launch protests against Ottawa.

On 28 September 1981, in a televised scene that could have been taken from a Hollywood movie, the nine justices appeared in their splendid robes to give their verdict. It was a classic Canadian compromise, with both sides getting a nugget of gold. By a vote of seven to two, the court ruled that, while there was no legal requirement to prevent Ottawa from proceeding, by another vote among the nine justices, six to three, the court said that this constitutional measure changed provincial powers without their consent, so defied constitutional convention and should require "substantial" support, without defining it. It was a brilliant decision, perhaps more diplomatic that legalistic, reflecting Canada's constitutional history, where no province has its legislative powers altered without its own approval. This third mega-package also included an escape addendum, the notwithstanding clause, inserted at the behest of the western premiers. It eventually received approval, without Quebec's signature, but allowed the prime minister to proceed, justifying his approach by the overwhelming support of Liberal Quebec MPs.

While English Canada celebrated the new package, especially the immensely popular Charter, it never received much legitimacy in Quebec, even beyond the vocal, educated, and defeatist *séparatiste* political circles in Montreal and Quebec City. While Ottawa was quick to fund any number of pro-Charter groups – environmental associations, ethnic and linguistic minorities, Indigenous associations and peoples, and Status of Women – each with its own grievances but often extending to areas well outside the briefs, many legal scholars, constitutional experts, and political scientists took a fresh, non-partisan look at the 1982 package and its second-order effects on future reform. Close inspection of the 1982 events exposed legacy flaws, not only leaving out founding province Quebec, but adding unwieldy and inadvisable constraints to making future constitutional changes. Certain amendments would require approval of every provincial legislature. In western Canada, there were already signs of discontent, and new stirrings in the Aboriginal community suggested that its needs were not addressed.

Given past norms and conventions, Ottawa had to take the lead on constitutional reforms, but any province could hold out as a bargaining strategy – a recipe for stalemate. Patrick Monahan, the former dean at Osgoode Hall Law School and adviser to the Ontario government, described the outcome succinctly: "The Canadian constitution is, for all practical intents and purposes, virtually unamendable." Prime Minister Trudeau, despite his personal frustrations at constitutional deal-making in three mega-rounds, and knowing that timing was crucial to potential success, felt that in Canada's constitution, starting with the BNA Act, "intergovernmental relationships are indispensable from the outset, between the executive, the legislative, and the judicial organs." In reality, he never forgave the Supreme Court for its judgments in 1982.

Fast forward to 1986. Prime Minister Mulroney faced similar political pressures and grievances. There was the growing desire in western Canada for Senate reform. Alberta media outlets were giving coverage to fringe but vocal bodies like the Alliance for the Preservation of English in Canada and to the rise of protest groups in the Aboriginal community, where new leaders with a rising and vocal consciousness sought a louder voice in Confederation. Many Conservative supporters argued against any new constitutional reforms, but the new government had no other option. In fact, the 1982 constitutional package included a clause that Ottawa and the provinces agreed to hold federal–provincial meetings, without Quebec, to examine changes to the century-old Indian Act of 1878. On its own, Quebec established an all-party study of the legitimacy of the 1982 pact and laid bare the high bar to address Aboriginal issues and changes to the Senate without Quebec. Quietly, the western premiers realized that the 1982 package, without Quebec's active involvement and participation, unwittingly gave Ontario a de facto veto on any future constitutional changes.

IX

Brian Mulroney is, as in many matters of public policy, a conservative vis-à-vis the constitution. Like previous prime ministers, he accepted the flexible nature of the BNA Act, the history of piecemeal changes, such as the 1912 agreement to allow Prince Edward Island no fewer MPs than it had senators, or the legacy of Manitoba becoming a province in 1870, not by Parliament's enacting article 146 of the BNA Act involving "powers to admit" or a possible Manitoba Act of 1870, proclaimed in Ottawa on 15 July 1870, but by an imperial statue, the British North America Act, 1871. His long-held view that any initiatives towards constitutional reform should be incremental, not unilateral, came from his reading of Canadian history and the many failed attempts since 1945. He held strong views on the rights and jurisdictions of the provinces, and he believed changes required federal–provincial consensus. When he first ran for the Tory leadership in 1976, his own province demonstrated sharp political divisions, after Réné Lévesque had left the provincial Liberal party and the separatist threat was real. When Lévesque became premier in the autumn of 1976, with a platform calling for a referendum on sovereignty-association, the political and language divisions extended well beyond Quebec. Mulroney's personal and family friendships in Montreal and across Canada covered the political spectrum, starting from his student days at Laval, and no one ever doubted his deep sentiments as a strong federalist, and anyone who knew him understood that he also identified himself as a Quebecer, a charter Québécois, with a flair for Irish humour in both official languages.

In the leadership campaigns both in 1976 when he lost, and in 1983 when he won, he never expected to initiate a mega-round of constitutional discussions. He did resent the fact that Quebec was not a signatory to the 1982 package, he was never a fan of the notwithstanding clause, and his famous Sept-Îles speech on August 1984 was a testimony to his honest attempt to bring his province into the constitutional family, "with dignity and enthusiasm." The original draft of this speech was written by Lucien Bouchard, a prominent Montreal lawyer and Laval classmate. His draft, written in stylish French, called for massive decentralization of the Canadian federation, leaving Ottawa with limited powers, like defence, the central bank, and some aspects of external affairs.

In Baie-Comeau, Mulroney's hometown, in the constituency he would represent, Manicouagan, Jean Bazin and I argued over Bouchard's draft, with its discussion of future process and reform proposals. Starting on the Friday night, despite the relaxed mood in the campaign team, I was in fervent opposition to the main themes, despite the brilliantly written opening. Bouchard had a real flare for the written word, a master wordsmith, but I wanted any reform proposals of substance, especially on decentralization, deleted in subsequent drafts. The future prime minister-elect inserted his own views, which represented a turning point for the party and the election results in Quebec: "Aware of the importance and complexity of federal–provincial issues, I will not entertain an ambiguous or improvised approach to constitutional initiatives. To proceed otherwise would do more harm than good." Even René Lévesque, usually dismissive of federal positions, called Mulroney's Sept-Îles speech a *"beau risque."* But, contrary to academic and media comments after the Meech Lake Accord failed, neither Mulroney nor the cabinet was in a hurry when they assumed office on 17 September 1984, and other issues took priority, especially the competitive agenda and putting the financial books in order. But the event cycle took over.

The Supreme Court of Canada, rather diffident vis-à-vis practices in London, but with new justices appointed and now in charge of its own agenda with the new, patriated constitution in 1982, was now the final arbiter of federal–provincial disputes, or what Bora Laskin, the first Jewish member, called "the umpire of the Canadian constitutional system." Public opinion in western Canada was warming to calls for Senate reform and the triple-E Senate – elected, effective, and equal. New awakening by Aboriginal leaders put pressure on Ottawa to make massive changes to the Indian Act, or even to disband it, in favour of new constitutional protection and autonomy. In his own province, Quebec, the provincial Liberal party in March 1985 published *Mastering Our Future*, setting out its five constitutional demands, the main planks in the party platform for its election victory in December 1985. These five conditions became the minimum acceptable to the National Assembly in a new round of constitutional negotiations with the federal government. They were recognition of Quebec as a "distinct society"; limits on the federal spending power in fields of provincial jurisdiction; a guarantee of increased powers to the provinces in immigration; a provincial role in making appointments to the Supreme Court; and a full Quebec veto over any and all constitutional changes.

In truth, there was nothing novel in these demands, given the decades of federal–provincial meetings. The history of Quebec's demands, according to respected jurist Edward McWhinney, involved "relatively modest reforms … [and] would have accommodated most of Quebec's demands as they were then presented." Two meetings, the first in Edmonton hosted by Premier Don Getty at the annual premiers' conference, and another in Vancouver, agreed to negotiate these Quebec terms. Prime Minister Mulroney, following previous practice, sent his minister for federal–provincial relations, Lowell Murray, to visit each provincial capital, just as Marc Lalonde and Gordon Robertson had done in 1971, to test the elements of a package. On 30 April 1987, the federal government and the 10 provinces agreed to the terms, settled at Wilson House overlooking Meech Lake, in Quebec near Ottawa, with plans for another federal–provincial meeting in June to finalize the legal text. This meeting was held in the Langevin Building, a twenty-hour marathon session, with several breaks to allow the premiers to confer with their legal advisers, and each delegation recognizing that the final agreement was an integrated, balanced but seamless package, consistent with constitutional agreements approved in 1982. Early in the morning, Friday 3 June 1987, the parties came to an agreement, with a minor amendment, where on matters of major amendments unanimous provincial approval was necessary.

The following Tuesday, after cabinet, I had lunch alone with the prime minister at 24 Sussex Drive. He was in a good mood, and on such occasions, I often pressed ahead with items on the policy agenda, sometimes providing a countercyclical view of his temperament: when he was down, I was up, when he was despondent, I was an optimist. Despite the gruelling marathon of intense discussions, negotiations, and a touch of bickering, he, as chair, managed to reach an agreement. The purpose of our lunch was to finalize the details of the ACOA announcement, a series of files on the competitive agenda, including plans for the Western Diversification agency, and my pending departure from the PMO, as I had promised to stay only two years after the 1984 election. We discussed briefly the signed, finalized constitutional agreement, which I thought was an amazing accomplishment. He asked my thoughts about eventual ratification by the legislatures, knowing my long-held view, echoing Harold Wilson, that a week is a long time in politics, and three years for ratification is an eternity. It was an open secret that the Hatfield government in New Brunswick was in serious political trouble. There was to be an autumn election in Newfoundland, one was expected in Manitoba, and I mentioned talks with Fred Dickson and Nigel Wright over dinner the previous week about the real political headwinds facing Premier John Buchanan in Nova Scotia.

The prime minister, ever the optimist, saw the road ahead for approval of the constitutional file as a vehicle to address other issues – Arctic sovereignty, major initiatives for Aboriginals, Senate reform, and the free-trade agreement. We both knew, as did many members of the cabinet, especially articulate spokesmen like Don Mazankowski, Charlie Mayer, and Bill McKnight, of the plans for Preston Manning's Reform party, arising partly from the cabinet decision to support Bombardier in Quebec, rather than Bristol Aerospace in Winnipeg, and the deep resentment in British Columbia, where Premier Bill Bennett was unabashedly against an Ottawa bias that favoured central Canada. Indeed, at a meeting the previous September at the Hotel Vancouver, attended by only the premier, the prime minister, and me, he accused the federal government of spending so little money in his province – scarcely 2 per cent of total federal spending, much less than proportionate to its population, a point partly confirmed in a memo two weeks later, quite reluctantly prepared by the Federal–Provincial Relations Office (FPRO), that showed 2.3 per cent of total federal spending going to that province, which had 8.3 per cent of the total population – and one of the reasons that senior members of the PMO recommended so strongly that Norman Specter, born and raised in Quebec and deputy minister in Premier Bill Bennett's Office of the Premier, should succeed the highly respected Gérard Veilleux at FPRO.

Once Quebec's National Assembly ratified the Meech Lake Accord, on 23 June 1987, that date set in motion the three-year deadline for all other legislatures – Ottawa and the nine provinces – to do the same. Both the NDP and the Liberals, to their credit, supported the government's motion to ratify in Parliament, and within a year eight provincial legislatures followed suit. Then followed, over the next two years, a series of events that weakened the public's resolve to bring the province of Quebec back into the constitutional foal, "with dignity and enthusiasm." Each event provided a cascading momentum against public acceptance, not one single, titanic attack, like a giant excavator tearing down a house, but a series of blows, often regional events that reinforced grievances elsewhere in the country. For instance, the New Brunswick legislature voted disapproval of the Meech Lake agreement when the Liberals assumed power in the autumn of 1987, after Premier Frank McKenna vaporized the Conservatives, winning every seat in the legislature. In Manitoba, Gary Filmon won a minority government in April 1988, taking his own seat by only 123 votes.

In Parliament, the Liberal-dominated Senate advanced a series of amendments to the bill approved by the House of Commons that would have gutted the agreement. On 15 December 1988, the Supreme Court announced its decision on Bill 101, Quebec's language law, ruling that parts of the bill restricting English signs were unconstitutional, inflaming passions in Montreal and Quebec City, including Claude Ryan at *Le Devoir*, and offering a pretext to Liberal Premier Robert Bourassa to invoke the notwithstanding clause – its first usage under the Constitution Act of 1982. Bourassa, despite ample warnings from the prime minister, his own constitutional advisers, and other premiers, invoked the clause, precisely the signal for Lucien Bouchard to bolt from the Mulroney cabinet, and inspiring a view in parts of English Canada that constitutional reform is a game of heads, Quebec wins, tails, Canada loses.

In truth, the appetite for constitutional reform after a decade of federal–provincial squabbling was diminishing fast. The Meech Lake deal was becoming a symbol of regional grievances, personality clashes, and ad hominem arguments that questioned people's motives and integrity. The three-year deadline for ratification saw a succession of voices picking and choosing their favourite point of opposition, from Aboriginal groups, the Status of Women, the Reform party under Preston Manning – what political scientist Alan C. Cairns calls "Charter Canadians" – i.e., individuals and groups who see the Charter of Rights creating a political consciousness to vent their views. However, no event galvanized public opinion against Meech Lake more than the appearance before a Senate committee of Pierre Trudeau, on the same day he published an article in the *Toronto Star* in English and in *L'Actualité* in French, containing factual errors and ad hominem attacks on the premiers and the prime minister – "a bunch of snivelers." A far more realistic assessment came from an article in a *Globe and Mail* opinion piece by Gordon Robertson, Trudeau's former mentor when he joined the civil service and a key civil-service adviser on the 1982 pact. Preston Manning and the Reform party launched a campaign against Meech Lake, but focusing on the Supreme Court appointments, less on the role as the arbiter of jurisdictional disputes, and more against activist, non-elected judges making policy, not a political process where "policy must be made by persons who are elected by and accountable to the people." The ambiguity of many criticisms of Meech Lake, with attacks on narrow political elites deciding Canada's future, was a forerunner to claims later made by Prime Minister Paul Martin about the "democratic deficit" in Canada.

X

As the three-year deadline of 23 June 1990 for ratifying Meech Lake by all provinces and Parliament approached, I attended the annual meeting of the New England Governors and the Eastern Canadian Premiers – Quebec and the Atlantic provinces, plus Connecticut, Maine, Massachusetts, New Hampshire, Rhode Island, and Vermont. These gatherings were a case study of U.S.–Canada relations at the state–province level, serving as a forum to improve dialogue and cooperation in this northeastern region of North America, and even David Peterson attended a session after he won the Ontario election in 1985. The first meeting took place in 1973, in Prince Edward Island, an initiative of Premier Alex Campbell to coincide with the 100th anniversary of his province's entering Confederation, and a fitting tribute to the Canadian region's historic links to what are still sometimes called the "Boston States." Each year the agenda varies, but includes such topics as economic development, energy, tourism, trade, and matters of mutual cooperation, both internationally and bilaterally.

In June 1990, the meeting was held in the seaside resort town of Mystic, Connecticut, in a large resort hotel that included a convention hall and a separate aquarium. I was an invited guest and speaker, as the author of a report for the Atlantic premiers, entitled *Standing Up to the Future*, which seemed to be better received by the governors than by the premiers. U.S. Federal Reserve chair Paul Volcker was the featured speaker, and I looked forward to renewing my acquaintance with Massachusetts Governor Michael Dukakis. The session on Sunday 17 June started with an open bar and smorgasbord dinner in the Aquarium building, with each guest helping themselves to a wide range of culinary delights, including barbecued beef, lobster, mussels, seafood chowder, and a panoply of desserts.

When I checked in to the resort, I was told the reception started at 6 p.m. For once, I arrived on time, only to find that guests were coming at the appointed hour, 6:30. The only other person caught with the same time mix-up was Premier Clyde Wells of Newfoundland, dressed informally in a bold red sweater, attending with his assistant. We struck up a conversation, but the topic quickly turned to the national speculation – whether Meech Lake would pass in Manitoba and Newfoundland that week, to meet the deadline. The prime minister didn't help his cause when he gave an interview to the *Globe and Mail* on 12 June, a relatively benign accounting of the events leading up to approval on 3 June 1987 by the provinces and Ottawa, and the time constraints of the process. Unfortunately, one phrase – "roll the dice" – reflected the false stereotype of Mulroney's character: feckless, shallow, and too interested in power, too careless with national unity.

No doubt this interview was on Clyde Wells's mind when he attended the conference in Mystic. I can't say I knew him well, but I had met him when I was conducting interviews in Corner Brook and St John's, and at the final meeting with the Maritimes premiers he agreed that Newfoundland should become a full member, so the name was changed to Council of Atlantic Premiers. He also knew my background as the twin brother of the Canadian consul-general in Boston, and my policy work in the Mulroney PMO, especially on issues dealing with Atlantic Canada, including the establishment of ACOA and the Atlantic Energy Accord.

To my surprise, when only the two of us were standing together, he blurted out that he wasn't going to have a free vote in the legislature, as he had promised. I was stunned by his comment, so forthright, despite his past promises. He openly admitted that the Meech Lake deal, which needed Newfoundland's assent, was as good as dead. I decided to say nothing, but, as the guests began to assemble, John Buchanan and Frank McKenna arrived together. We four had a short huddle, and we were soon joined by Joe Ghiz, also wearing a bold red sweater. To their collective surprise, as I informed them what the Newfoundland premier had just told me, each man was mulling over his province's reaction. It didn't take long for Joe Ghiz, a very strong supporter of the deal and a purported constitutional expert – he took a master's in constitutional law at Harvard – to confront Wells directly in front of the open bar, and they had a loud, open, and personal encounter. McKenna and Buchanan, furious and a tad annoyed, reacted in a more measured way, but McKenna admitted that he had been planning to fly to St John's later that week, to meet the Liberal caucus before the vote on Friday. Buchanan suggested the four of us – the three premiers and I – get some food and discuss the matter over dinner.

I checked to see if Premier Bourassa had arrived, but I was told he was taking a private plane from Montreal. Over dinner, on Frank McKenna's suggestion, we decided that I would call the prime minister and inform him what had transpired. I suggested the best time was 10 p.m. Ottawa time, since the prime minister would likely have watched the CBC news on the Atlantic satellite feed at 9 p.m. Before calling, I wrote down the four points agreed over dinner: why we were meeting together in Mystic, what Clyde Wells had said about his not holding a vote, that Frank McKenna wanted to go to St John's to speak to the Liberal caucus, and that Robert Bourassa had not yet arrived so knew nothing of that evening's discussions. We all agreed I would convey these four points as matters of fact, without offering any advice, given the dynamic events about to unfold.

At precisely ten o'clock, in my own room, I called the PMO switchboard, and was put right through to the prime minister. I explained why I was calling and who knew I was calling, and I recited the evening's events and the four points, explaining that I was acting as a messenger, not as a political adviser. Alone or separately, the premiers were prepared to talk strategy with the prime minister on a conference call, and I gave him the number of the resort.

The prime minister was as shocked by Premier Wells's admission of his decision as I was. I also conveyed the collective message that a meeting in St John's with Wells was now a political set-up, as the premier had no intention of calling for a vote. Personally, I was not too concerned about the well-worn public and media criticism of Meech Lake, namely that the deal was an elitist attempt by eleven politicians to decide issues of extreme importance to Canada's future. I never paid too much attention to that criticism – what was the 1864 and 1865 Charlottetown and Quebec conference all about, where, in the words of Edmund Burke, politicians owe not industry but judgment? The prime minister did ask my opinion, and I gave it: arrange a scrum in the morning and have a question planted, indicating that if Premier Wells wasn't going to call a vote, the prime minister would reconsider the decision to visit the premier if he refused to allow a vote. Mulroney indicated that Lowell Murray was on his way to Manitoba to confer with Premier Gary Filmon and his advisers. Privately, my personal premonition – that the week would end in constitutional failure – was borne out by events.

After this call, I went for a walk around the resort grounds, mulling over our conversation, the events that had already unfolded, and what was likely to take place in the next 48 hours. Returning to the resort, I entered the front hallway, just as Premier Bourassa and his entourage arrived. Without hesitation, I went over to introduce myself again (we had met several times before, the first time when I was a visiting professor at Laval University in 1980). Sitting on a nearby sofa, we reviewed the events of the past six hours – Clyde Wells's admission, our dinner session with the other premiers, and my call to the prime minister. I could tell in the premier's face that Wells's refusal to hold a vote would likely end in another constitutional failure. For a moment, Bourassa switched topics, first to the conference agenda and then to a clever but mischievous discussion about why politicians and legislatures should be addressing big issues and events, but often get bogged down on policies that have no real answers – guns, abortion, religion, capital punishment, language – where both sides resort to the moral high ground to please their uncompromising supporters.

The next morning, at breakfast, I spoke to the three Maritimes premiers about my call to the prime minister and my late-night meeting with Premier Bourassa. But the real events of the week were happening elsewhere. In Calgary, where the Liberals were holding a convention to anoint Jean Chrétien as leader, all the Newfoundland delegates supported his anti-Meech Lake stand. On Thursday, in St John's, the prime minister spoke for an hour in the legislature, largely without notes, itself a rarity, and he had dinner that night at Clyde Wells's home. In Winnipeg, where the Conservative premier, Gary Filmon, himself a very lukewarm supporter of French-language rights and bilingualism – in February 1984, when Brian Mulroney planned to visit Winnipeg, he advised that he not visit Manitoba – and a reluctant backer of Meech Lake, simply adjourned the legislature. Now back in Ottawa, the prime minister and his advisers were regrouping, encouraged by public support for his televised speech in the legislature and a favourable reaction in a provincial poll. But when Wells adjourned the Newfoundland Assembly on Friday 23 June, without allowing a vote, he effectively killed a three-year constitutional effort of eleven governments and a process so typically Canadian, an imperfect but highly workable compromise where provinces put the national interest first, even more so when the enemies of a united Canada, the separatists in Quebec, were watching every move with quiet glee. Wells then flew to Calgary to attend the Liberal convention, to be greeted on stage by Pierre Trudeau and Jean Chrétien. The only missing item on the stage was a Liberal banner, "Mission Accomplished."

XI

In the aftermath of Meech Lake, the end of a twenty-five-year period of constitutional haggling and mega-rounds of talks, the main participants – premiers, the prime minister, and the federal cabinet, the plethora of advisers, but, most important, the public at large – were exhausted. In the short term, despite the blame game, where politicians and the media love to speculate on winners and losers, the nation's business continued, and the event cycle took its course. Public opinion turned on politicians, political elites, and the prime minister. It became open season for all sorts of groups to voice their grievances, and in many cases it became personal and vitriolic towards the participants, especially the prime minister. The ultimate failure of the Meech Lake package led to a period of balkanization – disgruntled opinion, distortions as a form of analysis, and Quebec separatists rising in the polls. Certainly the constitutional file was, by its nature, more than substantive changes but also truly symbolic, indeed almost metaphysical, and reaction to that series of events defied reason and immediate understanding. The federal Liberals knew the political advantage of polarizing the Quebec electorate between federalists and separatists, because they had a monopoly among the first and suspected the province would never go to the ultimate extreme, outright separation. Mulroney himself was a polarizing leader, and his reform agenda was akin to emptying a glass filled with political capital with each month in office. Private polls showed he was deeply unpopular, offering a chance to various groups to exploit their political advantage: the Liberals, and a series of groups that felt their grievances were not being addressed. There were lingering after-effects of the divisive free-trade debate and, as with two other events in Canadian history – the execution of Louis Riel in 1885 and the conscription crisis of 1944 – a deep psychological divide split English and French Canada.

Across Canada, pollical sentiments give way less to calculation, analysis, and a reality check on other alternatives than to emotions, tribalism, and passion, which became the currency for voters to see issues not in facts, choices, or options but as a surrogate, where what they believe is true is what they wish to be true. Politicians, parties, insiders, the media, and pundits all offered their own perspectives, sifting through their own biases and flagging opposing views, often seeking out opportunities to confirm hyper-partisan claims and fling emotionally charged barbs, to cast blame. The time constraint, even though more legislatures representing many more Canadians approved Meech Lake than the 1982 reform package within twelve months, the accord's policy dimensions gave way to other criticisms. For the public at large, as on any topic where regional tensions and partisan views are never far from the surface, each element of the package, instead of projecting a path to national reconciliation, became a chokepoint for zero-sum calculation. It was easy for armchair critics to cherry-pick sections of the accord for deletion, change, or additions, but the negotiated package was a careful balancing to meet Quebec's minimum demands, all-province agreement, and alignment with the Constitution Act, 1982. It was a package approved by elected leaders, subject to legislative approval by their parties representing various political interests, even though the deal was blocked by a single person, Clyde Wells, who had offered a solemn promise to hold a vote in the Newfoundland legislature.

In response to these events, the Mulroney government operated on a number of fronts, almost echoing the views of Hamlet:

Let us go in together, And still your fingers on your lips, I pray.
The time is out of joint – O cursèd spite,
That ever I was born to set it right!
Nay, come, let's go together.

When Joe Clark took over the constitutional-reform file, the Mulroney government made a decision to address two criticisms of Meech Lake. Instead of focusing on a narrow agenda, i.e., the five minimum conditions put forward by the Bourassa government, the new mega-round, dubbed the Charlottetown Accord, sought to bring in groups left out, from women to Aboriginals, or what was called "Charter Canadians," and address anxieties about Senate reform and even the Bank of Canada's decisions on monetary policy, It tried also to address the criticism of "arrogant elitism" by opening up the political process to public participation. In November 1990, five months after the final 23 June deadline, the prime minister appointed Keith Spicer, head of the CRTC and former commissioner of official languages, to chair the Citizen's Forum on National Unity (Spicer Commission). Spicer was a fluently bilingual former editor of the Ottawa *Citizen*, who had a sharp tongue, a way with words, and a nonpartisan view of Canada as a bilingual, multicultural nation. He held hearings across the country, or, as his Final Report of June 1991 stated, a forum for "a dialogue and discussion with and among Canadians ... to discuss the values and characteristics fundamental to the well-being of Canada."

The report found Canadians angry, confused, and displaying a motherlode of immense discontent with their institutions and the existing mode of elite accommodation, as well as "a fury in the land against the Prime Minister." In English Canada, the central assumption of Confederation, that English and French must stick together to avoid absorption by the imperialistic United States, was no longer true – and Quebec, equipped with new opportunities, including access to the U.S. market because of the free-trade agreement and mobile global capital, would choose association with English Canada as an option, within a range of other options, including outright independence. Reports in Quebec, from the Bélanger–Campeau Commission, named for prominent businessmen Michael Bélanger and Jean Campeau, and the Allaire–Dumont Commission, named for MNAs Jean Allaire and Mario Dumont, called at a minimum for massive decentralization of federal powers to Quebec, and by extension to the other provinces, and a majority of the submissions preferred outright independence.

Joe Clark also travelled across the country, met his counterparts in provincial capitals, and then submitted his report to his cabinet colleagues, a last attempt for constitutional reform. Mulroney was in Europe when Clark announced his recommendations, so when he returned to Ottawa the cabinet had little choice but to proceed with another round. It was easy for armchair quarterbacks to argue that the prime minister and the cabinet should have recognized the intractable nature of constitutional reform, but Mulroney knew that separatists led by Jacques Parizeau were regrouping to plan another referendum and a potential declaration of independence, regardless of entreaties by the Supreme Court or the niceties of constitutional decorum. Mulroney proceeded with another round with the ten premiers, the leaders of the two territories, Yukon and Northwest Territories, and four Aboriginal leaders.

Their new reform agreement, approved in Charlottetown at the end of August 1992, was voted and passed in the House of Commons 233 to twelve, and then submitted to a national referendum on 26 October 1992, with the entire cumbersome package reduced to a single referendum question. It failed, 54.4 per cent nationally to 45.6 per cent, with similar results in Quebec, 55.4–42.7, but the Aboriginal community in Alberta, for instance, voted almost 70 per cent against, despite the optimistic statements of its leaders. A full-page ad by Aboriginal communities in the *Globe and Mail* against the deal was an early signal of the deep unease and a show of rising consciousness of the Aboriginal community on its treaty rights. In the end, the Charlottetown Accord and national referendum ended the five mega-rounds. The aftermath brought home to all Canadians that constitutional engineering is a complicated part of nation-building. The complex issues addressed in Charlottetown and Quebec in 1864, and the resulting agreement submitted to the British government, involved compromises, tradeoffs, and the high art of political leadership, despite voters' anger, frustration, and suspicion, but often with a measure of altruistic discipline.

Pierre Trudeau, who fought again against the Charlottetown Accord, might accept that his constitutional deal of 1982 remained intact, unlikely to be changed in another mega-round, preserving his life's work against the separatist cause, but he proved unwilling to provide any magnanimous gestures to his federalist opponents, least of all to fellow Quebecer Brian Mulroney. The latter, disappointed because the Meech Lake deal, if passed, might have halted separatist sentiment in Quebec and allowed constitutional reform to address the rising demands of the Aboriginal community and western Canada. During the protracted negotiations over the Charlottetown Accord, Mulroney, meeting the premiers who initially opposed Meech Lake, like Frank McKenna, and the one who accepted only one approach to constitutional unit, his own, in the person of Clyde Wells, Mulroney kept his cool, despite occasions to vent his anger and deep frustration. He could take some comfort that his nationwide view of Canadian federalism still included a strong central government with strong provinces.

In June 1993, the federal Conservatives had another leadership convention, and they chose Defence Minister Kim Campbell, who became Canada's 19th prime minister and first female. She appointed a new, smaller cabinet, put some policy difference between her approach and the Mulroney government's, and spent the summer touring, with the party leading in the polls. She called an autumn election, and the Tories were obliterated after their inept campaign and at the end their attack ads mocking Jean Chrétien's partial facial paralysis that offended virtually everyone, including Conservatives. The party was reduced to two seats, Jean Charest's riding in Sherbrooke and Elsie Wayne's in Saint John. Kim Campbell's subsequent book, *Time and Chance* (1996), places the blame on Mulroney, but others' analysis is more unforgiving of her, indicating she was never a party insider and didn't understand the Conservatives and their traditions, and proposing that a Mulroney–Chrétien clash instead would have produced a very different outcome, which she now admits.

The Reform party, which had become a strong force in western Canada, triumphantly played the "we the people" card to win popular support, advancing ideas of elected senators, recall of MPs who differed with their riding associations, and an undisguised scorn for federal institutions, including the Supreme Court, the Charter, the Senate, cabinet government, and many aspects of federalism. In truth, the Reformers and their various transformations – the Canadian Alliance, the Conservative party – became the party of resentment, where criticisms of and anger about all the ills of the federation found a voice in the top echelons, backed by supporters in the media, and the oil-patch in Alberta, only too willing to use delicately balanced government positions on abortion, capital punishment, gay marriage, gun control, and Supreme Court appointments as wedge issues for temporary, partisan political gain. In Quebec, fissures divided the federal Conservatives, and Lucien Bouchard bolted from cabinet to establish another protest party, Le Bloc.

Jean Chrétien won three consecutive majorities, in 1993, 1997, and 2000, against regionally fractured opposition parties, and three weak opponents, all from western Canada, Kim Campbell, Preston Manning, and Stockwell Day, respectively. From his first days in Parliament, under the careful tutelage of Mitchell Sharp, Chrétien, like Mulroney, had street smarts, and quietly they had a mutual admiration society of two, and both loved campaigning in both official languages. But Chrétien, playing a key role, with Ontario's Roy McMurtry and Saskatchewan's Roy Romanow, in breaking the constitutional log-jam in 1982, appreciated that, after a generation of constitutional fighting, he brought – in style, speech, and limited objectives – a less confrontational approach to solving national problems.

In 1993, knowing the deep divisions within the opposition, Jean Chrétien campaigned against free trade, the new value-added goods and services tax (GST), and Meech Lake, election promises made purely for partisan gain, and advancing other measures in the Liberal Red Book, a compendium of promises, which largely expanded policy initiatives of his predecessor. He knew the widespread political fatigue on constitutional issues and assured anyone who would listen that he would put that file on the back burner.

But. as for two of his predecessors, Pierre Trudeau and Brian Mulroney, constitutional issues framed federal–provincial relations, and Chrétien couldn't avoid the subject, especially with the now-entrenched Charter of Rights and the role of the Supreme Court as dispute settler. As the memory of London's Privy Council rapidly receded. Chrétien did a volteface on the free-trade pact, which was rechristened the North American Free Trade Agreement (NAFTA) after Mexico was added in 1994, and constitutional change came with the 1995 referendum in Quebec. This vote was a near thing, in part because Chrétien lacked the political gravitas that French Canadians in Quebec saw in Pierre Trudeau, whose spellbinding speeches during the 35-day 1980 referendum campaign, especially his intervention on 14 May at Paul Sauvé Arena in Quebec, showed his gunslinger style at its best. The 1995 vote, on 30 October, went 50.6 per cent No to 49.4 per cent Yes, with a turnout of 93.5 per cent, and only 55,000 votes separating the two camps. On referendum night, Premier Jacques Parizeau blamed the loss on money and the ethnic vote.

Parizeau, of course, was now an unashamed separatist, wanting to win at any cost, and paying only lip service to negotiating with the rest of Canada, with Lucien Bouchard as chief negotiator for Quebec, and he was prepared to make a unilateral declaration of independence had he won. He had hoped that other countries, including France, would accept this unilateral approach, not appreciating Canada's close ties to France, French investments in Canada outside Quebec, and France's leadership in the European Union, which had little interest in separatist parties, or unilateral diplomatic moves on anything, least of all calls for independence. This very close call, and a potential and irreversible split in the federation, with Jacques Parizeau and then Lucian Bouchard exposing their long-held separatist beliefs, was a bridge too far. The fact that Jean Chrétien, responding to statements by former premier Daniel Johnson that Quebec was a "distinct society," announced on 24 October, a week before the vote, his acceptance of that most controversial element of the Meech Lake Accord, which he opposed, doing so without cabinet approval, revealed the earlier degree of complacency on the federal side.

In 2003, the premiers, meeting in Charlottetown, set up, partly on the initiative of Quebec's Jean Charest, the Council of the Federation with a staff and research group to formalize the Annual Premiers' Conference, but adding the premiers of the three northern territories. In form and intent, this new council was a parallel to the proposal first advanced by Quebec's Premier Robert Bourassa, who submitted a paper as a private citizen in 1984 to the Macdonald Commission proposing a Federal Council to replace the Senate as "a permeant inter-government forum that has real powers in areas where governments operate concurrently." Given the wide range of shared programs between Ottawa and the provinces, and a general view in provincial capitals about Ottawa's overreach, the Council of the Federation became a forum to discuss and develop common positions, but also to improve coordination and initiate policies within provincial jurisdiction. Many provinces had joint programs with their neighbours – the four western provinces signed a pact to remove internal trade barriers, for instance.

Historically, Ontario and Quebec have had close relations, working at several levels and covering a range of issues from language and education to health and economic development, often fostered by close contacts between premiers – George Drew and Maurice Duplessis, Bill Davis and Robert Bourassa, Mike Harris and Lucien Bouchard – regardless of party affiliation or partisan leanings. A measure of this close affinity and friendship surfaced at Robert Bourassa's funeral, when Premier Harris and four of his predecessors (Bob Rae, David Peterson, Frank Miller, and Bill Davis) attended the moving ceremony at Notre Dame Cathedral in Montreal. Jurisdictional rivalry, e.g., over the national-securities regulator or international relations, doesn't obstruct close links between these two neighbours, a legacy of the friendships and working relations between John A. Macdonald and George-Étienne Cartier. For instance, the governments of Jean Charest in Quebec and Dalton McGuinty in Ontario initiated a joint meeting of their cabinets on 2 June 2008, and the two provinces signed am Ontario–Quebec Trade and Cooperation Agreement, as well as sectoral agreements on culture, the environment, French-language issues, labour mobility, public security, tourism, and transportation.

The Council of the Federation has accelerated participation by the northern premiers. In 2006, the ten provincial premiers started meeting with the main leaders of national Indigenous organizations, such as the Assembly of First Nations, Inuit Tapitiit, and the Métis National Council, but in 2017, these leaders boycotted the sessions, wanting full participation in the annual proceedings, a new wrinkle for the future of intergovernmental meetings in Canada, and a far cry from the lament of political scientist Robert McGregor Dawson, in *The Government of Canada*, who saw federal–provincial meetings as "grotesque unreality, untrammeled by logic."

XII

After five mega-rounds of constructional talks, two referenda – one in Quebec, one national – the Clarity Act (2000), and lingering legal and constitutional arguments that the notwithstanding clause encroached on individual rights more than the distinct-society clause in the Meech Lake agreement, the event cycle took over. There truly was constitutional fatigue among voters. Several provinces, including Quebec, signed agreements with Ottawa on immigration policies. In retrospect, there was widespread recognition that Pierre Trudeau's vision, despite his opposition to Meech Lake, was a classic model of a federation, with a powerful central government enacting federal programs and executing policies for regional and local administration in the provinces without the taxing policies to fund them. Brian Mulroney was in the mould of the classic federal model of a balanced federation, with a strong central government and strong provinces, with mutually defined areas of jurisdiction, spending powers, and agreement on future changes. The end of constitutional changes didn't prevent future amendments or bilateral amendments between Ottawa and a province or territory. A case study is Prince Edward Island, but there were others, like creating Nunavut, a new territory in the north, another Mulroney initiative.

Prince Edward Island ranks high in the constitutional scheme, not only because Charlottetown hosted the Fathers of Confederation in 1864, but because, as an island, it has worried about transportation for over 150 years. In 1984, as the fifty-eight-day election campaign showed steadily rising support for the Conservatives, especially after the first debate between Brian Mulroney and John Turner, it was clear earlier in August that the public had decided to vote for change after twenty-one years of Liberal rule (except for Joe Clark). The new Conservative leader tried to visit as many ridings as possible, with events scheduled from early morning to evening. On 18 August, a Saturday, his Air Canada chartered flight had left Corner Brook after a serious of rallies, landing in Charlottetown for a big campaign event at a community college – the same hall where Prime Minister John Diefenbaker made an election promise to build a causeway to replace the CN ferry service. By this time, Brian Mulroney and his campaign team were making most strategic decisions at 35,000 feet, showing a combination of quiet exhilaration at voter reception and the fatigue that comes from eighteen-hour days with fifteen more to endure.

I wrote the draft campaign speech, but, for once, Brian Mulroney took the draft as final and dealt with three PEI issues – high electricity prices, tourist promotion, and transportation, an island obsession for over 100 years. It was the only address so far where Mulroney didn't open with his famous "You had an option, sir," line that audiences loved about Turner's patronage appointments, and the overflowing crowd waited in anticipation. His closing argument included this legacy item – a fixed link – and the province's four Conservative candidates entertained huge prospects of winning, including Pat Binns, a Saskatchewan-born future premier.

Fast forward seventeen months to Ottawa, at a breakfast where the prime minister was hosting his Japanese counterpart, Yasuhiro Nakasone, at 24 Sussex. In their conversation, Mulroney asked about Japan's experience in dealing with large budget deficits. Nakasone, fresh from a formal dinner the previous evening in Toronto, indicated that his government was encouraging the private sector to undertake large projects such as the bridge across Tokyo Bay. The bridge, he indicated, would be 57 kilometres long, and would cost $7.5 billion. Two hours later, at a budget meeting in the Centre Block of the Parliament Buildings, Mulroney recounted this story and wondered about potential projects in Canada. Seeing the opportunity, I boldly interjected and offered him two cases, the PEI bridge crossing and large airport terminals. He asked Paul Tellier, clerk of the Privy Council, to prepare a written briefing on the PEI link from the relevant departments.

When Minister of Transport Don Mazankowski first heard about this initiative and the source, he thought it especially idiotic, particularly because of the potential, ballpark cost of $1 billion. Within a week, however, as the bureaucrats did their homework, he learned that replacement ferries would cost $400 million each if built in Canadian shipyards (but only $175 million in South Korea). Eventually, the federal government received six formal proposals (one involving a combined causeway / train system). Prolonged protests divided the island, and Premier Joe Ghiz initiated a plebiscite in 1988. Opponents of all sorts campaigned against the bridge, declaring that a fixed link would destroy the "island way of life" and ruin the underwater habitat for lobsters and marine life, while school teachers and other spokespeople spread rumours that the bridge would bring in motorcycle gangs, aiming to rape senior citizens and schoolchildren. The premier quietly opposed the project, while Premier McKenna supported it enthusiastically (while seeking to maximize construction work on the New Brunswick side of the Northumberland Strait, across from Borden). Islanders voted 59 per cent in favour, overwhelmingly in the Borden region, which would lose its ferries and gain the bridge, but less so in the east, where many residents wanted to retain the existing ferries from Wood Islands to Pictou, NS. Eight years of financial negotiations followed, and years of construction.

Today, the Confederation Bridge, opened 31 May 1997, is the defining feature of the province's island identity: a 13-kilometre ribbon of concrete, a vast engineering marvel of steel, cement, and electronic wizardry that measures tides, ice flow, wind, air pressure, snow flurries, and anything that affects the traffic. From New Brunswick, it looks like a highway that rises more than 30 metres above the treacherous waters. From the island, it's far more majestic, a sweeping stretch of forty-four suspended pillars like a vast Roman aqueduct, joining the province to the mainland. The structure won a gold medal from the Canadian Council for Public–Private Partnerships, recognition both of its remarkable engineering and the even more remarkable public-policy innovation that went into this great feat.

Transportation has been an island obsession and matter of contention for more than two centuries. Governor Walter Patterson commissioned a boat to take the mail across to Pictou in the 1780s. The first advocate for a fixed link was Senator George Howlan, who proposed in the 1880s a subway on top of the seabed. A decade later Father Alfred Burke suggested a tunnel. Vast ice-breaking ferries included the MV *Abegweit*, launched 1947, which carried train cars, trucks, campers, and automobiles.

Premier Walter Shaw and John Diefenbaker promoted a proposed causeway. In the 1965 federal election, Lester Pearson promised to build a causeway / bridge / tunnel that would cost $148 million – which ballooned to twice that from estimates by engineering consultants.

The Northumberland Strait, as an extension of the Gulf of St Lawrence, is a fast-flowing waterway that deceives the eye. Below the water is a staggering diversity of God's marine jewels – oysters and lobsters, herring and bluefin tuna. Clearly, a causeway or a bridge or some form of link would attract stakeholders who preferred the province as a hard-to-reach island. But infrastructure requires financing and engineering prowess, because, in some winters, the ice could strand even the famed *Abegweit* for up to thirty hours. The huge tourist market and the movement of goods by trucks and trains eventually led to the practical issues of ferry replacement and the huge upkeep of the terminals at Borden and Cape Tormentine. This was the problem facing the Mulroney government in 1984. Replace the ageing ferries, or find another means of transportation.

The Confederation Bridge remains a testament to Canadian engineering ingenuity. Today, it's hard to find islanders who were originally against the fixed link, because it has enhanced small business, exporters, and tourism. The bridge is a great case study of a truly successful public–private partnership, costing $840 million, built by Strait Crossing Inc., and financed entirely by the private sector, using the revenue stream from tolls, the former ferry subsidy, and the financial obligations of the federal government for maintenance. When the bridge opened, two ministers from the Mulroney government were invited, Elmer MacKay and Lowell Murray, but not the former prime minister, who took the initiative to settle this longtime transportation irritant, and launched sundry other initiatives for the island – the national GST tax centre in Summerside, the Slemon Aerospace Park on the former air-force base, or the airport terminal and an expanded runway in Charlottetown.

The bridge also required a constitutional amendment, using the bilateral formula for Ottawa and a province (section 43). Senator Orville Phillips moved the amendment in the Senate, but two Conservative senators, Heath Macquarrie and Eileen Rossiter, both refused to second the motion, so Liberal Senator Lorne Bonnell did so. In the debate, Liberal Senator John B. Stewart, former MP from Antigonish and elevated to the Senate by Pierre Trudeau, asked puzzling questions about lobsters, including whether their forward movement would be impeded by the bridge. Orville Phillips gave a trenchant reply: "Lobsters move backwards. They're like Liberals in that respect." Prime Minister Mulroney could take some little solace from the fact that in 1993, Prince Edward Island's Terms of Union, first enacted in 1873, were amended, from requiring ferry-boat service to the Confederation Bridge.

5

Constructive Internationalism in a Changing World Order

*Post-1945 Reconstruction – Founding of NATO – NORAD –
Pearsonian Internationalism – Trudeau's "Third Option" Foreign Policy –
The Commonwealth – The Apartheid Fight – German Unification –
Breakup of the Soviet Union – The Arctic Council – The Acid-Rain Debate –
The Montreal Protocol – The Third World – Canada's Soft Power*

I have never heard a Canadian refer to an American as a 'foreigner.' He is just an 'American.' And, in the same way, in the United States, Canadians are not 'foreigners,' they are 'Canadians.' That simple little distinction illustrates to me better than anything else the relationship between our two countries.
Franklin D. Roosevelt

INTRODUCTION

In the months and years immediately after 1945, Canada's international reputation in the corridors of power – but especially in Washington and London – had little to do with the size of this relatively small nation. With a population then under 12 million, Canada emerged during the Second World War with the fourth largest navy – over 500 ships used for escort duty across the Atlantic – battle-hardened troops, with over a million people serving, and more than 100,000 casualties. This awesome, painful legacy included the first armed wave that stormed Sicily in 1943, the troops captured in Hong Kong, the botched, heroic raid in Dieppe, and Canadian formations that became the fifth leg in the invasion of Normandy, at Juno Beach. Canadian troops liberated much of Holland and parts of France and Belgium and formed the spearhead with Montgomery's combined forces crossing the Rhine and defeating Nazi Germany. In the Pacific war, Canada had paid the ultimate cost in blood and treasure, in Hong Kong and along Canada's Pacific coast, winning the plaudits of American soldiers, airmen, and military brass. It was no accident that when British Prime Minister Clement Attlee visited Ottawa, he had no doubt about Canada's contribution to the war effort. His immediate predecessor, Winston Churchill, first visited Canada after the Boer War, and this vast country left an indelible impression on this young war correspondent. On another visit in 1930, Churchill spent time in Ottawa during the new year, staying with the Willingdons at Rideau Hall, before heading west in a car provided by the CPR, visiting the Rockies, and painting two scenes of the Bow River in Calgary.

Attlee's visit in 1946, so soon after hostilities had ended, was enlightening for Prime Minister King and his senior ministers, who received an insider's look at the war's costs to Britain. Despite his quiet but clever wit, Attlee left little doubt about his country's financial plight. Canada was not a member of the sterling-currency area, like Australia, New Zealand, or South Africa, which had lent Britain their currency reserves to pay for its imports (mostly food and materiel) which amounts grew steadily during the war, initially £250 million. Canada gave the United Kingdom $1 billion in 1942, another $1 billion in 1943, and later another $2 billion towards war expenditures, making its *financial* support for the beleaguered islands, carried out quietly and efficiently, so much greater per capita than the celebrated American support through Lend-Lease — mostly fifty obsolete destroyers from the Great War and Americans taking over British bases in Bermuda and Newfoundland.

From the meeting of forty-four countries at Bretton Woods, New Hampshire, in July 1944, that created the International Monetary Fund (IMF) and the International Bank for Reconstruction and Development (IBRD, later part of the World Bank), and led to the General Agreement on Tariffs and Trade (GATT) and the founding of the United Nations (UN) at San Francicso in October 1945 – in effect, the launch of the postwar order – Canada played a prominent role. King's successor, Louis St Laurent, led Canada during a series of events that required a judicious diplomatic touch and a clear understanding of his country's limited influence and of how present events might require future obligations, financial, military, and diplomatic. But it was Winston Churchill, turfed from power in the June 1945 election, who captured the postwar environment that would last a generation, speaking in Fulton, Missouri, in March 1946: "From Stettin in the Baltic to Trieste in the Adriatic, an iron curtain has descended across the Continent ..."

World-changing events – the declaration of the state of Israel in 1948, Mao Zedong's founding of Communist China in 1949, the first Soviet detonation of an atomic bomb in 1949, the Korean War (1950–53), the death of Soviet dictator Joseph Stalin in 1953, the defeat of the French at Dien Bien Phu in Vietnam in 1954, the abortive Anglo–French invasion of Suez in 1956, the abortive revolt in Hungary in 1956 – all occurred on St Laurent's watch. He managed to direct his cabinet, his diplomats, and the country at large to offer help where it was needed, to mediate where required, and to strengthen Canada's reputation in the capitals that really mattered, London and Washington. Well past the events of 1945, it became clear that the world had moved from a military-industrial wartime footing against Nazi Germany to one of Soviet aggrandizement, with the wartime Allied coalition in disarray, and rumblings of a new era of revolt against colonial rule in the Middle East, Africa, and Asia. Like his own country, Churchill, returning to office in 1951, saw Canada's role in special terms, as a mediator, a go-between, vis-à-vis the powers in Europe and the democratic superpower, the United States.

In this tense era, geopolitics became a Cold War match of wills and rhetoric, with the United States designing a containment strategy against its adversary, the Soviet Union. A set of institutions – militarily, the North Atlantic Treaty Organization (NATO) and North American Aerospace Defense Command (NORAD); in trade and finance, the General Agreement on Tariffs and Trade (GATT), the IMF, and the World Trade Organization (WTO); and for diplomacy, the United Nations – became the framework for American policy, with nonpartisan support at home, to outcompete the Soviets on the economy, outclass them with superior weapons emerging from scientific pre-eminence, and outmanoeuvre their communist ideology in the less developed world in concert with ideals of freedom and democracy. The establishment of NATO with a central command led by an American was a move as much to lower tensions within Europe because of a powerful West Germany, successor state to France's old nemesis, as to ease fears in central and eastern Europe, particularly in Poland, of a powerful West German military. The welcome news came from West German leaders, starting with Chancellors Konrad Adenauer and then Ludwig Erhard, who were pro-democratic, market-oriented politicians. Their policies were as much pro-Europe as pro-German, and their path for a generation was clear and far-sighted.

Canada's first peacetime military treaty, signed in Washington on 4 April 1949, was that to establish NATO. Its launch coincided with deep unease in Europe, Germany divided between east and west, and Berlin itself under siege, requiring a heroic airlift in 1948-49 to avoid mass starvation in the city. NATO first had twelve members: Belgium, Britain, Canada, Denmark, France, Iceland, Italy, Luxembourg, the Netherlands, Norway, Portugal, and the United States, but the treaty contained an unambiguous clause, in article 5: "An armed attack against one or more of them [members] in Europe or North America shall be considered an attack against them all."

In the 1960s and 1970s, the Vietnam War and Watergate delivered strong blows to American prestige on the world stage and weakened morale at home. The rejuvenation of the European and Japanese economies, and the emergence of the powerhouse economies of the BRIC (Brazil. Russia, India, and China) – a term not then in wide use – hinted at a new world order. The fall of the Berlin Wall in 1989, the breakup of the Soviet Union in 1991, and the reawakening of China all affected the new and large role of emerging markets, as the BRIC nations joined the global trading system. "China is a sleeping giant. Let her sleep, for when she wakes, she will move the world." So said Napoleon Bonaparte over 200 years ago, but he could have been also talking about Japan and the Pacific Rim countries, which in population, economic dynamism, technological prowess, and educational achievement were a competitive rival.

Canada, with so much territory, almost 10 million square kilometres and bordering three oceans, had to adjust to new global realities. If it has "too much geography," in the words of Mackenzie King, while other countries have too much history, its location was the ham in the Cold War sandwich, with the United States to the south and the Soviet Union across the North Pole. By the late 1970s, Ottawa faced new obligations, with public opinion following events in the Arctic, discord in Asia, and what Norman Macrae, the deputy editor of the *Economist* heralded in 1975, the "Pacific Century," which "could bring startling changes to the ways in which we handle our affairs politically, environmentally, commercially, technologically, and culturally." In the Pacific, Canada became a laggard country.

From the beginning, Canada helped set up NATO, starting with internal memoranda from Canada's ambassador in Washington, Hume Wrong, a hard-headed realist, aware of communist infiltration in many European countries, including Italy and France, and only too cognizant of the strong postwar isolationism in the U.S. Senate. Congress had members who were international sceptics, including Rep. Emanuel Celler (D–NY), who spoke for many when he called Britain a country with "too damned much socialism at home and too much imperialism abroad." President Harry Truman, with no experience in international affairs, became a quick study and fully appreciative of the new global threats. Three individuals played a particularly active role in the diplomatic and political discussions leading to NATO's founding: U.S. Secretary of State General George Marshall, who became the greatest advocate for the economic recovery of Europe (the Marshall Plan); British Foreign Secretary Ernest Bevin, from Attlee's Labour government; and Canada's Lester Pearson, then deputy minister of external affairs. Each had the strong backing of his government. Canadian negotators like Pearson and Escott Reid thought that the NATO treaty might include a clause for closer economic ties, but this approach was dropped, partly for fear some members couldn't afford their military obligations. General Hastings "Pug" Ismay, Lord Ismay, chief of staff during the war under Churchill and then under Attlee, became NATO's first secretary general. By the mid-1950s, Canada had a military presence of 10,000 troops in France and West Germany.

I

In this Cold War climate, international political and diplomatic relations were tense, with few avenues to communicate privately, amid continuing Soviet military threats, subversion, and spying. Communist hardliners controlled the Kremlin, even after Stalin's death in 1953 and despite Premier Nikita Khrushchev's famous 1956 speech denouncing his predecessor's crimes. The United States had its own hardliners, as it increased its defence spending – President Dwight Eisenhower, after all, was a former supreme commander of Allied forces, but even he, like the rest of the world, was surprised by the Soviet launch in October 1957 of Sputnik, the first satellite ever. A group of Allied politicians and military experts, including senior U.S. defence official Paul Nitze and General Howard McCormick, head of the U.S. Air Force's R&D lab, meeting at a Bilderberg Conference in the Italian spa town of Fiuggi in October 1957, were flabbergasted at Soviet advances in missile technology. Such a turn of events put a new wrinkle in Canadian–U.S. military cooperation, when the two countries launched the bilateral defence agreement known as NORAD on 12 May 1958. Unlike NATO, in which defence experts worried about a potential Soviet land-based attack with tanks and troops, NORAD set up an advanced-warning radar system – a "trip wire" – to provide a clear alert to manage command and control of military force, including long-range aircraft, missiles, and forces.

The 1950s saw a series of cooperative defence agreements between the two neighbours: three radar networks across the north – the famous

Distant Early Warning (DEW) Line, the Mid-Canada Line (sometimes called the McGill Fence), and the Pinetree Line – while the Royal Canadian Air Force (RCAF) and the U.S. Air Force (USAF) worked closely together, exchanging liaison officers and meeting to focus on a common military system for command and control. By 1957, the military of both countries approved the establishment of the North American Air Defense Command (NORAD), at Ent Air Force Base, in Colorado Springs, Colorado. This location, home of the U.S. Continental Air Defense Command, included USAF Air Defense Command, led by General Earl Partridge, later commander of NORAD, and the senior RCAF official, Air Marshal Roy Slemon, who became deputy commander, NORAD. The NORAD agreement established the political connections in Washington and Ottawa for approval to review undertakings or to take steps for a state of readiness, called "Defcon," where, on a scale of 1–5, Defcon 0 was a nuclear attack, and Defcon 3 readiness. Once these systems became fully operational, the RCAF and CF-101 Voodoos intercepted Soviet planes, usually TU-95 Bear Bombers, flying near or even over airspace buffer zones.

The Soviet Union's 1957 launch of Sputnik effectively set off a technological arms race, with both the Soviets and the Americans having access to nuclear scientist Werner Von Braun's Nazi weapons secrets and blueprints and the Germans' launching-pad systems for their V-1 (cruise) and V-2 (ballistic) missiles. But the Americans had their own ace card, capturing Von Braun himself, whisked away secretly in 1943 with much of his senior team, from his base at Peenemunde, the launch site, which employed 12,000 people during the war. This high-powered team was put on the U.S. payroll and eventually employed at the National Aeronautics and Space Administration (NASA), in Houston, Texas, established in 1958.

A new vocabulary emerged in policy circles – arms control, global thermonuclear war, graduated deterrence, unilateral disarmament – and thinkers like Herman Kahn, Henry Kissinger, and Thomas Schelling wrote compelling but abstruse tomes on nuclear war and its fallout. Denis Healey, Britain's Labour defence secretary 1964–70, a multilateralist and strong NATO advocate, saw the need to combine clear-headed defence thinking with political appreciation of the arms race. He formulated what he called Healey's theorem, "It takes only five per cent credibility of American retaliation to deter the Russians, but ninety-five per cent credibility to reassure the Europeans."

By the late 1970s, NORAD's system – eight control centres, 100 radars, and 300 interceptors – had become obsolescent, but not its mission: to warn about and assess possible attacks, which by the mid-1980s required a joint cost-sharing agreement, including investments to replace the DEW Line with an Arctic radar line – the North Warning System (NWS). New in office, Brian Mulroney's Conservative government had in 1984 to confront this issue, which created long-term implications for defence deployment and spending. The relevant systems included Over-the-Horizon Backscatter radar; greater use of USAF Airborne Warning and Control System (AWACS) aircraft; and the assignment of newer aircraft, specifically American F-15s, F-16s, and Canadian CF-18s, stationed in Edmonton, to NORAD. Over time, Canada and its NATO allies faced a constant political battle over defence spending, to match American commitments, and treaties with Japan and South Korea. Today, NATO's 29 members spend about $900 billion each year on collective defence, in contrast to Russia's $66 billion, with Britain, France, Germany, and Italy committing more than two-and-one-half times what Russia does (see Figure 5.1).

Lester Pearson's promise to embrace a policy of nuclear weapons, made in a speech in Scarborough on 12 January 1963, only weeks before the Conservative convention in Ottawa, was an attempt to publicize Conservative divisions. It backfired and exposed Liberal rifts. The nuclear issue had come to a head at the Ottawa convention, when Diefenbaker had an ambiguous resolution passed promising "negotiations with the United States ... to make readily available for the Canadian installations and equipment that form part of NATO and NORAD forces such nuclear weapons as are required for the defense installations." As Yukon MP Erik Nielsen remarked, paraphrasing W.L.M, King on conscription, "Nuclear weapons if necessary, but not necessarily nuclear weapons." In *Cité Libre*, a disgruntled academic and polemicist, recognizing Pearson's reversal of established Liberal policy, called him "the defrocked Prince of Peace," a reference to his Nobel Peace Prize. The writer was Pierre Elliott Trudeau.

II

The fifteen years of Pierre Trudeau's time as prime minister, extending from April 1968 to June 1984 minus Joe Clark's nine months in 1979–80, overlapped with five U.S. presidents – Lyndon Johnson, Richard Nixon, Gerald Ford, Jimmy Carter, and Ronald Reagan – a period of deeply divisive social and political discord in American society. The war in Vietnam, the civil-rights movement, Watergate, and the resignation of Richard Nixon coincided with rising inequality, riots in the inner cities, gun violence, and high rates of crime (murders, robbery). An

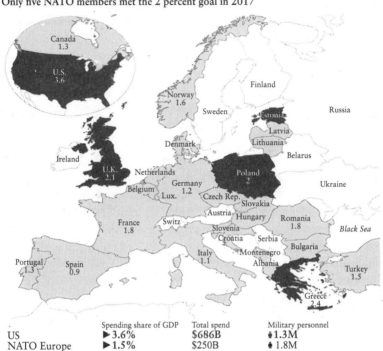

Figure 5.1 NATO Defence Spending as a Percentage of GNP.

uncompromising political culture emerged in the United States, and controversial social issues like abortion, capital punishment, gun laws, and immigration spilled over to other countries, including Canada. U.S. domestic issues also influenced American foreign policy in the Cold War and affected Canadian and European approaches to exchange rates, foreign aid, international competitiveness, military spending, and the role of government.

From his first days as prime minister, Pierre Trudeau wanted to create distance from his Liberal predecessors, especially Pearson. Perhaps owing to his personal experience as an outsider to Liberal orthodoxy, or his extensive travels to exotic places like Bukhara and Samarkand in Uzbekistan on the old Silk Road in central Asia, and visits to China, India, Cuba, and Africa, he had a vision of the world beyond the stereotypes of

North American and European leaders. In foreign affairs, most were classic "Atlanticists," linking European capitals with North America as a common heritage and shared destiny, reinforced in international institutions like the IMF and the World Bank. Trudeau felt other countries might view economic development and progress in a different light,

Pearson, of course, had helped create and animate the postwar, liberal global order, defined by the rule of law, international cooperation, and institutions like GATT (which became the WTO) the IMF, and the World Bank, military alliances like NATO, and the United Nations. Pearson, in short, knew the world of diplomacy; Trudeau knew the world at large. There was never any doubting among Canada's elites, or even among its citizens at large, about which side Canada was on, despite ambivalence on actual spending. In the Cold War struggle for military and economic supremacy, Canada's position was clear and unequivocal. In many ways, the Ottawa foreign policy consensus was best illustrated by Winston Churchill's 1946 Iron Curtain speech: "It is necessary that constancy of mind, persistency of purpose, and the grand simplicity of decision shall rule and guide the conduct of the English-speaking peoples in peace as they did in war." For Canada, a middle power, so close by history and tradition to the power centres of Washington, London, and Paris, the role of "helpful fixer" – an ambiguous phrase implying a quiet but effective adviser, illustrated by its (and Pearson's) role in the Suez crisis of 1956 and, decades later, its early support for the U.S. military coalition to remove Iraqi troops that invaded Kuwait in 1990 – is a vital element in what is called "Pearsonian diplomacy."

During the 1968 campaign, Trudeau promised a foreign-policy review, a full-scale assessment of policy since 1945, given the changes in the world in matters from defence spending and foreign aid to Canada's role in international institutions and alliances. In Calgary, Trudeau asked why NATO commitments should determine defence policy, which in turn determined foreign policy: "The basic pillars of [Canadian foreign policy] are not NATO, NORAD and the United Nations ... They are disarmament, non-proliferation and the development of a special role in foreign aid and assistance, related both to our unique capacity and our special interests." As in domestic policy, so in international affairs, the Liberal government reflected Trudeau's own philosophy, and his foreign ministers – Mitchell Sharp, Alan MacEachen (serving twice), Don Jamieson, Mark MacGuigan, and Jean Chrétien – and his closest advisers – bureaucrats like Louis Delvoie, Ivan Head, de Montigny Marchand, Michael Pitfield, and Gordon Smith – brought a measure of idealism, moral enthusiasm, and an Atlantic mindset to their views of Canada's foreign policy. The 1970 review of foreign policy, actually a series of papers (the one on NATO wasn't published) illustrated a confusion of core assumptions, including relations with the Great Republic to the south, but this exercise, which was also a prolonged, frustrating, and time-consuming process designed to produce better outcomes, did anything but.

The machinery of government for foreign policy linked expertise in the PCO, Finance, and External Affairs, which also incorporated international trade and foreign aid (the Canadian International Development Agency, or CIDA) and was really a super-ministry, or what Lord Moran, the British high commissioner called "a huge, sluggish bureaucratic conglomerate." Allan Gotlieb, ambassador to Washington, expressed his own frustrations with "official channels" – "an utterly preposterous proposition, a power play, a flexing of bureaucratic muscles. The Canadian Ambassador is supposed to be a puppet of the Ottawa bureaucracy." Trudeau's five foreign ministers brought their own skills to the job, but there was little doubt that the prime minister was in charge of foreign policy, a lesson well known in Ottawa circles when five prime ministers (Borden, Meighen, King, Bennett, and Diefenbaker) also served as their own foreign minister.

In the late 1960s and the 1970s, the Trudeau government regularly faced a series of crises in the United States that constrained actions at home. The deep American cleavages stemming from U.S. involvement in Vietnam, the Watergate hearings, Nixon's resignation, and the civil-rights movement emboldened some Canadians to take a strong anti-American perspective, push for an independent foreign policy, and ask for more resources devoted to disarmament, aid to the Third World, potential withdrawal from NATO (an NDP policy, like British Labour's seeking unilateral nuclear disarmament). Trudeau called for support of the North–South dialogue, a feature of his Mansion Houses speech in London in March 1975, and funded an agency in Ottawa with the same name. He also added an item on the G7 meeting hosted by Canada at Montebello in June 1980 and at the North–South Summit of twenty-two countries in Cancún, Mexico, in October 1981.

Trudeau co-chaired the Cancún sessions with Mexico's president, José López-Portillo, which was the first and last time such gatherings discussed redistributing wealth from the rich North to the poor South. Among the participants were Prime Minister Indira Gandhi, happy to receive the largest loan ever issued by the IMF, and Julius Nyerere from Tanzania, unhappy with the IMF's stiff terms over his misaligned public finances, high tariffs, and over-valued currency. Nyerere openly led the charge to place the IMF and the World Bank under UN supervision, while ignoring which countries funded them. Both British Prime Minister Margaret Thatcher and U.S. President Ronald Reagan attended the meeting, and it soon became clear that not only was there no necessary divergence between support for market mechanisms, private property, and open trade, but Western support for Third World countries didn't have to be a tradeoff for U.S. economic policies or the American nuclear umbrella.

"Trade, not aid," was a nifty and even seductive slogan, but most Third World countries – especially from Africa – had neither the economic capacity nor the institutions to become export-led economies. In frustration, Japan did its own study under the rubric of the Asian Development Bank to cultivate export capacity in southeast Asia, backed by its own extensive foreign aid. It may be an overstatement, but the 19th-century saying, "Providence is always on the side of the big battalions," has a certain resonance in the diplomatic world. Traditional socialist policies of self-reliance, import substitution, and high tariffs, a mantra of development economics taught in Britain, now found little resonance in the British and American delegations. The first draft of the Cancún summit communique, prepared by Canada, was largely discarded. Foreign policy is often domestic policy with a flag and an embassy. Trudeau's Liberal government enacted a series of measures, such as the Foreign Investment Review Act, that became a red flag to the American business community and its members of Congress, which unwittingly reinforced anti-American sentiment on Canadian campuses and among political elites, including Walter Gordon's Committee for an Independent Canada, a motley group with ten thousand members, with luminaries like Eddie Goodman, Jack McClelland, Peter Newman, Abe Rotstein, Claude Ryan, and Bruce Wilson and ample coverage by the CBC, *Maclean's*, and the Toronto *Star*.

The Trudeau government coped with these events, generating mixed results at home, and even disquiet in foreign governments, especially among Canada's closest friends. From his foreign travels, writings, and listening to debates within the Pearson cabinet, Trudeau developed only two interests in foreign policy – nuclear disarmament and help for the Third World. Canada had been part of disarmament talks since 1945, but, as even Winston Churchill discovered, the United States had its own approach to dealing with the Soviet Union and tolerated, but rarely welcomed, help to restrict nuclear proliferation in other countries. Paul Martin, Pearson's secretary of state for external affairs, first announced Canada's commitment to spend 0.50 per cent of GNP on foreign aid, much less than Scandinavian countries, but power politics often intruded on the politics of aid. Pearson preferred a target of 1 per cent but settled on 0.7 as a benchmark. The Trudeau government increased foreign aid, once reaching 0.6 per cent, but other countries were growing faster and increasing their aid budgets. At one point, Japan was the top aid donor. In absolute numbers, the United States is by far the biggest donor for humanitarian aid ($30.9 billion per year), followed by Germany ($20.85 billion), Britain ($19.98 billion), France ($10.9 billion), Japan ($10.4 billion), and Sweden ($8.5 billion) – see figure 5.2.

In the recent past, donors debated how best to channel foreign aid, with many Third World countries preferring a direct donation to government, hence a licence to use the money for other purposes, such as purchase of military hardware to support those in power or send a portion to offshore accounts in Switzerland. Japan, by contrast, prefers tied contracts, whereby aid agencies oversee construction of hospitals, schools, and water-treatment plants. Today, most donors channel foreign aid through multilateral agencies, including those of the UN, or NGOs like the Red Cross or those from donor countries, which increases the transparency of reporting and accountability. Africa illustrates the Third World challenges of industrialization, with a per-capita income of about $1,000 per year, but 40 per cent of the population is urbanized.

Trudeau was a star on the international stage, but his government rarely made a difference, despite his exhortation at the University of Alberta in 1968, "Never before in history has the disparity between the rich and poor, the comfortable and the starving, been so extreme." He used his superstar image to give a voice to Third World concerns, but he failed to appreciate that many recipient countries faced rent-seeking from aid donors, i.e., much of the foreign aid actually went through contracts for domestic companies, and Canada and firms like SNC and Lavalin were legendary. Like FIFA's antics in the soccer world, Canada often provided aid to curry support for a seat on the UN Security Council. To a degree, Trudeau and other foreign leaders failed to appreciate, or at least publicly admit, domestic politics often intrudes in foreign policy.

|||

More by general design that by the force of events, Brian Mulroney decided to stay in Canada during his first year as prime minister, concentrating on the economic and competitive agenda. Only two months in office, he saw the event cycle in action when he addressed the famine in Ethiopia,

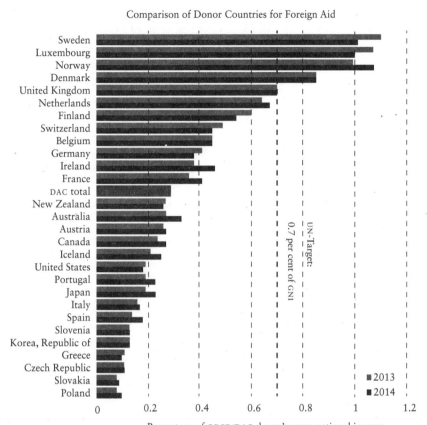

Source: Adapted from OECD

Figure 5.2 Comparison of Donor Countries for Foreign Aid.

a result of heavy rains and government incompetence. But as any new leader quickly learns, the schedule also includes international events prescheduled years into the future, such as G7 Summits, Commonwealth Conferences, and bilateral meetings with foreign leaders. The bilateral in Washington with U.S. President Reagan in September 1984, only a week after the cabinet was sworn in, followed visits to Canada by the Queen and Pope John Paul II. The meetings at the White House included a private lunch in the presidential quarters, which included Defense Secretary Caspar Weinberger, a hawk on the Soviet Union. The meal started with jocular banter between the two leaders, each upping the other with Irish jokes, a sign of a relaxed atmosphere and warm personal relations. As Weinberger wrote in his memoirs, *Fighting for Peace*, "For once the President had encountered a memory bank for jokes almost as an extension as his own. When we reached item one of the agenda, the discussions sailed along far more smoothly and quickly than anyone had expected." The agenda focused on NATO, defence, trade, and Reagan's attempts to control government spending by appointing the Grace Commission, a foretaste of Mulroney's Nielsen Task Force.

In February 1985, Mulroney had a short rest with his family in Florida before his first foreign trip, joining the annual session of the Caribbean Commonwealth countries in Kingston, Jamaica, the largest member of the sixteen-nation, English-speaking grouping, which consists of Anguilla, Antigua, the Bahamas, Barbados, Belize, Bermuda, the British Virgin Islands, Dominica, Granada, Guyana (not attending), Montserrat, St Kitts-Nevis, St Lucia, St Vincent and the Grenadines, Trinidad and Tobago, and the Turks and Caicos. Trudeau had promised the grouping a five-year foreign-aid target of $260 million for 1982–87, with $148 million already delivered, and the rest arriving in 1985. The region had suffered economically, with the decline of the East Caribbean dollar, the closure of two aluminum smelters in Jamaica, drug trafficking, and over-reliance on the American market for exports.

The full meeting of all Commonwealth leaders was to take place that October in Nassau, Bahamas, and the Caribbean leaders had wanted to meet the new Canadian leader in advance. The Kingston meeting lasted one day, on Sunday 24 February, with a bilateral meeting planned for Trudeau on Monday with Jamaica's popular Labour prime minister, Edward Seaga, a Harvard graduate with a record for innovative transformation of depressed inner-city areas, including in his West Kingston constituency. There was political tension after the U.S. invasion of Grenada in October 1983, which became a case study of conflicting signals, crosspurposes, and confusion over advance consultations. Granada, a British colony, achieved independence in 1974, keeping the Queen as head of state. Five years later, a Marxist coup, led by Maurice Bishop, allowed a growing Cuban presence on the small island, but the deputy prime minister and the military commander revolted against Bishop, and he and his supporters were executed. Over a thousand Americans lived on the island, many attending St George's Medical School. The U.S. military, through its Crisis Planning Group, received a request from the Organization for Eastern Caribbean States (OECS), so President Reagan contacted Margaret Thatcher in London and promised her advance warning of U.S. action. However, a series of mishaps, perhaps intentional secrecy by the White

House to present a fait accompli, left the British unaware of the invasion until it was over. Thatcher had a wider view, worried about U.S. application of the Monroe Doctrine (excluding external influence from the Americas) to other areas, including Nicaragua.

In February 1985, External Affairs sent draft remarks to Prime Minister Mulroney in Florida for his opening remarks in Jamaica, an anodyne text of platitudes and nostrums. When Lee Richardson, travelling as part of the advance tour, informed the prime minister about the logistics for the two-hour flight to Kingston on the Saturday night, Mulroney asked him to contact me, to rewrite the speech. I had taken the opportunity to take my family for a short holiday at Ochos Rios, a beach resort in Jamaica, before the Caribbean Commonwealth gathering. The previous night, I had a pleasant dinner with Keith Spicer, a staunch critic of the prime minister, and explained the rationale for the agenda, Mulroney's views on bilingualism, and his uncompromising views on the role of Quebec in Confederation. The next afternoon, while I was on route to Kingston, the young driver outlined the workings of the drug trade in Jamaica. I spent that evening in the Canadian high commissioner's office drafting the revised text. In the opening paragraph, I added a telling sentence, first prepared by my assistant, Nigel Wright, "Canada is not a neutral country," before having dinner with Lee Richardson, discussing the drug problems and the extreme poverty in this incredibly beautiful island, where so many famous people spent their winter holidays, including John Diefenbaker, John Turner, and Lester Pearson.

At the opening session of the conference, after the usual perfunctory remarks, the prime minister made his address, including remarks on his personal attitude about Canada's neighbour, the United States, much to the chagrin of some of the External Affairs bureaucrats. What unfolded after his remarks was totally unexpected, but the leaders spoke as one. They had supported the Reagan administration's moves in Grenada, and talked about the seditious material infiltrating their schools, mostly printed in North Korea, and the serious problems each faced with the drug trade, radical Cuban influence, and Soviet documents fomenting social unrest. The most forceful presentation came from Prime Minister Tom Adams of Barbados, as well as the host, Edward Seaga, who, in his private bilateral with Mulroney, said he saw Canada as a mediator with G7 leaders and the White House, particularly about harmful U.S. trade policies barring imports of Jamaican sugar, another protectionist trade policy helping rich American farmers. The Kingston conference led to a new trade grouping within the British Caribbean, CARICOM. The conference offered Canada a lesson in foreign policy beyond Europe and North America: Canada had, in Latin America, large investments but no trade strategy, in the English-speaking Caribbean, vital interests but no policy, and elsewhere, a foreign policy with no clear strategies. As ever, global issues were changing the event cycle, and Canada had to catch up.

IV

At his first G7 summit in Bonn, the West German capital, in May 1985, not only was Brian Mulroney the only first-timer, but all the other leaders had long experience in politics – over forty years for the Japanese prime minister, for instance. President Reagan was in his fifth year in office, after serving two terms as governor of California, a state that ranks 10th or 11th in the world in GDP. Margaret Thatcher, first elected to Parliament in 1959 and with personal insight about five prime ministers, had led her country since 1979. All the other leaders had attended several annual meetings, in a G7 rotation system, where the host chooses the site and arranges for security, media, and local logistics. Canada, like Italy, was a new player, not attending the first conclave in Rambouillet, near Paris, in 1976.

By chance, Mulroney had unexpectedly been to Moscow in March 1985 to attend the funeral of Premier Konstantin Chernenko. Leadership in the USSR had been in turmoil since the death in November 1982 of Leonid Brezhnev, who had been general secretary for 18 years, a hardliner who frowned on dissent within the Soviet bloc. Weak, pliant leaders in such countries as East Germany, Hungary, and especially Poland, where the Solidarity union movement was on the march in 1980 and 1981, backed by the new Polish pope, John Paul II, was a threat to the hawks in the Kremlin. Brezhnev was succeeded by the geriatric Yuri Andropov, former KGB head and a hawk, but he died soon, replaced by another hardliner, a Siberian-born chain smoker and severely ill Konstantin Chernenko, Brezhnev's former chief of staff, who managed Soviet propaganda. Chernenko was yet another old-school leader who had never travelled to the west, saw things in black and white, and typified Stalin-style leadership. Brezhnev, Andropov, and most members of the Politburo had little grasp of the reforms required for a moribund, sclerotic, closed economy. He in turn died in March 1985, leading Ronald Reagan to quip, "How am I supposed to get any place with the Russians if they keep dying on me?"

Chernenko's funeral in Moscow's Red Square took place on a bitterly cold day, and anyone unfamiliar with a Russian winter, like Napoleon and Hitler, had no idea what 40 degrees below (on either scale) plus wind chill does to the human frame. The Americans, who monitor carefully such matters, had known Chernenko's days were numbered, so his death was not unexpected. More important, his successor, Mikhail S. Gorbachev, named only four hours after the announcement of Chernenko's death, was a decision made in advance, unlike the machinations following Lenin's death in 1922. The funeral was a useful occasion for Mulroney not only to meet the new Soviet leader, but for visits with other G7 leaders (i.e., "bilaterals") before Bonn. For Brian Mulroney, these four months (February–May 1985) were a useful prelude to eight years on the world's diplomatic stage. Moscow, a city of 13 million, typified Churchill's comment about Russia: "A riddle, wrapped in a mystery, inside an enigma." The funeral, occurring after the Kingston conference and before the Quebec Summit (with Reagan, in Quebec City, in March) and Bonn, was part of Mulroney's crash course in international diplomacy.

In Moscow, he wore a Russian fur hat, a rarity for a person who usually goes hatless. Given the extreme cold, Mulroney welcomed a small gift, a battery-operated hand warmer to wear inside his gloves, from a leader once depicted by French President Charles de Gaulle as a transistor salesman: Prime Minister Yasuhiro Nakasone of Japan. Nakasone was now presiding over a booming economy and a rising yen relative to the U.S. dollar. Japanese–Soviet relations were marred by mutual claims over the four islands of the Northern Territories, and while Soviet hawks could dismiss the Japanese for their weak military stance, their compatriots might well hope to learn from the Japanese ability to master new technologies.

The Mulroney–Nakasone bilateral was propitious, because the G7 summit after Bonn would be in Tokyo in 1986, and in the formalized sequencing of visiting leaders, it was the turn of Japan's to go to Canada. Japan was a "priority" country for Canada, not only for two-way trade but for the potential to attract large investments, especially in the auto sector. Even in industries where Canada had competitive strengths – energy, mining, pulp and paper – Japan had awesome capacities to import the raw feedstock, e.g., crude oil, newsprint, or timber, and upgrade it into advanced materials, fine paper, and plastics, using their powerful trading companies, unparalleled logistics capabilities, and a new logistics system: just in time. In the specially lined, eavesdropping-proof meeting room in the Japanese embassy in Moscow, their leaders hit it off, a good sign for future cooperation on investment, science, and trade, and agreed to talk again in Bonn.

The May summit in Bonn was hosted by Chancellor Helmet Kohl, a very tall, big man with a mischievous sense of humour but a politician with a clear sense of West Germany's postwar place, an economic superpower but recognizing NATO Secretary General Lord Ismay's dictum: keep the Soviets out, the Americans in, and the Germans down. In the hierarchy of international meetings, time-consuming affairs where global issues are studied, assessed, and decided, the G7 was at the top, and included both national leaders and finance and foreign ministers as well, who held separate meetings. The final summit declaration reflected a consensus of the gathering. For the G7 leaders, the global economy faced new challenges, with few easy answers for currency misalignments and trade imbalances, due not only to domestic policies, but issues like energy exports and imports, international flows of capital, and Third World policies.

At his first summit, Mulroney was there to participate, but also to observe, to grasp the personal dynamics between and among the leaders, and to figure out how each leader played to his or her own strengths but also their views on global issues. Despite the experience and sophistication of the participants, as Paul Volcker recalled in *Changing Fortunes*, there was no common agreed framework to address fiscal and monetary coordination, capital flows, exchange rates, and the debt crisis in the Third World. At Bonn, the two big economies reflected the quality and prestige of Ronald Reagan and Helmut Kohl. At the opening reception, at Schaumburg Castle, as the leaders entered with their entourages, a cameraman almost knocked aside French President François Mitterrand; Mulroney, who was standing with Bill Chambers and me, noted the obvious: the strong economies confer strength in everything else.

While history cannot be rewritten, it is clear today, just as it was in the 1980s, that the root cause of structural payment imbalances starts in the United States. A generation ago, American over-consumption and Japanese over-saving, thanks to a temporary bilateral trade surplus and very high domestic savings, led to restrictive U.S. trade practices and calls for a stronger yen relative to the U.S. dollar. Today, the American policy issue is identical, but with China, flowing from massive U.S. over-consumption (deficits in government, energy, and trade) and Chinese under-consumption. As depicted in Figure 5.3, IMF projections show dramatic reordering of countries in the global pecking order, measured not only by GNP output, but by influence in the global economy.

The Bonn Summit helped form Mulroney's view of the world economy, the key players, and the levers that each country can play to shape outcomes. On his watch, the G7 and its leaders became the focus of Canada's

Constructive Internationalism in a Changing World Order 211

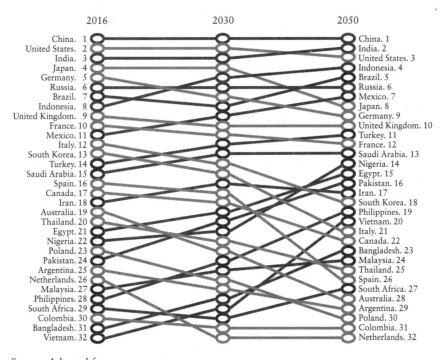

Source: Adapted from IMF

Figure 5.3 The Shifting Fortunes of Globalization.

place in the world, as each developed a relationship with Canada concerning a variety of issues, national objectives, and points of leverage. In this sense, his thinking was closer to Pearson's than to Trudeau's, as Canada's wartime sacrifices had given it a unique place at the table, and other countries looked to it, often quietly and without media attention, for advice and opinions. Trudeau had provided an opening to Canada in the Third World – in Africa, the Caribbean, and even in China. But global forces, and the unique U.S. role, necessitated new leadership and a new mindset, as Mulroney learned in face-to-face meetings in Kingston. Even Caribbean leaders had little use for Trudeau or for Jamaican Prime Minister Michael Manley's "democratic socialism" and "burden sharing," which reflected style over substance, often cloaked with a touch of anti-Americanism, government edict over market solutions, and a seeming blindness to the role of security and defence in the calculation of friends v. foes. Further, as other countries achieved the elixir of rapid economic growth, the world order of the G7 and, thanks to Prime Minister Jean

Chrétien and Paul Martin, the later G20, Canada would have to run faster to hold its place in global political and economic forums. At the end of the Bonn Summit, as Canadian delegates were preparing to travel to the airport in buses provided by their German hosts, I was surprised to hear a remark from Robert Fowler, then in the PCO, who wasn't returning on the government aircraft. "After a week of summitry, I always take a holiday. I am spending a week at the Canadian embassy in Rome."

V

It is almost a truism that the Conservative party and belief in the Commonwealth go hand in hand. John A. Macdonald always saw the British connection as reinforcing Canadian independence from the Great Republic. Canada's political evolution to a federated, independent country and a powerful image as a protector of minority rights had a resonance with leaders as diverse as Cecil Rhodes in the 19th century and Jawaharlal Nehru and Nelson Mandala in the 20th. History shows that leaders ranging from Benjamin Disraeli in the 19th century to Lord Beaverbrook in the 20th had advanced arguments for a free-trade zone within the empire and later Commonwealth, but Britain pursued other priorities. In the post-1945 period, Britain's economic plight forced its gradual retreat from global responsibilities, even as some Commonwealth citizens' passports allowed holders to migrate to Britain, which many holders from Africa, India, and Pakistan did, enlivening many of its cities, like London, Birmingham, Bradford, and Leeds, much to the distress of some voters and MPs. In truth, the quiet policies of the Foreign Office reflected one of squeezing the colonial possessions to satisfy the middle classes of England, like limited immigration and support for apartheid in South Africa.

The Commonwealth Conference in London in March 1961 dealt with South Africa, setting the stage for a 25-year struggle within the Commonwealth. South Africa had applied to rejoin the Commonwealth because it was planning to abolish the monarchy and become a republic on 31 May 1961. Britain and some white dominions attempted a compromise, allowing it to stay as a republic, while African members such as Nigeria and Ghana preferred expulsion because of the Nationalist government's racist policy of apartheid (Afrikaans for "apartness"). Fearing a deep split on racial lines, John Diefenbaker proposed a resolution on racial equality, and the final communique reflected this new principle of the Commonwealth, much to the chagrin of the British delegation. South

Africa withdrew its application and left the Commonwealth when it became a republic. Britain's ambiguous policies on matters of race reflected past views, as in 1924 Japan had proposed a resolution at the League of Nations on equality of races, only to be thwarted by Britain, and quietly supported by the United States. John Diefenbaker returned to Canada in triumph. He addressed a large Conservative audience at Ottawa's Château Laurier Hotel, and spoke movingly about South Africa: "My hope is that they will return to the Commonwealth in due course. There will always be a light in the Commonwealth window."

Few of Britain's citizens realized how much their country's economy, depicted sometimes after 1945 as the "sick man of Europe,' relied on trade and investment with the old members of the British Empire, especially in the Caribbean and in Africa, particularly in the south, where British firms dominated mining, with reserves of diamonds, gold, oil and gas, platinum, and rare metals, and Britain worked with firms such as De Beers to protect British interests, with low tax rates and friendly governments to mitigate threats like nationalization. Over 100 British firms were listed on the London Stock Exchange having mineral rights in the region worth over a trillion dollars. but their operations had controversial disputes over environmental issues, pay scales, racism, and deplorable working conditions. More recently, NGOs in Britain and Africa, such as Global Justice Now, have published reports setting out the asymmetric payments from African countries to Britain. Estimates vary, but examples include the $162 billion African countries received in 2015, mainly in loans, aid, and personal remittances, while foreign firms withdrew $203 billion, directly from multinational firms that repatriate profits and illegally shift money into offshore tax havens, or through costs imposed through adaptation and mitigation for climate change, which generates an annual deficit of $41.3 billion from the forty-seven African countries, according to one group, Honest Accounts 2017.

In this post-1945 era, passports in many Commonwealth members, including Canada, stated that the holder was a British subject. Many holders from some of those countries had British nationality or claims to it, and some migrated to Britain, especially when their own nations erupted in political unrest, civil war, or challenges to dictatorial rule. In the 1960s, such immigration, starting from Jamaica, expanded because of political unrest in India, Nigeria, Northern and Southern Rhodesia, Pakistan, South Africa, and Uganda. The British government, attempting to provide a colour-blind approach, instituted policies that were anything but. Immigration is always a delicate political issue, but in the rhetoric of a populist flame-thrower, extremist views arouse sensitive chords, which was precisely the aim of Conservative MP and former minister Enoch Powell in 1968. At an afternoon meeting of Conservative activists in his constituency of Wolverhampton, with the media present and warned in advance of provocation, Powell, a war hero and keen student of Greek who served as shadow defence secretary, delivered his notorious "rivers of blood" speech. His inflamed rhetoric removed all ambiguity about his views: "The West Indian does not by being born in England become an Englishman ... he is a West Indian or an Asian still," and he quoted a constituent: "In 15 or 20 years' time, the black man will have the whip hand over the white man."

His history and background became widely known around the English-speaking world in the weeks and months leading up to the Commonwealth Conference in Nassau in October 1985. In June, the powerful South African military attacked bases of the armed resistance African National Congress in neighbouring Botswana; France reacted angrily and imposed a unilateral freeze on new investments in South Africa and asked the UN Security Council for voluntary sanctions. American banks refused to roll over loans to South African companies, and Desmond Tutu, the articulate, media-savvy Anglican bishop of Cape Town, received the Nobel Peace Prize for his advocacy of peaceful change in his country. Britain and the United States pressed Soviet leader Mikhail Gorbachev to release prisoners like Nobel laureate Andrei Sakharov, but did nothing to aid South African resistance leader Nelson Mandela, in jail since 1963 on the infamous Robben Island. South Africa and its apartheid policy put the issue of apartheid in stark, moral terms, and policy analysts and the global media wondered at what point support for the Nationalist government of President P.W. Botha might end. The status quo allowed trade and investment policies that favoured British industry and imports of South African coal for West German electricity plants, while the U.S. government and New York-based financial firms continued profitable loans to South Africa. Meanwhile, the "front-line states" in southern Africa, most of them Commonwealth members, called for punitive sanctions, the release of Nelson Mandela, and the end of apartheid rule.

Before the conference in Nassau in September 1985, other G7 nations, but especially Britain, knew Canada had a mixed record, a combination of past hypocrisy and duplicity, supporting IMF loans to South Africa and letting Canadian companies, including crown corporations like Canadair, remain active in South Africa and bordering states, especially in mining. In the PMO, Dalton Camp, seeing briefing notes prepared by

External Affairs, remained skeptical about progress, repeating his scathing comment that the only real difference between the Canadian civil service and South Africa's was that some of Canada's spoke French. British companies were very active in, and some very dependent on, the South African market. British policy was unequivocally against sanctions, despite rising antipathy against the South African government, apartheid, and Nelson Mandela's imprisonment. Margaret Thatcher herself, often with the support of her husband, Denis, who referred to South Africa as "God's own country," was quite caustic and dismissive of some black Commonwealth leaders. Denis wasn't the author, but smiled at the private jokes told in London pubs where the British media referred to the Commonwealth Conference as "coons holidaying on government money." In short, there was no shortage of hypocrisy, deceit, and racism in the diplomatic cocktail of the anti-apartheid saga. Public statements made for one audience had little to do with the reality for another audience, as when the front-line states publicly called for economic sanctions against South Africa, while trading (and bartering) with that nation.

In London, in advance of the Nassau conference, the Queen hoped for a private meeting with Margaret Thatcher. The prime minister was more interested in her travel arrangements, refusing to take the Concorde, and flew with the British delegation on British Airways. At the three days of testy meetings, with righteous arguments on both sides, mixed with a degree of moral pretension and hard realities on the ground, leaders who were autocrats at home looking for racial justice and democracy in South Africa and democratic leaders clashed with Britain's hard-line policy favouring no sanctions and South Africa's right to make its own choices for future action. The leaders agreed to a compromise, appointing an Eminent Persons Group (EPG). Thatcher wanted British Foreign Secretary Geoffrey Howe to take the lead, but she settled on Anthony Barber, former chancellor of the exchequer, and Malcolm Fraser, former prime minister of Australia. It wasn't clear that the South African government would cooperate, but both Thatcher and German Chancellor Helmut Kohl had their own sources of information on the fractured nation – from bankers, former officials, and the shady world of Swiss finance. Botha remained truculent, uncompromising, and dogmatic about white rule, and only too willing to blame outside rebellious forces, including Marxist subversion. Unwilling to meet the EPG, which interviewed Nelson Mandela in his prison cell on Robben Island, he received a message from Thatcher that "frustrated nationalism" was the breeding ground for communism, and he relented.

But the event cycle was pushing leaders before they were ready. On 19 May 1986, just as Brian Mulroney was finishing his tour of Japan, China, and South Korea, having met Margaret Thatcher in Vancouver for Expo 86 a few weeks earlier, South Africa unleased its military with raids on ANC offices in Botswana, Zambia, and Zimbabwe, creating a media firestorm. This action put Thatcher and her pro-South Africa policy in a squeeze, and she decided to send Geoffrey Howe, now a much-disgruntled foreign secretary, to buy time before facing Commonwealth leaders at the Commonwealth Games in Edinburgh early in August. Despite confronting Brian Mulroney's pleadings in Vancouver, Thatcher was becoming isolated, apparently even from her own monarch. A *Sunday Times* exposé included the headline, "Queen Dismayed by 'Uncaring Prime Minister'" and set out the case that "the Queen considers the Prime Minister's approach often to be uncaring, confrontational, and socially divisive."

The eventual release of Nelson Mandela, the end of apartheid, and the powerful moral message of leaders like Bishop Tutu were lessons in geopolitics that belied the *sotto voce* tones for the status quo, held by leaders like Reagan, Thatcher, and Kohl. Canada could stand tall, forcefully pressing the case against apartheid in the two capitals that mattered, London and Washington, but not antagonizing leaders there to make a media splash. The fact that Nelson Mandela looked to Canada for advice is testimony to the leadership it offered when needed most, in defiance of Canada's historic friendships and personal ties with the United States and Britain.

Not everyone would give Brian Mulroney much credit, including for his instructions to Ambassador Stephen Lewis at the United Nations, who had spent time in Africa. Nelson Mandela's visit to Canada in June 1990 was further evidence of Canada's leading role, but also confirmed his sense of humour and magnanimous gestures, despite his twenty-eight years in a jail cell. In Ottawa, meeting over lunch, he and Mulroney discussed the forthcoming election in South Africa and Canada's support at international agencies like the IMF and World Bank to secure trade credits for his new government. He pleaded for Canada's financial support to hold an election, at a cost of $10 million. Mulroney reluctantly agreed. Mandela then started to leave the room, opening the door, and then turned back. "Brian, I want to thank you again. And by the way, the $10 million in aid for the election is in American dollars!"

VI

Even before Pierre Trudeau undertook a review of Canada's foreign policy in the early 1970s, in the search for new approaches, Canada, like the Canadian Pacific founded in 1881, tried to put the Pacific into Canada's economic mindset. Partly arising from Trudeau's 1970 decision to formally recognize China, Canada and Japan have cultivated a range of policy initiatives to strengthen their own diplomatic ties, helped by Japan's magnificent pavilions at the New York World's Fair in 1964-65 and at Expo 67 in Montreal, stunning displays of that nation's electronics and technological prowess. One of the final initiatives of the last Trudeau government was the Asia Pacific Foundation of Canada, located in Vancouver, passed with all-party support in June 1984. The idea of a Pacific Rim initiative emerged after Joe Clark attended the G7 Summit in Tokyo in June 1979, and people like Jack Austin, Tom Axworthy, and External Affairs experts mulled over future direction, including such a foundation. This was an early signal of a more aggressive approach to attracting Japanese investment. Within the Mulroney cabinet, at least initially, there was far less interest in Japan, as an economic player generally, or as an importer of Canadian products. My own advice to anyone who would listen was the need for top people to visit Japan, tour the factories, meet senior executives, and see how the Japanese viewed Canada.

In 1984, there were only four Japanese specialists in Canada's universities, and two died that year. Joe Clark at External Affairs made Japan his first overseas visit. One minister who took my advice seriously was Sinclair Stevens, at Industry, who chaired the powerful Economics Committee of cabinet. At a meeting in Vancouver in late March 1985, he met a Japanese delegation led by Ejie Toyoda, president of Toyota Motor Corporation, whose Canadian Autoparts Toyota Inc. (CAPTIN), in Delta, BC, was the first Japanese manufacturing facility ever built in North America, to make aluminum wheels for Toyota's cars and trucks imported into Canada. But Toyota didn't say publicly that, with the yen steadily rising against the U.S. dollar, it had decided to build a plant in North America, but probably (like Honda, which invested in Ohio) not in Michigan, with its legacy of bad labour relations. Behind the scenes, I gave other advice, based on my own studies and interviews with Toyota in Nagoya: Toyota was thinking of building two assembly plants, one in Ontario, the second in a U.S. border state. Stevens's March 1985 meeting and tour in British Columbia, attended by Premier Bill Bennett, led to the minister's decision to visit Japan in late August 1985. By coincidence, the cabinet was meeting in Vancouver mid-August, and the prime minister asked me not to go to Japan with the Canadian delegation. I argued otherwise, citing the real possibility of obtaining more than one Japanese car plant, if the right moves were made. Reluctantly, he relented.

Stevens's August trip to Japan included a side visit to South Korea, and meetings with the four big *chaebols* (South Korean industrial groupings), similar to but not as big as the giant *Keiretsu* (Japanese counterparts) like Mitsubishi, Mitsui, and Sumitomo, each bank-centred, along with the massive Sogo Sosha (trading firms) with a global reach, each with offices in Canada. Stevens's meeting with Hyundai in South Korea at its headquarters led to an invitation for another gathering that evening attended by some Canadian business executives like the CEO of Bombardier, Laurent Beaudoin, with Hyundai's founder, Ju Yung Chung, at his home, a singular honour in the Asian tradition. Stevens and a few Canadian bureaucrats, including Bob Brown and Paul Labbé, also attended. In his living room, Chung agreed to build a car-assembly plant in Canada. After a tour of the vast Hyundai shipbuilding site in Pusan, South Korea, the delegation took the short flight to Osaka, for a dinner that night with Japanese corporate executives. For some unknown reason, the minister didn't like the remarks prepared for him by Canadian Ambassador Barry Steers and asked me to rewrite them, stressing the possibility of increased two-way trade and investment and Canada's competitive agenda.

On consecutive days, the Canadian delegation toured three car plants, two in Hamamatsu, a city about the size of Hamilton but with more engineering start-ups than all of Ontario, and corporate headquarters for Honda, Suzuki, and Yamaha. After plant tours, briefings, and discussions, the signals were very strong that the first two firms planned investments in Ontario. The final visit was in Toyota City, near Nagoya, which had ten assembly plants working flat out. A big welcoming sign outside the Toyota plant, showing the number of robots working on the assembly line, was meant as a briefing to visitors. The minister turned to me and asked what this number really meant. My answer was short and curt: "This assembly plant, and there are nine more Toyota plants near-by, has more robots than all of Canada." The discussions again were enormously successful, including the Toyoda CEO's mentioning to our group that, since I first met him in 1980, his firm, by holding off direct investments in North America, had made $720 million on the savings from the exchange-rate differential.

Arriving back home on 4 September, the anniversary of the 1984 election, I called the prime minister, to update him on the four potential assembly plants. There was a cabinet meeting the next day, and before the session, I gave him some speaking notes. During the first year, ministerial travel to foreign countries included forty-one trips to London, thirty-nine to Paris, forty to Rome, and three to Asia: two to Tokyo and one to

India, for a state funeral. Canada had some work ahead to give justice to its Pacific Rim heritage.

VII

In many ways, Canada–Japan is a case study in missed opportunities. Walter Light, the former president of Nortel, once said that, for Canadian business executives, international trade meant Palm Springs or Palm Beach. A generation ago, Canada had huge opportunities in Japan, such as the critical linkage between the Bell Canada subsidiary Northern Telecom as a supplier to Nippon Telephone, a Japanese superstar in a vital technology. But Northern Telecom's quality problems bedevilled the relationship. Nortel refused to invest in Japan or acquire a Japanese firm as a supplier and partner so it could learn the quality principles of Japanese management, in the way pioneered by American firms like Texas Instruments. In other sectors, Canadian banks had opportunities with the massive disruptions of Japanese banks in the early 1990s, but only Manulife Financial, returning to its pre-1939 Japanese roots, acquired a sizable market share in Japan, which became the basis of its acquisitions in China, Vietnam, and later in the United States. The same lost opportunity applies to Canadian auto-parts firms, like Magna, which would have had to make slow, steady, and initially low-profit-margin investments in Japan to become tier-one suppliers to its car industry. By contrast, Air Canada, now privatized and taking over, through a forced merger, Canadian Pacific Airlines, with its landing rights in Tokyo, has turned its global cargo operations into a world-beating operation, and its aggressive marketing policies across Asia have made it the favourite carrier for foreign travellers to visit North America.

Academic interest, starting from a limited base, developed from joint government funding efforts. Japanese universities promote courses and programs on Canada and Canadian studies. Six Canadian universities – Victoria, UBC, Alberta, McMaster, Toronto, and McGill – offer undergraduate and graduate courses on Japanese studies, but have few faculty experts and students. (The same challenge applies in Australia, but with significantly larger numbers.) Provincial trade delegations to Japan, mainly from British Columbia, Ontario, and Quebec, elevated Canada's links with Japanese industry associations, and each province set up trade offices in Tokyo, within the Canadian embassy. Canada's sparse corporate presence means limited visibility and public awareness in Japan, let alone in Tokyo, a metropolis with the same population as Canada.

From the Trudeau years in the 1970s to Mulroney and Chrétien in the 1980s and 1990s, Canada cultivated close ties with Japan, mostly on the personal initiatives of the prime minister. The Japanese appreciated this relationship, in part as a window to understand Canada's close ties with the United States, across a range of national and local issues, as well as its more direct links to Washington. During the first Mulroney government, an official in the Japanese embassy in Ottawa wrote a book for a Japanese audience on what Japan could learn from Canada about relations with the United States. Despite government and corporate activity, there has been a singular lack of attention by Canada's media – from the CBC to Canadian newspapers (the *Globe and Mail* closed its Japanese bureau) – which collectively have shown little or no interest in Japan. The event cycle influenced the Mulroney government in the autumn of 1985. The infamous September meeting in New York, where finance ministers from Britain, France. Japan, the United States, and West Germany met at the Plaza Hotel to realign exchange rates for the leading currencies, but especially the yen–dollar rate, from 360 to a potential 100 (it actually dropped to 80 temporarily), steadied the global currency markets but forced rethinking about foreign investment, trade policies, and national competitiveness in Japan.

The announcement in November 1985 of three Japanese assembly plants in Ontario, by Honda, Suzuki, and Toyota (Hyundai built in Bromont, Quebec, a predictably unwise location, far from the supply chains in southern Ontario) was a wakeup call for Ontario's auto sector, including Canada's auto-parts suppliers and steel industry, just when Japanese imports were climbing and Detroit firms were steadily losing market share. I was a forceful advocate of technological upgrading among Canadian firms, and when Sinclair Stevens briefly thought about asking Toyota to invest in Collingwood, near the closed shipyard on Georgian Bay, to employ laid-off workers, or when Stelco's CEO heard my private comments in Ottawa that Toyota would never buy low-carbon steel from Stelco's obsolete blast furnaces, there was abundant ill-feeling towards the PMO in some corporate boardrooms.

The Canadian cabinet developed a Japan strategy, set out in a cabinet document, that reflected mutually reinforcing bilateral issues – the Arctic, arts and culture, education, the environment, foreign direct investment, health care, science and technology, security, and university exchanges. Prime Minister Nakasone's visit to Canada in January 1986 was transformative, when he visited Toronto and Ottawa, including a plant tour at Northern Telecom's site in Brampton. On his arrival in Toronto at Pearson Airport, after the long flight from Tokyo on his chartered DC-10, he was surprised to receive advance copies of the Canadian prime minister's welcoming remarks, written in Japanese, English, and French. That night, at the official dinner at Toronto's Westin Harbour Castle Hotel, Nakasone broke protocol, whereby Japanese leaders usually speak only Japanese. He spoke excellent French and appreciated that Canada was a bilingual country. His remarks in French were a shock to the travelling Japanese press corps, which immediately asked Bill Fox, the press secretary in the PMO, to explain. Bill asked me to meet the corps in an off-the-record briefing. I explained that Nakasone was a graduate of a prominent high school in Shizouka, which happened to be my wife's hometown, when a French teacher from Montpellier gave lessons to some of the aspiring students like the young Nakasone. Quietly, and unknown to many of his colleagues, Nakasone kept up his French and love of France, with its historic silk routes between Lyon and Kyoto, Nara, and Tomioka.

As part of its competitive agenda, the Mulroney government initiated a Pacific 2000 policy, a five-year, $250-million plan to enhance relations with Japan and Asia generally. Worried that cabinet might not approve the measure, even civil servants from External Affairs like Howard Balloch lobbied me to assure approval. Mulroney's official visit to Japan after the G7 meetings in Tokyo in May 1986, including his breakfast speech to the Keidanren (Japanese Business Federation), a visit to the imperial palace and meeting with Emperor Hirohito, and a speech to the Diet, was part of Ottawa's rethinking of both the Japanese and the Asian relationships. Some of Canada's largest enterprises had offices in Tokyo, but that involved mostly resource companies and offices of the banks and pension funds. Aggressive importing of Canadian goods by Japan's large trading houses has helped increase sales, but limits direct contact between the two countries' executives. Moreover, Canadian business still concentrates its sales efforts in Tokyo, where international competition is fiercest and where the chances of short-term success are limited. The Mulroney government opened four offices in strategic cities, with External Affairs bureaucrats serving as consul general. Official visits helped cement the bilateral relationship, by Nakasone in January 1986 and by Mulroney in May 1986. Two private-sector study groups, one initiated by Mulroney, and the second by Jean Chrétien, have made proposals to governments and private sectors about a possible future trade pact.

Yet Canadian exports have hardly kept up to the levels of European and Australian competitors. Fewer than 500 Canadians per year study Japanese there, while Australia has 15,000 students immersed in Japanese-language training. Twenty years ago, Japan aspired to have 100,000 foreign students at Japanese universities. Today, that number is pushing 300,000, led by the University of Tokyo and the leading engineering and technical schools, a magnet for Chinese and other Asian students.

Canada's diplomatic corps in Tokyo, despite the size and grandeur of Raymond Moriyama's embassy, remains small relative to its staff in London, Paris, or Rome – capitals with far less economic and commercial potential for Canada. Japan alone invents and registers more patents – a key indicator of subsequent commercial production – in the United States than Britain, France, and Germany combined. Only about 5 per cent of Canadian exports to Japan are manufactured goods. In 1986, Mulroney, standing in his suite at the New Otani, looking out over the lights of Tokyo after a long day of meetings, asked me two questions.

First, seeing a subway station, he asked me how many people go through it every day. My response was two million, more than the ridership of Toronto's subway and Montreal's *métro* combined. Second, he asked about the audience and the companies at the breakfast meeting the next morning. I replied that this was the cream of corporate Japan, whose executives controlled massive global operations. To cite one, the Mitsui keiretsu group consists of 525 companies, and the trading company Mitsui Busson does more annual trade than Canada's GNP. "My God," he relied, "that's big, even in Baie-Comeau!"

VIII

In 1988, at a meeting of the Asia Pacific Conference on Pacific Cooperation and Information Technology (PACIT 88) at the Atwater Institute in Vancouver, I was approached about an initiative to create a Pacific Economic Cooperation Council (PECC) secretariat in Vancouver. PECC's first meeting, as the Pacific Community Seminar, was held in September 1980 in Canberra, Australia, at the initiative of Prime Ministers Masayoshi Ohira of Japan and Malcolm Fraser of Australia. Delegates – usually one senior government official, one business leader, and one academic or professional – from eleven countries attended (Australia, Canada, Indonesia, Malaysia, Japan, New Zealand, the Pacific Island states [Fiji, Papua New Guinea, and Tonga], the Philippines, Singapore, South Korea, Thailand, and the United States). Also attending were representatives of the Asian Development Bank, PBEC, and PAFTAD. At this stage, PECC provided a regional forum to promote policy ideas and coordinate policy on economic development in the region. Over time, as agenda items expanded with regional economic growth, PECC built up staff expertise and provided information and analytical support to Asia–Pacific Economic

Cooperation (APEC) ministerial meetings and other working groups, including private-sector participants.

I sent the attached memo to the PMO, after talking to Peter White:

> September 19, 1988
> TO: Peter White,
> Principal Secretary, PMO
> RE: PEC Secretariat
>
> I just returned from Vancouver where I attended a meeting of the Asia-Pacific/Atwater Conference on Information Technology in the Pacific Rim. During the meetings, I was approached by Dr. Suburo Okita, an old friend who has covered the waterfront in Japan, as civil servant, University President, Foreign Affairs minister, member of Brundtland Commission, etc.
>
> His specific query to me was the possibility of placing the Secretariat of PEC in Vancouver. A word of background. Over the last few years, Japan has been promoting the idea of greater cooperation/collaboration among the Pacific Rim countries. Japan does not want to be too aggressive, obviously with overtones of a Greater Co-Prosperity Sphere in the ears of many Asian countries. PM Nakasone, and more recently Takeshita, have advanced the idea of a Pacific OECD Secretariat, among other initiatives as a means of providing more collaboration among the Pacific Rim countries.
>
> Like all such initiatives there is lots of tension, hand holding, and hesitancy. The Japanese want to advance the idea but are reluctant to push it. The Americans, sensibly, see the merit in the approach but can't get too close to the Japanese.
>
> Okita's message to me is that both the Americans and the Japanese see Canada's role as both central and vital. They would back the secretariat in Vancouver. Canada has been pussyfooting, although I understand Joe Clark was forthright in favour on his recent tour in Japan.
>
> When the PM called me last week, I mentioned Okita's remarks to me. In my view, Canada should get out on this initiative and publicly, through diplomatic channels, and perhaps publicly be aggressive on a) the need for a Secretariat, b) offer to have it in Vancouver.
>
> I suggest you ask PCO for an update and inter-departmental assessment, and the pros/cons of a 'Vancouver initiative'.

IX

Few experts in the academic world, the diplomatic corps, and even the CIA expected, let alone foretold, the extraordinary events that would lead to the implosion in 1991 of the USSR, a federation of fifteen states. The biggest, Russia, itself with seventy-six republics and Moscow as its capital, has eleven time zones, shares a border with fourteen countries (more than any other), has the largest land mass (bigger than western Europe), and has 275 million inhabitants (roughly equal to Canada and the United States combined) and a GNP equal to Ontario's. Military and space expenditures drained the real economy, and rising imports of food illustrated the severe limits of Soviet central planning, as more goods were bartered, foreign currency was in short supply, and television (a domestic tool for propaganda) was gradually revealing the economic discrepancies between the West and the Soviet Union, which lacked most consumer goods.

In fact, internal political tensions were rising in Soviet society. Most young citizens, with men conscripted for the massive military forces, knew about past rebellions in Hungary and Czechoslovakia. Before the Soviet Union imploded in December 1991, the entire postwar Soviet empire, like a chair with four legs – Russia, Ukraine, eastern Europe, and central Asia – was held together by Communist control from Moscow, backed by the military and the KGB. The whole set-up was actually perverse: in past colonial empires, the colonies provided raw materials to the home country to be turned into manufactured product, like the old British Empire, but here countries like East Germany and other central and eastern European nations manufacturing, while the Soviet Union produced the feedstock, like aluminum, coal, oil and gas, and other raw materials. In this Cold War atmosphere, with nuclear threats a constant worry, underscored by the Cuban missile crisis of 1962, various Western leaders attempted to lower the temperature and instill a climate of detente. U.S. President Ronald Reagan, elected in 1980, was seen as a hardliner, and openly called the sprawling bloc an "evil empire." In truth, it was much worse, illustrated by gulags and the police treatment of Soviet citizens at home without access to justice.

Soviet leaders like Brezhnev, Chernenko, and Andropov had collective memories of Soviet sacrifice during the Second World War, including their own personal experience fighting the Nazi invaders. President Reagan's planned for a renewed military build-up and a missile defence system, the Strategic Defense Initiative (SDI), often belittled as star wars, which was a technological investment intended to protect the United States against Soviet intercontinental ballistic missiles flying over Canada and submarine-launched missiles. Assuring the American public on 23 March 1983 about the doctrine of mutual assured destruction (MAD), which he described as a "suicide pact," the president called on American scientists and engineers to develop the SDI and invited allied countries to join, in an effort to make nuclear weapons obsolete. Clearly, the Soviets simply could not afford this kind of financial investment and required new thinking. By design, the Kremlin approved a recommendation from First Secretary Konstantin Chernenko, to allow the minister of agriculture, the relatively young, abstemious, and knowledgeable Mikhail Gorbachev, to visit Canada, secretly carrying a letter to Prime Minister Trudeai, asking him to be a helpful mediator in the corridors of power in Moscow and Washington.

Gorbachev visited Canada in May 1983, stopping first in Ottawa, where he met Trudeau and opposition leaders Erik Nielsen (interim Tory leader) and Ed Broadbent (NDP). He then travelled with Canada's ebullient agriculture minister, Eugene Whalen, to visit farms around Ontario and Alberta in a chartered, forty-year-old, propeller-driven Convair, leased from Air Ontario, because External Affairs and Treasury Board refused to lease an Air Canada DC-9 to host the agriculture minister of one of Canada's biggest customers of farm products. Gorbachev was accompanied by Alexander Yakovlev, the former Soviet ambassador to Canada and an outcast to Kremlin hardliners, but a Gorbachev confidant, who largely drafted his new approach, based on *glasnost* (openness) and *perestroika* (reform). In Ottawa, as Soviet ambassador, Yakovlev had met with Pierre Trudeau frequently, often over dinner, and he explained to him the inner workings of this secretive, almost paranoid society, with a third-rate economy but first-rate scientific and military capabilities, including in space. Trudeau listened intently and learned much from a reputable source about the desire for change in traditional Soviet policies. When he met Gorbachev in Ottawa, they struck up a close friendship. Gorbachev knew he now had a close, knowledgeable contact among Western leaders.

Gorbachev and Trudeau held two meetings, a private dinner at 24 Sussex Drive and a 90-minute session about issues well beyond Gorbachev's official purpose, agriculture. Speaking without notes, Gorbachev discussed arms control, cruise-missile testing, and the Geneva talks on intermediate-range missile deployment, and, while sticking to the conventional Soviet positions, privately he showed much more flexibility. Trudeau, to his credit, when asked about Reagan's hardline rhetoric, indicated the political climate he faced at home. During the visit to Eugene Whalen's farm,

Trudeau, Yakovlev, and Gorbachev spoke about the need for Soviet reforms, like liberalizing the economy from the strait-jacket of central planning (i.e., *perestroika*) and more individual freedom and political changes (i.e., *glasnost*). Shortly after his Canadian trip, thanks to Gorbachev's interventions with General Secretary Yuri Andropov, Yakovlev was brought back to Moscow to run the Institute of World Economy and International Relations, a unit of the USSR Academy of Sciences. In Ottawa, his replacement was his close friend, Yevgeny Primakov, who arrived in Canada in 1985.

A week after Gorbachev's visit, Trudeau attended the G7 meetings in Williamsburg, Virginia, hosted by President Reagan. In the two days of talks, among both the leaders and the foreign ministers, Canada stood alone, almost a personal indulgence of the prime minister, despite his glowing congratulations to the president at the end of the conclave. It was up to Margaret Thatcher to recognize the growing gap between the NATO partners in North America, the hardline, hawkish U.S. position on nuclear deterrence and Canada's softer approach. When she visited Ottawa on 25 September 1983 and had her first meeting with the new Conservative leader, Brian Mulroney, and spoke to Parliament, she also listened intently to Pierre Trudeau's account of his discussions in May with Mikhail Gorbachev. Her trip occurred shortly after the Soviets had shot down a Korean Airlines commercial airliner, killing 269 people aboard the flight heading to Seoul, about which the Soviet military, not the Kremlin or Foreign Affairs. issued a statement. Who, in fact, was in charge in the Soviet government – the hardliners following in the footsteps of Andropov, who had died on 23 February 1983, his successor, Konstantin Chernenko, or other political rivals in the Kremlin? Taking advantage of Trudeau's insights about Gorbachev, Thatcher adopted a new mission, to become an expert on the Soviet system. She hosted two seminars in London, inviting mostly outsiders – academics who had travelled to the Soviet Union – and ignoring the list given her by officials in Whitehall. She was emboldened by her election win on 9 June 1983, the largest majority since 1945, owing in part to the collapse of the Labour vote, by over 3 million, but her real confidant was the U.S. president. The fact that Gorbachev visited 10 Downing Street in mid-December was a signal from the Kremlin that Thatcher, not Trudeau, was the key bridge to the U.S. administration. Her memorable phase after the meetings, "Yes, he's the sort of guy you can do business with," won plaudits in both Washington and Moscow, a sign of a new opening in East–West relations, a reduction in Cold War tensions, and a potential step-by-step approach to disarmament.

Trudeau continued his international travels as part of his plan to focus on disarmament, meeting leaders in Third World countries, including China, but at this point, the media speculated whether this peace initiative was inspired more by domestic politics than by a serious approach to foreign policy. The Reagan administration, and the president himself, knowing the hardliners were still in control in the Kremlin, had mixed reactions, but quietly accepted this travel as a bit of self-indulgence by a retiring prime minister with novel ideas on serious global issues. As Opposition leader, Brian Mulroney gave quiet but constrained support, saying the Conservative party was always in favour of peace. In another sense, Trudeau's timing was terrible, with growing unrest among provincial governments, key ministers departing Ottawa for the greener patches of the private sector, and no movements in the polls (in October 1983, Gallup gave the Conservatives 62 per cent favourability). Despite Martin Goldfarb's private polling advice that he could win re-election, Trudeau took a walk in the snow on 29 February 1984 and announced his resignation.

In the months immediately after the September 1984 election, the new Conservative government didn't see the Soviet Union as a policy priority, despite being a neighbour across the Arctic border. In the years following Mikhail Gorbachev's emergence as general secretary in March 1985, as his *glasnost* and *perestroika* took hold, tensions eased, as foreign leaders like Margaret Thatcher, who visited Moscow in March 1987, and Ronald Reagan, who hosted Gorbachev in Washington in December 1987, signed a new IFM treaty, a particular priority for NATO and other countries in Europe, so close to the Soviet border. In 1991, Ottawa was as surprised as other governments about events taking place in Moscow and other Soviet capitals. Clearly, the emergence of a Polish pontiff, John Paul II, in 1978, the Solidarity-led coalition of Lech Wałęsa in Poland, and the fall of the Berlin Wall in November 1989 generated intense media speculation about Communist hegemony, but experts assumed that Mikhail Gorbachev could negotiate a new, reformed Soviet Union. His plan, the Union of Sovereign States, a treaty discussed by deputies and the State Council, would have preserved common institutions like the Central Bank, control over the military, and macroeconomic functions. At a meeting in December 1991 in Belovesk Forest, near Minsk, in Belarus, Boris Yeltsin and the leaders of Ukraine and Kazakhstan put forward an alternative plan, the Commonwealth of Independent States, which in effect dissolved the Soviet Union. It was clear internally in Soviet capitals that Gorbachev was being sidelined. Western leaders, NATO commanders, and the media had little real understanding of Soviet events in this fateful year.

During the autumn of 1991, various Soviet republics declared their independence, but each new "state" had no central bank, no currency, no passport, and none of the other national institutions taken for granted in the West. A failed coup in August 1991, when Gorbachev was on holidays in the Crimea, with the nuclear button removed from his control, even if temporarily, as exposed by a BBC radio report, shocked Western nations, which knew that the USSR might be a third-rate economy, but was a scientific and military superpower. The coup leaders, conservative hardliners who detested Gorbachev's reforms, were members of the Politburo, the KGB, and the Defence Ministry. Leaders of NATO met in November, and British Prime Minister John Major, representing the G7 leaders, flew to Moscow to discuss a massive aid package, but it soon became clear that the event cycle was overtaking Gorbachev's capacity to mould an internal political consensus.

For me, the coup events made troubling news, because of my personal involvement in Poland and other countries of central and eastern Europe. I had travelled there in two capacities. First, when I was a consultant for a Japanese investment bank, working on privatization of state corporations, I visited several capitals and spoke to senior economic officials. Second, as an academic collaborating in research, I had very good contacts in Poland, including with the Polish Academy of Sciences. When I first visited that country in 1975, I witnessed at first hand communist rule, including Soviet troops in Polish cities. During the next decade, I made several visits to Warsaw and other cities in central and eastern Europe, but in Poland my hosts were personal friends of a young cardinal from Cracow, Karol Józef Wojtyła, who had transferred to the Vatican and was soon to become the first Polish pope, John Paul II. By 1991, I had returned to York University, but was still providing advice to Prime Minister Mulroney, often by written memos, background papers, speech drafts, and Sunday-night phone calls. On 18 December 1991, I walked in the front door of our Toronto home, remorseful that I yet again had been away for my daughter's birthday, on the 16th. Earlier that day, I had flown from Moscow to Paris, and then from Paris to Toronto, where I was studying my extensive notes from my three weeks in Moscow and central Asia, mostly in Kyrgyzstan. When I arrived at home, my wife asked me to call the prime minister.

He took my call and, after a few pleasantries, asked me what I was doing in the Soviet Union. I explained the sequence of my travel there. I had been asked by Monte Kwinter, former Ontario minister of trade in David Peterson's Liberal government (1985–90), and retained by the government of Kyrgyzstan, to write an economic-development plan for this new republic, which meant a trip to its capital, Bishkek. We would fly to Moscow, there meet the Kyrgyz president, Askar Akayev, and then travel to Bishkek – a major Soviet science city – a distance the equivalent of Toronto to Vancouver. In Kyrgyzstan, we met senior civil servants and university presidents and toured the country by car and helicopter, an Antinov 212, meeting civil servants, academic experts, and mining specialists. The republic had one of the biggest gold deposits in the world, called Kumtor.

When we first met President Akayev in Moscow, he had just returned from a meeting at the Kremlin, where the leaders of the fifteen republics decided to go their own independent ways, with a formal announcement to come on 25 December, with the Russian flag flying over the Kremlin. When I asked him naïvely where Gorbachev fitted in to this new arrangement, he was blunt: unemployed.

Prime Minister Mulroney, listening to this narrative, was speechless, a rare occasion for an Irishman. Catching his breath, he then asked why the Canadian ambassador in Moscow had not given notice, in a cable, and there was nothing equivalent to my story in the *New York Times,* or other media sources like the BBC. I mentioned that Monte Kwinter and I took the Canadian ambassador, Michel Bell, and his commercial officer for lunch the day after we first arrived in Moscow, told him our tour plans, and received a "Good luck" but a very doubtful, equivocal reaction to our mandate to study the Kyrgyz economy. Two weeks later, when we returned to Moscow from Bishkek, we took Bell for lunch at the Savoy Hotel, at a cost of $257, which I paid, and recounted to him what we had found in Kyrgyzstan – a fabulously beautiful country, which I later dubbed the "Switzerland of central Asia."

My conversation with the prime minister was quite long, but when we finished, he offered me and my family best wishes for the Christmas holidays, and that, I thought, was that. Early Boxing Day he called, this time a bit curt and to the point. He asked me to repeat, as best as I could remember, what we discussed on the 18th. I repeated the saga, including the story that the Russian flag would be flying over the Kremlin on Christmas Day.

Mulroney admitted that he had been shocked by my narrative on 18 December. He was even more shocked when, on Christmas Eve, Mikhail Gorbachev had called from his statehouse in the Lenin (now Sparrow) Hills outside Moscow, repeating exactly what we had been told by Askar Akayev. Boris Yeltsin indeed had become the president of Russia, but faced constant opposition from hardliners, including military generals, who had little use for democratic ideals, elections, and political dissent. The nuclear codes and the military transfer of supreme command was given to the new president of the remaining, though immense Russian Federation, and Gorbachev signed the decree removing himself from his job as president of the USSR.

The Yeltsin era created massive turmoil in Russia, with many supporters of the coup against Gorbachev now seizing power in many of Russia's seventy-six republics. American consulting firms received U.S. financial support to help Russia privatize vast corporate enterprises, and growing tensions emerged about who controlled the formerly Soviet nuclear arsenal. U.S. Vice President Al Gore toured the capitals of several former Soviet republics and had severe doubts about who was benefitting from American largesse: former Soviet citizens or American consultants? One of the mysteries of the new Russia was the rise of the oligarchs, and their sudden vast wealth. I heard many stories about them, including a high-sourced insight from a former KGB operative. On 14 July 1990, West German Chancellor Helmut Kohl flew to Moscow to meet Mikhail Gorbachev, and over long discussions, first in Moscow and then in Stavropol, in Gorbachev's private dacha, the two leaders discussed the role of East Germany, Soviet troops stationed there, and Kohl's plans for German unification. In Europe, Kohl faced deep unease from both Margaret Thatcher and François Mitterrand on an enlarged Germany, a view not held by Brian Mulroney, whose views he quietly shared with them to help assuage their worst fears, especially if Gorbachev would agree to Germany's remaining a member of NATO. Gorbachev did consent to the creation of the enlarged Germany, incorporating 16 million people and a territory bigger than Ireland and Israel combined, and the most prosperous country in the Warsaw Pact. Gorbachev also agreed to its staying in NATO, but in return Germany would pay some 50–80 billion Deutsche Marks, or about U.S.$31 billion–$50 billion today. But pay that to whom?

My information was that the money was paid not to the Soviet government but to the Communist party in Moscow. This large amount was gradually recycled to offshore accounts in Switzerland, Cyprus, and elsewhere. It was this pool of money that allowed Soviet insiders access to an enormous horde of U.S. dollars to buy up share coupons in aerospace, aluminum, forestry, mining, and oil and gas conglomerates. Insiders had the wherewithal to purchase, for pennies, shares distributed to individual former Soviet citizens as part of the privatization program, from a desperate populace suffering from massive unemployment and the collapse of health and education benefits provided free under the old system, and facing few prospects of employment in this "cold shower" economic reform.

Russia still remained a scientific and military superpower with a nuclear arsenal, despite its weak economy (equal to the GNP of Spain) and massive social problems. Yeltsin, in spite of his fondness for vodka, his total ignorance of a market economy, and his appreciation that Russia needed Western assistance, cultivated close personal relations with G7 leaders and walked a delicate political line between the fractious members of the Politburo, the secret service, the military, and Russian citizens thirsting for the freedoms and consumer comforts taken for granted in the West. Within the Kremlin, there was fear that Russia itself might break up, so a new KGB officer was appointed deputy head of management in Yeltsin's administration, in charge of the Kremlin's relations with the regional governments. Two years later, Yeltsin resigned and turned power over to the young KGB officer, Vladimir Putin, appointed on Christmas Day 2000.

After the breakup of the Soviet Union, Canada was a natural partner for Russia, a neighbour by geography and shared challenges in the Arctic and an economic powerhouse in the sectors vital for Russian industrial rejuvenation. Prime Minister Mulroney made forceful presentations to Russian and other leaders, hosted Askar Akayev in Ottawa, and offered an aid package. Ukraine, divided from Russia by language, religion, and history, first voted for independence on 3 December 1991, and Mulroney announced full diplomatic recognition, before other countries, including the United States, would follow similar measures after Secretary of State James Baker visited Kiev in 1992. Canada was an ideal host for the Yeltsin–Clinton summit in Vancouver in April 1993, the 24th time the leaders of the two superpowers met in fifty years of summitry. Brian Mulroney hosted the first day's lunch and offered a G7 aid package of over $30 billion, to be confirmed at the G7 summit in Tokyo, attended by Mulroney's successor, Kim Campbell.

X

In a metaphysical sense, the Conservative party has long had an attachment to the Arctic and the north. In 1872, Prime Minister John A. Macdonald sent George-Étienne Cartier, his preferred successor, to London to negotiate the purchase of Rupert's Land – the Hudson's Bay Company's territories, which encompassed what is now northern Quebec and northern

Ontario, Manitoba, and parts of Saskatchewan, Alberta, and Nunavut, covering about 3¼ million square kilometres – settling on a price of £300,000, payable by a forty-year loan from the British government.

Perhaps no Canadian leader put the Canadian north so front and centre as John Diefenbaker, who campaigned in the 1957 election on his Northern Vision, a list of promises to make the Arctic a part of mainstream Canadian society. With the help and advice of his visionary aides, Roy Faibish and Meryl Menzies, he laid out his promise, "Roads to Resources": "A National Highway policy should be launched to provide highways for peace and development wherein the Federal Government will make contributions to or share in cooperation with the provinces. The challenge of Communism now and in the years ahead demands that our vast northern resources be made accessible and available to industry ... (and) forge the shield of freedom and contribute to the survival of the Free World."

In practical terms, despite sporadic progress, Canada as an Arctic nation suffers from three defaults. First, most Canadians have never visited the Arctic, so the images of Arctic life, the potential for economic development, and other possibilities like the arts and education had no real champions, in the House of Commons, the Ottawa bureaucracy, or voters in the south. Second, post-1945 Canadian concern about the Arctic had a Cold War colouring, with the communist Soviet Union directing its long-range ballistic missiles across the Arctic towards Canada and the United States. Canadian public opinion often waivered, recognizing the need to join NORAD with the Americans in 1958, but also having an ambivalence over defence obligations for both North America as a three-ocean continent and article 5 of the NATO treaty. Diefenbaker's waffling during the 1962 Cuban missile crisis set a Cold War pattern for other prime ministers, where the more hawkish American officials insisted that Canada's policy positions necessitated financial commitments, so Canadian officials needed diplomatic nuance and political finesse to deal with the White House and congressional leaders.

The United States and Japan knew that people operating ocean-based trade and global supply were starting to realize that the shortest sea route between Pacific Rim countries and Europe ran across the Arctic: the legendary Northwest Passage (see Figure 5.4). Canada woke up to these possibilities in 1969, when, on orders from President Richard Nixon, the USS *Manhattan*, a 300-metre refurbished oil tanker, the largest icebreaker in the world, passed through the Northwest Passage during the summer, accompanied by the Canadian Coast Guard icebreaker *Sir John A.*

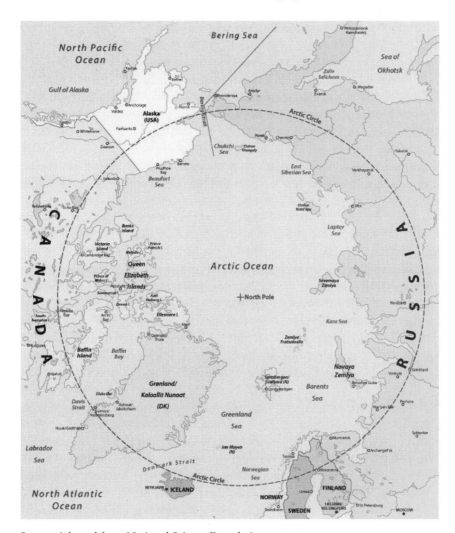

Source: Adapted from National Science Foundation.

Figure 5.4 *Les routes maritimes polaires.*

Macdonald, defying Canada's claim that the Arctic Archipelago was part of Canada's internal waters.

When Mikhail Gorbachev spoke in Murmansk in October 1987 about a "zone of peace" in the Arctic, various European leaders, NATO countries, and the media were taken by surprise. Canada, of course, had its own priorities in the Arctic, including the unsettled boundary of its north and the Supreme Court's admonition of "Use it or lose it." The Mulroney PMO had a satellite photo of the Arctic hanging in its boardroom, with competing boundary markers showing the disputed territories. In January 1987, the PMO and the Department of National Defence, and Minister of Health Jake Epp, following up on an idea put forward by Ian Shugart, decided to send a medical team to the high Arctic, in part to undertake medical checkups of families and children. To the surprise of the medical team, its findings showed very high levels of toxins in the children's stomachs, and also in some of the animals they studied, yet there were no chemical factories in Canada within 1,000 miles (625 kilometres). As subsequent events would show, the northern Soviet Union, including the areas around Norilsk, that country's second largest, most northern city above the Arctic Circle, was immensely polluted, with air, animals, fish, and water radiating towards Canada.

Scandinavian countries were serious about the Arctic, had cities in northern latitudes close to the Arctic Circle, and devoted resources for educational spending and economic development. In June 1977, three northern nations – Canada, Denmark, and the United States – established the first Inuit Circumpolar Conference, a successor to the Nordic Council, founded in 1952, and hoped the Soviets would join. The timing was propitious, when energy firms were shifting exploration from the Middle East to other areas, including the North Sea, the Atlantic offshore near Newfoundland, and the high Arctic, including Prudhoe Bay in Alaska. Canadian firms active at the time included Gulf Canada, owned by Paul Reichman, and Dome Petroleum, with close contacts to the Liberal party.

In 1989, Tom Axworthy, president of the [Walter and Duncan] Gordon Foundation and former principal secretary to Pierre Trudeau, recruited a group of policy advisers to examine the feasibility of a new Arctic Council, envisaged as an international organization dedicated to the non-military use of the Arctic, involving the eight countries that have land and territory there. The policy advisers included Bill Fox and me, with leadership from Franklin Griffiths, professor at the Centre of Eastern Europe and Russia (now part of the Munk Centre at the University of Toronto), Kyra Montagu (Walter Gordon's daughter), and Rosemarie Kuptana. The study plan was to hold hearings across Canada and schedule meetings with foreign experts from the Arctic nations. The initial report was given to Prime Minister Mulroney. Gorbachev was now general secretary of the Communist party, offering glimmers of a thaw in Cold War rhetoric. When he spoke in Murmansk, the Soviet's largest military base, calling for an Arctic "Zone of Peace," he signalled a striking change of tone and the potential for formal international cooperation with the West. He wanted to attend G7 annual meetings, the so-called G8, but behind the scenes desperately needed Western aid and financial support.

On a visit to Leningrad in 1989, Brian Mulroney endorsed the idea of Western support, and went one step further, calling for a council of Arctic countries. Arctic cooperation, especially in non-defence topics, was not a new concept. Maxwell Cohen, a law professor at McGill, floated such an idea, and conceived an Arctic Basin Treaty, which could foster economic, environmental, and scientific cooperation among Arctic nations. That approach became the legal framework of Mulroney's speech in St Petersburg. The Canadian prime minister was now the senior G7 leader, and he knew this initiative would take time, caught in the cross-currents of international energy policy, the legacy of Cold War defence policy, boundary disputes in the Arctic, and the treatment of the people who live there, the Indigenous inhabitants, including those in the Soviet Union. He also knew that some countries outside the region, like Japan, had a keen interest in it, not only to exploit minerals, and substantial scientific and engineering achievements in cold-weather technologies.

The Americans initially showed little interest, while Nordic countries, especially Finland, became policy activists after Gorbachev's speech and Mulroney's bold proposal. Negotiations proceeded, and the first initiative became the Arctic Environmental Protection Strategy in 1991. On his trip to the Arctic in 1992, Mulroney, now having the final report of the Arctic Council study group, spoke of the council as a vehicle to focus on multilateral issues in the region with Canada, Denmark, Finland, Iceland, Norway, Russia, Sweden, and the United States. To date, it was the only regional organization that included all eight countries and directly involved Indigenous peoples' organizations as "permanent participants." After a change of government in Ottawa in 1993, Prime Minister Jean Chrétien chose Mary Simon as Canada's first ambassador to the Arctic Council and lobbied President Bill Clinton to have the United States join, which it did.

XI

In the late 1970s, Canada and the United States established a Bilateral Research Consultation Group on Long-Range Transport of Air Pollutants. It produced a report outlining how large portions of North America were sensitive to acidic deposition, so both countries issued a joint statement making a commitment to reduce certain types of transboundary air pollution identified as injurious to human health, ecosystems, and property. In the more formal "Memorandum of Intent Concerning Transboundary Air Pollution," both countries in August 1980 agreed to negotiate a bilateral agreement by 1 June 1981. They passed legislation to regulate air pollution. In Canada, where property rights are provincial matters, the federal role is primarily advisory; when "the Environmental Minister determines that 'an air contaminant emitted ... in Canada creates or contributes to the creation of air pollution that may reasonably be expected to constitute a significant danger to the health, safety or welfare of persons in any other country,' that officer shall "recommend to the [cabinet] ... such specific emission standards ... as he [or she] may consider appropriate for the elimination or significant reduction of that danger."

When the Conservatives won the 1984 election, few in Canada would see the new prime minister as an environmentalist. His choice for the environment post, Susan Blais-Grenier – despite her credentials: attended the Sorbonne, government experience, MP from Quebec, where environmental issues had salience – became an instant disaster. In the early cost-savings measures, department by department, she chose cuts of $50 million to one of the most high-profile organizations, the Canada Wildlife Fund. At a meeting in the PMO boardroom to discuss the cuts, when Ed Clark from Finance announced these measures, little attention was paid to the political fallout, and more to ministers who refused to accept departmental savings, especially from Joe Clark at External and his forceful chief of staff, Jodi White. Meanwhile, morale in the Department of the Environment plummeted. In reality, despite these initial missteps, Mulroney knew and cared about the environment. He was born and raised in Baie-Comeau, a pulp-and-paper town, where this powerhouse industry had a history of generating effluents from washing and bleaching pulp and high sulphur discharges of wastewater and black liquor.

During the 1983 leadership campaign and the election campaign in summer 1984, Mulroney visited many paper towns and announced his promises on acid rain in Sault Ste Marie, standing with Jim Kelleher, the Conservative candidate. Moreover, as CEO of the Iron Ore Company, which had close relations with the steel sector, a huge consumer of coal, Mulroney knew well the economics of these industries, grasped the need for new investment in the latest technology and equipment, and understood that if the Americans acted on acid rain, Canada couldn't be a laggard. He said as much quite openly in cabinet and caucus, and in his first meeting, as Opposition leader, with President Reagan in 1984, he left no doubt that acid rain was a personal priority. When he became prime minister, he knew that the flow of sulphur dioxide from the United States vastly exceeded the flow in the opposite direction, by a factor of three or four to one.

During this period, despite growing public awareness of environmental factors on specific files and events – coastal erosion, shipping calamities, water shortages, weather disasters – the environmental movement consisted of single-issue pressure groups on matters like saving the whales, stopping the trade in furs, and protecting the elephant population and activist movements fighting child poverty and seeking shelter for the homeless. The 1980s was a watershed moment for environmental policies. Science had made huge progress, assisted by serious research in the universities, a better grasp of the disastrous effects of oil-spills, and new understanding about climate change. While environmental issues were on the margins in the political arena, the growing evidence, often fragmented and isolated, became more central to specific industrial sectors and groups. The media became a player, especially as 1980s' environmental catastrophes had a global reach, from India's Bhopal gas leak in December 1984 and Ukraine's Chernobyl nuclear disaster in April 1986 to Alaska's *Exxon Valdez* oil-spill in March 1989. Government-funded programs for conservation and preservation, illustrated by the focus on national parks and the control of water supplies, extended to public concerns on the fisheries, notably the disappearance of certain species like the cod in the North Sea and off Newfoundland, and air and noise pollution. Governments and leading corporations now faced new, practical struggles, echoing the insight of Victor Hugo: "Greater than the thread of mighty armies is an idea whose time has come."

The Canada–United States Air Quality Agreement (Acid Rain Treaty) of 1991 was a remarkable policy achievement for Canada. It illustrated persistence in dealing with the American political system, the need to align federal policy with the provinces, and the reality that lobbyists, NGOs, and do-gooders often speak with their own sense of righteous conviction, but are blind to the political realities of different points of view. In retrospect, the acid-rain deal is part of a history of cross-border solutions, such as the Boundary Waters Treaty of 1909, which set up the International Joint Commission (IJC), consisting of six members, three from each country, and a rotating chair. Sixty years later, both countries expanded the IJC's role to include protecting water quality in the Great Lakes, as well as creating two related advisory groups: the Great Lakes Water Quality Board and the Great Lakes Science Advisory Board. In 1972, the two nations signed the Water Quality Agreement, one of the first international accords to set water-quality standards for boundary waters, a prelude to other international agreements like the United Nations Convention on the Law of the Sea of 1983.

The United States and Canada updated the 1972 Water Quality Agreement in 1978 to establish new standards, but, while not providing any tools of enforcement, they added issues of transboundary air pollution, such as identifying pollutant sources and the contributions of substances that affect environmental quality. Canada, ever self-righteous against the United States, was not blameless on transboundary air pollution, as shown by Trail, BC, where the giant aluminum smelter was sending fumes to Washington state. While the IJC accepted American allegations to that effect, nothing serious was done to address the problems. These events took place in an international environment of growing awareness, in Europe, in Japan, and in Britain, which had in 1956 passed the Clean Air Act to address the smoke-filled air in industrial cities, where electricity was generated from coal-fired furnaces, belching out huge amounts of sulphur dioxide that even taller chimneys didn't dissipate.

In the November 1980 U.S. election, when American society was riveted by the Iran hostage crisis, Ronald Reagan defeated Jimmy Carter, who considered himself an environmentalist in the mould of President Theodore Roosevelt. Environment issues were not a priority for anyone senior in the Reagan administration, or in the new Congress. At best, the new president felt that the evidence on acid rain was inconclusive, and the Environmental Protection Agency allowed higher emissions, especially from coal-producing states like Pennsylvania and West Virginia and coal-fired electricity-generating states like Indiana. During Trudeau's last mandate and the early months of Mulroney's first, there was little action, indeed, little attention, to acid rain, mainly because of the U.S. policy stalemate – senators and representatives, even from the same party – differed widely, i.e., those from coal-producing states and those from the "green" states, with California being the outlier.

Policy stalemates in Congress always become a challenge for foreign governments, their embassies, and the diplomatic corps, given the extreme fragmentation of the Washington policy system, where often cabinet secretaries themselves differ with each other or with the White House. In the autumn of 1983, Pierre Trudeau launched his peace initiative at a conference held at the University of Guelph, coinciding with changes in the U.S. administration, with the Canadian file taken over by cabinet members like Secretary of Defense Caspar Weinberger and Secretary of State George Shultz, who had dealt with many Canadian business executives, including while dean of the University of Chicago's Booth School of Business, who ipso facto was really in charge of the Canada file and put bilateral issues on hold. He was less impressed with the Canadian prime minister's peace initiative, seeing it more as a personal indulgence to please the Third World and an unwanted intrusion into the crucial five-power summitry of the nuclear powers. Even worse, American coal lobbyists made sure that members of Congress knew Canada was more an environmental crusader against American policies than a serious player, unwilling to cut its own emissions. Canada did announce a change in the spring of 1984, a 50 per cent reduction in ten years from the levels of 1980, but, as exemplified by Trudeau's peace initiative, the political landscape in Ottawa and Washington had changed drastically, much more profoundly than many Canadians realized.

Governments, academics, scientists, and some politicians were starting to take another look at traditional views on economic progress, and in the 1980s new ideas, terminology, and a "paradigm of sustainable development" came to prominence. Bestselling books like Lester R. Brown's *Building a Sustainable Society* (1981) and Norman Meyers's collection *Gaia: An Atlas of Planet Management* (1984) offered a different model for environmental management. In 1984, the United Nations General Assembly commissioned a group of twenty-two people from developed and developing nations to identify possible long-term environmental strategies for the international community up to the year 2000 and beyond. This Brundtland Commission, chaired by Gro Harlem Brundtland, prime minister of Norway, spent four years and submitted its report, *Our Common Future*, in 1987. The report, written in non-technical language, expressed the belief that economic growth, environmental sustainability, and social fairness and equity are not in conflict, thus opening a new approach where the three components of sustainable development, economy, environment, and society, are compatible, but they require new measures to apply integrated, sustainable solutions to a wide range of societal issues – agriculture and food security, biodiversity, energy choices, greening industry, population growth, to cite highlights – and the report acknowledged the political and social tension between economic growth and environmental protection.

Despite the successful Canadian work on acid rain, the political impact was not recognized, especially among the new, forceful, and outspoken environmental lobbyists. But in time, a series of measures, including the acid-rain treaty, creation of new national parks, the Halifax harbour cleanup, and revision of various environmental regulations, showed a new face to the Mulroney record. A succession of three strong, activist ministers – Tom McMillan, who replaced the hapless Blais-Grenier, Lucien Bouchard, who assumed office when his predecessor was defeated in the 1988 election, and Jean Charest, when Bouchard resigned over the Meech Lake Accord – with strong caucus support, including outspoken leadership from MPs Stan Darling and Pauline Browse, McMillan's parliamentary secretary, advanced the environmental agenda. Many MPs came from rural districts and were strong environmentalists, only too willing to lobby the PMO and present and past members of the cabinet, so the environmental agenda started to take shape, including six new national parks: Bruce Peninsula, Ellsemere Island, Grasslands, Pacific Rim, Rouge National Urban Park in and near Toronto (an effort led by Pauline Browse, a Scarborough MP), and South Moresby.

Antiquated and obsolete laws and regulations were updated, strengthened, and consolidated, such as the Clean Act, the Environmental Contaminants Act, and the Water Act. The Montreal Protocol on Substances That Deplete the Ozone Layer (September 1987) is, to many environmentalists, the crown jewel of the Mulroney government's environmental record. The meetings in Montreal focused on ozone-depleting substances (ODSs), the greenhouse gases that spur the radiative forcing of climate change. The negotiations on ozone depletion, or in more technical language, "the threat of chlorofluorocarbons (CFCs) destroying the atmospheric layer that protects life on earth from the sun's most harmful rays" – a key plank in the treaty – were assisted by Dupont's decision to switch from CFCs to substitutes. The Montreal Protocol elevated these issues among governments worldwide and put Canada in the global spotlight. More significantly, it raised the profile of the federal environment ministry and emboldened the science community to advise policymakers on climate change, the Kyoto Protocol (1997), and new measures in the Arctic.

In retrospect, Mulroney's December 1984 speech to the Economic Club in New York was telling. He heard directly from leading American business executives about the growing protectionist forces sweeping across boardrooms, their obsession with Japanese competition, and the potential need to raise tariffs or quotas on Japanese imports, including steel. The American steel industry was a technological laggard, and a huge emitter of pollution. Senator John Heinz (R–Penn.) was an uncompromising advocate for his state's steel sector. A flurry of activity, including suggestions from Allan Gotlieb, the Canadian ambassador in Washington, led to a declaration at the Reagan–Mulroney Quebec Summit in March 1985 appointing two special envoys on acid rain, U.S. Transport Secretary Drew Lewis and recently retired Premier Bill Davis of Ontario.

Lewis was an ideal candidate, coming from industrial Pennsylvania, managing the president's campaign there, a superb administrator, and he had a science degree, a Harvard MBA, and a year at MIT. Eight months later, on 19 June 1985, at a lunch in the White House cafeteria with Bill Davis and Allan Gotlieb, Lewis openly admitted that acid rain was caused by high levels of sulphur dioxide and nitrogen oxide, a human-made cocktail of emissions. That evening, International Affairs Minister Jim Kelleher, Derek Burney from External Affairs, and I attended a dinner at Canada's embassy with Canadian steel producers (Algoma was in Kelleher's riding) to discuss potential trade barriers. Before the dinner, we met several U.S. senators in their offices, and when Jim offered to be a sounding board on the Canadian side, Ambassador Gotlieb took that as a slight, which even Derek Burney thought was rather childish. The Davis–Lewis report, released a year later, left little doubt about the nature of the problem, and President Reagan sent a request to Congress for $5 billion to address the problems, in part with new technologies to address coal use and abatements of acid rain.

By this time, the U.S. administration was preoccupied with a series of international issues: nuclear disarmament, negotiating nuclear-missile treaties with the Soviet Union, and China's awakening as a force in Asia. Despite the Mulroney government's persistence, and regular telephone calls between Mulroney and Reagan, the acid-rain file had few champions in the White House or Congress, and it took the election of George H.W. Bush in November 1988 to push the file, which, Mulroney forcefully argued, was the test of good relations between the two nations. It helped enormously that Mulroney had kept his word on the Canadian side, convincing seven provinces to accept a legally binding agreement on acid rain, with, paradoxically, Nova Scotia as the last holdout, until Premier John Buchanan, staying at a resort in Digby, NS, heard a telling remark. Noting the gorgeous vista from the front porch, the premier was informed by the bartender: "It used to be beautiful, but the view now is marred by so many dead trees, caused by acid rain." Converted, Buchanan decided to sign.

The successful free-trade negotiations had changed the minds of many people in the U.S. Congress, and when the new Bush administration put forward major amendments to the Clean Air Act, including authorizing the Environmental Protection Agency (EPA) to establish standards "twice as stringent if they are found to be necessary, technologically feasible, and cost-effective." Catching up with other countries, these proposals would establish clean fuel and clean-fuelled vehicle programs and a national pilot program in California, which required new industry standards for clean-fuelled vehicles by 1999 – path-breaking initiatives. The Senate approved these amendments by a stunning eighty-nine to ten on 20 October 1990, and the House followed, 401 to twenty-five, on the 26th. These amendments, and the changes on emissions in Canada, laid the foundations for the acid-rain treaty, signed in Ottawa on 13 March 1991 by Bush and Mulroney, only a week before the latter's fifty-fourth birthday, another major example of the slow, arduous journey to forging international agreements.

XII

In 1975, the Association of University and Colleges in Canada (AUCC) appointed a Commission on Canadian Studies, chaired by Professor Thomas Symons, president of Trent University in Peterborough, Ontario. The Symons Commission consulted widely and focused on selected fields, including environmental studies, science and technology, and Canadian-study programs in foreign universities, including the six in New England, as well as those in Britain, France, and Italy. The final report recommended more resources for Canadian studies and more support from policy-makers, including private actors. Federal governments after 1945 had understood the role of the foreign programs, but the real influence came from champions, starting with Prime Ministers Lester Pearson, a diplomat who saw the advantages for the country's image, and Pierre Trudeau, whose swinging image, playful character, and intellectual prowess brought international acclaim. Richard Gwyn makes a telling comment: "Pearson won it for what he did; Trudeau wins it for what he is."

Decades ago, these programs were appreciated as what we would call national "branding," whereby foreign students might take a course on Canada's political institutions, social values, and forms of behaviour. Such efforts are instances of what Harvard's Joseph Nye, Jr, labelled "soft power" – as a contrast and complement to "hard" military power – in *Bound to Lead: The Changing Nature of American Power* (1990). Soft power has many manifestations – cultural policy, including the arts, political values and institutions, and foreign policies to attract or influence citizens and governments in other countries. Unlike many sceptics, who see the word "soft" as a pejorative, even the U.S. military, after its (mis)adventures in Vietnam, Iraq, and Afghanistan, now admits the role of economic development and soft power, sometimes with hard power as a last resort, in enhancing the country's influence and sharing of values.

Many other countries – such as Britain, France, and Japan – harness soft power as part of their foreign policy and leverage cuisine, language, the media, music, the performing arts, and sports to advance their national interests. There is a clear understanding that while countries generate soft power as a national resource, they exercise it through relationships and institutions, not by government edict. Despite deep cuts in government spending, David Cameron's Conservative government in Britain in 2015 actually increased foreign aid, including spending on cultural programs by the BBC and aid to voluntary youth organizations working overseas. The report of Britain's Strategic Defense and Security Review offered a forceful statement on that country's soft-power capacity, as orchestrated by institutions and instruments of British public and cultural diplomacy, such as the BBC World Service, the British Council, and private schools and universities. Indeed, people on both sides of the Brexit divide demonstrate how soft power can help their bewildered and divided land prepare to deal with the European Union.

Starting with Brian Mulroney, and following the endeavours of prime ministers like Jean Chrétien, Paul Martin, and now Justin Trudeau, Canada's soft power is a notable and powerful tool in the diplomatic arsenal for quiet diplomacy, trade policy, human rights, and negotiations on global issues, where Canada can set the example, and other countries may follow. Even Conservatives were shocked when the Harper government cut funding for Canadian studies in foreign universities, a piddling savings of $7.5 million a year. The value of soft power as a policy tool is shown by annual studies that compare 61 countries through the soft-power index, compiled by Portland, a strategic communications consultancy based in London, and the University of Southern California (USC) Center on Public Diplomacy (CPD) at USC Annenberg in Los Angeles. Their annual report measures the influence and reputation using objective data across six categories – government, culture, education, global engagement, enterprise, and digital – plus international polling from twenty-five countries representing every major region of the world. Not unexpectedly, France comes first, but countries like China are rising fast, devoting huge resources to soft power. See Table 5.1.

Canada's challenge is to keep an eye on global trends, using the lens of North America and its close alliance with the United States to understand how diplomatic, economic, social, and technological policies affect Canada. Both in the public sector, but also in the private sector, Canada

Table 5.1
Comparative Country Ranking of Soft Power

Country	Score	2018 rank	Score	2019 rank
France	75.76	1	80.28	1
Britain	75.72	2	79.47	2
United States	75.02	3	77.40	5
Germany	73.87	4	78.62	3
Canada	72.90	5	75.89	7
Japan	71.66	6	75.71	8
Switzerland	70.45	7	77.04	6
Australia	70.15	8	73.16	9
Sweden	69.32	9	77.40	4
Netherlands	67.89	10	74.03	12
China	50.50	28	51.25	27

Source: USC Center on Public Diplomacy, 2020

can serve as a partner to countries that need help. Its experiences in diplomacy, its economic relations with the United States, and its work with the Commonwealth and la Francophonie, the Organization of American States, and Asia strengthen its capacity at home, but also can be costly. Yet Canadian legislation and judicial decisions on assisted dying, bilingualism and multiculturalism, gay marriage, and gun control, to cite examples, now influence events elsewhere – including in the United States, where the red state–blue state division is widening on these kinds of social issues – through the new worlds of social media, data management, and computer surveillance, and affect international legal issues regarding privacy and intellectual property. But that approach will require a new level of vigilance by Canada's private sector, an innovation laggard among advanced economies, as well as by governments – to ensure that Canada becomes a truly competitive North American economy, as well as a global power, in the 21st century.

PART THREE

Canada's Future

6

Aboriginal Peoples: Wards of the State or Full Citizens?

Canada's Aboriginal Peoples – The Age of European Empires – The French Regime – The Royal Proclamation of 1763 – The American Revolution and the Indian Removal Act – The Confederation Regime and the 1876 Indian Act – Decades of Amendments and Little Progress – Post-1945 Reforms and Voting Rights – The Constitution-Making Regime – Truth and Reconciliation – Land Claims

Q: What did Indigenous Peoples call this land before Europeans arrived?
A: "OURS."

INTRODUCTION

To most Canadians interested in history, the nation's economic and social development began with the first French explorers in the early 1500s and the dramatic influx of European settlers a century later. The military and colonial regimes of the French, the British, and the Spanish across North America antedated Confederation in 1867, but this narrative rarely puts Aboriginal peoples, their rights, and their forms of justice at the forefront. In a pointed contrast to the interpretations of this long history, John Amagoalik, a witness before the Mackenzie Valley Pipeline Inquiry, set up in 1974 and headed by Mr Justice Thomas Berger, gave a dramatic response: "To you, Mr. Berger, it is a frontier, but to us, it is a homestead." His story typifies the governance challenges Canada faces as a society, with its dark, recessed, and racist past. John Amagoalik was only five when he, his family, and other Inuit were relocated from their homeland in northern Quebec to Grise Fiord and Resolute, both in what is now

Nunavut, in the early 1950s. This was the start of a movement by new and forceful advocacy groups like the Inuit Tapirisat of Canada, now called the Inuit Tapiriit Kanatami, to change government policy to protect Indigenous languages, heritage, and ways of life.

In the past twenty years, the "rights" revolution arising from the Constitution Act, 1982, the Royal Commission on Aboriginal Peoples (1991–96), and the Truth and Reconciliation Commission (2008–15) serves as testimony to a new awakening for Canadians. Further, cases and rulings before the Supreme Court of Canada have left no ambiguity that new approaches are required, that the federal government's traditional colonial lordship over land titles, human rights, and styles of governance must change. Slowly, the courts and Parliament are crafting new legal frameworks that shape political decisions across the country. For the political system, the event cycle brings new policy challenges to help move Aboriginal peoples to the centre of national political decision-making.

Few Canadians know the four-century history of Aboriginal governance, even though Aboriginal peoples have essentially kept to their original views of treaty rights. Federal funding to help them press their arguments has been perhaps a mixed blessing, as the courts rarely sided with their legal philosophy and legal thinking. However, the Aboriginal community still faces Ottawa's bureaucratic lethargy, an entrenched willingness to accept old rules as an impervious pattern for future actions, and a general unwillingness to recognize rewritten histories and narratives as a basis for retrospective learning and innovation.

Across the country, there is both deep confusion and a range of opinions on the policy issues, in part because the historical record is so one-sided and there are divisions in the Aboriginal community. The media, especially the publicly funded CBC, were very late actors on the Aboriginal stage. Certainly, on such matters as the racism of the Indian Act of 1876, the shock and horror caused by revelations about residential schools, and the denial of fundamental rights to Indigenous peoples, there is growing awareness of the need for fundamental change, even if the speed and direction of policy change are open to debate. Public opinion shows a high level of optimism on this sensitive file – a comprehensive Angus Reid survey suggests that more than six in ten (61 per cent) people are hopeful about future relations between Indigenous and non-Indigenous citizens. On the general proposition that the country has a moral and legal obligation to maintain and improve the Aboriginal quality of life, including on Indigenous reserves, seven in ten (68 per cent) agree, but less so in provinces where conditions are in fact worsening – Manitoba, Saskatchewan, and Alberta.

The poll divides 2,455 respondents into hardliners, opposed to any special status, accommodation, or special consideration for Indigenous peoples; the wary, closer to the hardliners but more sympathetic on some issues; and the sympathetic, more aligned with the next category, advocates, who strongly favour rights for and amends to Indigenous peoples. Hardliners tend to be older, wealthier, and male from the prairies, while most advocates are younger, with university degrees, and live in Ontario and Quebec. Among Indigenous respondents – 6 per cent of the total, roughly equal to their proportion of the population – more are sympathetic or advocates, but some are wary or hardliners. On a fundamental question like Indigenous independence and self-governance, the divisions among the whole body of respondents are notable: hardliners and the wary are joined by the sympathetic, meaning that two-thirds share the belief that Indigenous communities should be "governed by the same systems and rules as other Canadians." Only the advocates feel that they should be "moving towards more independence and control over their own affairs."

As more young Aboriginals advance their careers as political activists, or indeed enter the political fray as legislators, their compatriots face a wakeup call for fundamental change (see Figure 6.1). Two recent books, *Unsettling Canada: A National Wake-up Call* (2015), by Arthur Manuel and Grand Chief Ron Derrickson, and *Surviving Canada: Indigenous Peoples Celebrate 150 Years of Betrayal* (2017), ed. Myra J. Tait and Kiera L. Ladner, convey the urgency for fundamental questioning and reflection. The days are long gone when young Indian Affairs Minister Jean Chrétien could rise in the House on 25 June 1969, with great anticipation among Aboriginal leaders sitting in the galleries, to present the White Paper, offering so many changes, including abolishing the dreaded and racist Indian Act of 1876. Almost immediately, the reaction of Indigenous groups was one of shock and dismay, saying the paper displayed a vast ignorance of core issues, leading to its total rejection by the Aboriginal community for its fundamental misunderstanding of Canadian history and Aboriginal rights. Even worse, when Prime Minister Pierre Trudeau spoke in Vancouver on 8 August 1969 at a conference on treaty rights, the community rejected his views, despite his wide-ranging consultations with its members and the work of the National Indian Council (founded 1961). "We can't recognize Aboriginal rights," said the prime minister,

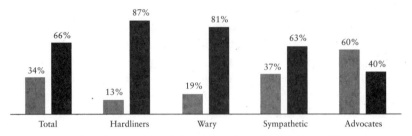

Source: Angus Reid, 2018

Figure 6.1 Rules of Governance: Four Views on Indigenous Independence and Self-Governance.

"because no society can be built on historical *might have beens*." And he explained his reasoning: "We must be all equal under the laws and we must not sign treaties amongst ourselves."

Almost half a century later, and despite Aboriginal misgivings, Prime Minister Justin Trudeau in August 2017 announced a major shift in the machinery of government vis-à-vis Indigenous peoples, following the recommendations of the Royal Commission on Aboriginal Peoples (1991–96). The renamed Ministry of Indigenous and Northern Affairs Canada (INAC) would become two distinct departments, each with a minister: Crown–Indigenous Relations and Northern Affairs, and Indigenous Services – the first to deal with treaty rights and land claims, the second, with federal services across departments. It remains an open question whether the bureaucratic ethos will change enough to address the long-standing complaints outlined in the commission report: an unresponsive, paternalistic culture and ongoing failure to meet treaty obligations and unfulfilled claims.

Like all leaders of the main political parties, Aboriginal leaders have varying views, timelines, and "stakeholders." The final report (2018) of the Truth and Reconciliation Commission proposed a powerful idea – a third level of government in Canada's federal system, an Aboriginal Parliament, to provide advice, self-rule, and shared values. Such a legislative body, as a work in progress, would include representatives of First Nations, the Métis, and the Inuit, with perhaps a system of both elected and appointed members. Its primary mandate might be to provide advice and consent on Aboriginal policy, legislative initiatives, and regulatory issues before the House of Commons and the Senate, as well as federal agencies, and possibly on matters before the courts, given the population data set out in Table 6.1, based on the 2016 census.

The fact that more Aboriginal peoples are now active in federal and provincial political parties bodes well for a new partnership that looks forward to righting wrongs, not settling old scores. British Columbia, for example, offered surprising initiatives two generations ago. The province was the first to allow all "Indians" to vote in provincial elections, in 1949, and that year Frank Calder (CCF / NDP) became the first Aboriginal elected to the Legislative Assembly, where he served for thirty years. John Diefenbaker appointed the first Aboriginal senator, James Gladstone from Alberta. Today, many Aboriginals run as candidates and get elected to the House of Commons or provincial legislatures and are appointed to the Senate, as well as working in the federal or provincial civil service. More recently, Stephen Harper appointed Patrick Brazeau, a member of the community of Kitigan Zibi in Quebec, to the Senate, while the new appointments committee for the Senate recommended Brian Francis, chief of the Abegweit Mi'knaw Nation in Prince Edward Island. Another sign of progress was the selection of Jody Wilson-Raybould in 2015 as the first Indigenous leader to become minister of justice and attorney-general, facing complicated files like assisted dying, legalizing cannabis, updating the Criminal Code, and redesigning federal Aboriginal policies.

Unfortunately, too many Canadians, including many policy-makers, are unaware of the history of Aboriginal policy in Canada, allowing a breakdown into five phases: French rule, c. 1534–1759; British rule, 1763–1867; Confederation, 1867–82; constitutional change, 1980s–2010s; and Truth and Reconciliation (see Table 6.2).

I

When Christopher Columbus, on the morning of Friday 12 October 1492, claimed the island of San Salvador in the Bahamas for Aragón and Castile, he redirected the seafaring nations of Europe from the Mediterranean Sea to the Atlantic Ocean, launching the race to conquer the Western Hemisphere. Few resources were spared to discover new lands and new sources of food beyond the staple European diet of grain and codfish, and a new slogan emerged: geography is destiny. Columbus kept a diary and wrote in 1493 of his encounters with Native Americans: "I discovered a great many islands, inhabited by numberless people."

Table 6.1
Aboriginal-Identity Population Canada, Provinces, and Territories

Area	Total population	Aboriginal identity†	Single Aboriginal responses	First Nations (North American Indian)	Métis	Inuk (Inuit)	Multiple Aboriginal responses	Aboriginal identities not included elsewhere	Non-Aboriginal identity
Canada	34,460,065	1,673,780	1,629,800	977,235	587,545	65,025	21,305	22,670	32,786,280
Newfoundland and Labrador	512,250	45,725	42,610	28,375	7,790	6,450	555	2,560	466,525
Prince Edward Island	139,685	2,740	2,660	1,875	710	75	20	65	136,950
Nova Scotia	908,340	51,495	49,940	25,830	23,310	795	835	720	856,850
New Brunswick	730,705	29,380	28,160	17,575	10,200	385	470	755	701,325
Quebec	7,965,450	182,890	175,960	92,655	69,360	13,945	2,760	4,170	7,782,565
Ontario	13,242,160	374,395	361,125	236,680	120,585	3,860	5,730	7,540	12,867,770
Manitoba	1,240,695	223,310	220,470	130,505	89,360	610	2,020	815	1,017,390
Saskatchewan	1,070,560	175,015	172,810	114,570	57,880	360	1,300	905	895,540
Alberta	3,978,145	258,640	253,460	136,585	114,375	2,500	2,905	2,275	3,719,505
British Columbia	4,560,240	270,585	263,540	172,520	89,405	1,615	4,350	2,695	4,289,650
Yukon	35,110	8,195	7,930	6,690	1,015	225	160	105	26,915
Northwest Territories	41,135	20,860	20,650	13,185	3,390	4,080	160	55	20,275
Nunavut	35,580	30,550	30,490	190	165	30,140	55	10	5,030

* The 2016 census counts are not based on adjusted counts for the incompletely enumerated First Nations reserves and settlements of previous census years, while the percentage change is based on adjusted counts.

† "Aboriginal identity" refers to whether the person identified with the Aboriginal peoples of Canada and includes those who are First Nations (North American Indian), Métis, or Inuk (Inuit) and/or those who are Registered or Treaty Indians (that is, registered under the Indian Act of Canada).

Source: Statistics Canada, Census of Canada 2016, 25% sample data

Aboriginal Peoples: Full Citizens or Wards of the State?

Table 6.2
Canada and the Aboriginal Community: Key Dates

Year	Event(s)
1492	Columbus lands in North America.
1534	Jacques Cartier arrives in New France – touches on today's Newfoundland, Prince Edward Island, Quebec.
1663	Royal edict creates Sovereign Council, establishes New France as a royal province.
1763	Treaty of Paris and Royal Proclamation deal with Aboriginal claims to lands.
1764	Niagara Wampum Diplomacy with William Sumner
1774	British Parliament passes Quebec Act, extending boundaries of Quebec to the Ohio River.
1783	United States signs Treaty of Paris with Britain on American independence.
1860	Britain cedes Indigenous jurisdiction to Canada.
1867	British Parliament passes BNA Act with federal jurisdiction for Aboriginals and their lands.
1871–75	Ottawa signs five numbered treaties with Aboriginal peoples in northwestern Ontario, Manitoba, and southern Saskatchewan and Alberta.
1876	Alexander Mackenzie's Liberal government shepherds Indian Act of 1876 through Parliament, making Aboriginals wards of the dominion government through the Department of Indian Affairs.
1870s	Manitoba starts the first residential schools.
1885	The Northwest Rebellion of the Métis people of Saskatchewan under Louis Riel
1951	Amendments to the Indian Act remove some discriminatory features.
1960	Diefenbaker government gives Aboriginals voting rights in federal elections.
1969	Pierre Trudeau's government issues white paper, later withdrawn.
1973	Supreme Court of Canada upholds Aboriginal rights to land, citing the Royal Proclamation of 1763.
1975	Quebec signs the Baie-James / James Bay hydro agreement with Cree and Inuit communities.
1982	Parliament passes Constitution Act 1982, with Charter of Rights and Freedoms.
1984	The Inuvialuit Claims Settlement Act gives the Inuit of the eastern Arctic control over resources.
1985	Under Mulroney government, Parliament amends the Indian Act of 1876, extends formal Indian status to Métis, all enfranchised Aboriginals living off reserves, and Aboriginal women who marry a non-Aboriginal man.
1990	The Oka crisis, near Montreal, focuses attention on Aboriginal land claims. Royal commission established.

Table 6.2 (*Continued*)

Year	Event(s)
1990	Meech Lake Accord fails to pass.
1992	National referendum votes no to Charlottetown Accord.
1999	Nunavut is created, giving Inuit in the eastern Arctic land rights and control of sub-surface resources.
2000	The Chrétien government approves the Nisga'a Treaty, with a payment of $196 million, which creates communal self-government and transfers control of natural resources in much of northwestern British Columbia.
2005	The Martin government signs the Kelowna Accord, committing $5 billion over five years for Aboriginal education, healthcare, and living conditions.
2008	Prime Minister Stephen Harper offers a formal apology in the House of Commons over residential schools.
2010	Canada signs the UN Declaration on the Rights of Indigenous Peoples.
2011	The Attawapiskat winter housing crisis in northern Ontario stirs national media attention on Aboriginal living conditions on reserves.
2012	Prime Minister Stephen Harper holds a summit meeting with First Nations chiefs.
2018	Royal Commission on Truth and Reconciliation Final Report
2018	Justin Trudeau's government splits Department of Native Affairs into two ministries.

Thinking he had arrived in India, he called them "Indians." Data are utterly unreliable, but some estimates are as high as 3.8 million native "Indians" populated the hemisphere in 1492, perhaps many more, but there were only one million by 1800, decimated by disease, fighting and slaughter, and land speculation through broken treaties, when European settlers began to arrive in large numbers.

A series of explorers, missionaries, navigators, and traders followed Jacques Cartier's 1534 voyage up the St Lawrence. For Europeans, North America posed a new challenge apart from the weather, the vast territory, the English / British, Dutch, French, and Spanish rush to colonize, and violence, a spillover of European and Aboriginal disputes. Unknown at the time, the Europeans introduced lethal germs – influenza, malaria, measles, smallpox, syphilis, typhus, tuberculosis, and yellow fever – to a world that lacked genetic resistance, and these microbes devastated both European settlers and Indigenous tribes. The small numbers of French settlers spread French influence well beyond the proselytizing work of the missionaries, By the 1660s, forty years after the *Mayflower* from

Plymouth had arrived in Massachusetts with the Pilgrim settlers, half of whom died in the first year, French adventurers, *coureurs de bois*, explorers, missionaries, and traders established a network of forts, missions, trading posts, and alliances with Indigenous peoples spanning the Great Lakes, the Mississippi Valley, and the Great Plains, and as far west as Missouri and the Saskatchewan River, with French place names that survive today.

English settlements along the Atlantic and in the major ports such as Halifax, Boston, Newport, Philadelphia, Annapolis, Charleston, and Savannah, were small, compact, and militarily protected. Each was a multi-layered maritime hub for coastal and transatlantic commerce, often with very diverse populations working variously as land agents, manual labourers, merchants, seamen, shipbuilders, and wholesalers. By contrast, New France was a territorial empire, neither won by conquest, usually by military means, nor a colonial power with political masters. It spread across a vast geography, enjoying an ambiguous relationship with Aboriginal peoples. Native chiefs accepted the governor as their "father," a dispenser of gifts and a go-between as mediator with the French king, who assumed their formal submission. Policy-makers in France and Quebec knew that their complex relations with Indigenous peoples required a blend of policies – assimilation via intermarriage, religious conversion, and francization, to educate Indigenous people to European civility – in dress, food, medicine, and trading. The French appreciated Indigenous people's physical strength and endurance in harsh weather. While cooperation was the norm, the French kidnapped Indigenous leaders for display at the royal court in Paris and Versailles.

Overall, the French population was tiny, perhaps numbering only 3,000 souls. The conflict between what Paris wanted – colonialization, via settlements – and what the monopoly traders desired – the lucrative fur trade, usually in concert with Indigenous peoples – forced Paris to act. In consequence, France's colonial ambitions required an understanding with the Indigenous peoples, and to meet the twin goals of expanding the fur trade and defending the settlements. The Indigenous peoples thus played three roles – as partners in the fur trade, as warriors in defence of the settlements, and agents of demographic reproduction via interracial marriage. Intendant Jean-Baptiste Colbert, writing in 1666, set out his aims: "To increase the colony ... it seems to me that, instead of waiting to benefit from the new settlers who could be sent from France, the most useful way to achieve it would be to try to civilize the Algonquins, the

Hurons, and the other Savages who have embraced Christianity; and to persuade them to come to settle in a commune with the French, to live with them, and educate their children in our mores and our customs."

A monopoly called the Compagnie des Marchands operated 1613–20 but was replaced by the Compagnie de Montmorency. By 1663, Paris and the king had lost confidence in past actions. The British had become aggressive competitors in commerce and trade, and warfare against the Iroquois disrupted the fur trade. As a countermeasure, in addition to setting up a new Sovereign Council, the edict of 1663 established the French West India Company and the position of intendant, who would be an informal member of the council, but made ex officio in 1675. This official, at Quebec, was powerful, in charge of finance, justice, and policing. For 100 years, France occupied the lands along the St Lawrence River and Great Lakes from Quebec City to the Ohio valley, but faced two challenges. First, in 1618, it entered a new Thirty Years War in Europe, and thereby became preoccupied with expensive land wars in Europe, against Austria, Holland, the German states, and of course England. Second, it lacked one key strength the English / British possessed – a powerful navy. Successive defeats in Gibraltar (1704), Malaga (1704), and Toulon (1707) sealed the fate of Louis XIV's imperial ambitions in Europe and overseas. France was encircled, and its crushing debts would cripple the state for two generations and then provoke a revolution and rejection of the monarchy in 1789. French naval power became confined to Mediterranean ports like Toulon and naval bases like Cherbourg, just as Britain was laying the groundwork for its new overseas empire in North America and India, backed by the Royal Navy, giving its sovereign an unrivalled geopolitical advantage over all European rivals.

The Treaty of Paris of 1763 ended France's territorial ambitions in Canada. It was only a matter of time before it would cede its remaining holdings in North America, the vast Louisiana Territories. The arrangement was negotiated by Foreign Minister Talleyrand in 1803 but approved by Napoleon for only $12 million, to a surprised Thomas Jefferson. The president then ordered two members of the regular army, Meriwether Lewis and William Clark, to search for a sea route to the Pacific, in company with Indigenous interpreters and help from the Shoshone peoples.

II

Britain's military victories in the French and Indian War, or Seven Years' War (1756–63), and France's cession to Britain of all its land east of the

Mississippi in 1763 forced London to reconsider its land holdings and territorial ambitions, with specific emphasis on the political, legal, and military challenge of incorporating this vast area into its North American empire, including the Aboriginal inhabitants.

In the 1760 "Articles of Capitulation Between their Excellencies Major General Amherst, Commander in Chief of his Britannic Majesty's troops and forces in North America, on the one part, and the Marquis de Vaudreuil, &c., Governor and Lieutenant-General for the King in Canada, on the other," signed on 8 September 1760, article XL read: "The Savages or Indians of his most Christian Majesty shall be maintained in the Lands they inhabit if they choose to remain there; they shall not be molested on any pretense whatsoever."

The First Nations allied with "his most Christian Majesty" included Algonquins; Mohawks from Akwesasne, Kahnawake, Kanesatake, and Oswegatchie; and some Chippewas, Hurons, Mississaugas, Odawas, and Potawatomis. The Royal Proclamation of 1763 placed a boundary down the spine of the Appalachian range, separating the millions of square kilometres of the American west. Roughly, the territories from the Appalachians north to the Great Lakes, west to the Mississippi River, and south to the Gulf of Mexico were to remain "Indian territory." London allowed Indigenous peoples to transfer lands by sale, but only to the crown and its representatives, i.e., local governors, and prohibited all private individuals from buying "any Lands reserved to the said Indians."

However, Britain was never clear about its North American territories, because the main decision-makers in the Colonial Office had never visited that continent and received their information principally from military officers who knew only certain areas where they were stationed. The legal position on these colonial regimes varied, but the French royal court, like those in London and Madrid, adopted a European legal theory called *terra nullius*, i.e., nobody's land, where uninhabited or uncultivated territories could be brought under Christian dominion. *Terra nullius* was a foundational tenet of *The Law of Nations* (1758), one of the first works of its kind in international law, written by Emmerich de Vattel, a Swiss legal scholar, philosopher, and diplomat, and published in French in 1758. The work isolated the core feature of a state: "It is sufficient that it really be sovereign and independent, that is it governs itself by its own authority and laws." Vattel's book was circulated in Philadelphia, and U.S. founders like John Adams and Benjamin Franklin made several references to it in speeches and written commentaries.

For the British, exhausted by lost blood and treasure in the Seven Years' War, their North American holdings presented many political and financial challenges. The military imperative was straightforward: unlike the people at home, who tended to accept rule from London, the American colonists displayed a more unruly, self-assured individualism, even cantankerous opposition. London imposed measures like the long-standing Navigation Acts, the Sugar Act (1764), and the Stamp Act (1765). Such initiatives were attempts to limit smuggling and illegal trafficking of goods and, as in wartime, allow Royal Navy men and officers to collect half the value of captured vessels as prize money. But this approach left much of the population seething with anger, and leaders like Benjamin Franklin, a polymath and publisher from Boston who had moved to Philadelphia, Sam Adams, and John Hancock, expressing their outrage, cited the actions of the Royal Navy. "There seems to be direct and formal design on foot to enslave all America," John Adams would write in the Boston *Gazette*. "Have we not been treated formerly, with abominable insolence, by offers of the Navy?"

Despite great naval power, British authorities knew the extreme vulnerability of their control in the American colonies – a restless population with no secure ports and territories to source supplies of food, equipment, and materiel. In many of the thirteen colonies, Indigenous peoples had little trust in British forces, or their commanders. Britain's North American commander-in-chief, Jeffery Amherst, conqueror in 1758 of the great French fortress of Louisburg in Cape Breton, sought to limit or cut off financial support for diplomatic gift-giving to Aboriginal leaders, which he considered bribery. He had disallowed any supplies of guns and ammunition to their peoples, much to the disgust of an Ottawa chief, Pontiac, who in 1763 started an uprising that spread to the British northwest frontier. Amherst, caught unawares, had plans to send him supplies and blankets infected with smallpox, but the intervention of William Johnson, the superintendent of Indian Affairs in the northern district, allowed Wampum diplomacy, whereby offering gifts, a measure of political theatre, eased dissension within the Indigenous peoples. Johnson also managed to convince London to recall General Amherst.

King George III, much maligned in American ports, issued a Royal Proclamation on 7 October 1763; it is today part of Canada's Constitution Act, 1982. The new special envoy, William Johnson, went from Connecticut and was put in charge of all diplomatic negotiations with what the proclamation described as "the several Nations or Tribes of Indians" as self-contained "political societies" and apologized unequivocally for "great

Frauds and Abuses" committed in the pursuit and purchase of Indigenous lands. France's colonial holdings in the part of New France protruding south to the Ohio Valley were ceded to British rule by the Treaty of Paris (signed 10 February 1763), and the Royal Proclamation guaranteed that all lands and territories therein not already ceded or purchased by Great Britain were considered "hunting grounds" for the Aboriginal peoples – essentially all the lands from the Appalachians west to the Mississippi. At this time, the legal philosophy and arguments for property rights were in turmoil and went beyond ownership of land to issues of political control and the jurisdiction for distribution of land. Envoy William Johnson was well aware of the situation in Connecticut, where the Mohegans had lost a much-disputed legal battle in a decades-long dispute with the colony, which argued its autonomy in the British Empire extinguished the Mohegans', the law of conquest in action. Johnson knew the implications and worried that the "spirit" of that case might lead "all the Indians in America to make claim & introduce the utmost confusion and mischief."

Pontiac's rebellion was a symptom of growing political and thus military tensions, and the Royal Proclamation was a valiant attempt to slow colonists' settlement and dull their sense of liberty, which thwarted and denied the rights of Indigenous people.

The 1743 decision in favour of Connecticut broke the long-standing alliance between the Iroquois nation and the British, and unfolding events, including the Seven Years' War, Pontiac's Rebellion, and aggressive colonial settlement, allowed far less agreement and less tolerance for Indigenous rights. The rebellious thirteen colonies fought Britain for many other issues, but collateral damage was a pluralistic legal philosophy, including recognition of Indigenous rights, accepted by the crown in Britain, succumbing to a new revolutionary order, a republican federation based on popular sovereignty, colonial settlement westward, and aggressive military expansion.

More tellingly, the Royal Proclamation set out a new attitude and policies for the future – settlement would be allowed only on lands purchased by the crown from the "Indian bands," all unlawful settlers would be removed, and a new assembly would be convened. The result was the famous treaty council at Niagara in July 1764, representing twenty-four Indigenous nations, with two thousand delegates attending. William Johnson commissioned the Algonquin and Nipissing Anishinaabe Nations to tour the vast territories and waterscapes with a printed copy of the Royal Proclamation, plus strings of white Wampum as a sign of peace, with an invitation to attend the Niagara meeting. Johnson, himself now a large landowner, knew that Anishinaabe Chief Pontiac had fought British soldiers, destroying many forts and killing or wounding many European settlers. His mandate also included assurances for the landholdings of the French settlers in Lower Canada who remained after 1759, part of which was Algonquin Anishinaabe traditional territory.

The treaty council at Niagara included two groups, the Haudenosaunee and Seven Nations – Algonkins, Canoys, Cayugaes, Coghnawageys (Kahnawake), Ganughsadageys (Kahnasatake), Mohawks, Mohicanders, Nanticokes, Nipissengs, Oneidaes, Onondagaes, Senecas, and Tuscaroras. The Western Confederacy included the Algonkins, Chippawaes, Christineaux (Cree), Hurons, Menomineys, Nipissangs, Ottawaes, Outagamies (Fox), Puans (Ho-Chunk – Winnebago), Reynards, Sakis, and Toughkamiwons. This treaty council was a first, even if it actually consisted of a series of mini-councils, each dealing with common issues but focused on specific circumstances, leading to some eighty-four Wampum belts exchanged during the conference.

Clearly, Johnson had the personal touch and diplomatic skills that military commanders like Amherst had lacked, and he managed to negotiate a series of British concessions and gained pledges of loyalty. Timing was one advantage he used, offering to suspend any trade for foreign entities until he was satisfied that his terms were met. He also promised that the British army and its close allies, the Six Nations, would destroy any foreign settlements. He hoped to present a large Covenant Chain belt as the result of his Wampum diplomacy, with 84 separate agreements. The separate treaty on 6 August 1764 with the Geneseo Senecas' Chenussio (Pleasant Valley, or Genesee Castle), which had harboured insurgents in Delaware and part of the Devil's Hole Massacre of 1763, where twenty-one teamsters and eighty-three English soldiers were killed, with total casualties possibly as high as 121.

For the Aboriginal nations attending this Niagara conference, and the exchange of the Two Row Wampum Belt, Johnson and the British delegates had agreed to a symbolic arrangement, a nation-to-nation relationship rooted in non-interference, mediated by peace, friendship, and respect. This meant that Indigenous Nations' right to self-government included their rights to define their own citizenship laws and to an equal distribution of land and resources necessary for self-governance. Symbolically, the three Wampum Belts – the British and Great Lakes Covenant Chain Confederacy Wampum Belt, the Twenty-four Nations Wampum Belt to the Indigenous Nations, and the Two Row Wampum Belt – embodied Indigenous agency as sovereign Nations, not as subjects of the British Empire.

In North America and elsewhere, the Royal Navy became the world's chief law enforcer, controlling the key ports, with Real Admiral Alexander Colville in charge in Halifax, supervising captains and navy frigates against smuggling and illicit trade, and operating as policeman, judge, and jury. In Acadia, the British encouraged interracial marriage, especially for British men with Native women, a military measure to challenge French–Abenaki friendships and alliances. Benjamin Franklin echoed the sentiment of merchants' wrath, eventually spilling into street agitation: "By putting Frigates all along the coast, ... the officers of which were all vested with Custom-House powers ... executed their Commission with great Rudeness and Insolence, all Trade and Commerce, even the most legal between Colony and Colony, was harassed, vexed, Interrupted." London also faced another challenge, how to incorporate into its growing North American empire its military allies and territories of the Indigenous peoples that inhabited them. Parliament passed the Quebec Act in 1774, seen by many historians as a landmark of tolerance, a measure that guaranteed Quebec's seignorial system and civil law and the rights of the Catholic church, including control over education. In the American colonies, the law was seen as part of a series of coercive acts – along with the Boston Port Act (1774), blockading Boston, and the Quartering Act (1774), empowering the governor to commandeer private homes for soldiers, an ideal pretext for Samuel Adams to spread his whispering campaign that King George III sided with "Popery" – a lethal slur among Protestant American patriots.

III

The American Revolutionary War of 1775–83 reinforced Britain's worst military fears. This revolt, as much economic as political, against the British monarchy opened up new alliances, but also created new foes, and the Indigenous peoples were caught in a vise. Benjamin Franklin and Patrick Henry both knew it would not be a short war, and urged the Aboriginal Nations to remain neutral, oblivious to their past alliances with the French and the British, but their entreaties were largely ignored. By 1783 when the conflict ended, the revolutionaries assumed most Indigenous peoples had supported the British and would be treated accordingly. Many Americans who supported the crown either went to Britain or moved north, to Canada and Acadia. With its naval support and massive loans and subsidies, France was the first ally of the United States of America, and the Treaty of Paris of 1783 recognized this new state and its territorial claims, after its forces surrounded General

Cornwallis's at Yorktown in October 1781, and a French squadron of twenty-six ships cut off any reinforcements. Britain granted the thirteen colonies their independence.

George Washington might be celebrated in U.S. history and mythology as "first in war, first in peace, and first in the hearts of his countrymen," but as a former surveyor of Aboriginal lands, then as a military commander fighting both the French and the British, his record is blemished by his grabbing of Native lands. He had decidedly military views of Britain's edicts to isolate the western region as an expedient to placate Indigenous residents of the area, as a means both to confine the thirteen colonies to the Atlantic seaboard and to isolate their settlements from trade with the French in Louisiana and the Spanish in the distant southwest. Washington was doubtful that the Royal Proclamation of 1763 would hold. He was fully aware that he, like many colonials and others, including the Earl of Dunmore, the royal governor of Virginia and later of New York, would probably move westward, setting off a land grab, with Native inhabitants paying a huge price. Landholdings had become a formidable currency of wealth, as aggressive new settlements allowed land speculation to spread with few restraints, and Washington thus predicted the proclamation "must fall of course in a few years."

American colonists would appropriate land, including those occupied by Indigenous leaders – Bloody Fellow, Joseph Brant, Little Turtle, Red Jacket, Shingas, and Tanaghrisson – and the peoples they represented, such as the Creeks, the Delawares, the Iroquois Confederacy, the Lenapes, and the Miamis. George Washington summarized, in a letter of 1783, the prevailing American attitude: "The Indians should be informed, that after a Contest of eight years for the Sovereignty of this Country G: Britain has ceded all the Lands of the United States within the limits described by ... the Provisional Treaty."

Across the former colonies, Indigenous leaders were astonished to discover that a foreign (French) treaty between Britain, which they considered an ally, and the United States was signed without their knowledge, advice, or consent, even more so when the new government now allowed sale, seizure, or distribution of their land. During the Revolutionary War, some Nations were allies of the British; some supported the rebels; and many stayed neutral. In 1783, when the new republic found that the national government, which occupied a series of cities in the 1780s, not the states, had jurisdiction for "Indian policy," many Americans citizens had harsh views of their opponents and saw Native peoples as part of the defeated enemy. That vengeful sentiment explains why many British loyalists moved north to Canada, and, after the Civil War, former slaves left the Confederate states. Given widespread anti-Indian sentiments among many of the American settlers and citizen armies, in 1789 Congress gave authority for Indian relations to a division of the War Department, a signal of new battles ahead. Nevertheless, many Europeans realized that perpetual war could not be sustained.

Thomas Jefferson, the main author of the Declaration of Independence, thought the new nation would be a peace-loving, agrarian society, yet he bowed to political pressure as president to seize Indigenous property across the Mississippi. He often expressed benevolent rhetoric while white settlers committed wanton acts of cruelty against the Native inhabitants and allowed frontier justice to reign supreme, and the new republic seized over 48 million acres of their territory between 1795 and 1809. Twin brothers, sons of a Shawnee chief, appalled at the loss of their hunting land, decided to take action, suggesting a new Confederacy of all tribes as a defensive measure. The two, a stately warrior called Tecumseh, the second a medicine man called the Prophet, hoped to obtain British support. In the Battle of Tippecanoe, fought on 7 November 1811, General William Henry Harrison, governor of the Indian Territory, with support from President James Madison, destroyed Tecumseh's forces.

The British reconsidered and met Tecumseh in June 1812 at Fort Amherstburg (near Windsor and Detroit) in Canada, where the British commander-in-chief, soon to be governor general, Sir George Prevost, predicted war with the United States. There was no shortage of war hawks in the American population of about seven and a half million, compared to half a million in British North America, so the temptation to fight the British, and grab the lush lands of Canada, would also end the Indigenous menace on the frontier, liberate the Americans residing in Canada and the Maritimes, and take control of the military base in Halifax. Chants shouted the call to arms, "Canada! Canada! Canada!" when war was declared on 18 June 1812, when an American war hawk like Henry Clay could boast that the Kentucky militia alone could conquer Canada. Yet the British won victories at Baltimore ("The rockets' red glare ... ") and Lake Champlain, and at sea, including capture of a revolutionary new schooner-brigantine, the *Prince de Neufchatel*, with a unique hull and sail design. The Royal Navy seized the ship at sea, took her to drydock, where she was badly damaged and had to be broken up, and stole her technical secrets, a gift for its shipyards. In August 1814, the British set fire to parts of Washington, including the Capitol and the Executive Mansion (restored and repainted as the White House). The two years of land war and sea battles ended with the Treaty of Ghent, signed in Belgium on Christmas Eve 1814,

In 1814, the British prime minister, Lord Liverpool, wanted to turn military command over to the Duke of Wellington, but he knew he was needed in Europe and saw the North American conflict as a draw: "I think you have no right from the state of war to demand any concession of territory from America." This unnecessary war brought few real gains for either side. However, the American public did not fully appreciate that the British had defeated Napoleon at his pinnacle in 1815, with the French economy in shambles after his Continental System failed against the Royal Navy, and Britain's booming economy made the Americans more dependent than ever on it. Serious folks in Washington now knew Canada would never join forces with the new republic. New England, less warlike than the southern slave states, more attuned to British trade interests, considered a go-it-alone, separate peace at a convention in Hartford, Connecticut, an initiative endorsed by the London *Times*: "New England allied with old England would form a dignified and manly union well deserving the name of Peace."

The Ghent treaty allowed Britain to dominate the oceans, consolidate its empire, and establish a new global order and permanent balance of power within Europe that would last a century. In the United States, successive administrations ceded to the demands for continental expansion and white settlement and to a widely held sentiment that "the country is a land for cattle." Indigenous landholdings became fair game in the frontier territories, as government agents became hacks for land companies, land speculation, and a common view that "Indian tribes" were allies of "foreign influence" – the British, the French, the Spanish – a useful premise to break treaties, seize land, abuse Indigenous inhabitants, and treat them as what Governor William Henry Harrison, later briefly president, called "the most depraved wretches on earth." Such confiscatory policies were codified when President Andrew Jackson signed the Indian Removal Act (1830). It was indeed an odious measure that removed entire communities of Delawares, Shawnees, Sioux, and Wyandots, and, in the southwest, Cherokees, Chickasaws, Choctaws, and Creeks, devastated by famine, a cholera epidemic, other diseases, and wanton massacres of men, women, and children. The view that Indian tribes might not survive was widespread, and certainly the one held by Sir Francis Bond Head, the lieutenant-governor of Upper Canada in 1830. De Tocqueville, in his *Democracy in America*, gave his own view and that of many American politicians: "I think that the Indian race is doomed to perish, and I cannot prevent myself from thinking that on the day when the Europeans shall be established on the coasts of the Pacific Ocean, it will cease to exist."

In 1960, in a U.S. Supreme Court case involving the Niagara Power project, in which the Tuscarora band lost an appeal to preserve its reservation, a dissenting opinion from three justices – Hugo Black, joined by Earl Warren and William O. Douglas – summarized the injustices of 150 years of broken treaties, outright theft, and a devastating absence of basic decency by the American nation:

> The record does not leave the impression that the lands of their reservation are the most fertile, the landscape the most beautiful or their homes the most splendid specimens of architecture. But this their home – their ancestral home. Their they, their children, and their forebears were born. They, too, have their memories and their love. Some things are worth more than money and the costs of a new enterprise. I regret that this court is the governmental agency that breaks faith with this dependent people. Great nations like great men, should keep their word.

IV

The Congress of Vienna in 1815 placed Britain in an unrivalled global position, with territories home to a quarter of the world's peoples. London was forced to redesign colonial subjecthood to encompass the vast colonies in North America, Africa, India, and Asia. In places like Canada, Australia, and New Zealand, colonial governments had to rethink the legal and political role of Indigenous peoples, no longer needed as military allies, but a financial burden for Britain's over-extended Treasury. Each colony had different requirements, but its authorities now had great powers to deal with local circumstances, including land holdings. In British North America, the main authority, the governors or lieutenant-governors, such as Sir Peregrine Maitland (in office 1818–28) and Sir John Colborne (1828–36), in Upper Canada, were heavily influenced by the civilizing influence of British diplomacy, as expressed by Foreign Secretary Lord Castlereagh: "The power of Great Britain to do good depends not merely on her resources but her impartiality and the reconciling character of her influence."

Both Maitland and Colborne were war heroes, friends of the Iron Duke, and placed in Canada to assist war veterans. Both combined a military discipline with a Christian philosophy, only too willing to allow Protestant sects, each battling for land grants, and support for Indigenous peoples as part of their evangelical philosophy – advancement and civilization to foster Christian values. There was no shortage of suggestions from religious leaders to advance this civilizing cause, including plans to allow intermarriages, an Anglican university, and permission for First Nations to become "white" farmers and give up their lands for colonial settlement. Lord Dalhousie, governor general 1820–28, aware of the tensions about future policies, asked his military secretary, Major-General H.C. Darling, to write a report. Darling did his own investigations with tours in Upper and Lower Canada and submitted his findings. In July 1828, he suggested a system of fixed locations for Aboriginal territory, an idea proposed by many Indigenous chiefs, as well as practised in Lower Canada, as at Sillery, established in 1637. He also advocated keeping the Indian Department as the indispensable tool to deal with the First Nations; otherwise they would "turn with vengeance in their hearts into the arms of the Americans." This recommendation essentially was the approach applied by Lieutenant-Governor John Graves Simcoe in Upper Canada in 1796, to allow the Indian Department independence, to apply clear instructions to Indian agents, and to retain proper records of meetings, transactions, and orders.

Unfortunately, the Indian Department was caught in a malaise of political crossfires – patronage appointments for former military personnel, limited financial resources, and the centralizing nature of decision-making in a chain of command extending up to the lieutenant-governor, the governor general, and then – weeks' travel away – the colonial secretary in London, which instilled deep frustration, thwarted initiative, and caused endless delays. In addition, the status of First Nations became part of the military conflicts between Britain and France and, later, military and diplomatic struggles with the United States and its attempts to seize land in Rupert's Land / North-West Territories and beyond, as far north and west as Alaska, which the Americans purchased from Russia in 1867. In both cases, the various Aboriginal peoples thought they had huge leverage – they were great fighters, they knew the land, waterways, and key points for defence.

Canada's current Aboriginal treaty systems flowed from this experience, but always engaged the "crown," not individual governments, colonial, federal, or provincial. These treaties assigned rights, including hunting and fishing, in perpetuity. Before Confederation, and after the Treaty of Paris in 1763, the crown conferred protected status on Canada's Aboriginal residents through the Royal Proclamation of 1763, which confirmed the existence of their rights, recognized their title to lands, and specified that

Aboriginal Peoples: Full Citizens or Wards of the State?

they could cede their lands and territories to the crown by way of treaties. In 1850, as European settlement in British North America grew, the British Parliament defined "Indians" in a revised act to protect them in Canada West, as well as in Canada East, and defined whom it considered "Indian" and entitled to use "Indian" lands and property.

Rupert's Land, the vast territories of the Hudson's Bay Company, presented a special challenge to the colonial administration in British North America. There were few formal "Indian" treaties there, so a system emerged called "reserves," not unlike the U.S. "reservations." Indigenous people viewed the reserves as protected places, their homeland, with clear hunting and fishing rights, but colonial officials saw them as a vehicle for assimilation and a political expedient to seize land for settlements. In 1839, further south, the Act for the Protection of the Indians in Upper Canada allowed for a last name for Indigenous males over twenty-one, approved by a commissioner, with wives and children to adopt that name, and that person would give up membership of a tribe, unless acquired through another marriage. He could receive a parcel of land up to fifty acres on a territory allocated for Indian Reserves, which came with "a sum of money equal to the principal of his share of the annuities and other yearly revenues receivable by or for the use of such tribe," but on the condition that this grantee would "forgo all claim to any further share in the lands or moneys then belonging to or reserved for the use of [their] tribe, and cease to have a voice in the proceedings thereof."

In 1857, the Parliament of the Province of Canada passed the Act to Encourage the Gradual Civilization of Indian Tribes in this Province, and to Amend the Laws Relating to Indians (the Gradual Civilization Act):

> The third section of the Act passed in the Session held in the thirteenth and fourteenth years of Her Majesty's Reign [1839], chaptered seventy-four and intituled, An Act for the protection of the Indians in Upper Canada from imposition and the property occupied or enjoyed by them, from trespass and injury, shall apply only to Indians or persons of Indian blood or intermarried with Indians, who shall be acknowledged as members of Indian Tribes or Bands residing upon lands which have never been surrendered to the Crown (or which having been so surrendered have been set apart or shall then be reserved for the use of any Tribe or Band of Indians in common) and who shall themselves reside upon such lands, and shall not have been exempted from the operation of the said section, under the provisions of this Act; and such persons and such persons

only shall be deemed Indians within the meaning of any provision of the said Act or of any other Act or Law in force in any part of this Province by which any legal distinction is made between the rights and liabilities of Indians and those of Her Majesty's other Canadian Subjects.

The preamble sets out the assimilationist intentions: "Whereas it is desirable to encourage the progress of Civilization among the Indian Tribes in this Province, and the gradual removal of all legal distinctions between them and Her Majesty's other Canadian Subjects, and to facilitate the acquisition of property and of the rights accompanying it, by such Individual Members of the said Tribes as shall be found to desire such encouragement and to have deserved it."

The complexity of the act's stipulations, written in a legalese (still standard) not readily understood by the average person, at a time when most people had little or no schooling, put awesome powers in the hands of Indian Department officials. Other British colonies were struggling with the complexity of Indigenous rights, inasmuch as they recognized them. Property ownership, and the balance between ancient property rights and the surrender of these rights recognized in treaties, went to the core of citizenship, and in exchange for private property, with settlement and voting rights as a British subject within the British Empire, was it implicitly if not explicitly a policy of assimilation?

During the 1850s, the British government became more accommodating in domestic and foreign policy, its assertiveness as an imperial power checked with inglorious defeat in the Crimean War, where its Light Brigade charged into the "Valley of Death." This decade saw the end of Lord Palmerston's imperial ambitions, and cries for responsible governments in Australia and New Zealand led to the South Wales Act of 1842 and the Australian Colonies Government Act of 1850, just as Reformers Robert Baldwin and Louis LaFontaine had achieved responsible government for the Province of Canada in 1848. London was keeping a close watch on events in the United States, on the tensions between the north and the slave-holding south and the military implications for British North America and Rupert's Land. Palmerston's cabinet was decidedly pro-south, hoping to protect the booming British textile trade, dependent largely on cheap cotton imported from the slave states. The gold rush on the British Columbia's Fraser River in 1858, with many American settlers moving north, forced Britain to act, by combining, on 2 August 1858, the colony on Vancouver Island, granted to the Hudson's Bay Company in 1849, and the mainland to become British Columbia – a name chosen by Queen Victoria. The Colonial Office appointed a new governor, James Douglas, not realizing his imperious ways, more interested, as he was, in European settlement as a spur to economic progress, and not terribly concerned about the traditional rights of Indigenous people. In truth, Douglas was an autocrat, governing by executive order and proclamations, anti-British and keen to side with the Hudson's Bay Company, and, as one critic put it, "unsuccessful as a statesman," a paragon of "masterly inactivity."

The Royal Navy's budget was the biggest expenditure in the British government, which launched a wave of cost cutting, decentralization, and autonomy in the colonies, so decided in 1858 to lessen crown control over "Indian lands." The Colonial Office, by granting the North American colonies fiscal autonomy in 1860, meant to empower the Indian Departments there, entrench past practices, and facilitate assimilation. Britain's Indian Lands and Property Act of 1860 transferred responsibility to the Aboriginal communities in Canada, despite various warnings that this measure would mar the crown's traditional approach. In fact, this bill diminished the influence of the Royal Proclamation of 1763, whereby the crown acted as a mediator between colonial settlements and Indigenous communities in the delicate balance between empire, colony, and Aboriginal organizations. In practice, it went much further, leaving the Aboriginal community to the whims and powers of colonial legislatures. And the Aboriginal chiefs were well aware that their fate was tied to colonial authorities, whom they deeply distrusted. That measure would haunt future policy a century later.

V

By the spring of 1867, when the three British colonies – Canada, Nova Scotia, and New Brunswick – successfully appealed to the British Parliament to pass the carefully worded British North America Act, control over Indian policy was designated a federal responsibility. The new dominion's secretary of state became the superintendent-general of Indian Affairs, and the relevant legislation, the first passed under the new Macdonald government, essentially consolidated previous bills. The regulations, such as the patrilineal rules adopted in Canada East in 1851, defined "Indian" to exclude European men who married "Indian" women, but include European women who wed "Indian" men. An 1868 law created the Department of the Secretary of State of Canada, which was to manage Indian and Ordnance Lands and funding for Aboriginal communities.

In the six years after Confederation, Canada expanded, adding three new provinces – Manitoba in 1870, British Columbia in 1871, and Prince Edward Island in 1873 – and Rupert's Land, which became the original North-West Territories. Treaties 1–7 with First Nations in western Ontario and the North-West Territories were approved by amendments to existing laws and by orders-in-council. In negotiations, ceremonies and symbols played a powerful role, especially to the Indigenous people, including religious practices, tradition, the pipe ceremony, and reference to the crown, translated as the "Queen's Hat," an image of Queen Victoria as a woman and mother not taking away land but sharing it. These treaties, and others like them, showed the ambiguity of meanings, often using words that aren't easily translated and that may complicate implementation, such as Indigenous families choosing land against the bureaucratic rule-making of surveyors. Dominion legislation of 1874 extended the existing "Indian laws" to Manitoba and British Columbia and strengthened earlier legislation prohibiting the sale of alcohol to Aboriginal people and making it an offence for them to be found "in a state of intoxication," with additional punishment for refusal to name the supplier. The fact that there were no internal rebellions and uprisings in Canada, like the "Indian wars" in the United States, after 1763 inspired the U.S. Congress to send an emissary north to probe this contrast. Commissioner F.N. Blake concluded that in Canada there were no treaty violations or forced removals of Aboriginals from their homelands, a stark contrast to American practices.

Under the Liberal government of Alexander Mackenzie, the Indian Act of 1876 set up the Department of Indian and Native Affairs. By coincidence, the bill was presented during the Battle of Little Bighorn, in Montana, on 25 June 1876, when Lieutenant-Colonel George Armstrong Custer led his U.S. federal troops to a devastating defeat against a band of Cheyenne, Lakota, and Sioux warriors. In Ottawa, the minister in charge was PEI Liberal MP David Laird, elected in 1874, a native of Charlottetown, founder and editor of the *Patriot*, and one of the new MPs sent to Ottawa when the province joined Confederation on 1 July 1873, on "better terms." Laird won Liberal friends when his paper scolded the Conservatives for their lack of "integrity" in the CPR scandal, and when they resigned, Mackenzie appointed him minister of the interior and superintendent-general of Indian Affairs. He retained his seat in the Liberal victory in 1874 and now faced two big challenges, despite his limited knowledge of the files and a lack of enthusiasm for the national railway or the people and territorial government in western Canada. The Indian

Act of 1876 consolidated previous legislation, but the minister didn't participate in the debates, noting merely that "the Indians must either be treated as minors or as white men." William Spragge, deputy superintendent of Indian Affairs, added a comment after the act was passed: "The legal status of the Indians of Canada is that of minors, and the Government is their Guardian."

In 1875, the North-West Territories Act was passed, with the real drafting coming from Prime Minister Mackenzie and Deputy Minister of Justice Colonel Hewitt Bernard, Sir John A. Macdonald's former secretary, his travelling companion, and his brother-in-law. The railway needed titles to the land, so Interior Minister David Laird had to negotiate treaties. The first three agreements were with the Cree and Ojibwa, and they provided a framework for future treaties, settled in September 1874 with a Canadian delegation that included Laird, a military contingent, interpreters, and Manitoba's lieutenant-governor, Alexander Morris, who took the lead in the negotiations. Treaties No. 4 and No. 5 covered the huge area between the Qu'Appelle valley and the Cypress Hills in what is now Saskatchewan, 75,000 acres of rich land, in return for land grants, cash payments, and the promise of tools, seed, and cattle. The Treaty 6 negotiations took place at Fort Carlton, a Hudson's Bay trading post about sixty-five miles north of present-day Saskatoon, situated on the Carleton Trail between the Red River colony in Manitoba and Fort Edmonton. The new North-West Mounted Police leased the fort as its main base of operations. The negotiations for the Plains and Woods Crees and the Assiniboines were led by Chief Mistawasis and Chief Ahtahkakoop, respectively, but in English, and went beyond previous treaties by offering the starving, buffalo-hunting Crees protection from famine and pestilence, more agricultural implements and oxen, and on-reserve education, plus the right to exploit resources on crown lands, including timber. Every family of five living on the reserve was to receive one square mile of land.

When Sir John A. returned to power after winning the 1878 election, his government faced new challenges, with more European immigrations arriving in Canada, many Indigenous peoples moving north from the United States, and later the building of the Canadian Pacific Railway (CPR) placing strains on Ottawa's finances. Smallpox was spreading across Canada, and under Macdonald's watchful eye, all Aboriginals were vaccinated. He wanted a peaceful settlement of the west, a contrast to U.S. practices, and the challenge became greater with the near-extinction of the continent's buffalo herds, the main source of food for Aboriginal peoples. He doubled, then quadrupled the budget allocation to assure food, despite criticisms of his excess generosity by his Liberal opponents. His simple retort: "When they fall into a state of destitution, we cannot allow them to die for want of food."

The slow but rising population in western Canada opened the issue of schooling for children of new immigrants, mostly poor and uneducated, and Aboriginal children. Education is a provincial responsibility, but in the North-West Territories Ottawa could set up a Department of Education, and Protestant and Catholic school systems emerged. Most Aboriginal leaders promoted this education initiative, which was also in keeping with Ottawa's treaty obligations, including both on-reserve schools (185 in total) and residential schools (20 in all) when requested – "whenever the Indians of the reserve shall desire it." Attendance was voluntary. In practice, the 1876 Indian Act gave total control to the civil servants in the Department of Indian and Native Affairs, including all aspects of family life, schooling, and management of land and resources. The law also enacted regulations defining "status Indian," thereby determining membership in Aboriginal bands. The law forbade certain traditional ceremonies, public meetings to discuss Aboriginal affairs, and Indigenous people hiring lawyers to pursue egregious offences and land claims, which emphasized the male line, while women could receive monies and income but only with the band's consent, and those who married status Indians from other bands or non-treaty Indians became members of their husbands' band. The act gave the secretary of state control over Indigenous lands and property, in a new position called superintendent general of Indian Affairs, which controlled all aspects of Aboriginal life. While immensely controversial within the Aboriginal community, it remained in place for almost 100 years, guiding all aspects of governance, such as land tenure, cultural practices, voting "privileges," and who was a "status Indian."

By 1951, despite various amendments – in 1884, 1894, 1906, 1991, 1927, and 1936 –officials in the Indian Department, moved to Mines and Resources in 1936, controlled virtually all aspects of the reserve lands, with the bands and chiefs largely sidelined. The Royal Commission on Aboriginal Peoples reported on and acknowledged this dire situation in 1993:

> By the time of the 1951 Indian Act revision, bands and band councils were no longer in a position to exercise any real control over their reserve lands beyond refusing to consent to land surrenders for sale or attaching conditions to such surrenders. This situation has continued almost unchanged to the present day. Many bands complain that the high degree of federal control over their land

use decisions is preventing them from taking advantage of commercial and development opportunities in the modern Canadian economy.

Fortunately, some changes were in the air after the Second World War. Near war's end, three events influenced federal Aboriginal policy in Canada. First, the defence forces and many other Canadians publicly recognized that Aboriginal citizens had participated in combat, in fact far beyond their numbers in the total population. Over three thousand members of Inuit, Métis, and other Indigenous peoples enlisted, including more than 70 women, and many received medals and decorations for bravery in action. A Joint House of Commons–Senate Parliamentary Report in 1948 outlined this contribution for the historical record. Second, in 1946 Liberal Secretary of State Paul Martin, introduced a Citizenship Act designating all the country's inhabitants, including Aboriginal people, as citizens. He intended this measure to celebrate Canada's wartime role and alleviate growing racial and religious tensions. There was a hopeful air in the Commons in 1949 when the Indian Branch shifted to the Department of Citizenship and Immigration. In 1950, when Citizenship Minister Walter Harris presented Bill 267, he confirmed its goal as "integration of the Indians into the general life and economy of the country," with recognition "that during a temporary transition period ... special treatment and legislation are necessary."

Third, improvements to the welfare system included family allowances, available to all families, including Aboriginal, but this exposed the growing disparity in national standards of community services, education, health, and housing between Indigenous and other communities.

The problem for Ottawa was two-fold. First, Indian and Northern Affairs delivered virtually all federal services for Aboriginal communities, and its culture, organization, and mandate flowed from a 100-year legacy of paternalistic colonial practices and what many even then called "racism." In social terms, past practices had disastrous social consequences: despite an enormous increase in births, double the national average, there was a breakdown in the family structure, with high divorce rates, babies born to single mothers, baby and children's adoptions by non-Aboriginal people, and juvenile delinquency and suicides. Later, oral testimony as well as written submissions to the Parliamentary Joint Committee from a wide range of witnesses – government officials, medical personnel, missionaries, social workers, and teachers – exposed a common pattern: appalling housing conditions, lack of clean water, and decrepit infrastructure like deteriorating or non-existent sewers and neglected hunting lands.

Doctors and nurses testified to the prevalence of diseases – influenza, measles, pneumonia, and tuberculosis – far in excess of national averages, plus levels of malnutrition, poverty, and unbalanced diets.

The second issue was legal jurisdiction. Traditionally, Ottawa had sole jurisdiction for Aboriginal policy, as laid out in section 91 (24) of the BNA Act, 1867. Now Ottawa wanted to share responsibility. Liberal minister Jack Pickersgill, born in Ontario, a former civil servant and chief of staff to the prime minister, expressed his personal views of policy changes: "My interpretation of section 91, Item 24 of the British North America *Act* is that the jurisdiction over Indians which was given to the Parliament of Canada refers to Indians domiciled on reserves." In short, after 1945, as Canada urbanized, with higher levels of travel and mobility, federal Aboriginal policy had to involve cooperation with the provinces, as "Indians should be accepted on an equal footing with other citizens as they move from their own communities into non-Indian towns and cities throughout Canada."

As in all matters involving federal–provincial constitutional issues, money, budgets, and taxing power sit at the heart of the matter, and this new proposal put more financial onus on the provinces. It was one thing to argue federal jurisdiction for on-reserve communities, but another to look at provincial funding and expertise for health, education, and community infrastructure. Section 87 of the act set out the terms: "All laws of general application in force in any province are applicable to and in respect of Indians except where such laws are inconsistent or duplicate provisions in the Indian Act or other federal legislation."

By mid-1951, during widespread consultations with Indigenous bands and chiefs across the country, which helped shape legislative content, Bill 267 went to the Commons. Its elements received unanimous, all-party consent for 103 sections, a majority for 15 sections, six opposed by a majority, and two unanimously opposed – widening the tax exemption that Aboriginal supporters wanted and narrowing of the franchise. Despite many wording changes, such as removal of harsher Victorian-era provisions, the revised Indian Act of 1951 followed a series of changes, almost a regular ten-year-or-so updating, in 1884, 1894, 1906, 1927, and 1936. These alterations included changes in the machinery of government, such as transferring the Indian Affairs branch from the Ministry of the Interior to the Department of Mines and Resources in 1936, but often with little appreciation on the impacts on Aboriginal communities, and their traditional rights for hunting and fishing. Despite sundry changes, the 1951 bill remained remarkably similar to the 1876 Indian Act, both in content and in intent. For example, it lessened the minister's power, by reducing his or her discretionary powers from seventy-eight sections to only twenty-six, but still leaving the cabinet with discretionary powers over half the provisions. The definition of "Indian" and control of band membership remained in non-Aboriginal hands, yet were tightened up for fiscal reasons: an "Indian Register" became a centralized record of registration and for receipt of federal benefits. The new bill reduced expropriation powers, yet Aboriginal bands in western Canada still needed permission to sell their livestock and produce.

VI

The election of John Diefenbaker in 1957 was a watershed moment in Aboriginal policy. For only the second time, Canada had a prime minister from the west. Diefenbaker's Saskatchewan roots, his long-held interest in Aboriginal affairs, and his background as a noted civil libertarian and lawyer offered new hope for changing the colonial legacy of the Indian Department. Two early initiatives suggested change – his appointment of James Gladstone, a Blood Aboriginal from Alberta, to the Senate, and a new Joint Committee of the House and Senate "to investigate and report upon Indian administration in general, and, in particular, on the social and economic status of Indians." Conservative committee members hoped to avoid the example of the 1948 committee, which created a forum for the Aboriginal community but then largely ignored its opinions.

Some parliamentarians knew the Indian Affairs Branch was run largely by civil servants with huge leeway, using even definitions of "status Indian" as leverage to dispense funds, to manage Indigenous resources, from oil to minerals, and even to supervise individual bands, their financial resources, and family practices. Yukon MP Erik Nielsen saw "a native bureaucracy that obtains most of the benefits of government assistance, while the need beneficiaries, the families in the communities, receive the least." Implicit in Canada's paternalistic thinking – among civil servants, politicians, and much of the public, despite efforts of various churches to convert and "educate" Aboriginal Canadians – was assimilation and integration, despite code words like "self-government."

Within the civil service, especially the Indian Affairs Branch, perhaps recognizing a new government would force internal reforms, new efforts began to support selective financial funding for band councils to establish school committees and allow them to deliver childcare, education in Branch schools, social assistance, and support for governance. The external environment had changed, if slowly. Provincial governments could not ignore media and public criticism and rising anger over the state of housing and disease on reserves and the appalling schools. The closing of residential schools, starting in 1949, led to agreements to allow local school boards to accept Aboriginal children. Between the late 1940s and the mid-1960s, about 44 per cent of Indigenous children were enrolled in provincial schools, up from only 7 per cent. New federal–provincial funding led to other administrative changes,

Growing public awareness generated suggestions for other reforms, such as a federal–provincial conference to discuss Aboriginal social services, the establishment of a claims commission, creation of Indigenous advisory boards, and a new parliamentary investigation of social conditions on reserves. Many MPs worried that Aboriginal people and communities were victimized in the justice system, which reality was alienating young Indigenous people, many of whom, however, were enrolling in university, where more academic programs covered Indigenous history critically.

Under John Diefenbaker, the main initiatives in Aboriginal policy were two legislative measures. The first, to much public acclaim, was revision of the Canada Elections Act, repealing section 14 (2) to allow status Indians to vote, despite misgivings among many Aboriginal leaders that voters might lose their historic treaty rights. Diefenbaker, despite some opposition, offered this right on 18 January 1960: "The provision to give Indians the vote, is one of those steps which will have an effect everywhere … As far as this long overdue measure is concerned, it will remove everywhere in the world any suggestion that color or race places any citizen in our country in a lower category than the other citizens of our country."

However, in 1959, a joint parliamentary committee conducted a review of the Indian Act and Aboriginal administration, and no one had any doubts, except about residential schools: "Your Committee is in full accord with the program and would strongly urge and recommend that it be continued and expanded. We look forward to the day, not too far distant, when the Indian Affairs is not engaged in the field of education, except insofar as sharing in costs." All parties recognized that Aboriginal voting rights could affect election results in ridings with a large Indigenous population in the west, the north, and northern Ontario. The prime minister also contracted his long-time friend, and army associate, Chief Joseph Deaver of the Mistawasis First Nation in Saskatchewan, to assess the new voters' impact, which in the end seemed minimal.

The second measure in 1961 amended the Indian Act to delete compulsory enfranchisement, in section 112, a change that was later improved by the Mulroney government in 1985. By 1962, the government faced serious cabinet disputes on many policies, yet sought to change the Indian Act to reform bands, protect women's rights when they married non-Aboriginals, and set up a claims court to adjudicate Indigenous land claims.

The idea of a claims commission – a quasi-legal body to adjudicate grievances and land claims, beyond the department's reach – produced numerous meetings within Indian Affairs, including the considered views of the minister, Ellen Fairclough, and Justice Minister E. Davie Fulton, who jointly signed a cabinet memorandum in November 1961. The idea had been recommended by the Special Joint House–Senate Committee in 1948 and mentioned by various submissions in the second committee appointed by Diefenbaker. In fact, C.I. Fairholm, who drafted a plan in 1949, prepared a new plan, for a three-member body, one of them a lawyer or judge.

The commission mandate would adjudicate four categories of Aboriginal claims: (a) claims arising out of the acquisition of original "Indian lands" where the crown and Aboriginal people had disputes over the extinguishment of title; b) claims based on alleged non-agreement of terms of any treaty; (c) claims based on *any* alleged violation of trust arising out of any treaty or surrender in relation to the use, management, or disposition of Indigenous lands or money; and (d) other claims that might have no foundation in law or might be open to defect upon a technical or formal objection, but might merit consideration on grounds of honourable dealings and fairness and good conscience. For each claim, the commission would render written decisions and advise the cabinet on monetary compensation, which could be reduced by payments already made on behalf of the claimants (not to include money for administration, education, health care, relief, or road construction). There would a ten- to fifteen-year time frame for claims. Deputy Minister George Davidson, on seeing these terms, sent a handwritten note to the minister: "This is a proposal which deserves very serious consideration. In my opinion, no single act of the government would do more to regain the confidence of the Indians."

When the Liberals assumed power after the 1963 election, the new prime minister, Lester Pearson, took up the Conservative legislation and ideas for changes in Aboriginal policy. In the autumn of 1963, Ottawa hosted a federal–provincial meeting, and for the first time Aboriginal affairs and administration were discussed, a sign that cost-sharing by Ottawa and the provinces for services to Indigenous communities was more than a short-term solution but exposed the tensions between Indian Affairs and provincial officials, with their expertise in health and education. Ottawa circles understood that Indian Affairs was its own internal "silo," with more bureaucratic say over financial resources and program spending than the people it was meant to serve. The conference proposed some initiatives, but, after consultations, they were revised, and the cabinet allowed the bill to die on the order paper.

The Pearson government became preoccupied with three issues – introduction of national health insurance, revisions to the Canada Pension Fund, and a new national flag – but it worried about growing Quebec demands to intrude in areas of federal jurisdiction. What did this mean for changes to Aboriginal policy, just when the Aboriginal community wanted to retain federal jurisdiction over traditional treaty rights? In 1966, the prime minister finally shifted Indian Affairs from Mines and Resources, its home since 1936, to Citizenship and Immigration.

The government also followed up on Diefenbaker-era plans to introduce claims legislation in Parliament, but a high turnover of ministers – five in six years – put most initiatives on hold. However, when Arthur Laing, a popular MP from Vancouver, established a study group at the University of British Columbia to investigate all aspects of Canadian "Indian citizenship," chaired by anthropologist Harry Hawthorn, with M.A. Tremblay as his associate, Aboriginal expectations remained high. Three years later, the group released its massive, two-volume report. During members' detailed interviews with Indigenous bands across the country, they raised a lot of basic issues, including the performance of religious schools, just as the new government of Pierre Trudeau, elected in May 1968, was launching its own consultation exercise, with plans to make major changes to the Indian Act. The Hawthorn–Trembley Report catalogued the atrocious conditions in Indigenous communities, high-school drop-out rates exceeding 9 per cent, and the utter lack of real autonomy on the reservations, a sign of the veto power of Indian Affairs officials, but more damningly, of a real absence of governance mechanisms, as many families were not involved with departmental officialdom.

VII

The palpable optimism that came with Pierre Trudeau's election victory in 1968, and a mandate to break from past approaches, the nasty rivalry between Pearson and Diefenbaker, and the hope of Trudeau's election slogan, a Just Society, suggested change was in the air. Indeed, new legislative measures flowed in the first two years, similar to Diefenbaker in 1957-58. The new government published a new white paper in 1969,

Statement of the Government of Canada on Indian Policy. It set aside the Hawthorn–Tremblay recommendations and concentrated on its white paper, which reflected the prime minister's long-standing views on individual rights – the context for long-waited reforms: abolishing any barriers or legal distinctions between Aboriginal Indians and other Canadians, scrapping the Department of Indian Affairs and Northern Development, and redirecting existing federal programs for economic, medical, and social assistance to other departments or decentralizing them by sharing costs with the provinces.

Despite Trudeau's embrace of individual rights and freedoms and his hopes to enshrine a Bill of Rights in the constitution, and Minister Jean Chrétien's nationwide consultations with the Aboriginal community, the latter rejected the white paper, which activated Indigenous groups, led by the Congress of Aboriginal Peoples. Some of the provincial governments were equally unimpressed, and BC Premier W.A.C. Bennett, fully aware of the Hawthorn–Tremblay Report, went further. Prior to the release of the white paper, he set off a political firestorm, offering to take over Indian Affairs: "If Ottawa will agree, we will set up a provincial department of Indian affairs and all services available to our native Indians, plus special benefits which must go to our native people forever because this was their land." He also didn't contradict the Hawthorn–Tremblay findings of government discrimination and seemed to denounce the province's long history, starting with the first governor, James Douglas, who favoured the Hudson's Bay Company against Aboriginal treaty rights: "If the Indian citizens of our province ask for it and are willing to keep their lands in perpetuity so that no person can take them away, and will set up municipal governments in these areas which they will own forever – and they must own them forever – then this government is willing to take over all matters relating to Indians in the province."

Some of the reaction to the white paper was virulent, seeing it as an old approach that simply put a new face on assimilation. But an issue more profound presented itself – the need to preserve Ottawa and the crown's direct fiduciary role and responsibility, including treaty obligations with the crown. However imperfect the 1876 Indian Act and its paternalistic, patriarchal, and discriminatory features, any alternative policy, new legislation, or amendments could not be imposed unilaterally and had to address Aboriginal rights and land claims. Harold Cardinal, in his influential book, *The Unjust Society: The Tragedy of Canada's Indians* (1969), sets out the case: "We would rather continue to live in bondage under the inequitable Indian Act than surrender our sacred rights.

Anytime the government wants to honor its obligations to us, we are more than ready to help devise new Indian legislation ... How could even the most stupid Indian create a worse mess than has been handed to him over the past 100 years?"

For the next fifteen years (except in 1979-80), the Liberal government, in addition to providing extra financial support for land claims, accepted federal primacy and helped empower Aboriginal communities to provide their own essential services. The new claims court, conceived in 1962, was established in 1974 as a result of the BC Supreme Court's denying a claim by the Nisqua'a First Nation, ruling that no Aboriginal title existed there. This decision was appealed to the Supreme Court of Canada, which, while ruling against the Nisqua'a, divided evenly on pre-existing title based on long-term possession, occupancy, and use. The new Office of Native Claims also provided funds for legal investigations.

Brian Mulroney faced his first lesson in Canada's Aboriginal history on election day, 4 September 1984, at a morning meeting in his hometown, Baie-Comeau. A fifteen-member delegation of his own constituents, members of the Cree Nation, arrived promptly, for a friendly meeting with the candidate. The session was informal, harmonious, and informative. Both as a lawyer and as a businessman, Mulroney was more than familiar with the Crees' legal battles with Quebec, including over its land claims surrounding the giant hydroelectricity project at Baie-James, dating from the early 1960s. He offered his help to solve their problems and put the main emphasis on economic development and job creation, knowing the pressures the Aboriginal community face on a range of issues. This meeting was yet another reminder of the political battles to come in his first mandate.

In 1985, Minister of Indian and Northern Affairs David Crombie introduced amendments to the Indian Act, Bill C-31, to outlaw sexual discrimination and restore "Indian status" and band members' entitlements. The measure also recognized band control over membership but provided a second-generation cutoff of parenting with non-status individuals. The immediate imperative came from an aggressive appeal from Mary Two-Axe Early, born in Mohawk Reserve in Kahnawake, and denied her Aboriginal status after she married a non-status man. Critics argued in subsequent court appeals and bureaucratic representations that Bill C-30, while easing discrimination, exacerbated conflicts over who decided "Indian status," which now meant bands had to accept or deny reserve residence.

In April 1985, the prime minister hosted a federal–provincial conference, the first of twenty-two during his two mandates, on Aboriginal rights. This gathering was his first on the Aboriginal file, one of three flowing from an agreement in the 1982 constitutional package to address Aboriginal issues. The protracted negotiations for the 1982 constitution empowered Aboriginal leaders to claim national recognition of their traditional rights and land claims, and in the final deal, the premiers of Saskatchewan and Alberta insisted on adding the word "existing," diminishing long-held rights. Now roused, Aboriginal leaders became suspicious of provincial intentions and determined to preserve federal jurisdiction. In short, the debate had moved from issues of Aboriginal Affairs and the administration of the Indian Act, with all its faults, to treaty rights, land claims, and self-government in the north, where Ottawa had exclusive jurisdiction, and in the south, where the provinces, especially in the west, had no intention of sharing jurisdiction.

The three national parties, the federal government, the provinces, and the Aboriginal community each were caught in a catch-22 – Ottawa wanted to strengthen Aboriginal control and repeal the Indian Act, but needed the provinces to make any constitutional changes. The provinces had control over land rights, which included pipeline construction and energy development, but Aboriginal support was essential, because individual bands could block many land routes. Aboriginal peoples, deeply suspicious about provincial motives, had no intention of accepting lessening of federal jurisdiction and their rights in treaties signed with the crown and felt they had won clear acknowledgment of their inherent rights. The future constitutional battles of 1987–92 brought out more discordant provincial voices, especially in the west, and the Alberta-based Reform party on inherent rights.

When the Mulroney government appointed the Royal Commission on Aboriginal Peoples in 1991, the result of the crisis at Oka, near Montreal, where the Mohawk nation resisted development on traditional burial grounds, the debate focused on treaty negotiations as a national political exercise, not a legal fight, with over eighty agreements under way. Further, two new agreements, one between the Inuit people, allowed the creation of a new territory, Nunavut, meaning "our land." as a self-governing territory, consisting of 23 per cent of Canada's total land mass, with collective ownership of 350,000 square kilometres, bigger than Norway. The other territory, the Northwest Territories, with 44,500 people, is over five times as big and encbmpasses diverse language groups – Chipewyans, Crees, English, French, Gwich'ins, Inuinnaqtuns, Inuktituts, North Slaveys. South Slaveys, and Tłįchǫs. The Chrétien government followed the same path with treaty negotiations in areas of federal jurisdiction, accepting the Supreme Court's prescription of a "generous, liberal interpretation" (*R. v. Sparrow* [1990], sec. 35 [1]) in negotiating individual Aboriginal treaties with the crown.

Responses to the complex, complicated issues of Aboriginal inherent rights are guided by history and political philosophy and by differing interpretations of the constitutional obligations from Canada's former colonial status within the British Empire. For the government of Paul Martin, who succeeded Jean Chrétien in 2003, Aboriginal issues became a priority file. In November 2005, the prime minister and the premiers signed the Kelowna Accord, a comprehensive plan, negotiated over 18 months, which included funding to address Aboriginal issues, but also to right past wrongs and elevate Aboriginal issues for the Canadian electorate. However, the timing was not auspicious, occurring in the final months before the 2006 election. After the Conservatives won a minority government on 23 January 2006, Stephen Harper withdrew from the Kelowna Accord, largely a decision made by him, Aboriginal Affairs Minister Jim Prentice, and Gerry St Germain, a Métis and former Conservative MP first elected in 1983. The Harper Tories ran on a strong law-and-order platform, and their leader's personal views favoured limited spending, market-based economic development, and Ottawa's addressing only the unambiguously federal powers, leaving the provinces to theirs, including property rights. The new government and its caucus also reflected ideas of the Reform party, which had deep ties to the petroleum industry and funding from the U.S. Koch brothers and American oil barons. Spillovers from the Canadian Alliance party included its visceral opposition to the Meech Lake Accord, especially Quebec's "distinct society."

The Reform–Canadian Alliance ideology inflicted policy ambiguity on the Conservatives in government. Election-campaign promises of a Triple-E Senate, seen as a new balance of ten equal provinces against imperious Ottawa, reinforced a clear separation between federal and provincial responsibilities, whereas in practice many areas like health or Aboriginal policy were shared. Did the individual rights of citizens apply with equal force to Aboriginals? For example, Preston Manning, when he spoke in Parliament in 1999 as leader of the Opposition, sided largely with the views of the Trudeau–Chrétien white paper of 1969, calling for an end to Aboriginal "separate status" and "dependence" – that dreaded Reform party epithet, politically loaded and sure to inflame debate – but implying a policy of individual equality and assimilation. This policy angst related to past Indian Affairs colonial policy, enforcing collective land policy through reservations, so that land claims were a collective right of individual bands, enshrined in treaties, not individual property rights. Equating economic definitions of property rights, seen as possessions for sale in market transactions, conflicted with legal definitions of property rights, which, as Ronald Coast put it, depend on the "legal system of the state."

This Reform party approach, by this time ingrained in the Conservative caucus and the party at large, stressed a pan-Canadian model, with no distinctions – equality of all citizens under the law – leaving little room for self-government, with different rules and regulations for the Aboriginal community. It also left a clear impression that Indigenous claims to land represented the demands of only one of many groups that settled in Canada, a view set out by Harper's policy adviser and campaign manager, Tom Flanagan, in *First Nations? Second Thoughts* (2008): "Europeans are, in effect, a new immigrant wave, taking control of the land, just as earlier Aboriginal settlers did." In the nine years of Harper government, with first a minority, and then a majority, Aboriginal relations with Ottawa went from cautious optimism to outright hostility.

Towards the end of Harper's second mandate, trust between him and the Aboriginal chiefs bordered on zero, according to party insiders and Minister of Aboriginal Affairs and Northern Development Bernard Valcourt. Cutbacks to programs, including environmental regulations, reduced the size and spending of the federal government as federal spending dropped from about 24.5 per cent of GNP to 20 or less, a level that remained until the Wall Street banking crisis of 2008. The Harper government put its faith in pipeline development to move Alberta oil to tidewater, and one of the biggest projects, the Northern Gateway to Kitimat, BC, met open hostility from Aboriginal groups. Even Ralph Klein, a former Tory premier of Alberta, publicly criticized the government's over-zealous design and execution of pipeline policies and the obdurate actions of Natural Resources Minister Joe Oliver. In the end, none of the four pipeline projects were realized in the nine years of Conservative rule, and it was left to the next government to heal Aboriginal wounds under a new policy of Truth and National Reconciliation.

VIII

Justin Trudeau's new government in 2015 promised fundamental change in Aboriginal policies, and coincided with aggressive Indigenous pursuit of land claims. The legal issues are complicated, as is the history of Aboriginal rights, and new elements intrude, such as climate change, environmental protection, pipeline politics, and regional tensions over carbon fuels. Canada and many of its citizens have made a break from the traditional 19th-century approach to addressing Indigenous peoples, their rights, and the legal and political processes necessary for economic development. There is now almost universal acceptance and recognition that command and control from Ottawa or the provinces must give way to new approaches. Such changes also include an appreciation of Indigenous laws, protocols, and conventions in addition to those of common and civil law.

Despite visible progress, political tensions remain high, especially in Alberta and British Columbia, where advances in Aboriginal treaty-making and land claims are caught in the headwinds of national policy priorities – the environment and climate change, pipelines, fiscal restraint, and energy initiatives to convey Alberta oil to tidewater. Political cleavages come from diverse quarters – the traditional clash between Ottawa's national perspective and the resource provinces, interprovincial rivalry, an NDP minority government in British Columbia surviving on support from the Green party, and conservative opposition parties hoping Ottawa will use its constitutional authority to override provincial objections. Quebec stands in firm opposition to a Canada East pipeline through its territories to move Alberta oil to New Brunswick's refineries. However, not everyone agrees with the need for new political processes, including many Liberals and Conservatives. The word "consultations" is now highly charged in the political vocabulary. First, as mandated by the Supreme Court, federal and provincial authorities must consult in advance with Aboriginal communities, before deciding on certain policies. Second, consultations can mean endless delay, deep uncertainty, even abandonment of projects. Going further, it is one thing to speak about Truth and Reconciliation between the federal government and Aboriginal people, but another to reconcile Indigenous communities and the rest of the population.

Critics of the Aboriginal claims process include think tanks like the Fraser Institute, some legislators in Ottawa and the provinces, and some spokespeople in the business community, especially in Alberta's oil industry. Land claims illustrate the political problem facing governments, namely the general acceptance by the Canadian public that Indigenous claims require adjudication and settlement, given past administrative practices and violations of the Indian Act of 1876 and successor acts, but not to the point of endless confrontation and ransom demands. Since 1974, Ottawa has spent almost $6 billion, exclusive of settlements in the provinces or through shared costs. With about 450 cases settled, the federal government still faces a large backlog, including court litigation. In 2008, Minister of Aboriginal Affairs Jim Prentice set up a Special Claims Tribunal – a judicious measure to accelerate settlements – with a ten-year budget amounting to about $250 million per year.

Two main criticisms of the way land claims are settled involve the process itself. The first issue is an unending list of Aboriginal grievances, and broken treaties, so that there is little real awareness that each involves a clear list of matters that have to be adjudicated, with potential costs for the process itself. Tom Flanagan observed in the *Globe and Mail*: "Specific claims were originally thought to be a stock of historical grievances that could be settled once and for all, but the stock has turned into a never-ending flow." The second criticism relates to the huge industry surrounding Indigenous land claims – the retinue of highly paid lawyers, consultants, academic advisers, and retired bureaucrats – that has become part of a perpetual money machine that forestalls any time limits. Federal spending 2012–16 was about $8 billion, but increased by $3 billion, starting in 2017. Further, by extending the consultations, negotiations, and adjudications process, the exercise, noble for its settlement of historic grievances, becomes a tool for political activism on other files, including environmental policy, infrastructure development, pipelines, and other industrial projects, such as mining, port development, and railways and highways.

Whether the adjudication and expenditures actually increase the well-being of Indigenous citizens remains an open question, but the 2017 splitting of the department into two ministries is a good start. Clearly benchmarks for issues such as education, health care, infrastructure, and self-government can't be assessed yearly. But a warning against splitting economic development from improvements to basic living conditions comes from Mary Simon, Canada's first ambassador to the Arctic Council: "These politics have centered on the quest for social justice, cultural autonomy, ecologically sustainable development, and self-government – the package often called 'self-determination' in international indigenous circles. Inuit strategies have been so successful that sometimes it seems as if they have done more to reform Canadian political culture than to fulfil their primary aim of bettering Inuit lives and communities."

As more reforms take place, such as better access to universities and community colleges, new methods to assess land claims, and a general willingness by all Canadians to make amends for past wrongs, failures, and even racism, the salience of Aboriginal issues in the Canadian political system is clear, overdue, and unstoppable. Long gone are the days when these matters were secondary concerns for cabinet and the prime minister's policy agenda. Since the first minister, Superintendent-General of Indian Affairs Hector Langevin, there have been fifty-five successors, for an average tenure of less than three years. And the office has been held by five current or future prime ministers: Macdonald (twice), Laurier, Arthur Meighen, R.G. Bennett, and Jean Chrétien (for six years, 1968–74). Since 1945, following the ten-year tenure of Thomas Crerar, a staunch defender of 19th-century-style capitalism, short terms have been the norm; only four ministers have served for four years: Walter Harris, Ellen Fairclough, Bob Nault, and Carolyn Bennett. Lester Pearson had five ministers from 1963 to 1968.

Changing conditions in the Arctic now create pressing challenges. Prime Ministers Pierre Trudeau and Brian Mulroney had to address Arctic sovereignty after international bodies and Canada's Supreme Court insisted on "use it or lose it" for Canada's north, with implications for international ocean cargo transport, international shipping within Canada's boundaries, military air surveillance, and underwater detection of submarine traffic. Trudeau created the Nahanni National Park, Northwest Territories, in 1972, now a UNESCO World Heritage Site. Mulroney openly challenged the Reagan administration and pressed for Coast Guard and military air surveillance against Soviet intruders. His government announced two major initiatives with long-term consequences for Canada's role in the Arctic, the eight-country Arctic Council, and the Canadian Polar Commission. Both bodies have mechanisms to study a wide range of diplomatic, economic, social, and technological issues – virtual checklists for a modern Arctic agenda. Both Jean Chrétien and Stephen Harper stressed Arctic sovereignty as a national issue: Chrétien appointed Mary Simon ambassador to the Arctic Council, but Harper left the position open when she returned to become more active in Inuit political life. Increasingly, the Arctic is destined to become a global hotspot (as it were) as countries vie for short-term gains in commodity resources, military occupation, and supply routes for cargo shipping, often at the expense of Indigenous peoples.

Aboriginal voter turnout has traditionally been low, but the 2015 federal election saw a breakthrough, with record levels of participation. There were fifty-seven Aboriginal candidates, and ten of them won election. For the first time, campaign teams had access to social media, and #Rockthevote and #RocktheIndigenousvote targeted fifty-one ridings, including pushing against Minister of Natural Resources Greg Rickford and Minister of Aboriginal Affairs Bernard Valcourt. Such developments are a contrast to only two generations ago, when Prime Minister Louis St Laurent contemplated giving "status Indians" the vote, and was blocked by Industry Minister C.D. Howe, who feared that would endanger his electoral prospects. Howe lost his re-election bid in 1957.

Canada must now focus on Arctic sovereignty and Aboriginal issues. Unfortunately, despite political rhetoric, and most Canadians' ignorance of conditions in the Arctic, the region is now a priority internationally. China is perhaps the most aggressive player, hoping to link Arctic endeavours to its global Beltway Initiatives via a year-round gateway to link cargo shipping in the Pacific to Europe. In Canada, airships could transport food and cargo to northern communities and require little infrastructure, as scientists and engineers at the University of Manitoba have proposed. Books like Whit Fraser's *True North Rising* (2018) and Tony Pennikitt's *Hunting the Northern Character* (2018) display guarded optimism, recognizing perhaps Robert Service's "spell of the Arctic":

It's the great, big, broad land 'way up yonder,
It's the forests where silence has lease;
It's the beauty that thrills me with wonder,
It's the stillness that fills me with peace.

7

A Digression on Trade Policy

Global Trade in History – The Splendid Exchange – Historical Perspectives on Free Trade – Canada's National Policy – Free-Trade Negotiations – The Role of Personalities in Trade Promotion – NAFTA – The WTO – The TPP – CETA – American Mercantilism – Gravity Models of Trade-Export Promotion – Protecting the Global Trading System

Free trade, one of the greatest blessings which a government can confer on a people, is in almost every country unpopular.
                                              Thomas Babington Macaulay

Canada, like other advanced economies of Europe, the Americas, and southeast Asia, faces a growing dilemma. In terms of economic output, while representing about 13–15 per cent of the world's population, these nations generate about 60 per cent of its total output, and 40–41 per cent at purchasing-power parity. Only a generation ago, they generated more than three-quarters of world output: 78 per cent at market prices and 64 per cent at purchasing-power parity. Thanks to a number of immutable global forces, like the internet and ocean cargo shipping, regional economic groupings now foster technology diffusion and broad acceptance of rules and regulations to govern trade. NICs (newly industrialized countries) are both customers for imported goods and competitors for markets once dominated by advanced nations. Such 21st-century trends are transforming the global economy. The list of emerging countries affecting Canada directly – Brazil in aerospace and mining, India in advanced electronics and communications, Russia in energy, South Korea in autos and communications, Ukraine in wheat and aerospace – illustrates the need for a global mindset. And Africa, soon to have more people than China, beckons.

A Digression on Trade Policy

International trade, of course, has existed for millennia, since long before international institutions and trade agreements. In his brilliant book, *The Splendid Exchange: How Trade Shaped the World* (2009), William Bernstein traces the history of trade in its various guises, from brutal force, through colonialism and mercantilism, to managed trade, and documents that urge the exchange of goods form a fundamental and essential part of human development. The evolution of trade exchange from simple barter to today's global supply chains involved a colonial order and violently enforced monopolies. The use of force, for instance, was frequent in the development of the Roman, Arab, Mongol, Spanish, Dutch, and British empires, including the millennia-long slave trades. But the advantages of trade were real, and many of the pioneers showed remarkable doggedness and courage. To cite an example, for over seven centuries, the pax Islamica underwrote Arab supremacy from the western Mediterranean to the Far East. In this era, naval supremacy and bold military action established a lasting and sophisticated trading empire. But in 1498, Vasco da Gama, a greedy religious bigot, sailed round the southern tip of Africa to regain European access to the Indian Ocean and beyond to acquire spices and other exotica to build a fortune for himself and his Portuguese masters, setting an influential precedent for the centuries to come (see Figure 7.1).

Yet Bernstein, after chronicling centuries of trade, and following many great economists like Paul Samuelson, who wrote a definitive article on trade theory in 1941, points out that the case for free trade is not so straightforward. In fact, he comes to this slightly lame conclusion: "The dilemmas of free trade are reminiscent of Churchill's famous assessment of democracy: 'The worst form of government except all those other forms that have been tried from time to time.'"

In many ways, the history of Canada is a chronicle of trade policy, from the schools of codfish that stopped Jacques Cartier's ships in the North Atlantic to the fur trade of the Hudson's Bay Company. Elsewhere, Japanese trading enterprises, the British East India Company, and the Dutch East India Company (whose flag was very similar to the flag of Holland) carried goods from distant markets to the home country, from spices and food to silk and opium. Across the Eurasian continent, the Silk Road from China to Europe via central Asia illustrated the intersection of conquest, military action, and trade over several centuries. In the 18th and 19th centuries, trade became part of the Great Game, a name applied to the alliances of Napoleon of France and Catherine the Great of Russia that aimed to conquer the land routes over three mountain ranges – the

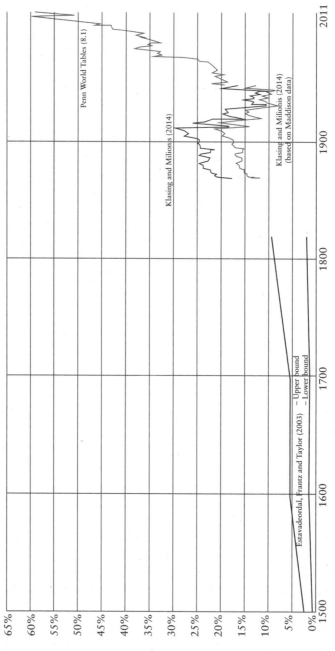

Figure 7.1 Globalization over Five Centuries.

Tien Shen, the Pamirs, and the Himalayas, the roof of the world – to help them, they hoped, grab India from Great Britain.

Trade policy therefore rarely can be isolated from other political matters, real or imagined. In the late 19th century, with John A. Macdonald's National Policy firmly in place, backed by the Montreal and Toronto business community, other options, such as unrestricted reciprocity, commercial policy, or free trade, were seen as a ghastly affront to Canadian nationhood. In 1887, controversial British MP Joseph Chamberlain visited Toronto. In a speech in Belfast, Chamberlain had warned his audience that Canada, with its reciprocity policy with the United States, "must be made to know that it means political separation from Great Britain." In Toronto, he told a packed house at the Imperial Federation League, with prominent Conservatives and members of the Orange Order sitting in the audience: "I refuse to make any distinction between the interests of Englishmen in England, in Canada, and in the United States. Our past is theirs. Their future is ours. You cannot if you would break the invincible bonds that bind us together. It may yet be that the federation of Canada may be the lamp lighting our path to the federation of the British Empire."

Reading the Chamberlain text in Ottawa a few days later, Liberal leader Wilfrid Laurier recognized that, with trade and language now associated in the public mind, commercial reciprocity with the United States would be a long shot. And the Americans, only too eager to shoot themselves in the foot, did just that. In 1890, the McKinley Bill would have increased U.S. tariffs up to 50 per cent – a measure to help wealthy industrialists, but hurt Canadian barley, cereals, and farm products. On 3 January 1890, U.S. Secretary of State James Blaine proposed a conference in Washington to discuss a treaty with Canada, a "British possession," but the Americans were really trying to make their neighbour break off ties with "the homeland." A proposed trade deal with Newfoundland, then a British dominion, was seen on both sides of the Canadian–U.S. border as a "divide and weaken" strategy to force Canada's hand. Secret plans to arrange these meetings, seen in Ottawa with forbearance, especially given former British Liberal Prime Minister William Ewart Gladstone's support of free trade, were leaked to the media through Edward Farrar, editor-in-chief at the Liberal-leaning Toronto *Globe*.

At the request of an American friend, Farrar wrote a pamphlet calling for unrestricted reciprocity and advocated measures for American retaliation towards Canada, such as duties on Canadian ship tonnage or breaking rail connections of the CPR border crossing at Sault Ste Marie. The Conservatives obtained copies of draft proofs, enough to do political damage, and Prime Minister Sir John A., now seventy-six, was flooded with requests for speaking events. In Halifax, addressing a large audience, the Old Chieftain laid out the case against Farrar's pamphlet: "A document points out every possible way in which Canada and its trade can be injured, and its people impoverished, with the view of eventually bringing about annexation." On 5 March 1891, he turned the tables on all his foes. Despite his age, he campaigned at a rapid pace to win his final election, extolling the Conservative slogan, "a great and powerful nation." It was a close thing, but the victory put reciprocity on hold, and as Laurier listened to his political foe addressing Parliament, Sir John mischievously told the members: "I tell my friends and I will tell my foes, *J'y suis, j'y reste!*"

|

Trade policy in general and free trade in particular have been a focus of study for centuries. The most celebrated tract in economic history, Adam Smith's *The Wealth of Nations* (1776), was a wholesale attack on Britain's mercantilist policies and a summons for unfettered trade. Unfortunately, the economic case for free trade runs up against the brick wall of the politician, whose main goal is to get elected and, once in power, re-elected. Against the clearly enunciated economic case for free trade based on a cost-benefit analysis stands a glaring problem: while the benefits of free trade are wide but diffused, the costs (in lost jobs, or factory closings) are highly focused and direct. To the political class, this latter factor means that competitive threats are real, the local factory will close, jobs will be lost, and the taxes paid by workers won't be available for community projects, government services, and infrastructure. In the extreme, too many factory closings lead to the rustbelt syndrome, where entire regions have factory closings, high unemployment, and little money to support community projects, which in modern terms forms the rationale for Donald Trump's mercantilist trade policy.

Clearly, there is a symmetry to these arguments, as economists often overstate free trade's benefits, falling back on the inimitable phase "long run." Politicians and anti-free traders understate the benefits of cheaper and more varied goods for consumers, lower prices of inputs like parts and components, and a check on producers' tendencies, clearly set out by Adam Smith, to collude and follow monopoly practices.

In Canada, four election campaigns were fought on these trade issues: 1878, 1911, 1949, and 1988. The first, in 1878, established Sir John A.

Macdonald's National Policy, of tariff protection to foster economic growth, encourage immigration to populate the west, and help pay for the national railway. John A. campaigned from the opposition benches, after losing power when defeated in the House because of the CPR scandal. The Liberal government and the opposition differed over the effects of higher tariffs. The Liberals believed that they would increase manufacturing costs and prices for consumers while reducing imports and hence government revenue. By contrast, the Conservatives argued their proposed tariff policy would improve the economy, which had been in recession, discourage emigration to the United States, foster infant industries, and promote trade between east and west. Increased revenues from tariffs would also help pay to complete the national railway. The election was principally about the National Policy, but also perhaps about the two chief protagonists, the dour and rather boorish Alexander Mackenzie and the witty, affectionate, and shrewd Macdonald.

The Conservatives won, and Thomas Galt's 1879 budget increased existing tariffs of 14 per cent to 21 per cent. Indeed, the average tariff rose from 14 to 21 per cent, eventually increasing to 32 per cent by the time of John A.'s last campaign in 1891.

The election of 1911 was fought on trade reciprocity with the United States, a deal negotiated that spring, with Liberal Finance Minister William Fielding in charge. At the last caucus meeting before the campaign, he said presciently, on reciprocity, "to fight upon, to win upon, and even to fall upon." U.S. President William Howard Taft, his secretary of state, and members of his administration were pushing dollar diplomacy in Latin America, another instance of the Monroe Doctrine's urge to keep European powers out of the U.S. zone of influence. Both the British and Canadian governments had agreed to the free-trade terms. Facing his own Republican party, which took tariff protection as an article of faith, Taft sent a message to Congress in December 1910 that was forward-looking and magnanimous:

> My purpose in making a reciprocal trade agreement with Canada has been not only to obtain one which would be mutually advantageous to both countries, but one which also would be truly national in its scope as applied to our own country and would be of benefit to all sections ... The entire foreign trade of Canada in the last fiscal year, 1910, was $655,000,000. The imports were $376,000,000, and of this amount the United States contributed more than $223,000,000. The reduction in the duties imposed by Canada will

largely increase this amount and give us even a larger share of her market than we now enjoy, great as that is."

But other Americans took a different view. U.S. House Speaker Champ Clark and William Bennett, a Republican member of the House Foreign Relations Committee, gave the Conservatives the ammunition they needed. "I look forward," argued Champ, to thunderous applause in the chamber, "to the time when the American flag will fly over every square foot of British North America up to the North Pole. The people of Canada are of our blood and language." Bennett introduced a resolution calling for talks with Britain on measures to annex Canada. Even the *Montreal Star,* a strong backer of Laurier and the free-trade agreement, changed its stance and, in a blunt editorial, castigated the master bargainers in Washington: "None of us realized the inward meaning of the shrewdly framed offer of the long headed American government when we first saw it. It was as cunning a trap as ever laid. The master bargainers of Washington have not lost their skill."

Backed by the business community in Toronto and Montreal, Robert Borden, the Nova Scotian leading the Conservatives, seized on the annexation threats and started a filibuster in the House of Commons that brought business to a standstill. Stymied in Parliament, Laurier called an early election, even though he had two more years in his mandate. The Conservatives won, and while Laurier stayed as leader for six more years, hopes of free trade were lost, for three generations at it turned out. An attempt in 1935, after the U.S. Smoot–Harley tariff bill hit Canada hard, came with a new agreement – confirmed in Canada's Reciprocal Trade Agreements Act – when the two countries limited their tariff wars. Both Britain and Canada hoped for better trade deals with the United States. An agreement signed in 1938 lowered tariffs in all three countries, a measure hailed by the *Economist*, a leading free-trade advocate, as "the largest operation in trade liberalization that has even been undertaken."

Wartime brought new Canadian agreements with the United States on corporate investment, defence cooperation, joint planning, and security measures, which shifted the balance of Canada's trade and investment from Britain to the United States. W.L. Mackenzie King's government was aware of this change, even if public sentiment viewed Canada as a charter member of the British Empire. In 1945, King was warming to the new Truman administration and took a personal interest in a bilateral trade deal. In 1948, the year of his retirement, he considered formal talks, but backed off when cabinet cleavages became public. One pro-U.S. faction, led by C.D. Howe, plus civil servants like John Deutsch, faced opposition from Louis St Laurent and his deputy, Lester Pearson. The compromise was a policy of trade multilateralism and an emphasis on the new, rules-based GATT. Pearson was prime minister in 1965 when the United States and Canada signed the Auto Pact, a managed trade deal limited to transborder investment and trade for cars and trucks.

II

The 1980s were a difficult decade for the international trading system. Seemingly unrelated events coalesced to test the will of many politicians who liked open markets and open borders. Antecedent conditions, i.e., those political and personality factors necessary for momentous change, seemed to be in place. Those conditions are instructive vis-à-vis bilateral Canadian–U.S. trade negotiations. Much has been made of the Reagan–Mulroney personal relationship, and despite their reputation as neoconservative ideologues, they were remarkably pragmatic politicians. Their friendship began during Mulroney's June 1984 visit to Washington, only a week after the strongly pro-American John Turner succeeded the enigmatic Pierre Trudeau as prime minister.

Mulroney had campaigned for the leadership throughout the spring of 1983 on a strong pro–United States platform and called for policy change on issues largely inimical to private- sector companies – namely, on crown corporations, energy, foreign investment, intellectual property, and international trade. In Canada, the media, many academics, and each political party recognized that close to the surface were strong pro-Canadian, nationalist conceits disguised as anti-Americanism. Personally, Mulroney was initially lukewarm on comprehensive free trade but spoke openly and critically on bilateral trade restrictions in sectors like agriculture, energy, lumber, and steel. Shortly after his election victory on 4 September 1984, Mulroney accepted the U.S. president's invitation for bilateral talks in Washington. At those meetings, President Reagan reiterated his 1980 initiative for a free-trade zone encompassing Canada, the United States, and Mexico, however vague the details. At this point, exhausted by the 58-day campaign and preoccupied with forming a cabinet, Mulroney pushed only for a new bilateral process – an annual meeting of president and prime minister, and a quarterly meeting of Canadian and U.S. foreign ministers. The new government recalled Parliament in early November to present a Throne Speech and announced major initiatives, including policies to encourage competitiveness and liberalize trade. Finance Minister

Michael Wilson's Economic Statement on 8 November detailed an economic framework based on downsizing of government, improved tax incentives, market liberalization, and social-policy reform. *A New Direction for Canada: An Agenda for Economic Renewal* reframed national purpose, after a century of Macdonald's National Policy, to reposition Canada in a global economy.

The government launched massive, all-encompassing consultations involving 18 industry sectors, such as energy, financial services, fisheries, forestry, health care, housing, mining, small business, and tourism. The policy areas covered a wide spectrum – export financing, international trade, regional development, science and technology, tax reform, and welfare policy – with each new minister, aided by the civil service, the PMO's Policy Unit, and the exempt staff, offering possible policy options. However, given the widespread protectionist sentiments in the U.S. Congress, and wide media coverage of these, trade policy became a central priority of the worried Canadian corporate community.

Over the next year, a series of events set the stage for launching bilateral trade talks. They are instructive for understanding the political dynamics of how the free-trade negotiations actually began and what they imply for other bilateral negotiations. When the new prime minister spoke in New York on 10 December 1984 to the Economic Club – a group of elite American industrialists and bankers, hosted by David Rockefeller – the policy context for free trade had started to change dramatically. For one thing, Mulroney was listening to his friends in Congress and hearing about ministers' talks with the U.S. administration and congressional leaders, and he began to realize the sheer depth of U.S. protectionist sentiment, as witnessed by the spate of bills introduced in Congress. Moreover, the lobbying efforts of Canadian business groups – on agriculture, fisheries, lumber, and steel – exposed the desperate, "finger in the dyke" nature of the exercise. The Americans were in no mood for trade rhetoric – least of all from their largest trading partner. "Canada is open for business," the theme of his New York speech, gave a strong pro-free trade signal to both sides of the border. Ironically, a concrete statement on free trade was deleted from the text of the speech.

Mulroney's public views on free trade were heavily influenced by Ontario's traditional protectionist stance, often cloaked in the guise of Canada's national interest. Even though the prime minister himself had opposed free trade during the leadership campaign in 1983, not so much on its economic merits as on its political perils, he knew only too well that it was a Conservative government under Robert Borden that had defeated the Liberal initiative of Wilfrid Laurier on trade reciprocity. Mulroney's personal views paralleled Laurier's in 1892: "The party would not follow me, and there is no use thinking of it." In 1984, Ontario's premier, William Davis, was a strong Mulroney ally during the federal election campaign, but in spring 1985 he announced his resignation. Davis left a leadership vacuum, not that he was against holding talks, but he, like the Ontario members of the Mulroney cabinet, remained doubtful that the Americans would accept Canada's minimum demands. Alberta's strongly pro-free trade premier, Peter Lougheed, quickly seized the initiative.

Indeed, at the federal–provincial conference in Regina, Saskatchewan, in February 1985, Lougheed led the charge, with a forceful televised speech calling for a dramatic new initiative on bilateral trade. Privately, Lougheed thought a U.S. deal could have been achieved decades earlier, while Canada now needed to pay more attention to Japan, China, and the rest of the Pacific Rim. Ontario's new premier, Frank Miller, was largely mute on the trade question. The pendulum quickly shifted in federal-government circles, especially after David Peterson's Liberals defeated the Conservatives in the Ontario election in May 1985.

Reform of social policy had become the biggest issue for the new government in Ottawa – universal programs v. targeted spending on the poor. After Mulroney's famous remark that Medicare was "a sacred trust," the defiant mood of social activists, reinforced by seniors with strong memories of double-digit inflation, challenged the new government's attempt at policy reform, which focused on a scheme to de-index seniors' pensions. The government's ardour for dramatic reform in social policy soon died, especially after a rancorous Question Period in December 1984.

Free trade, by default, now moved to the forefront. But other events were also at work – another instance of Mulroney's good luck. The federal civil service was divided on a bilateral trade agreement, not only in External Affairs but in the PCO, departments like Industry, and crown corporations. Sylvia Ostry, the deputy minister at Trade, remained a committed "multilateralist," and peripatetic deputy minister Arthur Kroeger worried about Canada's energy autonomy. Many other deputies – Bob Richardson at Investment Canada, Stanley Hartt at Finance, Derek Burney and Gerry Shannon at External – became early advocates of a bilateral deal. In 1982, the Trudeau government had appointed a blue-ribbon Royal Commission on Canada's Economic Future, almost a replay of Walter Gordon's 1957 endeavour. Trudeau chose Donald S. Macdonald as chair.

Macdonald was a close friend and political confidant of Trudeau's, as finance minister, energy minister, go-between to the Canadian business community, and possible successor. But as a Liberal politician, he had strong credentials as a staunch nationalist, a defender of Canadian interests, despite his strong temper and no-nonsense demeanour. His report was released in September 1985. Mulroney could have shut down the commission when he won his election in 1984, but most of the research had been completed, even if the findings were then unknown. I recommended that the commission continue, and the new prime minister sent me to meet Macdonald to discuss options. Quiet, confidential meetings in his downtown law office in Toronto shortly after the election quickly led to a government decision to proceed with the final report. Its major recommendation was a comprehensive U.S.–Canadian free-trade agreement.

|||

The 1988 election, the fourth fought on trade policy, was a watershed moment in Canadian history, and the campaign was a rare occasion when the parties focused on a single issue, free trade with the United States. Other issues, such as Medicare and the social safety net, intruded to support the arguments presented on both sides. However, there was little ambiguity or confusion about what was at stake, so nebulous responses or inscrutable rhetoric received unfavourable media attention. The campaign itself was a learning exercise, as each side recognized the shifting mood of voters, between the nationalist ideology, seen in the academic community, the anti-free trade rhetoric of the dubious, doubtful, and leftish politicians in the NDP, as well as many Liberals, including their leader, John Turner. It coincided with a 100-year-old debate about annexation by the American republic and Canada's capacity to remain a viable country. The United States–Canada Free Trade Agreement (FTA), and its later extension, the North American Free Trade Agreement (NAFTA), to include Mexico, were celebrated by free-trade proponents as a second-best outcome to a new multilateral agreement, the failed Doha Round of the World Trade Organization (WTO) (2001–08), and chided by opponents as the steady slide to economic dependence on the vast American marketplace.

The two North American countries sharing the largest trade flows in the world broke new ground on several fronts in the 1980s – in agriculture, in dispute settlement, in investment, in services, and in tariff reduction. At the time, bilateral trade coincided with an enormous build-up in global protectionist pressures, and, paradoxically, a deal with Canada was the first significant U.S. bilateral trade agreement passed by Congress.

The world's mood for negotiating a new round of multilateral trade had also changed, with the United States pressing for agreements on agriculture and intellectual property, and India, speaking on behalf of the less-developed countries, refusing to bend to U.S. terms and the economic norms of the Washington consensus.

For Canada, despite the numerous studies assessing free trade, including by the *bête noire* of nationalists, economist Harry Johnston, born in Toronto, trained at Cambridge and Harvard, who became a chair at the London School of Economics and the University of Chicago. A prolific writer and a speaker at the Liberals' Thinkers Conference in Kingston in 1959, he released *The Canadian Quandary* in 1962, berating traditional tariff policies and nationalist political pretensions. Despite the 1971 study *Looking Outward* by the Economic Council, and the main recommendations of the Macdonald Commission in 1985, there was little sign that either Ottawa or the provinces were prepared to make any bold policy leaps. Indeed, with the single exception of Peter Lougheed in Alberta, none of the premiers saw free trade as a policy winner, and most provinces were prepared to hide behind the implicit framework of tariff protection acceptable to the leading manufacturing centre, Ontario. Despite occasional rantings of policy analysts and a few Canadian CEOs, such as Walter Light of Northern Telecom, free trade was simply not a priority on the national agenda.

In the U.S. capital, trade talks were only one side of a larger economic agenda (see Figure 7.2). Historically, while international trade is sizable in certain sectors of the American economy, it was less than 4 per cent of total output when John F. Kennedy became president in 1961. Starting in the 1970s, the United States was starting to feel the first signs of dramatic postwar changes, and in 1973 Richard Nixon confronted the first shift, the forced devaluation of the U.S. dollar, by abandoning the gold standard and the postwar Bretton Woods framework established in 1944. Only a few years later, President Ronald Reagan started an inexorable trend to a "managed trade" framework for key sectors like automobiles and semi-conductors, headed by the two biggest economies, the United States and Japan. They were mirrors of each other, with, respectively, rising trade surpluses and deficits and creditor and debtor status, where their joint policies affected the global economy in such areas as capital flows, exchange rates, and Third World debt. Severe imbalances, in part influenced by OPEC, required new international policy coordination and led to annual meetings of leaders, the G4, then the G5, and later the G7, including Canada. The political impact of intense Japanese industrial

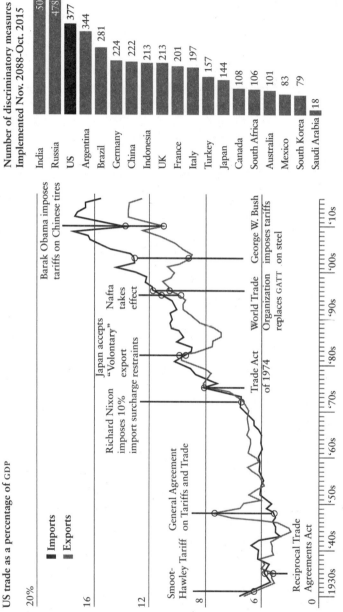

Figure 7.2 Presidents, Protectionism, and Free Trade.

competition (e.g., autos, cameras, motorcycles, radio and TV, robots, steel), forced American industrial groups to see the FTA with Canada as a side issue, secondary to trade pacts with Japan and Europe.

While the new government in Ottawa offered no specific promises or direct interest in bilateral free trade, four years later, in 1988, Mulroney's Conservatives became the leading proponents of an FTA. It remains a paradox that neither the Americans nor the Canadians were pushing for this agreement, and it wasn't the primary goal of either nation's leader in 1984. Indeed, the forces pushing the U.S. administration were quite different from those in Canada. So why did the agreement happen? As Harold Macmillan would say, "Events, dear boy, events." In the run-up to Ronald Reagan's sweeping victory in 1984, two issues dominated the American economy. The first was the deep recession of 1982, when interest rates climbed to double digits, and Paul Volcker, chair of the Federal Reserve, declared war on inflation. The second was competitiveness, against the accelerating inroads of Japanese firms across a range of sectors: automobiles, consumer electronics, semiconductors, and steel.

Across the industrial world, policy-makers recognized the fragility of the growing integration of market economies. The symptoms of the problems were (and remain) deeply embedded within the problems themselves, namely, the value of the stock market, the devaluation of the world's most important currency (the U.S. dollar), the debt crisis of the Third World, and monetary instability, i.e., major currency fluctuations and huge gyrations in capital flows. In the 1980s, the United States and Japan were in fact at a watershed in their postwar relationship and had allowed their trade to be seen as a zero-sum industrial struggle with political overtones. The media exacerbated the tensions, encouraged by such polemics as Ezra Vogel's *Japan as Number One: Lessons for America* (1979) and the Freidman–Lebard diatribe, *The Coming War with Japan* (1991).

A far more measured assessment came from Fred Bernstein, a leading economist at the Council of Foreign Relations: "Japan is already challenging the United States with a major new drive toward creativity and leadership in advanced technology ... Japanese bureaucrats and politicians will be sorely tempted to seek new avenues for national advancement. American officials will find it harder than ever to ward off self-defeating protectionist measures. The media will have a field day publishing the charges and countercharges of angry politicians. Public opinion in both nations could take an ugly turn. Traditional diplomacy will fail."

By 1983, Japan, riding a crest of phenomenal productivity and investment growth, found its trade surplus in one year equalled that of the previous two decades. In 1987, the figure approached $101 billion – the largest of any nation in recorded history. Between 1971 and 1986, U.S.–Japanese trade in merchandise increased to $115 billion per year from about $54 billion. Of this increase of $61 billion, Japan's exports to the United States accounted for $53 billion, and U.S. exports to Japan for only $8 billion, or less than 13 per cent. Of this low amount, $3.5 billion, or almost half, came not from car exports, nor from sophisticated electronics, but from gold, sold for re-export from Japan. Growing competitive problems at large, and the hollowing out of the manufacturing centre in the U.S. Midwest, in key states like Michigan, Ohio, and Illinois, created severe political pressure for protection from both state governments and members of Congress. President Reagan responded with a series of "managed trade agreements" limiting Japanese imports to mutually agreed levels based on talks in Washington.

For Canada, these U.S. tactics were particularly ominous. Canada's dependence on the American market, and the centrality of bilateral integration in sectors like cars, energy, and pulp and paper, forced governments at all levels to worry about the trade environment in Washington. Events were also changing in Canada, but for different reasons. Competitiveness had seriously deteriorated; unemployment was at historic highs; government deficits and national debt were virtually out of control. In early 1986, as the Canadian government decided to enter into trade talks with the United States, a succession of politically delicate problems flowing from "managed trade" started to emerge with force. Bilateral Japanese–American disputes added to the tension, especially in agriculture, automobiles, and steel, which affected Canada.

However, there were also other U.S.–Canadian disputes in sectors such as carbon steel and softwood lumber. They greatly added to the impetus for a "managed trade" approach, especially in light of the application of U.S. trade-remedy laws, which, perversely, defined unfair trading practices unilaterally. It was in this politically charged climate that the two countries undertook negotiations for a bilateral free-trade agreement. In 1985, it started with Brian Mulroney phoning Ronald Reagan at 1:30 p.m. on 24 September, and making a statement to the House of Commons at 3 p.m. There was no time for turning back, and the prime minister mobilized the cabinet, the bureaucracy, and a consultation process of unprecedented scope. The essence of the deal for Canada was about *process* as much as *substance*, in particular, a new mechanism for settling disputes, especially a binational review panel for appeals. The other policy objectives were straightforward and, within the general framework of multilateral trade deals, were hammered out (or not) as specific "chapters" were drafted on major topics, such as reduction of tariffs over a ten-year period, free trade over time in energy and in certain agricultural products and services; and liberalized investment and government procurement.

From a multilateral perspective, the U.S.–Canadian trade agreement offered a number of policy signals, some ominous and foreboding, about U.S. views on its future trade policy. The first had worldwide interest: was this bilateral trade agreement the latest, but most concrete, evidence of a U.S. retreat into a Fortress North America, reinforced by bilateral agreements with Mexico and Canada? (These agreements followed earlier U.S. trade arrangements – a bilateral deal with Israel in 1985 and the Caribbean Basin economic initiative.) Second, was the trade agreement a clear policy alternative to the post-1945 multilateral approach (see Figure 7.3), wherein the United States negotiated bilateral agreements with like-minded countries? In fact, Treasury Secretary James Baker spelled out this approach quite boldly: "If possible, we hope ... liberalization will occur in the Uruguay Round [of GATT]. If not, we might be willing to explore a 'market liberalization approach', through unilateral arrangements or a series of bilateral agreements ... Other nations are forced to recognize that the United States will devise ways to expand trade – with or without them." Third, was the U.S.–Canadian FTA initiating a broader policy framework for American trade relations that dropped the traditional multinational agreements that started with GATT? Would the United States prefer these bilateral deals, perhaps with Japan and the European Community, as the basis for trade, or for a broader agenda of military, political, and technological issues, between the world's largest market economies?

The visit to North America by Japanese Prime Minister Yosuhiro Nakasone early in January 1986, to Toronto and Ottawa, and then to Washington, was a forceful reminder that his government objected to a Fortress North America, discriminating against third countries, especially Japan. Clearly, Nakasone, advised by the ambassador to Canada, Kiyoaki Kikuchi, appreciated the underlying bilateral issues facing Canada and the United States, including the two-way trade and capital flows across subsidiaries of companies located on both sides of the border, i.e., within the framework of multinational subsidiaries, and also the special arrangements in other areas, such as the Auto Pact, NORAD, and the defence-sharing agreement.

Any U.S.–Canadian free-trade agreement, aside from being better than the status quo, where protectionist forces were spreading to industries vital to Canada, had to meet three other tests. First, it had to advance

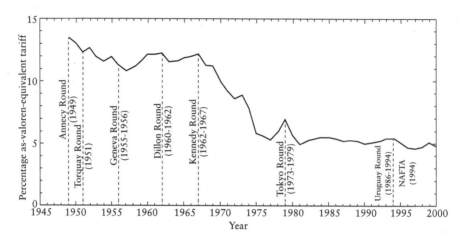

Source: Adapted from WTO

Figure 7.3 Tariff Reductions in the Post-war Era.

multilateral negotiations at the GATT (which later became the WTO). In fact, the final accord broke new ground on tariff barriers, investment, agriculture, and services – a possible model for multilateral or regional trade talks. Second, it should create, not destroy trade, by advancing rationalization of industry and production. Thus it should encourage domestic subsidiaries on both sides of the border to specialize and seek new market niches, rather than closing, as suggested by apocalyptic reactions from nationalists, such as academics at York University and the University of Toronto and much of the NDP, including the Waffle wing led by James Laxer and Mel Watkins. Third, because exchange rates, rather than trade barriers, shape investment flows, further Japanese and North American integration will increase trade as each country adjusts its industrial structure based on real comparative advantage.

The starting points are obviously different. Canada, like most European countries, depends on trade for up to 30 percent of its GNP. Canada, alone among the G7 countries, relies heavily on offering unprocessed raw materials and a limited range of services. Except for automobiles, Canada has a relatively weak manufacturing sector, especially on such criteria as R&D performance, export marketing, and financial capitalization. Its domestic economy features high foreign ownership, strong interprovincial trade barriers, and a small-scale industrial base outside the Toronto–Montreal corridor. For high-tech sectors, where economies of scale in production runs are vital to gain lower unit costs, Canada was the only

G7 country without secure access to a market of at least 100 million consumers. Further, Canada's micro corporate problems in the 1980s, where domestically controlled companies had lower levels of production in research-intensive sectors than international competitors, reflected an accumulation of neglect over the previous two decades, possibly a result of the "millpond tranquility" in corporate boardrooms. And politically, the domestic forces challenging the deal were uncompromising, not only from nationalists, but from provincial governments like Ontario's. As Allan Gotlieb, Canada's ambassador to the United States, neatly summed it up, "In the U.S., there are those who believe that unilateralism is strength; in Canada, there are those who believe that bilateralism is surrender."

IV

By coincidence, the release of the Macdonald Report occurred the same week in September 1984 that Mulroney flew to Washington for his post-election meeting with President Reagan. It was in this larger context that the most radical policy agenda item surfaced – free trade with the United States. The Macdonald Commission, widely reported and praised in the Canadian media, paralleled the policy initiatives launched in the Throne Speech and Economic Statement of November 1984, despite their separate origins. By the early spring of 1985, Mulroney and his cabinet had begun to rethink and refocus Canada's trade policy. They had launched major initiatives in areas such as promoting and financing exports and enhancing trade in the Pacific Rim. But the central role of U.S.–Canadian trade policy – and the Canadian options of functional trade, bilateral sectoral trade, or comprehensive free trade – had become the basis of the government–industry consultations launched in January 1985.

To the surprise of International Trade Minister James Kelleher, his department, and indeed the entire cabinet, the consultations produced, via briefs, letters, meetings, and open forums, an overwhelming consensus in the business community to push for a bilateral, comprehensive trade agreement – the cause, lest it be misunderstood, of the Liberals' defeat on trade reciprocity in 1911. Curiously, at the Liberal policy conference in October 1966, despite Walter's Gordon's urgings, members actually backed a resolution in favour of free-trade talks. This time, in the spring of 1985, the private sector and many supporters among labour, academe, and some provinces, forged a constituency for such talks. The prime minister seized the initiative and announced the project on 26 September 1985. Canada's detailed preparations for the actual negotiations – including the monitoring work of a special cabinet committee, fifteen sector trade-advisory groups, and an umbrella advisory committee of private-sector personnel – all strengthened the government's hand for specific negotiating issues. Joe Clark was placed in charge of the special cabinet committee, which could draw on external and internal advice, including from the main negotiator, Simon Reisman, former deputy of most economic portfolios in Ottawa, including Finance, the prime minister's first and only choice to lead the talks, with Gordon Ritchie second in command.

At the start, the aim was to reduce the political pressures for exemptions by placing all issues on the bargaining table, including culture and investment subsidies. The negotiators on both sides soon recognized what the political masters were only too quick to underscore: threatened industries, after all, have not only many jobs, but lots of voters. In a perfect world, for a small country like Canada negotiating bilateral free trade with the biggest economy in the world, all instruments of government need a central focus. Unfortunately, in the practical world, other factors are at work. The Mulroney government faced these practical issues in a daily attack in Question Period and the rantings of the Liberal Rat Pack, led by Sheila Copps and Brian Tobin, where verbal felicity was often in indirect proportion to veracity and common sense. With its huge majority, the government, despite a succession of scandals and six ministers resigning, pressed forward with its policy agenda for two years. It also initiated a new constitutional settlement, the Meech Lake Accord, which on its own caused political discord among significant stakeholders. Constant budget deficits, amounting to $30 billion a year, and rising national debt angered Conservative fiscal hawks. Media foreplay by the trade negotiators, and some unfortunate media comments by Simon Reisman, angered many senior cabinet ministers and caused a distraction and a burden on the cabinet and the prime minister. Many Conservative MPs, worried by what a trade agreement might mean for industries in their riding, placed significant time burdens on the prime minister and the PMO.

The government had no doubt as the talks started about three deadlines. Each timeline was in fact well under way, and each had only some overlapping personnel to coordinate responses. The first, of course, was the negotiating period, where both Reagan and Mulroney were totally committed. For Ronald Reagan, who wanted a significant missile-defence agreement with Mikhail Gorbachev before his own second term expired in January 1989, a failure to sign a deal with Canada was not a preferred option. The second timeline involved the next Canadian election, probably in 1988, and Mulroney's desire to have a deal in place, in order to win a two-term majority government. The third timeline related to implementing an extensive policy agenda, and supportive policy to adjust trade in such areas as science and technology, new regional economic agencies, and small business and labour training, while keeping Conservative MPs supporting the FTA. In Ottawa, behind the scenes, the political process was as important as the substantive trade measures.

The American trade negotiator, Peter Murphy, was a mild-mannered and unassuming lawyer, who knew little about Canada and its trade history. He wanted to focus on trade irritants, as seen by the American side. But many on his team knew a lot about Canada and the importance of this file for the Mulroney government. Many private meetings held in Washington and Ottawa, with support and encouragement by Simon Reisman, filled in the knowledge gap for the U.S. team. However, the prime minister and his trade advisers knew from personal experience that getting congressional leaders, the White House, and senior officials to focus on Canada, let alone the terms of a trade deal, was an ongoing challenge. The negotiations were occurring as other demanding U.S. events were unfolding, including defence and security meetings with Mikhail Gorbachev. The House of Representatives, forever in campaign mode, did not fully understand that the trade deal with Canada was the first instance after passage of new U.S. trade-remedy rules, so there were no precedents for members or committee chairs.

Even Simon Reisman, with his mood swings from calm and gentle to temper tantrums, was often exasperated by the U.S. negotiating team. After the prime minister chaired a meeting of his trade advisers, Reisman actually did walk away from the table on 23 September 1987 – his warning to take this file seriously, with the desired effect on the White House. On such delicate matters, those in the know weren't talking, and those outside the inner circle accepted media speculation, rumours, and potential defeat. In the end, the final elements of the deal were approved, including the pivotal chapter on dispute settlement, a classic example of the top two negotiators, Mulroney and Reagan, closing the deal.

The 1988 Canadian election campaign, for the vote on 21 November, proved a turning point for the economy, and, more important, for voters, on whether to prefer a relatively closed economy or an open, trading economy. There were two back-to-back TV leaders' debates, the first in French, with John Turner giving a dramatic, almost poetic closing in very good French, the second in English, where Mulroney, unlike his cool, relaxed appearance in 1984, looked nervous, over-briefed, and unsure, and Turner was seen as the winner. Even Mulroney admitted privately early the following morning that he had lost the debate. There was no other choice but to press on, out-campaign the other parties, and win the free-trade argument on its own merits.

To those who know him, Mulroney, when he is ahead, is unstoppable, and when he is behind, he is defiant, unburdened, and indomitable. Despite the faint-hearted in the party, where the Conservatives have no monopoly, Mulroney went all out, unyielding to Liberal taunts, even taking on hecklers in Toronto and actually sitting down to hear their pleas. He enticed retired Supreme Court Justice Emmett Hall, who had chaired the Royal Commission on Health Services (1961–64) that recommended Medicare, to show that Medicare was not in jeopardy with a free-trade agreement.

In the election, Mulroney won 170 seats in the enlarged House of Commons and carried all of Alberta's twenty-six seats, and most of Quebec's, sixty-three of seventy-five. Predictably, the six ministers who lost their seats came from regions vulnerable to trade competition and loss of local jobs, including Ray Hnatyshyn in Prince Albert, Diefenbaker's old seat, and International Trade Minister Jim Kelleher in Sault Ste Marie. Ironically, however, close analysis of the regional vote tallies shows that other factors were at work. Many people worried that an FTA might lead to abandonment of Medicare, and that pushed even some Conservative supporters to vote against their party.

Economic studies on the impact of the FTA and its extension to include Mexico in NAFTA (1994), after President Bill Clinton accepted the wider deal, thanks to Prime Minister Jean Chrétien's clever diplomacy, show they had positive effects. Trade openness not only increased exports and imports, but, less directly, reinforced comparative advantages in each country. Strategic changes within firms affected product specialization and helped integrate supply chains, as shown in aerospace, agricultural products, automobiles, auto parts, and food. More important in the longer run, the FTA changed many citizens' attitudes, allowing domestic firms to compete and win. The political culture also changed, with a marked decline in the anti-Americanism that impeded serious discussion on the need to make domestic firms competitive in the global market. More to the point, now that the FTA and NAFTA have become firmly entrenched, it is difficult to find politicians who had opposed the FTA in 1988 still feeling the same way, including former NDP and Liberal premiers. In 1993, Liberal leader Jean Chrétien had campaigned against not only the free-trade deal but other Mulroney initiatives, like the goods and services tax (GST), only to accept them once in office. Brian Mulroney might take comfort in the words of Winston Churchill: "To improve is to change; to be perfect is to change often."

V

Virtually all the shibboleths against free trade turned out to be illusory. Despite plant closures, as firms rationalized their production runs, they expanded production to meet new market segments, invested in new technologies, and created jobs, and trade expansion reached unprecedented levels, doubling every eight years. Canada's biggest provincial economy, Ontario's, overtook Michigan as the biggest producer of autos and trucks. Ontario has the largest information and communication technologies (ICT) sector in Canada, and the world's third biggest, rivalled only by New York and Silicon Valley in California. Canada's smallest province, Prince Edward Island, where all Conservative members lost their seats in 1988, experienced unprecedented export growth, high-tech job creation, and new business formations in aerospace and biotechnology, thanks to supportive national policies like the fixed link (the Confederation Bridge), new airport facilities, and R&D science policies.

Most of the tariff reductions, some from rates as high as 100 per cent, had a ten-year adjustment period, with certain sectors exempted (cultural industries, beer and wine), but the corporate communities on both sides of the border responded quickly and efficiently. In each country, they saw merits in focusing strategies to assure efficient production and competitive costs. The sheer size of the U.S. market and the fact that it has no true economic and financial centre, just a number of widely differing regions, forced Canadian companies to consider carefully issues such as plant scale, the need for long production runs to reduce unit costs, and the limits of price alone, compared to quality, speed, branding, and post-sales service, as competitive weapons. Indeed, Canada's small population, then only 34 million, slowly led some companies to consider other markets to achieve scale and scope and move away from a history of short production runs, high unit costs, and low productivity. Increasing two-way trade changed the domestic economic axis from east–west to north–south, as Canadian firms were forced to experience the brutal price competition in the open U.S. market.

After nine years of high-octane policy changes, Brian Mulroney announced his resignation (almost ten years to the day after he won the leadership in 1983). Kim Campbell beat Jean Charest and Jim Edwards for the Tory leadership and became prime minister in June 1993, the first woman to hold this office, and also the first Conservative to assume this role right after a leadership contest. Despite favourable polling during the summer, Campbell tempted fate and called an election. She ran a listless campaign, marred towards the end by negative and highly personal TV ads against Jean Chrétien that even many Conservative supporters found offensive. Her party was reduced to two seats, and she resigned. The Liberals had promised to reject the free-trade deal, and other Mulroney achievements, including the GST, but quickly changed their minds once in office.

Jean Chrétien, now firmly in charge of his party, and well-travelled from his time out of office, now put new emphasis on trade promotion, through a clever vehicle, Team Canada. He and the premiers would together visit foreign countries – Brazil, China, India, Pakistan– with a group of business executives, union leaders, and academics to pry open new markets, with the hope of signing trade, investment, and export relationships with local companies. This approach had three advantages, especially in most of the countries where they occurred, such as Argentina, Brazil, Chile, China, India, Indonesia, Malaysia, Mexico, Pakistan, the Philippines, Russia, South Korea, and Thailand. First, most Canadian firms don't export, regardless of size, and these delegations had a chance to learn about the opportunities for exporting. Second, commercial officers in Canadian embassies have mixed results, at best, in promoting Canadian products, especially for experienced firms that have their own local distribution networks. Third, small enterprises participating in government meetings, helped by big companies in each province, gain immediate access to the country's business and political elite, thus removing a challenging trade barrier for them. Unfortunately, Paul Martin's government cancelled this Team Canada approach.

Chrétien knew that too many firms, big and small, weren't export-oriented, as shown in Table 7.1. At home, another downturn meant that stagnant growth, high unemployment, and rising debt became the new realities for Canada and many other countries in the capitalist, developed world. Deficit-cutting and a balanced budget became a Chrétien cause, backed by Finance Minister Paul Martin. Exports and trade now seemed vital tools for breaking the downward spiral of debt and unmet expectations of disgruntled voters. Fortunately, leaders of both the richest economies and the developing world had learned the lessons of the 1930s. Through economic and financial forums like the G20 – in addition to regular meetings and international policy coordination – national leaders everywhere knew to avoid defensive measures like the disastrous U.S.

Table 7.1
Exporters and Non-exporters among Canadian Manufacturers

	Exporters	Non-exporters
Number of firms	13,538	34,138
Percentage of medium-sized and large firms	17%	2%
Average manu-facturing output ($) per firm	$3,380,000	$290,000
Total production workers	902,913	315,962

Source: Statistics Canada

Smoot–Hawley tariffs of 1930. With the failure of the Doha Round of the WTO in 2008, more countries were seeking bilateral and regional trade agreements, like that between Japan and the EU, the Trans-Pacific Partnership (TPP), and CEDA.

The Chrétien and Martin governments, from 1993 to 2006, accepted the advantages of a North American trading bloc. They became converts to global trends and the need to address the two countries with 40 per cent of the world's population, India and China. China, in particular, once it accepted the price system and capital markets in 1972, underwent spectacular economic change, growing at compound rates of 10 per cent a year. Massive amounts of foreign investment, at least $150 billion annually, and a relentless shift from low-wage assembly plants to higher value-added manufacturing, put a premium on upgrading worker skills. Lacking many raw materials to foster this growth, China became the biggest importer of commodity products – aluminum, coal, copper, iron ore, oil, and precious metals, as well as food products and potash for domestic agricultural production. Canada, like Australia, was a big winner in this export push, especially for western Canadian commodity producers.

Canada's private sector remained slow to recognize the economic rise of Asia, starting with Japan in the 1970s, and southeast Asia in the 1980s, followed by China and then India. Canadian firms focused primarily on NAFTA and internal adjustments to the free-trade agreement. The appearance of new firms like OpenText and Research in Motion and the aggressive strategies of giants like Air Canada, CN, the mining sector, and Scotiabank and of similar smaller firms in all regions was gradually reshaping the economy and redirecting it away from the managerial "culture of contentment" so derided by the country's global-minded thinkers. There was emerging an overwhelming consensus that the biggest economic challenges remained relatively low productivity and tepid innovation, and dependence on a few exportable products and services that rely mostly on the U.S. market (some 26 of 1,250 exported products accounted for over half of all exports) – see Figure 7.4. Even here, perhaps half of manufactured exports were coming from intra-firm transactions, such as Ford Canada selling to Ford United States.

The Doha Round at the WTO, involving about 160 countries, was launched in 2001, and took over seven years of talks before it failed. It reflected a breathtaking vision of global trade – the first WTO round of talks to include services, intellectual property and the politically sensitive agriculture sector – but broke down over disagreements between the United States and India, which spoke on behalf of the developed world. If the multilateral approach was not in the cards, trade agreements were still possible, where new alignments, sometimes called preferential trade agreements, became a second-best option.

Each participating country faced an awesome set of internal political challenges, as vested interests tended to prefer protection, not just for economic growth but also for managing demographic-influenced policy issues like health care, education, immigration, and an ageing population. They also had to deal with global and regional issues with no easy answers, and a scarcity of global statespeople to articulate bold solutions. As David Brooks, in a perceptive column in the *New York Times*, observed,

> It's not multi-polarity; it's multi-problemarity. As a result, this is more of an age of anxiety than of straight-up conflict. Leaders are looking around warily at who might make their problems better and who might make them worse. There are fewer close alliances and fewer sworn enemies. There are more circumstances in which nations are ambiguously attached. In this environment, you don't need big, bold visionaries. You need leaders who will pay minute attention to the unique details and fleeting properties of each region's specific circumstances. You need people who can improvise, shift and play it by ear.

The failure of the Doha Round in 2008 forced governments to seek bilateral and regional agreements, in part to forestall protectionist pressures at home, but also to formulate clear rules on a range of trade issues – e-commerce, government procurement, intellectual property, and industrial subsidies. Largely unknown to North Americans, Japanese banks, trading firms, and manufacturers had entered into strategic alliances and supply-chain networks to invest in new technologies, share

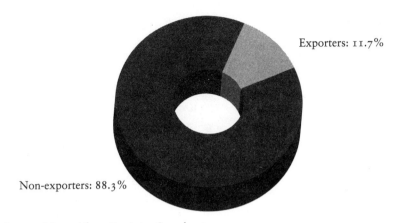

Source: Adapted from Statistics Canada

Figure 7.4 Share of Canadian SMEs That Export.

production and technology transfer, and enter new markets. Japan had become an aggressive exporter in telecommunications, nuclear power stations, and even high-speed rail (the Shinkansen, the celebrated bullet train), as well as in expanding fields like fashion, health-care products, and industrial design. In new areas like LED lighting and mobile-phone payment systems, Japan was ten years ahead of the rest of the world. A comparative study, published in the *Japan Times*, of 500 CEOs in American and Japanese firms asked about corporate priorities. The Americans highlighted return on investment (ROI), price increases, and market share; the Japanese CEOs, market share, ROI, and developing new products, with share price ranked tenth. Clearly, these CEOs have different time horizons.

Today, in the absence of a new multinational round at the WTO, a political non-starter in the face of a protectionist American administration from 2017 to 2021, even Canada, the EU, and Japan, which historically have preferred the multilateral approach and the rules-centred system of the WTO, now need other approaches to gain access to new markets (see Table 7.2 re Canada). That's why Prime Minister Harper's 2015 boast – "Under our Conservative government, Canada is going to have virtually unfettered access for our world-class products, workers and investors in forty-three countries across the world ... compared to just five when we took office" – is a bit vacuous, because Canada had been concentrating on the Doha Round, like most other advanced economies. Clearly the ground rules for trade have shifted; hence the move to bilateral and

Table 7.2
Canada's Trade Strategies (1867–date)

Key issues	1867–1985 Nation-building: east–west	1985–2010 North–south: FTA / NAFTA	2012+ Global: EU and Asia
International trade pacts	Commonwealth preference and GATT	WTO, NAFTA, CETA	WTO, TPP, and key bilateral
Exports	Traditional commodities in food, mining, pulp and paper	Commodities and high-value-added mfg (autos, ICT)	Commodities, energy; high-value-added mfg and services
Key markets	Britain and Commonwealth; United States	United States, Japan for commodities	50-50 balancing: United States and Asia
Immigration	British, European, and Commonwealth	Hong Kong, Asia, Caribbean	Global, based on skills and higher education
Special cases: industries	NORAD and defence (NATO) Auto Pact (1965) Wheat Board Bank Act, 1867	NORAD, NATO Supply management (dairy sector) Entertainment and arts and culture policy	CEDA NAFTA revisions TPP ASEAN
Defensive policy measures	Interprovincial trade barriers Crown corporations	Investment Canada Ownership restrictions in key industries (e.g., banking, telecommunications	Cabinet approval Crown corporations 3-P partnerships

regional agreements. Today there are almost 300 such deals in the world, some fairly small, like Mongolia's bilateral deal with Japan, and many of the Harper deals, such as those with Costa Rica, Jordan, and Panama, each amounting to a day's trade exchange for Canada with the United States or a week's with Asia.

VI

In 2011, winning a parliamentary majority after five years with a minority government, Stephen Harper and his Conservative cabinet made new trade agreements a front-burner issue. The FTA was now firmly in place, with companies on both sides of the border adjusted, and many branch plants closed. Harper planned to negotiate new trade agreements. Europe became a priority. Alas, provincial governments maintained high interprovincial tariffs and trade barriers, in areas as diverse as construction, education, government procurement, and the professions. The government started technical negotiations with Europe, but the actual initiative began with Jean Charest, by this time premier of Quebec, who had been a prominent minister in the Mulroney cabinet. Any Quebec premier keeps a close eye on events in Europe, especially France, where two-way trade and investment in aerospace, aluminum, forestry, and finance are tied not only to jobs and regulatory measures but to future trade pacts, such as an EU–Japanese agreement, or even an EU–United States agreement. Quebec's leading companies were key participants in the Canada Europe Round Table, then chaired by Roy MacLaren, a trade minister in the Chrétien cabinet and later high commissioner in London. His background in business and diplomacy, and his links with India, made him a strong free trader, and quietly supportive of Mulroney against Turner in 1988.

In 2006, Premier Charest invited MacLaren to his official residence in Quebec City. Over dinner, they discussed with some selected executives and his chief adviser, Dan Gagnier, a novel approach to planning talks with EU leaders, to see if a Europe-Canada trade deal had any political viability. A meeting in January 2007 in Davos, the small skiing outpost in Switzerland hosting the annual World Economic Forum, offered Charest the opportunity to broach the topic with Peter Mandelson, Europe's trade commissioner and a former senior minister in Tony Blair and Gordon Brown's Labour governments. Mandelson, more aware of Canada's federal system that most politicians in London, themselves rushing to decentralize British government, wanted to make sure the provinces as well as Ottawa would be part of the negotiations. Charest assured him that the provinces and the Council of the Federation, which he helped create in Charlottetown in 2003, would be involved. Returning to Canada, Charest recruited former premier Pierre-Marc Johnson, a lawyer and professor at McGill, to meet the premiers. Only later did he approach Ottawa to bring the prime minister up to speed. Harper agreed to launch the formal talks, but wanted to exclude the provinces, an unacceptable position when the Europeans knew that many contentious issues were under provincial jurisdiction.

The final agreement, known as the Comprehensive Economic and Trade Agreement (CETA), came into force on 21 September 2017. Canada had passed the deal on 26 May 2017, after the European Parliament approved it on 15 February, but each member country had to accept the deal, and each region within a country – and one in Belgium was reluctant. CETA, like the Canadian–U.S. FTA, shows why small, open economies like Canada's must have leaders who spend political capital to get approval of advantageous trade deals. Eventually, the deal was signed.

By late 2016, Europe was preoccupied with Britain's decision to leave the EU, after a national referendum called for 23 June that year by Prime Minister David Cameron.

Most of Canada's direct talks with the European partners, between about 2011 and 2015, were conducted by Minister of International Trade Ed Fast, whose junior portfolio meant he talked only to his equivalents in other countries. Advocates for the deal in Canada, including the business community, the provinces, and trade experts, were exasperated by Harper, who was willing to meet European leaders only in Ottawa, rather than holding a full-court press in each European capital. For fear of failure, Harper was simply unwilling to spend his political capital, which was already diminishing weekly from the Senate scandal and the loss of his chief of staff, Nigel Wright. His defeat in the election in 2015 left the final sprint to the new government of Justin Trudeau, who, unlike his father, was a strong free-trader. All the parties – Canada and the 28 EU members – ratified the pact in 2017.

Like other trade deals negotiated by the EU with Mexico or Japan, CETA provides two-way export opportunities free of tariff restrictions on 98 per cent of products, access to government procurement, and easier customs clearance by simplified testing and legal requirements. Like the FTA, CETA reinforces a rules-based system and allows firms to use other countries as a platform to expand elsewhere. For Canada, CETA offers a market of over 450 million consumers, and sectors in the industrial sectors – aerospace, agribusiness, financial services, military hardware, shipbuilding, telecommunications, and wind turbines – where European firms are world leaders.

VII

In Japan, the re-election of Prime Minister Shinzo Abe in 2017 opened a window for a trade deal with Canada, as part of his "three-arrow" economic reforms – monetary policy, fiscal policy, and deregulation and tariff reductions for industrial sectors. Two well-attended trade conferences, one in Toronto, hosted by the Canadian Chamber of Commerce, and led by Perrin Beatty from Ottawa, and one in Tokyo, hosted by the Canada Japan Chamber of Commerce, and led by Wilf Wakeley, a Canadian lawyer in Tokyo, indicated that most topics were open for discussion, unlike in other trade negotiations like CETA, which faced contentious issues like dairy products and supply management in Canada. Further, there was much to gain on both sides. Two dramatic examples came from the invited speakers. The first was better access for Canadian firms to Japan's phenomenal stock of intellectual property, gained over years of R&D investments, double the levels of Canada's private sector. The second, of special interest for western Canada's energy producers: the Fukushima nuclear disaster of 2011 and the resulting closing of nuclear plants (which produced more than a third of Japan's electricity) allowed Canada a favourable position as a natural partner for energy supplies (gas, oil, and liquefied natural gas, or LNG), technology, and organizational knowhow. What was widely seen in Canadian trade and executive circles as an optimal position – an FTA deal with Japan, full membership in the Trans-Pacific Partnership, and future bilateral free-trade pacts with India and even possibly China – meant that Canada was an ideal location for Asian investments to serve the Americas by direct trade, two-way investment, and partnership agreements in areas like science and technology and corporate alliances.

In reality, the bilateral trade deal with Japan had stalled. Changing currency alignments, notably the rise in the U.S. dollar against various currencies, including Canada and Japan's, had affected corporate tradeoffs between exports and investing abroad (a ¥1 decline against the U.S. dollar lowers Sony's ¥7-billion operating profits, so reduced tariffs are dwarfed by currency and treasury strategies). A trade deal with Japan was an ideal outcome, but a hard sell politically unless Canada took the same steps as it had to enhance the negotiations for the American trade deal, where the Mulroney–Reagan relationship was central, often at the cost of Canada's spending political capital, an approach followed by Jean Charest and then Justin Trudeau with European leaders over CETA. After all, Japan's corporate community is far more knowledgeable about Canada than Canada's is about Japan. Japan has huge direct and indirect investments in Canada, in every province, while Canada is represented in that country by only a few leading firms, like Air Canada, Manulife, and McCain, but the best-known Canadian brands there remain Anne of Green Gables, Banff, and the RCMP. Abe and Harper were not close, most ministers had limited knowledge of Japan, and the few that did, like Jim Flaherty, were preoccupied with other files. Despite regular meetings of both negotiating teams – seven in all – any deal was going to require serious commitment on the Canadian side, including the PMO, senior ministers, and the business community.

In reality, despite initial optimism, and despite seven negotiating sessions, Japan was shifting focus. For instance, it was preoccupied with a range of issues, including defence and security against China's aggressive maritime and naval reach. The issues over yen–dollar parity affected domestic economic growth and exports. And Abe saw an opening to negotiate a much bigger deal, the TPP. This initiative was inspired by Washington, in part as a pivot away from military preoccupations in the Middle East, in part to contain China, and reflecting general recognition that the leading growth economies were in Asia. Sadly, by any measure, this Pacific Rim trade initiative was not well thought through. First, the TPP didn't include Japan, by far the most advanced in Asia, or Canada. By actual GNP, China may be bigger than Japan or even the United States, depending on calculations, but Japan's global banks, global industrial reach, intellectual property, per-capita income, and multinational firms, including the trading companies, put its multilateral trade position on a higher plane.

Whatever the immediate commercial, job-creating merits of the TPP, virtually all serious analyses pointed to the long-term gains for all participating countries. Elements such as better access to markets, more effective division of labour, a legal framework for trade and investment, and a system of dispute settlement looked likely to open trade in a highly productive way. But opponents of the TPP, including those in the U.S. Congress, warned of potential job losses, a hollowing out of many industrial sectors, and a decline in real wages. U.S. critics saw parallels with the Midwest-rustbelt devastation wreaked by NAFTA. Other voices went further, presenting the TPP as a threat to Asian and American security interests. One commentator warned: "Because of the vast investments by U.S. companies there, they have often acted as lobbyists for the PRC because they are worried about protecting their investments. We can expect that, as U.S. company investments in the TPP countries increase, the potential for our firms to 'protect' their investments by advocating for the interests of their host country might be counter to some of our foreign policy or national security interests."

In Washington, where post-9/11 security and defence priorities overrode all other considerations, and after the election in November 2016 of Donald Trump, with his 18th-century-style mercantile mindset and "America First" mantra, both Democratic and Republican policy-makers started seeing the rise of China differently. China's two decades of industrial reform produced a new capitalist class among the political class in Beijing, and its members wanted more internal reforms, despite the fractious groups preferring the status quo. Around the world, few observers doubted China's emergence as an industrial power, a powerful regional power in Asia, attracting up to $150 billion a year in foreign investment, and growth rates of 10 per cent annually. It was producing annually goods and services equal to North America, Europe, and Japan combined. It has signed trade agreements with twenty-three countries, and has designs on its own Asian trade deal, including with Russia. As a result, it is ignoring international norms on labour rights and environmental benchmarks, and thus perpetuating substandard work conditions and practices, faulty machinery, and poor factory conditions at home, as is happening elsewhere in Asia, illustrated by the deaths of 1,134 people in the collapse of a garment factory in Dhaka, Bangladesh, in April 2013.

U.S. trade laws are, to put it mildly, very complex, involving procedural issues in Congress, committee votes with tit-for-tat exchanges to bring aboard reluctant members, and arcane workings between the two chambers of Congress. After his inauguration in January 2017, Donald Trump almost immediately pulled the plug on U.S. participation in the TPP (which had been shaped substantially to suit American interests). In May, Japan took the lead to revive the negotiations and forge a "TPP-11" – the original twelve interested parties, minus the United States: Australia, Brunei, Canada, Chile, Japan, Malaysia, Mexico, New Zealand, Peru, Singapore, and Vietnam. Japan, of course, has other trade deals in the works, including a new trade partnership with the European Union, a deal with the United States, and strengthening thirteen bilateral arrangements, including one with India. Japan had cleverly put a priority on completing its deal with the EU by the end of 2015, a real signal, with a publicly stated deadline, in contrast to its protracted trade negotiations with Canada.

Canada's signed (in 2018) but not-yet-ratified trade agreement with the EU (CETA) is another game-changer to certify Canada as an open-trade economy, and the fact that all provinces, from three political parties, are supporting Ottawa on renegotiating NAFTA is testimony to a sea change in citizens' attitudes since the free-trade election of 1988. But these and other deals now require a far more aggressive trade stance by Canadian firms. Few outside oil and gas or mining match the aggressive stance of enterprises like Air Canada, Bombardier, Manulife, and SNC in their Asian operations.

The TPP, in fact, became a national priority in Japan, while Prime Minister Abe cultivated good relations with President Trump. There were clear reasons for Japan's security concerns: nuclear tests by North Korea, Chinese military initiatives in the South China Sea, and the need to maintain Japan's military alliance with the United States, despite reluctant members of Congress. Abe saw the TPP as an effort to rejuvenate the domestic economy and reform dated institutions – the "third arrow" in what was dubbed "Abenomics." His government wanted to make Japan globally relevant and not marginalized within Asia by an aggressive China.

A trade meeting in Danang, Vietnam, in November 2017 finalized the revived TPP-11, coinciding with the APEC Summit. In some respects, the meetings were a turning point for Canada – and arguably a serious misstep with long-term consequences. By not fully endorsing the deal in Vietnam, Canada angered its negotiating partners – especially the Japanese, who knew that they couldn't afford to let their principal ally, the United States, see this initiative fall by the wayside.

To the Canadian public, the niceties of trade negotiations are a long way from everyday concerns, but insiders and many interested citizens understood that Canada had a lot at stake with the TPP. Canada's missteps in Danang intensely angered the Japanese delegates and their political, diplomatic, and industrial network in Tokyo. Even though the TPP started as an American initiative to "pivot to Asia," and originally excluded Japan and Canada, once the United States walked out in January 2017, Japan took the lead and expected help from countries like Canada. In the end, the eleven nations did forge a pact, which included new chapters avoided in other negotiations and offering a benchmark for other potential deals, such as EU–Japan, Britain–EU post-Brexit, Britain–United States, and United States–Japan. The other countries had even accepted Canada's proposal to rename the deal the Comprehensive and Progressive Trans-Pacific Partnership, a sop to placate potential adversaries in the Canadian labour movement and their NDP supporters. The eleven member countries have all filed their notices of ratification with New Zealand, which serves as the depository overseeing TPP implementation.

VIII

Canada–Japan EPA / FTA – Post Symposium Action Plan
TO: Nigel Wright
From: Charles McMillan
Date: November 7, 2012
Re: Canada Japan EPA / FTA

The Canadian Chamber of Commerce in Japan (CCCJ), with the support of the Keidanren and the Canadian Chamber of Commerce (CCC) hosted a high-level symposium on 2 November on the proposed Canada–Japan EPA / FTA. It was the first private sector conversation addressing the agreement tailored to the needs of the business communities of Canada and Japan, with negotiations between the two governments commencing on November 26.

The timeliness was carefully planned and brought key Canadian and Japanese stakeholders from the private sector to engage on pertinent issues / strategies / time frames to achieve a successful bilateral agreement. Among the keynote speakers were the Honourable Perrin Beatty, President and CEO of the CCC, and Yorizumi Watanabe, Professor, International Political Economy, Keio University, who was Chief Negotiator of the Japan–Mexico EPA and advisor on the Japan–India Partnership, among other duties.

The two panels included detailed discussions of Agriculture and Forestry, as well as Autos / Autoparts and Energy, including representatives from the Canadian Federation of Agriculture, Japan's Central Union of Agricultural Co-operatives (JA–Zenchu), Canada Wood Group, National Federation on Forest Owners Cooperative Association, Automotive Parts Manufacturers' Association, Japan Automobile Manufacturers' Association (JAMA) and Japan Oil, Gas and Metals National Corporation (JOGMEC). The detailed presentations / discussions were moderated by Japan's former Ambassador to Canada and Chairman of the CCCJ's Honorary Board of Advisors Sadaaki Numata and myself.

By any standards of comparison, the CCCJ Symposium on Canada Japan EPA was an outstanding success – the number and range of participants (including senior bureaucrats from the main ministries in Japan), the high-profile speakers from Canada and Japan, the organization (Receptions, Food, translations, open dialogue, publicity, media) so the issue now is to follow up this event with an action plan over the next six months to push the EPA / FTA forward. This event took careful planning, communications, and forward thinking, and this approach will be necessary as the formal trade talks take place later this month but will require sustained championing and support in the months ahead, particularly to get a deal signed, say in twelve months, and then executed via Parliamentary / Diet debates.

This memo is to brief you on the importance of this event, and what will happen over the next six months, with some suggestions:

1. CCCJ will contact existing members and their friends to brief their colleagues, MPs, Senators, academics, MLAs with background materials on Canada–Japan (one pagers) and local media asking for support;

2. The three Canadian political parties were represented on the Parliamentary trade committee visiting Tokyo and they were all in agreement of this free trade initiative – the CCCJ will provide them and their colleagues with background materials, and info and pictures for their monthly Householders that get mailed to their constituents, and key people – elected and staff – in each party (same for Diet members);
3. The CCCJ, with others, will compile a list of people (academics, business, bureaucrats, MLAS and MPS, media) who can push information, contacts, and feedback, province by province – regardless of party support;
4. Industry Associations – the CCCJ and the Canadian Chamber will contact various key industry associations on the results / takeaways of the Symposium and planned follow up with a 2013 Conference in Canada;
5. Briefing Materials – background papers, industry studies, speeches, media articles to be hosted on the CCCJ website and available to interested parties;
6. Media – ascertain key media in Canada and Japan – newspapers, TV, and cable;
7. DFAIT – the CCCJ should provide materials on the Symposium and suggest a SAGIT structure for the negotiating team to allow stakeholders' feedback on industry issues, similar to the US–Canada model. Possible sectors. Potential sectors might be Agriculture, Food and Agribusiness, Aerospace, Autos and Auto parts, Forestry, Alcohol and Beverages, Energy, Mining, High Tech (ICT), Tourism, Banking and Finance, Biotech and Pharmaceuticals, Medical Devices, Software and Gaming, and Business Services. Careful attention should be paid to both upstream and downstream issues in these sectors, as well as the presence, or the potential need, for scientific and engineering clusters of various stakeholders;
8. The CCCJ, possibly with the Canadian Chamber, should prepare briefings on the Conference for the Premiers and their policy staffs, and possibly have it discussed and regional meetings of Premiers, and their annual meeting in August;
9. Media – a list of Japanese and Canadian media journalists should be assembled, and regular contacts made in both countries, with background materials;

> 10 Japanese Embassy / Canadian Embassy should be briefed, with regular contacts made on on-going follow up, using a single contact with each Embassy;
> 11 March Conference – plans should begin soon for a major conference, with keynote, a high-profile speakers from each country, including sector panels and panelists, media, background briefings, and appropriate translation (French, English, Japanese) facilities. There are good arguments to have it outside Ottawa, say in Calgary (where regional and provincial support would be very high) or Toronto (where media attention would be high, and relatively easy to attract high profile folks from Ottawa). Special attention should be paid to bring various Premiers to participate (e.g. Alta, Sask, Ontario, NB, NS), as well as profile MPs from each party.
>
> PMO Briefing – a slide presentation should be prepared to brief Nigel Wright and his colleagues in the PMO on the Symposium takeaways, with key spokesmen in the Government Caucus.

IX

In the half-century between 1945 and 1995, in GATT, eight rounds of multilateral negotiations lowered tariff and non-tariff barriers in the advanced economies, but some countries preferred relatively closed borders. The failure of the Doha Round (2001–08) of the WTO (which replaced GATT in 1995) was traumatic, as the global economy evolved into geographically based trading blocs, even among former communist states like the Black Sea bloc. Other trading blocs also had a clear geographical focus – ASEAN, EU, MERCOSUR, and NAFTA. Falling transportation costs – over 90 per cent of global trade is ocean-based – coincides with new forms of communications, from cellphones to smart phones. The relentless speed of communications and frictionless cross-border passage suggest long-term trends, as Frances Cairncross suggests in *The Death of Distance: How the Communications Revolution Is Changing Our Lives* (1997). However, anti-globalist political trends also point to another force, a return to mercantilist-type pressure groups and political leaders who disown the wealth-creating advantages of global trade and open borders. As Canadian-born economist Jacob Viner put it presciently at the establishment of GATT in 1947, "There are few free traders in the present-day world, no one pays any attention to their views, and no person in authority anywhere advocates free trade."

Canada now faces challenging decisions on vital trade matters. The first – renegotiating NAFTA – was crucial, for trade and investment with the United States, Canada's biggest trading partner. It became more of a media showcase for Donald Trump, as he turned his back on three generations of U.S. economic priorities on trade promotion, the rule of law, and partnerships with allies. Presidents of both parties had put forward very similar positions. By contrast, Trumpism wasn't good for international trade and global trade agreements. All leading trading nations are scrambling to advance their trade agendas, without or without the United States, including through bilateral deals with the U.S. administration, a reminder of what John Milton observed, when "chaos umpire sits ... chance governs all." In this trade bazaar, negotiators receive a mandate from their political masters not only to proceed within a general framework, but to pay attention to certain chapters of any deal that are particularly sensitive at home or contentious for other partners.

The so-called NAFTA II, renamed awkwardly the United States–Mexico–Canada Agreement (USMCA), is arguably worse than its predecessor as a trade pact, but, given the deep protectionist sentiments in the White House, and the coal-fired fumes of "Make America Great Again" (MAGA), Justin Trudeau's government could take comfort that its negotiating team made the best of some bad options, including possible U.S. withdrawal from NAFTA. More hopeful, the fact that all provinces and federal parties supported the government's negotiating stance and made all-party support a signal to the Americans, shows how much Canada has shifted towards free trade, open borders, and dispute-settlement mechanisms, partly perhaps because of the 1988 election and the resulting FTA. One part of the "USMCA" – section 32.10 – was inserted at President Trump's behest and requires any signatory country to notify the other two partners three months in advance if it intends to negotiate a free-trade deal with a "non-market economy," clearly a code word for China. The early diagnosis of this clause was clearly misinterpreted, i.e., it purportedly gave the American government a veto over trade policy, a misreading.

The fact that many Canadians now fully realize the importance of the U.S. market for their economic future is encouraging, suggesting a real understanding of their country's competitive pressures and the need to orient its economy to global demands. The fact that the Liberal government recruited people like Brian Mulroney, who spoke to the U.S. Congress and to many of its members and to President Trump's cabinet privately, is a sign of bipartisanship at its best. But the trade basics remain the same: a rules-based system, where private firms compete in a global economy. Despite Chamber of Commerce rhetoric in the United States, there are many sectors where best commercial practice is not on display, a huge difference from the technological and economic environment of the 1960s and 1970s, so Canada needs to strengthen its global partnerships without jeopardizing its hard-won success in NAFTA and the United States.

Finalizing the TPP without the United States puts trade with Japan and the rest of Asia in play. In Asia, these political and trade machinations have another potential player – China. The TPP was originally conceived by the Americas as a tool to contain that powerhouse – or at least to put U.S. values, governance, and rule of law at the centre of new trade rules for the 21st century. The Trump administration saw China as the *bête noire* of trade, a predatory nation with mercantile instincts and government-sanctioned actions, both economic and military. Its huge trade deficits with the United States are blamed for the rustbelt decay of the American Midwest – the manufacturing heartland. "We have trade deficits with China that are through the roof," Trump said. "They're so big and so bad that it's embarrassing saying what the number is." In fact, the trade deficit – $274 billion for the first nine months of 2017 – included huge imports for American retailers like Walmart, a company that takes a huge share of China's exports to the United States.

It is facile to argue that the TPP is an "Asian" substitute for the stalled Doha Round at the WTO. The TPP is path-breaking and incorporates new standards on labour and the environment, intellectual property, and investment and rules of origin. Indeed, in any practical trade pact, following David Ricardo's iron rule of comparative advantage, the advantages (benefits) are small and widely dispersed; the disadvantages (costs) are large and highly focused. National trade protection has spiked in the past decade, and, according to the research group Global Trade Alert, the G20 countries have in total implemented more than 6,600 measures, at times disguising corporate subsidies as tax relief, and seriously threatened the global trading system. Even worse, in the United States, subtle forms of deregulation and tariff policy, justified as "America First" security moves, and efforts to defang the WTO allowed the Trump administration to avoid massive changes in U.S. private saving rates and the federal deficit, and for this deserved an international rebuke. China – no slouch when it comes to playing the game of geopolitics, with new forms of nuance and subtlety – has its own trade-infrastructure strategy, the "Silk Road" project, or Belt Road Initiative (BRI), and its Infrastructure Development Bank. These projects are stunning in their geographical reach and include both maritime and land corridors across most of Eurasia, from Beijing to Rotterdam.

Years ago, China established the ASEAN–China Investment Cooperation Fund, starting at US$10 billion, to support regional infrastructure construction, and another $15 billion in credit, including $1.7 billion in favourable credit terms. New funding partners now include Britain, Germany, and South Korea, but not the United States or Canada – the latter gap a strategic policy error by the Harper government, overturned by Justin Trudeau. In the short run, this infrastructure bank may help China's state-owned firms to design and construct Asia's infrastructure: dams, electrical plants, highways, pipelines, ports, and sewers, as well as, eventually, passenger train systems, subways, and superhighways.

Japan's focus on TPP-11 is seen as an interim project, along with the Asia–African Growth Corridor with India, a Japan–EU trade agreement, and future bilateral deals with APEC countries. Clearly, for Canada, TPP represents an opportunity that can't be dismissed, especially as other potential trade blocs may rival the TPP – a possible trade pact linking China, Japan, and South Korea, after the American disruptions from the Trump administration, or a Chinese-led rival trading bloc (including some South American countries), perhaps using the Chinese yuan as the reserve currency. Despite the historic trade imbalance, which has seen Japan export high value-added products like cars, electronics, and trucks to Canada (about $12.5 billion worth per annum) and Canada export about $4.5 billion in commodities to Japan, Canadian manufacturers can become part of Japanese global manufacturing by producing specialized parts and components or even sub-assemblies for sectors like advanced electronics, aerospace, and autos. They can also become a market platform for smaller Japanese firms to sell in North America. Estimates vary, but of the over 1,200 products Canada exports, more than half of sales come from only twenty-six products. Global marketing and distribution, in part because of the huge trading-house sector, are a global Japanese strength.

In the end, Canada signed the TPP agreement as the leaders met in Danang in November 2017, despite reluctance among special interests at home. To be fair, few countries have so many vital trade deals being negotiated simultaneously – with the United States, Europe, and Asia.

The issues have involved domestic politics (e.g., the dairy and auto sectors) and affect other files, such as the Paris Agreement on climate change, a potential seat on the UN Security Council, and, as always, relations with the White House. Of course, all parties to the TPP negotiations knew there was an elephant in the room: possible U.S. re-engagement. It is these arguments – the need for cooperation with China as a partner in Asian growth (see Figure 7.5), extending now to India and south Asia – the importance of the rule of law, protection of workers, health standards, worker safety, and a clear dispute-settlement mechanism – that provide the real rationale for the TPP and its expansion to other countries, especially China, the United States, and India.

Canada has a history of mobilizing internal resources – political, diplomatic, and provincial – to negotiate trade deals, such as GATT and the WTO framework. Today, few observers fully appreciate the extent of the Mulroney initiatives in the 1985–89 trade negotiations with the United States, such as establishing a cabinet trade committee chaired by the finance minister, allowing the negotiating team to have private meetings with political advisers to test potential clauses and chapters, and a fifteen-sector advisory committee on strategy in key industrial areas. Equally important was the personal Mulroney–Reagan connection, with each man knowing the other's preoccupations and the domestic fallout from failure to secure a deal. As Britain implements its Brexit plan, its formal withdrawal from the European Union, Canada must renegotiate its trade agreement with the EU (CETA). But Canada's future trade goes beyond such deals. Many of its private-sector firms must change their mindset from domestic and regional to global, to enhance their productivity and wealth creation, keeping in mind the sage counsel of Canada's first female MP, Agnes Macphail, "Canadians can be radical, but they must be radical in their own peculiar way, and that way must be in harmony with our national traditions and ideals."

Rank	Counyty	Stake (% of Total)	Voting Rights (% of Total)
	World	100.00	100.00
1	China	30.34	26.06
2	India	8.52	7.50.
3	Russia	6.66	5.93
4	Germany	4.57	4.15
5	South Korea	3.81	3.50
6	Australia	3.75	3.45
7	France	3.44	3.19
8	Indonesia	3.42	3.17
9	Brazil	3.24	3.02
10	United Kingdom	3.11	2.91
11	Turkey	2.66	2.52
12	Italy	2.62	2.49
13	Saudi Arabia	2.59	2.47
14	Spain	1.79	1.79
15	Iran	1.61	1.63
16	Thailand	1.45	1.50
17	United Arab Emirates	1.21	1.29
18	Pakistan	1.05	1.16
19	Netherllands	1.05	1.16
20	Philippines	1.00	1.11

Source: Adapted from *Wall Street Journal*

Figure 7.5 Contributors to China's Asian Infrastructure Bank.

8

Successful Governments, Successful Prime Ministers

Canada's Geography as Policy Constraint – The Canadian Electoral Cycle – Uncontrollable Events – Political Rankings as a Political Soapbox – Party Legacies – Political Electability – Style of Government and Policy Outcomes – Future Orientation – Canada's Post-Industrial Future

We should be grateful that we do not have the burden of violent revolution or civil war, which still cast their shadows over countries such as France or the United States.

Margaret MacMillan

INTRODUCTION

Like all democracies, Canada faces relentless pressures that define the cycles of history, often where sundry forces are propelled by uncontrolled and often uncontrollable events. The challenges are formidable – war and peace, economic downturns, terrorism, aggressive actions of other countries, viruses and disease, technology, trade protectionism, and migration. How the political system understands and reacts defines a nation's character and shape its values. Canada is a North American nation, so geography plays a vital role, with a three-ocean border, and a neighbour to the south with varying bouts of imperial impulses, isolationist tendencies, and a fundamentally conservative value system. In retrospect, it is one thing to criticize John A. Macdonald for his instincts about a strong central government, as against many people even in his own party and elsewhere who wanted divided, decentralized rule. But it is another matter when he had to take action against the likes of William Graham Sumner, the American social Darwinist, who opined, "If you want war, nourish a doctrine" and hoped that "the law of gravitation would bring in Canada" to the United States. Walt Whitman could write in *Democratic Vistas* (1871), perhaps anticipating his nation's second centennial, "There will be forty to 50 great states, among them Canada and Cuba."

To the north of Canada and around the pole, sits a country with the world's largest land mass, stretching across eleven and a half time zones (to Canada's five and a half), with a history that contrasts with Western political and legal norms. Canada's relationship with Russia, dominating the Arctic Archipelago with Western nations, has in recent decades been focused on the Kremlin, under the reformist Mikhail Gorbachev, the well-meaning but unstable Boris Yeltsin, and now the ruthless KGB-trained Vladimir Putin. Canada's political system struggles to find accommodation with Russia on a range of vital strategic issues, from Arctic boundaries and sovereignty, through climate change and nuclear proliferation, to energy and trade, still the central topics of Canadian foreign policy.

In 1984, over a century after Whitman's comment, after two decades of nationalist feelings, and with worries about possible American takeover via foreign investment, Canadians had these concerns:

> In the economic and cultural spheres, the 'interdependence' is also lopsided. Although Canada is America's best customer, the average American wallet would not be greatly flattened if all economic exchange between the two nations ceased. Canada, however, would feel a significant economic hardship. The distortions of reality inherent in the concept of 'interdependence' as applied to relations between Canada and the United States is epitomized in J.B. Brebner's unfortunate metaphor describing the two nations as the 'Siamese twins of North America.' It is difficult to image an elephant and a mouse as Siamese twins.

Canada's history gave its leaders a two-track development policy, namely, seeking economic relations with and military security from the Americans, while leveraging Britain for more autonomy but accepting the umbrella of British defence. Indeed, till the 1920s, British ambassadors in Washington dealt with Canada-related issues, so much so that the British government offered that job to a Canadian prime minister, Robert Borden. In 1929, with Canada entering its seventh decade as a Confederation, Winston Churchill travelled to Canada on a one-month national tour before visiting the United States, and was so impressed with the country's potential that he wrote his wife, "The Canadian national spirit and personality is becoming so powerful and self-contained that I do not think we need to fear the future" and then added: "Darling I am greatly attracted to this country ... immense developments are going forward. There are fortunes to be made in many directions."

Despite changes in voting patterns and political preferences of pockets of the electorate, Canada has remained in effect a two-party electoral system, with minority parties like the New Democrats and splinter parties from Quebec and western Canada gaining a minority of seats over time. Those latter parties existed as electoral forces, however, for one, maybe two elections in a first-past-the-post voting system. The electoral map is a product of the Charlottetown Conference of 1864, when George Brown, Clear Grit (Liberal) leader and briefly premier in 1858, and known best as editor of Toronto's *Globe*, fought relentlessly for representation by population, knowing that Canada West would likely gain the most. His prediction proved to be accurate: Ontario, as district boundaries change based on ten-year census counts, has always had the most seats of any province in the House of Commons, more than Quebec and more than all western provinces combined.

Curiously, only the Liberal party fully appreciated the changes in the electoral base after the era of Macdonald, when Laurier soon became prime minister. In retrospect, it was only a matter of the arithmetic of the electoral system. For fifteen years, Laurier built the Liberal party with support in all regions, including the west, and he watched the Conservatives morph into a regional party with only limited support in Quebec and French-speaking ridings elsewhere, especially in Ontario and New Brunswick. The fact that the Liberals after Laurier alternated (principally) English- and French-speaking leaders enhanced electoral discipline, not only in their caucuses in House and Senate, but in party headquarters as well. Since King's retirement in 1948, the Liberals have been in government for forty-five years, essentially by cultivating their electoral base in Ontario and Quebec. Put differently, the Conservatives faced then and now a huge electoral burden not only to gain power, but to stay in office beyond a single majority mandate, which has occurred only once since Macdonald's electoral success in 1878, by Brian Mulroney in 1988. See Table. 8.1.

For every generation, it seems, the politics of Canada involves a sea change in the electoral map. Just before the Charlottetown Conference of 1864, John A. Macdonald and George-Étienne Cartier developed a new political alliance between Canada East's *bleus* and John A.'s Tories in Canada West. That pact brought them government for a generation.

Table 8.1
Quebec and Rest of Canada (ROC) in Federal-Election Victories (1949–2015)

Year	Prime minister	Opposition leader	% vote	Total ridings	Seats won Total	QC	ROC
1949	Louis St Laurent	George Drew	49.15	262	191	68	123
1953		George Drew	48.30	265	169	66	105
1957	John Diefenbaker	Louis St Laurent	38.50	265	112	9	103
1958		Lester Pearson	53.66	265	208	50	158
1962		Lester Pearson	37.22	265	116	14	102
1963	Lester Pearson	John Diefenbaker	41.48	265	128	47	81
1965		John Diefenbaker	40.18	265	131	56	75
1968	Pierre Trudeau	Robert Stanfield	45.37	265	154	56	98
1972		Robert Stanfield	38.42	265	109	56	53
1974		Robert Stanfield	43.15	265	141	60	81
1979	Joe Clark	Pierre Trudeau	35.89	265	136	2	134
1980	Pierre Trudeau	Joe Clark	44.34	282	147	74	73
1984	Brian Mulroney	John Turner	50.03	282	211	58	153
1988		John Turner	43.03	283	169	63	106
1993	Jean Chrétien	Kim Campbell	41.24	295	177	19	158
1997		Preston Manning	38.46	301	155	26	129
2000		Stockwell Day	40.18	301	172	36	136
2004	Paul Martin	Stephen Harper	36.73	301	135	21	114
2006	Stephen Harper	Paul Martin	36.27	308	124	10	114
2008		Stéphane Dion	37.65	308	143	10	133
2011		Jack Layton	39.42	308	166	5	161
2015	Justin Trudeau	Stephen Harper	47.2	338	184	40	144

Source: *Parliamentary Guide*, author's analysis

Wilfrid Laurier then broke the back of the Macdonald-mourning Conservatives in 1896, setting up the Liberals as the true governing party for the 20th century, one of the most successful political machines in the democratic world. W.L. Mackenzie King continued Laurier's coalition of francophones and anglophones and cultivated strong regional ministers and power brokers in each province, the pattern of every post-1948 Liberal prime minister: St Laurent, Pearson, Pierre Trudeau, Chrétien, Martin, and

Justin Trudeau, helped hugely by governing experience, incumbency, and the feeding of the Liberal patronage machine without scruples.

John Diefenbaker's election sweep in 1958 left the Conservatives with a western-based rump when they departed office in 1963. Thanks to Premier Maurice Duplessis's Union Nationale machine, the Conservatives won fifty federal seats in Quebec in 1958. Five years of power had not taught the Conservative hierarchy to make francophones comfortable as party members, and its treatment of francophone ministers, including Leon Balcer, was shabby and unseemly. Subsequent leaders like Robert Stanfield and Joe Clark changed the party's attitudes for the better, much to the annoyance of many MPs and other party members. However, the fortunes of good timing in 1968 allowed the Liberals, with a new leader, Pierre Trudeau, to so dominate the electoral landscape in francophone Canada that in five successive federal elections he won huge majorities in his native province – in 1980 taking all but one seat. However, analysis of the results – in 1974 and 1980, for instance – show that the Liberals won only 30.5 per cent and 25.8 per cent, respectively, of the seats outside Quebec, mostly in Ontario, and they steadily lost ground in western Canada.

This pattern changed only when Brian Mulroney became Conservative leader in 1983. Flaunting his working-class background, party activism, and social network, and with his oceanic political ambitions, bold policies, and love of wading into crowds, he broke the Liberal stranglehold in 1984. He gained a landslide of 211 seats in a 282-seat House and legitimized Conservative candidates in the 110 ridings with francophone pluralities, helped in part because many francophone voters thought he was a francophone. With Canada's system of representation by population and first past the post, the idea of a national party being anything but a brokerage coalition of MPs is an academic pipedream. The Liberals' main base is in Ontario and Quebec, with some support in the west, essentially in British Columbia, as well as in parts of Atlantic Canada. However, in his first election as leader, Jean Chrétien won only nineteen seats in Quebec, a historic low for his party, and in 2004, Paul Martin, a francophone from Windsor, Ontario, who won a seat first in Quebec in 1997, took only twenty-one seats in that province, to form a minority government.

The 2011 election, however, showed a dramatic change, when Stephen Harper won his only majority government. His new caucus was widespread, by geography and by ethnic and language support, having attracted new suburban voters around the bigger cities, in the growth areas of Ontario and western Canada, but taking few seats in Quebec, fewer even than Diefenbaker in 1957 or 1962. Although Quebec has fewer than a quarter of Commons seats (seventy-eight of 338), traditional voting patterns by region make it unlikely that a party could win an overall majority with few Quebec seats – this was the subject of a controversial memo in 1957 to John Diefenbaker from Gordon Churchill, his confidant, who assessed winnable seats for the Conservatives. This possibility has implications for all parties. Harper's expectation and that of his party that the twenty-eight seats added by redistribution in Ontario and western Canada would vote Conservative was not borne out in the 2015 election, and the Liberals took most of them. Justin Trudeau won 144 seats outside Quebec, a number matched only by John Diefenbaker in 1958, Brian Mulroney in 1984, Jean Chrétien in 1993, and Stephen Harper in 2011.

I

During the first 150 years of Confederation, Canada has had twenty-eight prime ministers, but only four with a relatively long tenure. The first, John A. Macdonald, by any standards ranks at the top, because, without his cunning, forward-looking leadership, his close alliance and friendship with George-Étienne Cartier, his team of leading politicians from each of the six British North American colonies, his diplomacy in London, and his policies towards the Americans, there would have been no Canada as a federation, and most of western Canada would be American territory. Current approaches to belittle Macdonald's legacy, led ironically by academic members of the Canadian Historical Association, is a pander to political correctness and a shocking example of mindless naïveté. No politician gives Macdonald better tribute than his eventual chief rival, Wilfrid Laurier, who watched him closely for seventeen years. In fact, in many ways, the modern Liberal party borrows many of the features of Macdonald's Conservatives – a big-tent mix of francophones and anglophones that welcomes new members and seeks shrewd recruits to become MPs in the Burkean mould – members seeing Parliament as the arena to settle policy differences, where pragmatism and compromise lead to practical and pragmatic results.

Only Macdonald, Laurier, King, and Pierre Trudeau governed for more than a decade, and many prime ministers had very short spans in office, many less than a year: Tupper 69 days, Clark nine months, Turner 80 days, Campbell four and a half months. Macdonald's four Conservative successors, all appointed, lasted only a short time – Abbott, eighteen months, Thompson, twenty-four months, Bowell sixteen months, and Tupper, sixty-nine days, before losing the 1896 election. Two other prime ministers had short terms, Arthur Meighen (sixteen months and three months), Paul Martin (twenty-seven and a half months). Yet even briefly serving prime ministers can make a big difference: Joe Clark's letting in 50,000 Vietnamese boatpeople in 1979, Paul Martin's agreement on Aboriginal policies with the provinces – the Kelowna Accord, and Stephen Harper's motion to recognize the Québécois as a nation within a united Canada.

Similar trends shape the chronology of governments and prime ministerial leadership. For its first fifty years, the Confederation project took priority and dominated the policy agenda in Ottawa. The entry of new provinces, western expansion, and the transcontinental railway, the purchase and consolidation of Rupert's Land and beyond, the building of national institutions, such as the NWMP / RCMP and the Supreme Court, and enfranchising new groups of voters and designing an electoral system required ministerial focus and debates in Parliament. The First World War, along with the years just before and just after, similar to the Second World War a generation later, was a disruptive force and tested the historic connection to Britain. While the specific issues of funding a Canadian navy before the Great War and a role in the peace talks after made for divisive debates in Parliament, the larger issue of an independent foreign policy had greater consequences. Unfortunately for Robert Borden's Unionist government, conscription opened up new fissures and confounded relations between anglophone and francophone voters, collateral damage from wartime political debate. How to distinguish an independent voice in Ottawa from a shared voice with imperial policy in London – to declare war, to build a military, to negotiate with foreign governments, or, more simply put, to say *yes* or *no* to London? Such issues put a strain on the Canadian federation.

Every generation faces stresses on society, some from external events, like war, terrorism, or economic competition, but also from internal events within the polity, ranging from demographic change to new technologies changing social values and political tensions among regions, age groups, and political parties. Governments react in various ways to these dynamics – the appeasement policies of the British Conservatives before hostilities broke out in 1939 and the economic orthodoxy of the U.S. Republican party during the Depression are foreign examples – with Canada at times showing similar fault lines. The federal Conservatives had trouble with military events after 1939 and postwar reconstruction, just as the federal Liberals seemed blinded by the entrepreneurial forces in western Canada after 1970, with reverberations that lasted generations, a lesson facing Justin Trudeau today. Assessing national leadership can be a learning exercise, but not for the diehard partisan. Roy Jenkins, a powerful minister in the Wilson and Callaghan Labour governments, and author of a biography of Winston Churchill, whom he rates as the greatest prime minister ever, openly admits that the ranking exercise is a "game" – not far from the verdict of Peter Riddell, journalist, MP, and author of books on Margaret Thatcher and Tony Blair, who dismisses the "narcissistic world of academics writing for each other" and calls the assessment and rating of leaders "the ultimate parlour game for political junkies."

The event cycle often proceeds over generations, providing a "collective memory" of a country, with landmarks such as the Depression, the Second World War, Quebec's *révolution tranquille* and separatist movement, and the fight for Aboriginal rights. Personalities, individual acts, and political actions form elements of the parlour game of legacy ratings, not unlike the march of science. If science proceeds one funeral at a time, as Max Planck called the time progress of great scientists, revisionism is part of history, or as Oscar Wilde reminds us, "The only duty we owe to history is to rewrite it."

The most famous study, at least as a method to assess past leaders, was carried out in the United States by Arthur Schlesinger Sr. He conducted two surveys, the first in 1948, for *Time* magazine, the second in 1962, for the *New York Times Magazine*, using league tables of presidential performance, on five categories – great, near great, average, below average, and failure – fifty-five experts in the first and seventy-five in the second. But when he undertook the second survey, in 1962, he received a sharp response from the sitting president, John F. Kennedy, who responded, "How the hell can you tell?" The historically minded commander in chief had a good point, knowing the pressures of the office, the event cycle of the time, and the awesome burdens that descend in a crisis, the limited options available, and the unknowable about other actors.

This parlour game of ranking Canadian prime ministers now extends to the academic world, the media, and individual historians. Personal bias may play a role, and certain misdeeds can temper a verdict, but so can ignorance of both "hard" legacies, i.e., enduring policies, governing philosophies, and shared experience, and "soft" legacies, such as the accumulation of policies and programs that produce indirect payoffs for future policy direction. It may be a touch of narcissism and presumption to rate

19th-century leaders like Macdonald, Mackenzie, and Laurier, where their mandate was to complete the Confederation project, and where foreign policy played little direct role, because London called most of the shots. By this standard, Mackenzie faces a melancholy comparison with Macdonald, a man of the world, generous in spirit, well read, and well connected, while the Liberal leader, in the words of Governor General Lord Dufferin, had "the narrowness and want of lofty generosity inherent in a semi-educated man."

Laurier, by contrast, had two natural advantages. First, he was born an optimist, and in his family life, his business relations with his law firm, and in his adopted hometown in the country on the South Shore of the St Lawrence; he was popular – his neighbours saw his charm and abilities at first hand. An example of his generosity of spirit was shown when he intervened in 1884 to ask the local bishop to allow an inter-denominational marriage when one of his constituents, Minette Taschereau, wanted to marry Joseph Pope, a young Protestant from Prince Edward Island, whose main job was as Macdonald's private secretary. She was the eldest daughter of Justice Henri-Thomas Taschereau, whose wife, Pacaud, came from Laurier's riding, Arthabaska. Much later, Macdonald's advice to Pope was equally generous: "Laurier will look after you should you need a friend when I am gone." Laurier did: Pope served as Canada's undersecretary of state and assistant clerk to the Privy Council from 1896 to 1926.

Second, Laurier thus exploited his second advantage – he could see the great master, Sir John A., ever so strategic and canny, never unwilling to use the patronage machine to further his policies, to identify and recruit candidates to come to Ottawa and complete the Confederation project. In the House of Commons, on the campaign trail, and during his summer holidays near *Rivière-du-Loup*, Laurier saw Macdonald up close, and it is highly revealing that both eulogies given in the House of Commons when Sit John A. died were in French, the first by Hector Langevin, the second, by the eloquent Wilfrid Laurier.

The first fifty years after 1867 saw Laurier turn the Liberals into the national governing party, with only Robert Borden and R.B. Bennett upholding the Conservative cause. When King won a contested Liberal convention in 1919, after Laurier's death, his acolytes, such as H.S. Ferns, could confidently summarize his strengths: "In terms of understanding the political problems of Canada and in knowing what the Canadian people as a whole were willing to accept from a government, Mackenzie King was miles ahead of the active participants in politics." Others are less laudatory. Frank Scott, a constitutional lawyer and dean of law at McGill, a strong civil-rights activist, and a CCF social democrat, as well as a poet, gave another impression of King, six years after his departure:

> Let us raise up a temple
> To the cult of mediocrity
> Do nothing by halves
> Which can be done by quarters.

Unwittingly, as a historian, Ferns puts his finger on King's longevity and success, and less on the personality and cautiousness of this very devious and at times ruthless leader, but on his opponents in the House of Commons, the premiers who debated and challenged his policies, and the long list of Conservative politicians, including party leaders Arthur Meighen, R.B. Bennett, John Bracken, and George Drew, who fought him. King was lucky in two respects – he lost power to Bennett in 1930 just at the start of the deep recession, and he was in power when war broke out, guaranteeing him the awesome powers of a wartime prime minister. Yet King was never a real confidant of Winston Churchill, despite their almost-identical age (Churchill was eighteen days older) and same height, and, unlike the prime ministers of Australia and South Africa, never had privileged access to the Bletchley code-breaking of German communications.

The ranking of prime ministers, presidents, and men of action provides two lessons. The first, and the most important, is the learning process – how do governments, leaders, and individual behaviour respond to the force of the event cycle, the unexpected, and the crises at hand? Personalities play a role, where ability, ambition, mindset, preparation, short- or long-sightedness, and a sense of history often temper the ultimate policy outcome. History also shows that leaders differ in their capacity to mobilize a society at large, a political party, a civil service, or individuals. Great leaders learn from others, which explains why the examples of George Washington or Abraham Lincoln guide all incumbents in the White House. Winston Churchill is seen as a far better prime minister during war than in the early 1950s. In Canada, Wilfrid Laurier is rated near the top, because he saw the first prime minister at close hand, accepted his Confederation project, and turned it into his own, unlike the first Liberal leader, Alexander Mackenzie, who varied between the hapless and the hopeless.

Laurier's 15 years of office placed a burdensome hurdle before Conservative leaders in the 20th century, with a far greater challenge to gain elected office because those leaders made a series of bad decisions that severely weakened Conservative electoral prospects in francophone Canada, and not just in Quebec. Circumstances and events usually provide the framework for how top leaders respond, but so do their abilities, characteristics, mindset, and personalities. In democracies, leadership conventions, elections, and cabinet-making give signals about a leader's attributes, but often only faintly. Churchill described his cabinet colleague George, Earl Curzon, who served as viceroy of India and foreign secretary and almost became prime minister in 1923: "There was something lacking in Mr. Curzon. It was certainly not information or application, nor power of speech nor attractiveness of manner and appearance. Everything was in his equipment. You could unpack his knapsack and take an inventory item by item. Nothing on the list was missing, yet somehow or other the total was incomplete." In Canada, on such matters as electoral success, style of government, policy outcomes, and future orientation, the list of twenty-eight prime ministers narrows to a select few at the top.

Unlike Britain, France, or the United States, Canada lacks a plethora of biographies, memoirs, and easy access to public records for the main leaders, i.e., those who earned more than one mandate. Biographies of wartime leaders, generals, and public intellectuals like John Maynard Keynes can fill a library, but a person like Winston Churchill, with hundreds of detailed biographies, is a special case, not only with his published letters, telegrams, and memos, more than six million words, including his five-volume memoir of the First World War, his six-volume opus on the Second World War, and the four volumes of his *History of the English Speaking Peoples*. The two volumes on John A. Macdonald by Donald Creighton, or the two by his University of Toronto colleague J.M. Careless on George Brown, testify to the value of longer-term views on historic Canadian political figures. Journalists can play a useful role, often because they see a politician at close quarters. Peter C. Newman's masterful *Renegade in Power: The Diefenbaker Years* (1963) not only became a bestseller, but set a standard for insight, and history in motion.

Some biographies show the internal contradictions between the event cycle and character and personality. Denis Smith's study of John Diefenbaker, *Rogue Tory*, catalogues the long political career of this Saskatchewan lawyer who championed the common man and human rights. Often journalistic writings offer rare insights into politics as theatre, such as Lawrence Martin's two-volume profile of Jean Chrétien. Martin provides a journalistic account of this very lucky politician, winning power against three weak opponents and a Conservative party bent on self-destruction. Chrétien's time in office coincided with the term of a very pro-Canadian U.S. president, Bill Clinton, who had one of the best job-creating presidencies in 100 years, with spillovers for Canada. Yet during the second referendum in Quebec in 1995, which almost endorsed separation, Chrétien, as "Captain Canada," in the final days of the campaign proposed a "distinct society" clause and restoring Quebec's constitutional veto. He also offered Canadians two negative policies – not to send troops to Iraq in the ill-fated U.S. invasion, and not to be like Brian Mulroney. As (red) Tory adviser and wit Dalton Camp put it, "He is less like Mulroney than anyone in present day politics – in speech, manner, taste and style ... It can be remarked of him that he has decided nothing and disappointed no one." However, that is only one opinion of a very wily political operative, because Chrétien shares with Mulroney an unheralded record of fiscal probity after decades of spending profligacy.

However, premature judgment is a journalistic fault line, and Peter Newman's later *When the Gods Changed: The Death of the Liberal Party* (2011) was just that – a premature obituary. Four years later, the Liberals were in power in the two biggest provinces, Ontario and Quebec, plus the four Atlantic provinces, and Justin Trudeau swept the federal party to power with 184 seats. The Reform party, despite its conservative economic positions, was started and enhanced by Preston Manning, ostensibly to give the west a bigger voice in the federation. Its proposals included enacting American measures like an elected Senate, new ways to appoint the Supreme Court, and recall of MPs who voted according to their conscience or party line, rather than the *vox populi* of their constituents. In reality, Reform's goals were to replace the Progressive Conservatives, the party that defeated Social Credit, his father's Alberta party, then headed by Ernest Manning's successor, Harry Strom, in 1971.

II

Comparisons with the United States on presidential ratings, and similar studies in Britain on prime ministers, while interesting to political junkies, have no direct bearing on comparisons in Canada, where there are major differences in challenges for anyone in office in Ottawa. There is the regional basis of Canada's political system, the size and dominance of Ontario's electoral clout – far bigger than that of Quebec and larger than the west, and the country's French–English language duality, not just in Quebec, but in areas of Ontario, New Brunswick, and elsewhere. Canada is not easy to govern because of that.

However, it is a fair prediction that if current members of the Liberal party, the Conservative party, and the NDP were to rank their best leaders, Conservatives would rank John A. Macdonald at the top, the Liberals Wilfrid Laurier, and the NDP Tommy Douglas. The age of the members would probably shift rankings for each party, and include Laurier, King, and Pierre Trudeau among Liberals, Macdonald, Borden, and Mulroney among Conservatives, and Tommy Douglas, Ed Broadbent, and Jack Layton for the NDP. The Canadian electoral map still has only two parties vying for government in Ottawa, and third parties have a history of winning provincial elections – the Socreds (Social Credit) in Alberta and British Columbia, the CCF and now the NDP in all four western provinces, under Bob Rae in Ontario, and under Darryl Dexter in Nova Scotia, as well as amassing sizable representation in the House of Commons. Minor parties in Quebec date back to the Confederation era, and twenty-one authorized parties include in recent times l'Action Démocratique du Québec, the Alliance Provinciale du Québec, le Bloc Québec, the Coalition Avenir du Québec, the Nouveau Parti Démocratique du Québec, the Parti Conservateur du Québec, the Parti Libéral du Québec, the Parti Québécois, Québec Solidaire, and fringe parties – the Bloc Pot, the Parti 51, the Parti Culinaire du Québec, the Parti Marxiste–Léniniste du Québec, the Parti Nul, and Québec en Marche.

Ontario, the biggest electoral prize, has more seats and is growing steadily from internal Canadian migration and new immigrants. Ontario's seats in the House of Commons, 121, compare to 104 for the four western provinces, seventy-eight for Quebec, and thirty-two for the four Atlantic provinces, and this layout suggests the calculations necessary to gain a majority, hence the coalition nature of successful federal parties. Since the time of Wilfrid Laurier, the federal Liberals have dominated in Ontario and Quebec, with their shrewd strategy of alternating francophone and anglophone leaders, building strong provincial organizations separate from the national party, fund-raising, recruiting and cultivating young members, and, when in power, assuring a strong Quebec presence in the federal cabinet. New MPs often serve as parliamentary secretaries (e.g., Pierre Trudeau with Lester Pearson in 1965) or junior cabinet ministers (Jean Chrétien in 1968). W.L. Mackenzie King, knowing Justice Minister Ernest Lapointe was dying of cancer, quietly recruited a replacement at Justice and as Quebec lieutenant, prominent Quebec lawyer Louis St Laurent, who was sworn in as minister soon after Lapointe's death in November 1941 and the next year won a Commons seat.

Ontario's electoral base is central to federal parties for another reason. There is a historic pattern of the province having different parties in power at Toronto and in Ottawa. Starting in 1943, when George Drew took office at Queen's Park, Ontario had five Conservative premiers over forty-two years – Drew, Leslie Frost, John Robarts, William Davis, and Frank Miller – with the Liberals in power in Ottawa, except for 1957–63, 1979–80, and 1984-85. David Peterson's Liberal governments (1985–90) and Bob Rae's NDP (1990–95) coincided roughly with Brian Mulroney's prime ministership (1984–93). Mike Harris's provincial Conservatives ruled 1995–2002 while Jean Chrétien's Liberals held sway federally, and Doug Ford's Conservatives took over in Ontario in 2018 while Justin Trudeau's Liberals governed in Ottawa. See Table 8.2.

Quebec's engagement with the federal Liberals has remained the bedrock of the party, thanks to the legacy of Wilfrid Laurier, although "*rouge à Ottawa, bleu à Québec*" has been a general rule since 1945, notably for the years when Pierre Trudeau governed in Ottawa and René Lévesque was premier of Quebec. By contrast, the federal Conservatives in the 20th century faced an enormous barrier in francophone seats in Quebec and elsewhere. It didn't help when George Drew, federal leader and a former premier of Ontario, had in December 1936 called French Canadians a "defeated race." John Diefenbaker kept a distance from his French-Canadian ministers, such as Léon Balcer, and many of his francophone MPs, and francophones occupied few leadership positions in the party. For the party's electoral prospects, it was painful to have to acknowledge the charges made against Conservative leaders within Quebec political circles – Meighen as the "anti-Christ," R.B. Bennett as "*un mangeur de Canadiens français*," and even more enlightened ones such as Robert Stanfield.

The election barriers in Quebec were real, from party recruitment at the high-school level in ridings to building a campaign team in the province with deep knowledge of local issues and recruiting candidates well known because of their professional careers. In the Trudeau era after 1968, when issues of more powers for Quebec, or even outright separation, when separatists would hope for a WASP prime minister, or as Graham Fraser described that person in *PQ: René Lévesque and the Party Québécois in Power* (1984), "the one who speaks the least French." It did not work in the Trudeau years, as the federal Liberals managed to divide the Quebec electorate into pro-federalism and pro-separation, leaving little room in the middle, best represented in the 1980 federal election when they won

Table 8.2
Prime Ministers' Electoral Wins and Defeats (1949–2019)

Prime minister	Majority win	Minority win	Defeat
Louis St Laurent	1949, 1953		1957
John Diefenbaker	1958	1957, 1962	1963, 1965*
Lester Pearson		1963, 1965	
Pierre Trudeau	1968, 1974, 1980	1972	
Joe Clark		1979	1980
John Turner			1984, 1988*
Brian Mulroney	1984, 1988		
Kim Campbell			1993
Jean Chrétien	1993, 1997, 2000		
Paul Martin		2004	2006
Stephen Harper	2011	2006, 2008	2015
Justin Trudeau	2015	2019	

* As former prime ministers
Source: Elections Canada, author's analysis

all but one seat in Quebec, and Trudeau was seen in the rest of Canada, particularly in Ontario, as the best spokesmen to keep the country together.

That fact remains the key to understanding the role that Brian Mulroney played when he won the Tory leadership in 1983. He was the separatists' worst nightmare, a Quebecer by birth, fluently bilingual, who accepted bilingualism and the role of French power in Ottawa but also in the Conservative party. Unlike most other post-1945 leaders, he was hard-wired for political leadership and combined three distinct advantages – political experience, business experience, and professional experience. He had a thriving law practice in Montreal, but his training in labour law was ideal for becoming leader and prime minister in a fractious Conservative Party. While he sided mostly with management in labour disputes, he built up a following from striking workers and labour leaders, and one of the most militant of those, Louis Laberge, actually nominated him at his constituency nomination. As the CEO at the Iron Ore Company, Mulroney had the chance to travel and to see directly how foreign markets in Asia, Latin America, and elsewhere affect Canadian business and its competitive position in global markets. Like Diefenbaker and Clark, Mulroney had been a party activist from his teen years, easily made lifelong friends and contacts in the party from every province, participated in every leadership contest since the Diefenbaker win in 1956, and knew every Conservative premier on a first-name basis.

Unlike St Laurent, Pearson, Pierre Trudeau, and Harper, Mulroney was the ultimate insider in his party. Even though he had no parliamentary experience, his knowledge of the party's history, his friendships with premiers, cabinet ministers, MPs, and political foot soldiers in other parties, as well as media correspondents, made him more knowledgeable about party personalities and fiefdoms, skill sets, gossip and rumours, past and present, than any leader in Canadian history. Like all leaders, he had a memory for his friends and for his enemies, but unlike Diefenbaker, he didn't let his judgment be clouded by paranoia. Dalton Camp, a man who knew how to verbally bludgeon a political foe or offer sparkling praise, spoke for many in the party: "It was hard not to be charmed by his irresistible high spirits ... For a long time, one of the attractions of going to Montreal was in seeing Brian for a drink, or a meal, and long, lively, animated conversations. He was, everyone agreed, a joy to be with."

Political parties, like sports teams, need more than organizational charts, tour planners, and policy wonks. They need leaders who can give a psychological lift when the polls go down, when crisis is the order of the day, and can set out a winning hand that needs more than one father. Since 1945, Canada has had a scarcity of great campaigners, especially those who can turn low polling numbers into a winning formula. St Laurent in 1949 and 1953, Pearson in 1963 and 1965, Trudeau in 1972 and 1980, and Martin in 2004 all won their elections, even in minority status, mainly because of weak opposition and dissension in opposing parties, helped by their regional support in Ontario and Quebec. Diefenbaker's minority in 1957 was assisted by a shift of voting in Atlantic Canada, and he lost his majority in 1962 and power in 1963 mainly through declining support in Quebec, which had been, at best, on loan from Premier Duplessis, who died in 1959.

Joe Clark's minority win in 1979 again was short-lived – national polling and private party polls showed that the new government was more unpopular the day after the election than on polling day. Clark himself, and possibly the narrow circle around him, may have thought his pending defeat on the budget vote in December 1979 would be a repeat of the Diefenbaker experience, when the Liberals and their new leader, Lester Pearson (chosen January 1958), presented a motion to the House "of having a government pledged to implement Liberal policies. His Excellency's advisors should, in the opinion of the House, submit their resignations forthwith." Diefenbaker responded with what Jack Pickersgill, the author of the motion, called the best destructive speech ever made in Parliament and won the biggest election win in 1958 in Canadian history as a result. In 1979, Clark lost the confidence of not only the House, but also the population. The Liberals ran the 1980 winter election with a startling innovation – they kept their retired and now restored leader and their campaign plane flying at 30,000 feet, with few rallies, few press conferences, and few promises, allowing Canadians to discharge their duties and vote the Conservatives out of power.

From the earliest days of his leadership campaign in February 1983 to his first federal election win in September 1984, Brian Mulroney wanted two mandates, so the 1988 election planning started the day after the victory on 4 September. From the beginning, party headquarters was well staffed, well funded, and well organized. Many party members participated in provincial elections, and Conservative premiers and key operatives were part of the 1988 election planning. The big-tent approach was assured in patronage jobs, party fund-raisers paid the leftover bills of the leadership campaigns, and special attention was paid to involving new francophone MPs in party affairs at headquarters in Ottawa. Western MPs, especially Don Mazankowski from Alberta, Bill McKnight from Saskatchewan, and Charlie Mayer from Manitoba, invited Quebec MPs to their fund-raising and party events in their ridings, and Mulroney made caucus relations his personal priority.

For the Conservatives, Stephen Harper had a chance to build a national party with support in all regions after the merger of Reform with the Progressive Conservatives, which was perhaps more of a shotgun or arranged marriage than a match of equal partners, heading into the 2006 election. The deep division was led principally by Preston Manning, who founded Reform after his personal defeat in Edmonton in the federal election of 1988, when all Progressive Conservatives won their seats in Alberta and Brian Mulroney was returned with a second majority. The situation was reminiscent of the discord of western MPs under Robert Stanfield and under Joe Clark. Many westerners were deeply angered by the Tory government's awarding in 1986 of a major contract to Bombardier in Montreal, rather than to the British firm Bristol Aerospace, based in Winnipeg. But other factors were increasing westerners' alienation, including their opposition to the Meech Lake Accord of 1987, with its "distinct society" clause, and a rallying cry was emerging, "The West Wants In," as if the Conservatives had ignored westerners' policy priorities. Preston Manning's political machinations guaranteed Kim Campbell's defeat in

1993. What followed was twelve-plus years of Liberal rule under prime ministers from Quebec.

Harper was lucky in 2006, running a listless campaign but having a big scandal to run on, the result of the Gomery Commission of Inquiry (2004–06), appointed by Paul Martin, into federal Liberal sponsorship in Quebec under Jean Chrétien. For years, really since the Liberal leadership convention in 1990, there had been deep divisions between the Chrétien and Martin forces. In 2006, as prime minister, Martin won only thirteen seats in Quebec, and his successor as leader, Stéphane Dion, did little better in 2008, taking only fourteen seats. When the Bloc Québécois in 2006 and 2008 won fifty-four and forty-nine Quebec ridings, respectively, and then Jack Layton's NDP took fifty-five in 2011, Stephen Harper was able to gain power, with pluralities in the rest of Canada.

Unfortunately, the new Conservative party, despite the name, public promises, and intentions, and key ministers like Nova Scotia's Peter MacKay from the Progressive Conservative wing, had a Reform agenda and a style of conservative grandiosity. Perhaps in order to keep the more radical members in line, with many only too willing to air their personal views to the media, Harper centralized the government and the party apparatus as never before. Cabinet met less frequently than the normal weekly session, and mandate letters for ministers became policy wish lists, to be driven from the centre and compiled by political staff and the PMO and signed by the prime minister. By extension, ministers had little policy discretion, reinforced by an Orwellian communications mantra of "No comment," cabinet talking points, and government by press release. A combination of inexperienced ministers, party ideology, and PMO control soon revealed general disdain for civil-service advice, as well as for Conservative traditions and history.

In a short time, the public image of Harper's secret agenda made Parliament and the capital a locus of intense partisan divide and acidulous sentiments. When a scandal emerged in the late spring of 2015, an election year, involving expense payments to Conservative Senator Mike Duffy, repaid on his own account by Harper's chief of staff, Nigel Wright, a lawsuit and a series of court hearings ensued. During the extended seventy-eight-day election campaign (2 August–19 October), a lingering credibility gap – who knew what and when – drained Conservative morale and momentum. For Harper, as each day dragged on, he faced the ultimate challenge, as the passage of time threatened incumbent MPs. His Conservatives won only ninety-nine seats, a loss of sixty-seven, and leaving Brian Mulroney as the only Conservative prime minister since Macdonald to win two consecutive majorities.

III

Time and events help determine the policy outcomes of governing mandates, aided obviously by long periods in office, as shown with Macdonald and King, Laurier and Pierre Trudeau. But domestic agendas largely determine election outcomes, and here the divergence among Canada's twenty-one prime ministers since 1945 is striking. Economic issues are often the primary concern, with pocketbook issues of employment, salaries, discretionary income, and retirement planning as central priorities of the electorate. The gradual and general diversification of the national economy, as it evolved from dependence on primary sectors like agriculture, fishing, forestry, and mining, to encompass manufacturing and services, led to more economic and industrial integration across provinces, with annual output spurred increasingly by the rise in domestic demand. While exports still played a significant role, especially in certain sectors, exports actually fell as a percentage of total output.

Canada's post-1945 emphasis on social policy – education, health care, old-age pensions, youth strategies – flowed from federal initiatives, and while national leadership was vital, given regions' wealth differences, most of these endeavours intruded on provincial jurisdiction. Louis St Laurent centralized and extended Ottawa's spending powers, initiating new programs for the blind and the disabled and constructing the Trans-Canada Highway, thereby creating a model of cost-sharing in which Ottawa set the rules and conditions, but paid only half the cost. In some cases, the poorer provinces couldn't afford their 50 per cent, so Ottawa agreed to pay 90 per cent, a novel form of equalization. Some premiers were aghast at this approach, including Quebec's Maurice Duplessis, so St Laurent, without consulting the other provinces, introduced a new tax measure, allowing Ottawa more "tax room" by giving Quebec 10 per cent of the income tax Ottawa collected in that province and allowing it to establish a new tax-collection agency – a form of special status, or "asymmetric federalism." Both major parties supported these plans – indeed, it was John Diefenbaker and his Conservative majority (1958–62), disliking the word "welfare," which implied "dependency," who preferred a better term, "social justice."

How was Canada to cope with two conflicting forces after the Second World War? The first, the growing demands for social expenditures, such as health care, medical treatment in new hospitals, and educational endeavours, ranging from training programs to vocational schools, from universities to research labs, called mostly on the provinces. The second, economic growth, spurred rising tax revenues for the federal government, a trend established during wartime, when the provinces ceded it powers, so Ottawa now had to accommodate their spending needs, while keeping tax room for its own areas of jurisdiction, such as defence and security, foreign policy, and Aboriginal affairs.

Political scientists often use terms like "elite accommodation" and "brokerage politics" to describe how prime ministers, premiers, and the different levels of government negotiate fiscal arrangements through federal–provincial agreements. One policy, now in the constitution, is a program with an arcane name, "equalization," whereby Ottawa provides unconditional financial payments to provinces whose own-source revenue capacity falls below the ten-province average, and even Ontario has been a recipient. As its premier David Peterson could quip on the hustings, "What propels Canadian unity is that everybody in Canada hates Ontario, everybody in Ontario hates Toronto, and everybody in Toronto hates Bay Street." But Ontario was the motor of the nation's economy and saw the benefits of sharing the wealth.

Each prime minister had a polite term to describe this brokerage form of national unity. To Pearson, it was "cooperative federalism"; to Joe Clark, a "community of communities"; to Stephen Harper, "open federalism." In some cases, there were instances of "executive federalism," as when Pearson negotiated a deal in 1966 to allow Quebec to set up its own pension plan, where tax deductions would go to that province and allow it to invest as it saw fit, including in companies that would become part of what became known as Quebec Inc. Behind all these negotiations lay certain assumptions that everyone seemed to accept. The first, of course, was that Ontario wanted to pick up the expensive tab to redirect tax policies for poor provinces and regions. Second, all provinces wanted to play by this set of rules, with Ottawa serving as a brokerage referee to placate dissatisfied premiers. And third, contrary to federal–provincial relations being a zero-sum game, each jurisdiction had enormous fiscal flexibility in the Canadian constitution, a point that Pierre Trudeau kept telling Quebec.

Pearson was the first prime minister to face abrupt changes in all these assumptions. After a long rule, Maurice Duplessis's reign had come to a sudden end, when he died in 1959 and was replaced by Paul Sauvé, who died months later, only to be replaced by an even weaker leader, Antonio Barrette. Jean Lesage's Liberals won fifty seats and 51 per cent of the votes cast in the 1960 election and began to transform Quebec. With a talented, determined cabinet, which included a new minister in the person of René Lévesque, Lesage began a wholesale change with bold policies, *la révolution tranquille,* ranging from taking over the education and hospital system from the Catholic church to nationalizing hydroelectric utilities and introducing more modern, technocratic forms of decision-making, including a merit-based civil service and ensuring the French fact, starting in Quebec City. The Liberal cabinet and caucus had a radical edge to it, with the participation of aggressive labour leaders. It is a paradox of history that when René Lévesque visited the premier in his suite at the Windsor Hotel in Montreal during the second week of the spring campaign in 1960 to offer himself as a candidate, three other prominent Québécois were meeting in another suite only blocks away: Jean Marchand, Gérard Pelletier, and Pierre Trudeau. They decided to stay on the sidelines.

For the next two decades, under Prime Ministers Diefenbaker, Pearson, and Trudeau, Ottawa struggled to find the right mix of economic and industrial policies that would continue economic growth, job creation, and general prosperity without succumbing to American takeover of the major industrial sectors. While the policy outcomes differed, there were common threads pursued by Ottawa. The first was the politics of redistribution, by taking the sources of economic growth as a given but using government as the main lever to help poor regions obtain the services enjoyed by richer regions. Pearson's introduction of Medicare is seen as one of his legacy achievements. In practice, he succeeded only because he had the personal backing of Ontario's premier, John Robarts, who knew that previous Ontario governments had put a priority on health insurance, but also understood that Ottawa couldn't afford Medicare for the poorer provinces unless Ontario participated in a national system. Health-care coverage became a benchmark for an activist social agenda, which necessitated rising federal spending. Second, when Pierre Trudeau succeeded Pearson in 1968, the federal government and its departmental machinery pushed new programs and spending into areas as diverse as regional development, urban affairs, and policies in education, the environment, science, and training that often duplicated provincial initiatives, in an effort to have all Canadians recognize the advantages of a federal system, with Ottawa at the centre.

The election of René Lévesque and his Parti Québécois in Quebec in 1976 and his party's threat to leave Canada also had a severe impact on federal spending. As more private savings moved from Quebec to other jurisdictions, including outside Canada, Ottawa quietly compensated with federal programs, but politically had to spend in other provinces as well. The level of federal spending, which rose under Pearson, continued to do so 1974–79 under Trudeau, declined during Joe Clark's short time in office, and climbed again under Trudeau 1980–84. In the Trudeau years, the federal government reordered the machinery of government, and, as an extension of Parkinson's law, departments multiplied and so did spending. More than a hundred new agencies and commissions were created, seven departments, and fourteen secretaries of state, with salaries and pensions of federal employees, once on a par with the private sector, becoming 20 per cent more. By 1984, Ottawa's subsidies to finance crown corporations equalled half the defence budget, and annual payments on the national debt constituted 20 per cent of all federal spending.

It is telling that Trudeau fought the policies advanced by Robert Stanfield to impose wage and price controls as a battle against inflation in the 1974 election campaign, mercilessly belittling this promise, only to impose them afterwards. He then took outside advice, from German Chancellor Helmut Schmidt, on Canada's reckless spending and announced spending cuts without consulting his finance minister. When he stepped down in 1984, the annual deficit exceeded $37 billion, while the total federal debt almost doubled from 1968 to 1984, from about 26 per cent to 46 per cent of GDP. The Mulroney government started retrenchment, a painful, unpopular, and unforgiving political exercise, with a three-part approach to limiting any program spending increases – program review to assess the need for existing outlays, tax reform, and revenue-enhancing measures like privatization. The Chrétien government used similar methods, while ensuring that growth in spending did not exceed expansion in the economy, and it actually produced the first budget surplus in 1998, and a chance to pay down the national debt, from a peak of about $585 billion.

The shift in Canada's economic and industrial policies, like a good wine, improves with age. The Mulroney government, in its first six months of office, planted the seeds for fiscal rectitude, removing the barriers to future growth and putting forth policies for national competitiveness. It did this through a series of executive measures, legislative enactments, and federal–provincial agreements – mostly politically sensitive and controversial – in all the main industrial sectors – aerospace, agriculture, autos, energy, financial services, fisheries, northern development, space, and transportation. Many of these measures were time-consuming, required legislative enactment, and took time to implement, and thus consumed political capital, often against furious counterattack and personal invective. While critics of a conservative bent would argue the government didn't go far enough, quick enough, and deep enough in 1984 or during the first Mulroney mandate, critics across the aisle in the House of Commons, some provinces, and many in the public thought such an approach was going too far.

In 1984, the Planning and Priorities Committee of cabinet debated these issues, the timing of cuts, and the types of new expenditures to be allowed, including commitments to foreign aid, and Finance Minister Michael Wilson's first budget actually increased the level, approaching 0.7 per cent of GNP. It became clear early on that spending cuts alone would not address new challenges. one of them coming from new forms of international competition and another from a tax system that failed to address the fiscal imbalance. The growth in spending simply exceeded the increase in tax revenues, a formula for continuing annual deficits, high debt levels, and more borrowing to finance the debt. Tory Finance Minister John Crosbie's slogan on his budget measures in 1979 – "short-term pain for long-term gain" – might be catchy, but Canadians didn't appreciate the economic medicine, and the Mulroney cabinet remembered that well. A series of other initiatives like trade promotion in Asia, free trade with the United States, a consumption tax, funding National Centres of Excellence, and industrial measures to make domestic companies and industries competitive with their foreign peers were controversial and angered entrenched interests. But subsequent prime ministers accepted them, improved them, and extended them.

Collectively, however, these measures comprised a sort of 21st-century national policy, as sweeping as Macdonald's, of tariff protection, the transcontinental railway, and the opening of the west. Critics in other parties, the media, and university seminar rooms could and would decry the growing economic interdependence via shared policies, supply chains, and trade links taking place globally, as well as the growing but real protectionist sentiments in the U.S. Congress. Lawrence Martin, a *Globe and Mail* correspondent in Washington, lamented the approach of the Mulroney policies:

The [Canadian–U.S.] borderline was becoming more and more of a formality. Among the many arguments for its disappearance, perhaps the most convincing was common sense. In an increasing developed economic union, common sense would argue for a common currency, and a customs union; common sense, as in Europe, would argue for the elimination of border patrols and long waits at customs booths; common sense would argue that a single economic space needs to be regulated by common political bodies.

Common sense, in their vein, to quote Dr Johnson, is not so common, and none of these predictions – a single border, a common currency, a fusion of the political systems – ever took place or were even debated, let alone discussed in the Mulroney government. In fact, because developments forced an open debate on trade reciprocity, a 100-year-old controversy that bedevilled prime ministers from Macdonald to Pierre Trudeau was decided in the 1988 election. Not only has two-way trade increased, but Canadian firms do compete in the global marketplace, and Canadian attitudes on many issues have continued to diverge remarkably from American, as documented by studies such as Michael Adams's *Fire and Ice: The United States, Canada, and the Myth of Converging Values*. In 2019, a *New York Times* columnist could celebrate that "Canadians pursue policies that are preternaturally sensible. Canadians regulate guns, oversee the banking sector so as to avoid financial crashes, and nurture entrepreneurship and economic growth without enormous inequality. Typically, more Canadians use mass transit, and the country has better *traffic safety laws*, so that the vehicle fatality rate there is half that of the United States. If the United States had Canada's traffic death rate, we would save more than 20,000 American lives a year."

IV

Both Macdonald and Laurier shared three priorities, which have continued to engage every prime minister since their times, namely the Confederation project, Canada's place in North America and with the Great Republic to the south, and its place in the global community, starting in the 19th century with London and the British Empire, and later, with wartime responsibilities and obligations in two world wars, to allies and partners. Time and the event cycle largely allowed the Confederation project to reach completion, and all prime ministers built on the legacies of Macdonald and Laurier. In the pecking order of Canadian prime ministers, historians rank very highly King, who carefully managed to keep his caucus and cabinet united, not allowing his deep racism from marring his wartime record of accomplishment. His private views have become well-known, because he kept a diary. His meetings with national leaders, foreign ambassadors, and visiting diplomats gave him the opportunity to write down his thoughts on Canadian and foreign peoples, especially from Asia.

King made his only visit to the Far East as deputy minister of labour, a six-month tour in December 1908 as part of an effort to settle labour disputes in Vancouver. He travelled first to London, then to Egypt to catch a boat through the Suez Canal to Asia. The formal, public part of his trip involved attending the Joint International Opium Commission in Shanghai in February 1909, but his real task was to figure out how to restrict Asian immigration to Canada. In a note to his diary on departing Delhi, he expressed his real sentiments: "It is impossible to describe how refreshing it is to be again with people of one's own color. One becomes very tired of the black races after living among them. It is clear the two were never intended to intermix freely." From Shanghai, King visited Beijing and Manchuria, then travelled by ship to Kyoto and Tokyo, meeting the British ambassador there, and he later advised Prime Minister Laurier on policies to restrict Asian immigrants. Once in power, imbued with the white Anglo-Saxon sentiments of the American and British political elite, he introduced the Chinese Exclusion Act of 1923, and in 1928 he limited Japanese immigrants to 150 per year.

Once European hostilities started in 1939, King rejected a call for a national government representing all parties, and the National Resources Mobilization Act of 1940 copied the provisions of Britain's Emergency Powers (Defence) Act 1939, authorizing conscription of recruits for the military. This measure could have inspired a replay of the 1917 conscription crisis, when Laurier lost the election to Borden, and King had no intention of following that path. The issue was hard to ignore, especially after Arthur Meighen was re-elected to head the Conservative party on 12 November 1941, and Ernest Lapointe, King's loyal minister of justice and Quebec lieutenant, died of cancer the same month. King appointed Louis St Laurent to replace him, just as Japan attacked Pearl Harbor on 7 December, and before Winston Churchill, after visiting President Roosevelt in Washington, stopped in Ottawa at the end of the month and addressed the House of Commons. The January 1942 Speech from the Throne promised a plebiscite "to release from any obligation arising out of any past commitments restricting methods of raising men for military service." The results of the four by-elections that followed, when St Laurent won a seat in Quebec East and Meighen was defeated by an unknown high-school teacher, Joe Noseworthy, in York South, were an enormous relief for King, now largely unencumbered to run the war effort.

After the First World War, Canada had faced new obligations, including designing an independent foreign policy. Despite Britain's general acquiescence to Canada's needs, it took the work of Borden, King, and Bennett to assure complete control of foreign policy, starting with the Balfour Declaration in 1926 and the Statute of Westminster in 1931. Ever since, Canada has emerged well beyond a former colony and is seen by many people in former colonies like Australia, New Zealand, South Africa, many other African nations, the English-speaking Caribbean, and elsewhere as well, as a model – a federation, the first of several (some abortive) in Britain's decolonization process, and a country with two language groups and many cultures living together rather amicably. Like Meiji Japan in 1868, Canada had a unique capacity and used it to borrow ideas, institutions, and people from other countries and adapt them to Canadian circumstances, a point emphasized by U.S. President George H.W. Bush, who called Canada "one of the world's most respected forces for freedom, human rights, social justice, and – as I discovered firsthand as vice-president and then president – stewardship of the environment."

But the frayed symbolism of cooperative federalism became the growing, unrelenting, and increasingly provocative intrusion in foreign affairs of Quebec, starting in 1961 when its delegation in Paris was given the full immunity offered to foreign embassies and expanding with Quebec's Bill 33 (1967), which set up a new Ministère des affaires intergouvernementales in charge of "all relations that can exist between the Government of Quebec, its departments, and organisms and all other organisms or governments outside Quebec, as well as for the negotiations of 'ententes' that can be concluded between Quebec and these organizations or governments." French President Charles de Gaulle's famous, well planned, and provocative statements on the balcony of City Hall in Montreal on 24 July 1967 – "*Vive Montréal! Vive le Québec! Vive le Québec libre!*" – deeply annoyed the province's budding separatist leaders – René Lévesque told a reporter from France, "*C'est un mot de trop*" (It's too much), and the Liberal caucus of Jean Lesage, now in Opposition, normally sympathetic to France, at his insistence issued a statement criticizing de Gaulle. For many English Canadians, who knew the sacrifices their compatriots had made in two world wars – in blood and money – de Gaulle's statement deeply hardened their views on constitutional issues, a sentiment that would last a generation.

V

By the 1970s, Britain's place in the world had shifted – the government had gone through a painful decolonizing process: many colonies wanted independence (India and Ireland were classic examples), and in some, the British had to mediate between groups that wanted power. Britain basked in its "special relationship" with the United States, which became more and more one-sided, as the Americans assumed global responsibilities as policemen to the world, the former British role. Canada now faced a quandary. Many English Canadians felt a strong affinity to Britain and its monarchy, but many immigrants came from nations that had fought Britain, or freed themselves from it, and felt less or none. Relations with the United States were often fractious. Prime Minister Lester Pearson surrounded himself with advisers like Walter Gordon, who pressed for a wide range of measures against U.S. takeover of Canadian companies, and, during the Vietnam War, President Lyndon Johnson had little sympathy for any advice from Pearson concerning his war policy, and less for nationalist policies that would jeopardize American access to Canadian markets.

Pierre Trudeau had even less success in dealing with the Americans and Richard Nixon. The Vietnam War and growing defence spending put pressure on the U.S. dollar, backed by the gold standard, at $35 an ounce for gold. The U.S. administration devalued the dollar against other currencies – "the Nixon shock," 15 August 1971 – and ushered in a new era of floating exchange rates. An American academic, Ronald Kreiger, put the global turmoil to verse:

Humpty Dumpty sat on a wall, humpty dumpty had a great fall;
All the king's horses and all the king's men,
formed an ad hoc committee to consider the situation.

This measure had a profound implication for Canada, whose companies could face rising European and Japanese competition in the American market, and a higher Canadian dollar would make them less competitive against local rivals there. The two oil shocks in 1973 and 1979, with Middle East producers raising prices, placed massive deflationary pressure on Western economies. Ottawa was faced with pressures to address these issues. Pierre Trudeau's economic record was one of high annual deficits from profligate spending and ever-increasing national debt, ultimately placing an enormous budget burden on the government of Brian Mulroney.

Both Trudeau and Mulroney spent their careers in Montreal, they knew each other, and they shared many friends and acquaintances, from the Desmarais family to Roy Faibish, a conservative intellectual, a CBC producer at one time, and an adviser to prime ministers. Trudeau actually tried to recruit Mulroney as a Liberal candidate, but more as a way to weaken the Conservatives than accept him as a star in a Liberal cabinet. Both leaders knew Ottawa, their home province, and sundry leaders in government, politics, and the media, as well as in business and labour, and they were no strangers to the norms, protocols, and internal patronage of the Ottawa civil service. In some departments, such as the Privy Council Office and External Affairs, Trudeau brought in his own advisers, like Ivan Head and Michael Pitfield, but Mulroney digested the lessons of the inexperienced Clark government and left the direction of the civil service largely intact.

As a general rule, both men were outsiders to the Ottawa system, unlike King and Pearson, who were part of the "deep state" there, changing roles from civil servant / adviser to political adviser to politician with effortless ease, as demonstrated also by the careers of their senior ministers like Jack Pickersgill and Mitchell Sharp. John Diefenbaker, of course, was an Ottawa man, but a parliamentarian, and from the wrong side of the partisan divide until 1957. First winning an election in 1940, running as a Conservative in the political environment of Saskatchewan, against the powerful, ruthless, and unforgiving patronage machine of Liberal Minister of Agriculture (and former premier) James "Jimmy" Gardiner. This history partly explains Diefenbaker's paranoia as prime minister, knowing that the civil service, influenced by Gardiner, helped craft the Liberal campaign platform in the 1957 election.

Trudeau had some experience working in or with the Ottawa bureaucracy, first, 1949–51, in the Privy Council Office, under the tutelage of its formidable clerk (director), Norman Robertson, the ultimate mandarin insider, but his stint as justice minister in the Pearson government left him unimpressed with the traditions of Ottawa's decision-making, where civil servants write policy, the cabinet approves it, and self-selecting civil servants implement it. Ministers, like MPs, become salespeople for government achievements. During Liberal rule, royal commissions were the source of new ideas, helped by recruiting academics, and King was a master at using them to procrastinate, squelch party dissent, or buy time against petulant provincial governments. In the 1930s, as in the late 1950s, Bennett and Diefenbaker were the policy radicals, promoting new, bold policies for employment creation and new institutions for broadcasting and transportation, never quite accepting policy advice from the civil service. Pearson was the ultimate insider, civil-servant adviser to King and St Laurent and ambassador to Washington before becoming secretary of state for external affairs in 1948.

Trudeau's experience as Pearson's justice minister showed him the excessive caution of the Ottawa bureaucracy, and, given his personal obsessions and cabinet mandate on the Quebec file, he knew only too well the reality captured by John Porter's *The Vertical Mosaic* (1965):

"The low proportion of French Canadians would suggest that the demands for appointment on ethnic grounds *per se* have been kept in check. Or, conversely, the tendency to meet such demands by appointments from outside would suggest that ethnicity has been in some cases an overriding consideration." He knew this had to change, but ignoring advice on moderation from even his friends and colleagues, his uncompromising approach once prime minister made civil-service bilingualism a promotion boondoggle, and Official Languages Commissioner Keith Spicer said that Trudeau's sense of urgency "strains both optimism and pocketbook." However, bilingualism was only one feature of his attacks on the separatist cause in Quebec, and he, like Cartier during the Confederation debates in the 1860s, argued forcefully that francophones had better protection for their language, customs, religion, and legal system in a united Canada than they would in an independent Quebec. Fifty years of immigration, multilingualism, and additions to Canada's bilingual character have produced one of the most educated nations on the planet, and perhaps a key to a less polarized political environment. In short, Canadians enjoy non-partisan electoral rules and boundaries, judges, health care, policing, even arts and amateur sports.

Ignoring counsel to continue current policy, Trudeau as justice minister addressed contentious social-justice issues like abortion, capital punishment, homosexual rights, and marriage and divorce law, knowing that divisions across Canada tended to be age-related. Young people often differed from their parents, many of whom were themselves changing attitudes, and from some members of such traditionally often conservative institutions as churches and the military. Once he was prime minister, Trudeau and, on his urging, his cabinet brought in changes to immigration, making it much less discriminatory on race, country of origin, and religion, and those changes, along with new policies on bilingualism, dismantled King's approaches and effectively implemented Diefenbaker's "One Canada" vision. Speaking in the House of Commons on 8 October 1971, Trudeau set out his policy:

> It was the view of the Royal Commission shared by the government and, I am sure, by all Canadians that there cannot be one culture policy for Canadians of British or French origin, another for the Aboriginal Peoples and yet a third for all others. For altogether there are two official languages, there is no one official culture, nor does any ethnic group take precedence over any other. No citizen or group

of citizens is other than Canadian, and all should be treated fairly ... Sometimes the world 'bi-culturalism' is used but I don't think it accurately described this country. I prefer 'multiculturalism.'

These policies became immensely unpopular in some circles, and almost brought Trudeau's political career to an abrupt end in the 1972 election (a Liberal minority), but they appealed to many middle-aged and younger voters across Canada, including in Quebec. Every prime minister since has strengthened these measures, including by patronage appointments and by encouraging people from immigrant groups to run for elective office at all levels and become police chiefs, deans of universities, and leaders in volunteer groups and arts organizations. Trudeau's personal appeal, and the exciting results of these changes, gradually altered the minds of many Canadians, even some recalcitrant members of the "WASP elite" who only reluctantly changed their ways.

When Brian Mulroney succeeded Trudeau in 1984, after Turner's three-month tenure, he inherited a country deeply divided, not just on policy issues like energy, constitutional reform, economic competitiveness, and U.S. relations. He wanted to change the tone of political debate. Trudeau himself loved confrontation, and used rhetorical overkill as a political weapon, a Chicago-gangster approach to a gunfight, where opponents are enemies and compromise is a sign of weakness. Unlike Trudeau, Mulroney's background as a labour lawyer meant he was a skilled conciliator, who knew the value of personal relations, while arriving at a solution, inevitably a compromise, from the hard and even harsh lines on both sides. Perhaps his personal motto came from Louis Pasteur, "Chance favors the prepared mind." Both as leader of the Opposition for 13 months, and as prime minister, he excelled at his preparation, not only studying his briefing books, but harnessing his network of contacts, absorbing ideas and information with the compulsion of an addict. While Trudeau's early years in office were focused on social and constitutional issues, Mulroney faced a deteriorating economy, with high inflation and unemployment and dangerous levels of debt.

Trudeau had more understanding of economics than prime ministers like King, St Laurent, Pearson, and Diefenbaker, but learned much of it decades earlier, often taking in too much of John Kenneth Galbraith, I would suggest, and too little perhaps of Joseph Schumpeter and Paul Samuelson. Few people in his cabinet were entrepreneurs; only a few had business backgrounds, like Ed Lumley. Two were corporate lawyers – John Turner and Donald Macdonald. Hu Harries, elected in Edmonton in 1968, had a strong business background, had worked at the World Bank, and knew the oil and gas business, but had no real influence where it counted, with the prime minister and senior economics ministers.

Unlike King or Pearson, who both had lived and worked in the United States, or Trudeau, who studied at Harvard, Mulroney learned to deal with Americans in his hometown, Baie-Comeau, then as a student at Maritimes universities, and later as a lawyer in Montreal. As CEO of Iron Ore, he cultivated a wide network of American businessmen, trade-union leaders, and politicians. He developed an instinct for the American character, the nature of that highly conservative and decentralized society. But when he had to deal with the Reagan administration, he faced the anguish and wrath of the strong, even visceral anti-Americanism in Canadian society, whether on university campuses, with the media, or in Parliament. Congress was in a protectionist mood, and he knew Canada was unlikely to be exempted from protectionist trade measures and appreciated that the actual situation there was far more complicated and nuanced than many Canadians understood. Mulroney saw the faults and defects in American society – baseball pioneer Jackie Robinson was a hero in Montreal but not in his U.S. hometown – but he also recognized the admirable features of the United States, the entrepreneurial values, the technological and scientific prowess, the widespread philanthropy for the arts, education, and medicine, and the willingness to think big – the moonshot, a cure for cancer, the magnanimous gestures of Martin Luther King, Jr, or Ed Sullivan. Mulroney felt Canada could learn much from this very diverse society, believing that in so many areas, from trade and the military to culture and sports, Canada, given a level playing field, could compete with the best.

He also felt that Canadian diplomacy needed persistence as well as patience, whether on acid rain, cross-border trade, border security, the military, or the Arctic, and on specific bilateral agreements like the Great Lakes approaches to clean water and the environment. He accelerated contacts with Congress, governors, ambassadors, and media personalities, well aware of the divided American political system and the need for personal diplomacy and less public grandstanding. Whether dealing directly with the United States or in other forums, like the G7 and multilateral meetings, Canada had a welcome voice, but only if used strategically. It is a telling commentary on Mulroney's legacy that, when President Donald Trump wished to abrogate NAFTA, a government led by another Trudeau, from the same party that fought the FTA and excoriated Mulroney personally for selling out Canada, turned to him for help. Mulroney put past slights aside, attended a cabinet meeting, and then spoke openly and publicly before Congress and quietly and privately to the president, cabinet secretaries, and leading business groups in favour of Ottawa's trade approach.

VI

Canada's political system requires a careful balance between responding to the short-term needs for policy action, often as a reaction to the event cycle and electoral requirements, and developing forward-looking policies to address long-term imperatives, such as demographic changes, infrastructure requirements, trade policies, and investments in human capital. Canadians' perceptions of their leaders and their leadership qualities vary over time, and form part of those people's legacy. Among post-1945 prime ministers, only Pierre Trudeau and Brian Mulroney truly changed the mindset of most Canadians, and faced vitriolic and uncompromising criticism from certain quarters, but they serve as benchmarks for future governments and prime ministers. Governments and prime ministers have always built on past achievements, often with steady and incremental improvements on policy outcomes. Only Trudeau and Mulroney changed Canadian society in fundamental ways by pioneering new approaches and policies, whether at home or on the global stage. Unsparingly they used their political capital with an annoyance factor, audaciously advancing new policies that went beyond conventional tinkering or incremental reforms. From very different personal experience and on different issues, they extolled a largeness of vision that generated excited reactions and often personal vitriol, only to have their forward-looking outlook now acceptable, even conventional.

Timing, of course, is everything in politics, and so is luck. Trudeau's last mandate was his most successful, after a dismal start in office, when he almost lost power in 1972. He took on the separatists frontally in the 1980 referendum, and the Charter of Rights and Freedoms became immensely popular, in part as a check on the political class, even if his other constitutional initiatives left much to be desired, such as future amendments. Mulroney had the opposite problem, because his last years in office were in the middle of a recession, too many forward-looking policies drained his political capital, and the country had simply become exhausted with constitutional mega-reforms. Given the devastating loss of the Conservatives in the 1993 campaign, winning only two seats, it was easy to cast a wide net of blame and animosity towards Mulroney, conveniently ignoring the fact that Kim Campbell was ahead in the national polls before the election, the party ran a terrible campaign, and TV attack ads against Jean Chrétien were deeply offensive to most Canadians, including many Conservatives. Jean Chrétien could thank the political gods in 1993, running against Meech Lake and free trade with a heavy dose of anti-Mulroney bias, that he didn't have to fight against the real thing. The fact that the opposition parties could win elections running against Mulroney and his policies, only to accept them once in office, is perhaps the ultimate historical irony, or that two Liberal leaders' legacies – Medicare for Pearson, constitutional repatriation for Pierre Trudeau – both needed the endorsement of the Conservative Ontario premier. Curiously, Washington and other capitals – Paris, Bonn, Tokyo – appreciated Mulroney's legacy, even if London had mixed views, at least within Whitehall.

Classified documents sent by ambassadors and travelling senior ministers form part of the historical resources to assess retiring leaders and new people ready to take over. Recently declassified documents by British envoys reveal that Britain is a lot less sure of its role in North America and with Canada, and show pompous and paternalistic attitudes to the leaders of the "senior" member of the Commonwealth. Britain's Foreign office would describe Pierre Trudeau as a "very complex man, full of paradoxes and enigmas." Further, "He combines great personal charm with brutal insensitivity. He can be tough and robust, especially when it comes to Quebec about which he cares the most. But he can become bored with day-to-day politics and did not conceal his contempt for other MPs, the press and, sometimes the man in the street. This comes from his often bloodless and over-intellectual approach."

In contrast, the Foreign Office viewed the new Opposition leader, Brian Mulroney, in a different light, "an Irish street fighter," a man "who does not do things without a purpose," who could lead a country tired of 15 years of Mr Trudeau, and "who can mobilize the energies and resources of the country to an extent that none of his predecessors were able to achieve ... This watershed in Canada offers opportunities to us." Curiously, on Trudeau's last summit as Canadian prime minister in June 1984, held in London, he told Margaret Thatcher, "It was good for Canada to have a new prime minister, even in the event he was a Conservative, this would not be the ultimate tragedy." (At the same meeting Thatcher disparaged French President François Mitterrand, who advised the summit leaders that he expected the regimes in the Communist world to collapse within twenty years. Mitterrand was wrong only on the timeframe: all of those in central and eastern Europe collapsed after the fall of the Berlin Wall in November 1989, and the Soviet Union imploded in 1991.)

By any standards, other than party affiliation, Brian Mulroney and Stephen Harper have little in common, both as political leaders and in personality or policy. True, both wanted to win, but their means to achieve victory were polar opposites. Mulroney is complex, a bilingual Quebecer of Irish extraction who wears his heart on his sleeve, with a garrulous sense of humour that attracts long friendships from both sides of the aisle. Harper is the ultimate loner, with few friends, personal, family, or political, but he also has a sense of humour, though well hidden. After Mulroney swept the country in the 1984 election, more than a thousand staffers went to Ottawa as policy advisers, executive assistants, and employees for MPs, senators, cabinet ministers, and the party. Mulroney, only too aware of the mistakes of the Trudeau and Clark era, when campaigns were run from the Prime Minister's Office, kept the party machinery in place after the campaign. One of the new staffers was Stephen Harper, employed in the parliamentary office of Calgary West MP Jim Hawkes, first elected in 1979. Hawkes worked on a policy document on youth employment in 1983-84, while Mulroney was Opposition leader, but didn't make it to the cabinet in 1984, as Mulroney had 23 Alberta MPs to choose from, so selected the experienced ones, including Joe Clark, Don Mazankowski, and Harvie Andre.

Harper toiled in Hawkes's office, making few friends, and most staffers of the time have no memory of him. Later, he would run against Hawkes and defeat him in 1993, standing for the Canadian Alliance. Few recent prime ministers had so little international travel, even to the United States. If we assume that experience consists of formal education, travel, and the school of hard knocks, Harper's inexperience was stunning, and that was also true of his leading cabinet ministers in 2006. That exposes the contrast with the Mulroney cabinet, in which the prime minister was only one of many members with worldly experience and global travel (Energy Minister Pat Carney was actually born and raised in Shanghai, and Otto Jelinek born in Czechoslovakia), as well as having lived and worked outside their home province. Mulroney loved to quote Ronald Reagan's 11th commandment, "Never speak ill of another member of your party," but not even some ideological similarities could make former Ontario Premier Mike Harris be close to Harper. "They are an angry lot," he confided.

Mulroney, at heart, is a strategist, with a capacity to take the long view, who feels that personal relations dictate success, and, despite occasional fits of temper, he is mindful of human frailties, including his own. Harper, by contrast, is a master of the tactical move, where strategic considerations may be important but less worthy, while tactical victories are for the short term only. Long-lasting achievements of the Harper years were few indeed.

VII

As Canada enters the third decade of the 21st century, its record of achievement as a middle power is the envy of the world. Globalization, the relentless and perhaps-unstoppable force of growing interdependence, now extends well beyond economic issues like trade and financial flows to affect migration, travel, sports and culture, and idea absorption. When societies become a battle of nationalist tribes, as seen in the United States, each side seeks to mobilize the instruments of the state to support it, and deep polarization results. The polarization extends beyond the political arena to the media, the military, education, even sports, to divide the population into opposing teams. The narrative becomes zero-sum, a binary choice between winners and losers, friends and foes, progress and catastrophe, opportunity and decline, political tension and incompatibility.

Canada has been spared these polarizing forces because political leaders have fought for changes in Canadian society, even at the cost of personal popularity. Its political system is a careful instrument, like a magnet, to deal with internal grievances, disruptions, and errors, but, like sponge, a vehicle to listen, absorb, and change. Its parliamentary democracy is a work in progress. Perfection is confined to music and the arts. Politics is a messy, contested, and rough game, at times three steps forward, two steps back, and it takes leadership to make it go forward. Relative to most other countries, and despite political tensions, lack of trust, and at times personal animosities, Canadians have been blessed with a political system and a record of great accomplishment. By some standards, according to Britain's Institute for Governance, Canada's civil service is ranked first among democratic governments. But it also shows areas that need improvement, including bolder initiatives and more audacity from the country's private sector.

Individual Canadians should not let themselves become too comfortable, as societies can fail when complacency, hubris, and indifference hold sway in the political system. As a society or as individuals, Canada can learn from the sage advice of a recent governor general. In his book *Trust* (2018), David Johnston advises his fellow citizens to become knowledge diplomats at home and abroad: "Whether we are young or old, students or professionals, each of us has something worthwhile to share based on our particular education and experience. Canadians are excellent knowledge diplomats."

APPENDICES

APPENDIX A

Contested Liberal and Conservative Leadership Conventions (1948–2003)

Year	Place	Party	Candidates*	Voting	Ballots
1948	Ottawa	PCS	John Diefenbaker, **George Drew**, Donald Fleming	Delegates	1st
1956	Ottawa	PCS	**John Diefenbaker**, Donald Fleming, E. Davie Fulton	Delegates	1st
1958	Ottawa	Liberals	Lloyd Henderson, Paul Martin, **Lester Pearson**	Delegates	1st
1967	Toronto	PCS	John Diefenbaker, E. Davie Fulton, Alvin Hamilton, George Hees, John MacLean, Wallace McCutcheon, Duff Roblin, **Robert Stanfield**, Michael Starr, Mary Walkersaka	Delegates	5th
1968	Toronto	Liberals	Joe Green, Paul Hellyer, Lloyd Henderson, Eric Kierans, Alan J. MacEachen, Paul Martin, Sr, **Pierre Trudeau**, John Turner, Robert Winters	Delegates	4th
1976	Ottawa	PCS	**Joe Clark**, John Fraser, Jim Gillies, Heward Grafftey, Paul Hellyer, Jack Horner, Flora MacDonald, Brian Mulroney, Pat Nowlan, Sinclair Stevens, Claude Wagner	Delegates	4th
1983	Ottawa	PCS	Joe Clark, John Crosbie, Neil Fraser, John Gamble, **Brian Mulroney**, Peter Pocklington	Delegates	4th
1984	Ottawa	Liberals	Jean Chrétien, Don Johnston, Mark MacGuigan, John Munro, **John Turner**, Eugene Whalen	Delegates	2nd
1990	Calgary	Liberals	**Jean Chrétien**, Sheila Copps, Paul Martin, John Nunziata, Tom Wappel	Delegates	1st

Year	Place	Party	Candidates*	Voting	Ballots
1993	Ottawa	PCs	Pat Boyer, **Kim Campbell**, Jean Charest, Jim Edwards, Garth Turner	Delegates	2nd
1995	Hull	PCs	Jean Charest	Acclamation	1st
1998	Toronto	PCs	**Joe Clark**, Michael Fortier, David Orchard, Brian Palliser, Hugh Segal	Point system – 100 per district	2nd
2003	Toronto	PCs	Scott Brison, **Peter MacKay**, David Orchard, Jim Prentice	Delegates	4th
2003	Toronto	Liberals	Sheila Copps, **Paul Martin**	Acclamation	1st

* Winner highlighted in **bold**.

APPENDIX B

Contested Liberal and Conservative Leadership Conventions (21st Century)

Year	Place	Party	Candidates*	Voting	Ballots
2004	Toronto	Conservatives	Tony Clement, **Stephen Harper**, Belinda Stronach	Riding associations, preferential ballot	1st
2006	Montreal	Liberals	Scott Brison, **Stéphane Dion**, Ken Drydon, Michael Ignatieff, Gerald Kennedy, Bob Rae, Joe Volpe	Ranked ballots, plus riding associations (14 delegates), women's clubs (2), youth and senior clubs, 4)	4th
2009	Vancouver	Liberals	**Michael Ignatieff**	Uncontested	1st
2013	Ottawa	Liberals	Martin Cauchon, Deborah Coyne, Martha Hall Findlay, Karen McCrimmon, Joyce Murray, **Justin Trudeau**	Preferential ballot	1st
2017	Toronto	Conservatives	Chris Alexander, Maxine Bernier, Steven Blaney, Michael Chong, Kellie Leitch, Pierre Lemieux, Deepak Obhrai, Kevin O'Leary, Eric O'Toole, Rick Peterson, Lisa Raitt, Andrew Saxton, **Andrew Scheer**, Brad Trost	One-member, one-vote ranked ballot, each district with 100 points	13th

* Winner highlighted in **bold**.

APPENDIX C

Federal Cabinets, Size, and Committees since 1948

Prime minister	Number of ministers	Cabinet design
Louis St Laurent (1948)	20–1	Full cabinet, met weekly, selective committees as needed
John Diefenbaker (1957)	17–23	Weekly, sometimes daily
Lester Pearson (1963)	25–6	Nine standing committees, Planning and Priorities P&P, Treasury separated from Finance in 1966
Pierre Trudeau (1968)	27–33	Strengthened committees, separated FPRO from PCO (1975), separated OCG from Treasury (1975), MSEB established in 1979
Joe Clark (1979)	30	Inner cabinet + 12 committees, created PEMS, MSSD (1980)
Pierre Trudeau (1980)	32–37	P&P, PEMS extended, MSEB to MFEDC (1982)
John Turner (1984)	29	FDCDS to DRIE, PEMS cancelled
Brian Mulroney (1984)	40	P&P (18 members), emphasis on Economic and Social Affairs committees, cabinet committee on FTA; DPM appointed (1986) and chaired Operations Committee
Kim Campbell (1993)	23	Three committees on Health, Heritage, and Public Security
Jean Chrétien (1993)	22	DPM appointed, eight secretaries of state, new minister of intergovernmental affairs
Paul Martin (2005)	36	DPO appointed, eight cabinet committees
Stephen Harper (2006)	27	Secretaries of state joined full cabinet
Justin Trudeau (2015)	30	Gender parity in cabinet, regional ministries integrated as minister of innovation, science, and economic development, Climate Change Unit added to minister of the environment

APPENDIX D

A Performance Scorecard:
Canada and Other Industrialized Countries

	Avg annual growth of population (%) (1996–2016)	Avg annual growth – GDP / capita (%) (1996–2016)	Human Development Inde x 2 (2015)	Disposable income inequality Gini3 (2014)	Competitiveness % of top score (2017)	Innovativeness % of top score (2017)
Australia	1.42	1.70	98.9	33.7	88.6	77.7
Austria	0.46	1.25	94.1	27.4	89.6	86.4
Belgium	0.53	1.22	94.3	26.6	89.2	85.1
Britain	0.60	1.44	95.8	35.6	94.0	87.5
Canada	1.02	1.43	96.9	31.3	91.3	80.2
Denmark	0.43	0.91	97.4	25.6	92.0	88.1
Finland	0.56	1.63	94.2	25.7	93.7	97.8
France	0.58	1.00	94.5	29.7	88.4	84.0
Germany	0.11	1.26	97.5	28.9	96.4	97.1
Holland	0.46	1.38	97.4	30.5	96.6	95.4
Ireland	1.31	2.98	97.2	29.8	88.1	80.8
Italy	0.33	0.15	93.4	32.6	77.5	68.0
Japan	0.02	0.72	95.2	33.0	93.7	92.3
New Zealand	1.16	1.61	96.4	34.9	91.6	80.6
Norway	0.89	0.99	100.0	25.7	92.2	86.1
South Korea	0.59	3.48	94.9	30.2	86.5	82.1
Spain	0.76	0.93	93.1	34.4	80.2	63.9
Sweden	0.58	1.97	96.1	27.4	94.2	94.5
Switzerland	0.83	1.07	98.9	29.7	100.0	100.0
United States	0.93	1.37	96.9	39.4	99.8	100.0
CANADA'S RANK ORDER						
Among the G7	1st	2nd	2nd (tie)	3rd	5th	6th
Among the G20	3rd	8th	8th (tie)	13th	12th	17th

Source: Peter Nicholson, IRPP, 2018

Source References by Chapter

PREFACE

W. Christian and C. Campbell, *Political Parties and Ideologies in Canada: Liberals, Conservatives, Nationalists* (Toronto: McGraw-Hill-Ryerson, 1973); Winston Churchill, "The Duties of a Member of Parliament," *Parliamentary Affairs* 8 (1954), 302; James Gillies, "The Parliamentary Imperative," *Saturday Night* (June 1984), 55; Frank MacKinnon, *Postures and Politics: Some Observations on Participatory Democracy* (Toronto: University of Toronto Press, 1973); Michael McMillan and Alison Loat, *Tragedy in the Commons: Former Members of Parliament Speak out about Canada's Failing Democracy* (Toronto: Vantage, 2015); Rod Preece, "The Myth of the Red Tory," *Canadian Journal of Political Theory* 1 (2) (1977), 1–26.

CHAPTER ONE

Edward Bernstein, *The International Monetary System: Forty Years after Bretton Woods* (Boston: Federal Reserve Bank of Boston, May 1984); Michael D. Bordo and Barry Eichengreen, *A Retrospective on the Bretton Woods System* (Chicago: University of Chicago Press, 1993); Michael D. Bordo, and A.J. Schwartz, eds., *A Retrospective on the Classical Gold Standard, 1821–1931* (Chicago: University of Chicago Press, 1993); Andrew Boyle, *Montagu Norman* (London: Cassel, 1967); Barry Eichengreen, *Exorbitant Privilege: The Rise and Fall of the Dollar and the Future of the International Monetary System* (New York: Oxford University Press, 2011); H.C. Eastman and S. Skykolt, *The Tariff and Competition in Canada* (Toronto: MacMillan, 1967); Thomas L. Friedman, *The World Is Flat: A Brief History of the Twenty-first Century* (New York: Farrar, Straus & Giroux (2005); D.H. Fullerton, *Graham Towers and His Times* (Toronto: McClelland

& Stewart, 1986); John Kenneth Galbraith, *The Great Crash* (Boston: Houghton Mifflin Co., 1972); Walter Gordon, *Royal Commission on Canada's Economic Prospects* (Ottawa: Supply and Services, 1957); Charles P. Kindleberger, *The World in Depression, 1929–1939* (Berkeley: University of California Press, 1973); Allan H. Meltzer, "U.S. Policy in the Bretton Woods Era," *Federal Reserve Bank of St. Louis Review* 73 (3) (May / June 1991), 54–83; Donald Moggridge, *Activities 1941–1946: Shaping the Post-war World, Bretton Woods and Reparations* (London: Macmillan, 1980); Carmen M. Reinhart and Kenneth S. Rogoff, "Shifting Mandates: The Federal Reserve's First Centennial," NBER Working Paper 18888, National Bureau of Economic Research, Cambridge, MA, 2013, http://www.nber.org/papers/w18888 <27 July 2021>; Lionel Robbins, *The Great Depression* (New York: MacMillan, 1934); Paul Samuelson, "Full Employment after the War," in S.E. Harris, ed., *Postwar Economic Problems* (New York: McGraw-Hill, 1945), 000–00; M.L. Stokes, *The Bank of Canada: The Development and Present Position of Central Banking in Canada* (Toronto: Macmillan, 1939).

CHAPTER TWO

J.C. Abbegglen and George Stalk, *Kaisha: The Japanese Corporation* (New York, Basic Books, 1985); Walter Bagehot, *Lombard Street* (London: Henry S. King, 1873); Patricia Best and Anne Shortell, *A Matter of Trust, Greed, Government and Canada's $60 Billion Trust Industry* (Markham, ON: Penguin Books, 1986); William Black and George Lermer, eds., *Breaking the Shackles: Deregulating Canadian Industry* (Vancouver: Fraser Institute, 1991); Robert Bothwell and William Kilbourn, *C.D. Howe: A Biography* (Toronto: McClelland & Stewart, 1979); Richard Caves, Michael Porter, A. Michael Spence, with John T. Scott, *Competition in the Open Economy: A Model Applied to Canada* (Cambridge, MA: Harvard University Press, 1980); James L. Darroch and Charles J. McMillan, "Globalization Restricted: The Canadian Financial System and Public Policy," *Ivey Business Journal* (Jan.-Feb. 2007), 000–00; Michel Demers, "Responding to the Challenges of the Global Economy: The Competitive Agenda," in Frances Abele, ed., *How Ottawa Spends: The Politics of Competitiveness* (Ottawa: Carleton University Press, 1992); Peter Drucker, "The Changed World Economy," *Foreign Affairs* (spring 1986), 1–22; Economic Council of Canada, *A New Frontier: Globalization and Canada's Financial Service Markets* (Ottawa: Ministry of Supply and Services, 1989); Mathew Fraser, *Quebec Inc. – French-Canadian Entrepreneurs and the New Business Elite* (Toronto: Key Porter Books, 1987); Milton Friedman, *Capitalism and Freedom* (Chicago: University of Chicago Press, 2002); Ralph Hedlin, *Alberta Politics: Past, Present, Potential* (Calgary: Ralph

Hedlin Associates, 20 March 1989); Tom Jenkins, "A Simple Solution to Canada's Innovation Problem, *Policy Options* (Sept. 2011), 12–21; R.S. Khenani, D.M. Shapiro, and W.T. Stanbury, eds., *Mergers and Corporate Concentration and Power in Canada* (Halifax: Institute for Research in Public Policy, 1987); Paul Krugman, ed., *Strategic Trade Policy and the New International Economics* (Cambridge: Cambridge University Press, 20??); C. Ian Kyer, *From Next Best to World Class: The People and Events That Shaped the Canadian Deposit Insurance Corporation* (Ottawa: CDIC, 2017); Andrew Lambert, *Seapower States: Maritime Culture, Continental Empires and the Conflict That Made the Modern World* (New Haven, CT: Yale University Press, 2018); Robert MacIntosh, *Different Drummers: Banking and Politics in Canada* (Toronto: MacMillan, 1991); C.J. McMillan, "After the Gray Report: The Tortuous Evolution of Canada's Foreign Investment Policy," *McGill Law Journal* 20 (1974), 213–60; Charles J. McMillan, "The Pros and Cons of a National Trading Firm," *Canadian Public Policy* 7 (autumn 1981), 000–00; Tammy Nameth, "Pat Carney and the Dismantling of the National Energy Program," *Past Perfect* 7 (1998), 89–123; E.P. Neufeld, *The Financial System of Canada: Growth and Development* (Toronto: Macmillan, 1972); John Richards and Larry Pratt, *Prairie Capitalism: Power and Influence in the New West* (Toronto: McClelland & Stewart, 1979); O.D. Skelton, *The Life and Times of Sir Alexander Tilloch Galt* (Toronto, Oxford University Press, 1920); Donald V. Smiley, "Canada and the Quest for a New National Policy," *Canadian Journal of Political Science* 8 (1), 40–62; Walter Steward, *Dismantling the State: Downsizing to Disaster* (Toronto: Stoddard, 1998); George S. Watts and Thomas K. Rymes, eds., *The Bank of Canada: Origins and Early History* (Ottawa: Carleton University Press, 1993); V.S. Wilson, "What Legacy? The Nielsen Task Force Program Review," in K. Graham, ed., *How Ottawa Spends 1988-89: Conservatives Heading into the Stretch* (Ottawa: Carleton University Press, 1988), 23–47.

CHAPTER THREE

Richard Bird, "The GST / HST: Creating an Integrated Sales Tax in a Federal Country," School of Public Policy, Calgary, *SPP Research Papers* 5 (12) (March 2012), 1–36; Darrell Bricker and John Ibbitson, *Empty Planet: The Shock of Global Population Decline* (New York: Crown Publishing, 2019); Thomas J. Courchene, *Social Policy in the 1990s: Agenda for Reform*, Policy Study No. 3 (Toronto: C.D. Howe Institute, 1987); J.H. Dales, *Pollution, Property, Prices* (Toronto: University of Toronto Press, 1968); Michael Decter, *Tales from the Back Room – Memoirs of a Political Insider* (Winnipeg: Grant Plains Publications, 20180; Economic Council of Canada, *Economic and Social Impacts of Immigration* (Ottawa: Supply and Services Canada, 1991); A.G. Green and D.A. Green,

"Canadian Immigration Policy: The Effectiveness of the Point System and Other Instruments," *Canadian Journal of Economics* 28 (4) (1995), 1006–41; Masumi Izumi, "Lessons from History: Japanese Canadians and Civil Liberties in Canada," Graduate School of American Studies (Kyoto: Doshisha University, 1998); Roy Miki and Cassandra Kobayashi, *Justice in Our Time: The Japanese Canadian Redress Settlement* (Winnipeg: National Association of Japanese Canadians, 1991); J.G. Snell, "A Foreign Agent in Washington: George W. Brega, Canada's Lobbyist, 1867–1870," *Civil War History* 26 (1) (1980), 53–70; Nathaniel Rich, "Losing Earth: The Decade We Almost Stopped Climate Change," *New York Times Magazine* (2 Aug. 2018), 1–89; John Sawatsky, *The Insiders: Government, Business and the Lobbyists* (Toronto: McClelland & Stewart, 1987); Andrew Stark, "'Political-Discourse' Analysis and the Debate over Canada's Lobbying Legislation," *Canadian Journal of Political Science* 25 (3) (1992), 513–34; Ann Gomer Sunahara, *The Politics of Racism: The Uprooting of Japanese Canadians during the Second World War* (Toronto: James Lorimer & Co., 1981); Mabel Frances Timlin, *Does Canada Need More People?* (Toronto: Oxford Press, 1951).

CHAPTER FOUR

Louis, Balthazar, "Quebec and the Ideal of Federalism," *Annals: AAPSS* 538 (March 1995), 4053; André Bernard, *What Does Quebec Want?* (Toronto: James Lorimer & Company, 1978); Alan Cairns, "Citizens (Outsiders) and Governments (Insiders) in Constitution-Making: The Case of Meech Lake." *Canadian Public Policy* 14 (1988), 121–45; Andrew Cohen, *Lester B. Peterson* (Toronto: Penguin Canada, 2008); Margaret Conrad and J. Hiller, *A Concise History of Atlantic Canada* (Toronto: Oxford University Press, 2006); Graham Frazer, *René Lévesque and the Parti Québécois in Power* (Toronto: Macmillan, 1984; Alan Hustak, *Peter Lougheed: A Biography* (Toronto: McClelland & Stewart, 1979); Boris Laskin, "An Inquiry into the Diefenbaker Bill of Rights," *Canadian Bar Review* 37 (1959), 72–134; H.G. MacKinder, "The Geographical Pivot of History," *Geographic Journal* 23 (4) (1904), 421–37; David McLaughlin, *Poisoned Chalice: How the Tories Self-Destructed* (Toronto: Dundurn Press, 1994); Charles McMillan, *Standing Up to the Future: The Maritimes in the 1990s* (Halifax: Council of Maritime Premiers, 1989); Edward McWhinney, *Quebec and the Constitution 1960–1978* (Toronto: University of Toronto Press, 1979); Peter Meekison, Hamish Telford, and Harvey Lazar, eds., *Canada: The State of the Federation, 2002* (Kingston: Queen's University, 2004); Patrick J. Monahan, "After Meech Lake: An Insider's View," *Ottawa Law Review* 22 (1990), 317–63; Peter Nicholson, *An Action Plan for Atlantic Growth* (Ottawa: Privy Council Office, 2017); Steve Paikin, *Public Triumph, Personal Tragedy: The Biography of John Robarts*

(Toronto: Penguin, 2006); Lise Payette, *Le Pouvoir? Connais Pas, Québec-Amérique* (Montreal, 1982), 45-7; Peter Russell, *Constitutional Odyssey: Can Canadians Become a Sovereign People?* 3rd ed. (Toronto: University of Toronto Press, 2004); Donald V. Smiley, "The Case against the Canadian Charter of Human Rights," *Canadian Journal of Political Science / Revue canadienne de science politique* 2 (3) (Sept. 1969), 277–91; David E. Smith, Peter MacKinnon, and John C. Courtney, eds., *After Meech Lake: Lessons for the Future* (Saskatoon: Fifth Home Publishers, 1991); Gérard Veilleux, *Les relations intergouvernementales au Canada 1867–1967* (Montreal: Les Presses de l'Université de Québec, 1971).

CHAPTER FIVE

Stephen Clarkson, ed., *An Independent Foreign Policy for Canada?* (Toronto: McClelland & Stewart, 1968); David G. Haglund, ed., *What NATO for Canada*, Kingston, ON: Centre for International Relations, Queen's University, 2000; Denis Healey, *The Time of My Life* (London: Penguin, 1989); Paul Heinbecker, *Getting Back in the Game: A Foreign Policy Handbook for Canada* (Toronto: Dundurn, 2011); M, Kwinter and C.J. McMillan, "Central Asia's New Road to Riches," *New York Times* (12 June 1994); Maureen Appel Malot and Brian W. Tomlin, eds., *Canada among Nations – 1985: The Conservative Agenda* (Toronto: James Lorimer & Co., 1986); Nelson Michaud and Kim R. Nossal, eds., *Diplomatic Departures: The Conservative Era in Canadian Foreign Policy, 1984–1993* (Vancouver: University of British Columbia Press, 2001); Charles McMillan, "The Maple Leaf and the Chrysanthemum: 80 Years of Diplomatic Relations between Canada and Japan," *International Journal* 64 (Aug. 2009), 1075–94; Grant L. Rueber, "Canada's Economic Policies towards the Less Developed Countries," *Canadian Journal of Economics* 1 (4) (1968), 669–98; Richard Simeon, "Meech Lake and Shifting Conceptions of Canadian Federalism," *Canadian Public Policy* 14 (Supplement: The Meech Lake Accord) (1988), S7–S24; Brett Thompson, "Pierre Elliott Trudeau's Peace Initiative: 25 Years on," *International Journal* 64 (Aug. 2009), 1117–38; Caspar Weinberger, *Fighting for Peace – Seven Critical Years in the Pentagon* (New York: Warner Books, 1990).

CHAPTER SIX

Percey Moreau Ashburn, *The Ranks of Death: A Medical History of the Conquest of America* (New York: Coward-McCann, Inc., 1947); Nobel David Cook, *Born to Die: Disease and New World Conquest, 1492–1650* (New York: Cambridge University Press, 1998); Menno Bolt, *Surviving as Indians: The Challenge of Self-Government* (Toronto: University of Toronto Press, 1993); John Borrows and Michael Coyle, eds., *The Right Relationship: Reimagining the Implementation of Historical Treaties* (Toronto: University of Toronto Press, 2017); Michel Chaloult, *Les 'Canadiens' de l'expédition Lewis et Clark, 1804–1806: La traversée du continent* (Sillery, QC: Septentrion, 2003); William M. Denevan, *The Native Population of the Americas in 1492* (Madison: University of Wisconsin Press, 1976); Olive Patricia Dickason, *Canada's First Nations* (Toronto: McClelland & Stewart, 1992); Tom Flanagan, *First Nations? Second Thoughts* (Montreal: McGill-Queen's University Press, 2008); Allan Greer, *Property and Dispossession: Natives, Empires, and Land in Early Modern North America* (Cambridge: Cambridge University Press, 2018); LeRoy R. Hafen, ed., *French Fur Traders and Voyageurs in the American West* (Lincoln: University of Nebraska Press, 1997); Samuel Hearne, *A Journey from Prince of Wales's Fort in Hudson's Bay to the Northern Ocean* (Edmonton: Hurtig Publishers, 1971); Stephen J. Kunitz, *Disease and Social Diversity: The European Impact on the Health of Non-Europeans* (New York: Oxford University Press, 1994); John F. Leslie, "Assimilation, Integration, Termination? The Development of Indian Policy," PhD dissertation, Carleton University, 1999; Arthur Manuel and Grand Chief Ronald M. Derrickson, *Unsettling Canada – A National Wake-up Call* (Toronto: Between the Lines, 2015); Frank MacKinnon, "David Laird of Prince Edward Island," *Dalhousie Review* 26 (1947), 405–21; Carolyn Podruchny, *Making the Voyageur World: Travelers and Traders in the North American Fur Trade* (Lincoln: University of Nebraska Press, 2006); Peter H. Russell, "Can Canada Retrieve the Principles of the First Confederation?," in Kiera L. Ladner and Myra J. Tait, eds., *Surviving: Canada's Indigenous Peoples Celebrate 150 Years of Betrayal* (Winnipeg: ARP Books, 2017);, Peter Russell and Roger Jones, "Aboriginal Peoples and Constitutional Reform," paper prepared for Royal Commission on Aboriginal Peoples, Ottawa, 12 Aug. 1993; Denis Vaugeois, *America 1803–1853: L'expédition de Lewis et Clark et la naissance d'une nouvelle puissance* (Sillery, QC: Septentrion, 2002); Tangi Villerbu, *La conquête de l'Ouest – Le récit français de la nation américaine au 19e siècle* (Rennes: Presses Universitaires de Rennes, 2007); S.M. Weaver, *Making Canadian Indian Policy – The Hidden Agenda, 1968–70* (Toronto: University of Toronto Press, 1981).

CHAPTER SEVEN

Richard Baldwin, *The Great Convergence: Information Technology and the New Globalization* (Cambridge, MA: Harvard University Press, 2016); William J. Bernstein, *A Splendid Exchange – How Trade Shaped the World* (New York: Grove Press, 2008); C. Fred Bergsten, "What to Do about the U.S.–Japan Economic Conflict," *Foreign Affairs* (summer 1982), 000–00; Frances Cairncross, *The Death of Distance: How the Communications Revolution Is Changing Our Lives* (Boston: Harvard Business School Press, 1997); Jeffrey Frankel, "The Plaza Accord, 30 Years Later," Faculty Research Working Papers Series, RWB 15-056, Harvard Kennedy School, Boston, 2015; Gary Clyde Hufbauer and Steven Globerman, "The United States–Mexico–Canada Agreement: Overview and Outlook," Vancouver: The Fraser Institute, 2018; Harry G. Johnson, *The Canadian Quandary: Economic Problems and Policies* (Ottawa: Institute of Canadian Studies, Carleton University, 1977); D.C. Masters, *The Reciprocity Treaty of 1854* (London, 1937); Scott Lincicome, "Doomed to Repeat It: The Long History of America's Protectionist Failures," Number 819 (Washington, DC: Cato Institute, 2017); Charles McMillan, "How Free Trade Came to Canada: Lessons in Policy Analysis," *Policy Options* (Oct. 2007), 000–00; Robert Peterson, ed., *Canadian Regulation of International Trade and Investment* (Toronto: Carswell, Legal Publications, 1986); Paul Samuelson, "Where Ricardo and Mill Rebut and Confirm Arguments of Mainstream Economists Supporting Globalization," *Journal of Economic Perspectives* 18 (3) (2004), 135–46; Bruce Wilkinson, *Canada's International Trade: An Analysis of Recent Trends and Patterns* (Toronto: Private Planning Association, 1968).

CHAPTER EIGHT

Michael Adams, *Fire and Ice: The United States, Canada, and the Myth of Competing Values* (Toronto: Penguin, 2003); Stephen Azzi and Norman Hillmer, "Evaluating Prime Minister Leadership in Canada: The Results of an Expert Survey," *Canadian Political Science Review* 7 (1) (2013), 13–23; Conrad Black, *Duplessis* (Toronto: McClelland & Stewart, 1977); Winston Churchill, *Great Contemporaries* (London: Oldham's Press, 1937); Jennifer Ditchburn and Graham Fox, eds., *The Harper Factor: Assessing a Prime Minister's Legacy* (Montreal: McGill-Queen's University Press, 2016); Charles Foran, "Canada as Post-National Nation," *New York Times* (27 April 2017); Roy Jenkins, *Churchill: A Biography* (London: Macmillan, 2004); Ronald A. Kreiger, "The Monetary Governors and the Ghosts of Bretton Woods," *Challenge* (Jan.–Feb. 1975), 000–00; Margaret MacMillan, *History's People* (Toronto: House of Anansi Press, 2015); Lawrence Martin, "Continental Union," *Annals, ACPSS* 538 (March 1995), 143–50; John F. Myers and Mary H. Myers "The Elephant and the Mouse: Canada and the United States," *Bridgewater Review* 3 (3) (1985), 12–15; Peter C. Newman, *When the Gods Changed: The Death of Liberal Canada* (Toronto: Random House, 2011); John Price, "'Orienting' the Empire: Mackenzie King and the Aftermath of the 1907 Race Riots," *BC Studies* 156 (winter 2007-08), 53–81; Peter Riddell, "Winner of the Nation's Best Prime Minister Is ... ," *Times* (1 Dec. 2004); Andrew Roberts,

Churchill: Walking with Destiny (London: Allen Lane, 2018); Arthur M. Schlesinger, Jr, *The Cycles of American History* (Boston: Houghton Mifflin Co., 1986); Jim Stanford and Jordon Brennon, *Rhetoric and Reality: Evaluating Canada's Economic Record under the Harper Government* (Toronto: Unifor, July 2015); Kevin Theakston and Mark Gill, "Rating 20th Century British Prime Ministers," *British Journal of Politics and International Relations* 8 (2) (2006), 192–213; Walt Whitman, *Democratic Vistas* (New York: Kessinger Publishing, 1871).

Bibliography

There is now a growing bibliography of Canada's political and electoral system, seen from the perspective of academics, journalists, prime ministers, premiers, members of Parliament, and civil servants. The references below aren't meant to be comprehensive, but include works consulted for this book. Academic journals and journals of opinion regularly include helpful approaches, judgments, empirical studies, and theoretical works on specific topics: the *Canadian Journal of Economics*, the *Canadian Political Science Journal*, *Canadian Public Administration*, *Canadian Public Policy*, the *Canadian Review of Political Science*, and *Policy Options*. There are also biographies of all Canadian prime ministers, and memoirs by most prime ministers since 1945.

Armstrong, Sally. *Mila*. Toronto: Macmillan, 1992.
Axworthy, Thomas, and Pierre Elliott Trudeau, eds. *Towards a Just Society: The Trudeau Years*, Toronto: Viking, 1990.
Azzi, Stephen. *Walter Gordon and the Rise of Canadian Nationalism*. Montreal: McGill-Queen's University Press, 1999.
Bercuson, David, and Barry Cooper. *Deconfederation: Canada without Quebec*, Toronto: Key Porter Books, 1991.
Blake, Raymond, ed. *Transforming the Nation: Canada and Brian Mulroney*, Montreal: McGill-Queen's University Press, 2007.
Blakeney, Allan. *An Honourable Calling: Political Memoirs*. Toronto: University of Toronto Press, 2008.
Bliss, Michael. *Right Honourable Men: The Descent of Canadian Politics from Macdonald to Mulroney*. Toronto: 1994.
Borden, Robert Laird. *Robert Laird Borden: His Memoirs*, Vol. 1. Montreal: McGill-Queen'[s University Press.

Boyer, Patrick. *The Big Blue Machine: How Tory Campaign Backrooms Changed Canadian Politics Forever*. Toronto: Dundurn, 2015.

Brown, Robert. *Robert Laird Bordon: A Biography*. Toronto: Macmillan, 1975.

Camp, Dalton. *Gentlemen, Players, and Politicians*. Toronto: McClelland & Stewart, 1970.

– *Points of Departure*. Toronto: Deneau & Greenberg, 1979.

Campbell, Kim. *Time and Chance: The Political Memoirs of Canada's First Woman Prime Minister*. Toronto: Doubleday.

Careless, J.M.S. *Brown of the Globe*, 2 vols. Toronto: Dundurn Press, 1989, 1996.

Chrétien, Jean. *My Years as Prime Minister*. Toronto: A.A. Knopf, Canada, 2007.

Clarkson, Stephen, and Christina McCall. *Trudeau and Our Times*. Toronto: McClelland & Stewart, 1990.

Clippingdale, Richard. *Robert Stanfield's Canada*. Montreal: McGill-Queen's University Press, 2008.

Cohen, Andrew, and J.L. Granatstein. *Trudeau's Shadow – The Life and Legacy of Pierre Elliott Trudeau*. Toronto: Random House of Canada, 1998.

Cook, Tim. *Warlords: Borden, Mackenzie King and Canada's World Wars*. 2012.

Creighton, Donald. *John A. Macdonald: The Young Politician and the Old Chieftain*, 2 vols. Toronto: University of Toronto Press, 1952 and 1955.

Crosble, John. *No Holds Barred: My Life in Politics*. Toronto: McClelland & Stewart, 1997.

Dafore, J.W. *Clifford Sifton in Relation to His Times*. Toronto, 1931.

Davey, Keith. *The Rainmaker: A Passion for Politics*. Toronto: Stoddart, 1986.

Dawson, R. MacGregor, *The Government of Canada*, 5th ed. Toronto: University of Toronto Press, 1970.

Dawson, Robert, and H. Blair Neatby. *William Lyon Mackenzie King: Vol 1, 1874–1923*. 1958.

Diefenbaker, John G. *The Tumultuous Years 1962–1967*. Toronto: Macmillan, 1977.

Dorling, Danny, and Sally Tomlinson. *Rule Britannia: Brexit and the End of Empire*. London: Bitebike, 2018.

Economy, Elizabeth C. *The Third Revolution: Xi Jinping and the New Chinese State*. London: Oxford University Press, 2018.

English, John. *Just Watch Me: The Life of Pierre Elliott Trudeau 1968–2000*. Toronto: Knopf Canada, 2009.

English, John, and J.O. Stubbs, eds. *Mackenzie King: Widening the Debate.* Toronto: Macmillan of Canada, 1977.

Esberey, Joy E. *Knight of the Holy Spirit: A Study of William Lyon Mackenzie King.* Toronto: University of Toronto Press, 1980.

Ferns, Henry, and Bernard Ostry. *The Age of Mackenzie King.* Toronto: James Lorimer & Company.

Flanagan, Tom, *Waiting for the Wave: The Reform Party and Preston Manning.* Toronto: Stoddart, 1995.

Forsey, Eugene A. *Freedom and Order.* Toronto: McClelland and Stewart, 1974.

Fox, William. *Spin Wars: Politics and the New Media.* Toronto: Key Porter Books, 1999.

Gollner, Andrew B., amd Daniel Salée, eds. *Canada under Mulroney: An End of Term Report.* Montreal: Véhicule Press, 1988.

Gotlieb, Allan. *The Washington Diaries, 1981–1989.* Toronto: McClelland & Stewart, 2006.

Graham, Ron. *One-Eyed Kings: Promise and Illusion in Canadian Politics.* Toronto: Harper Collins Canada, 1986.

Granatstein, Jack. *The Ottawa Men: The Civil Service Mandarins, 1935–1957.* Toronto: Oxford University Press, 1982.

Gratton, Michel. *So What Are the Boys Saying? An Inside Look at Brian Mulroney in Power.* Toronto: McGraw-Hill, 1987.

Greenspon, Edward, and Anthony Wilson-Smith. *Double Vision: The Inside Story of the Liberals in Power.* Toronto: Doubleday, 1996.

Gwyn, Richard. *The Northern Magus: Pierre Trudeau and Canada.* Toronto: McClelland & Stewart, 1980.

Harris, Michel. *Party of One: Stephen Harper and Canada's Radical Makeover.* Toronto: Viking, 2014.

Heinbecker, Paul. *Getting Back in the Game: A Foreign Policy Handbook for Canada.* Toronto: Dundurn, 2011.

Henderson, George F. *W.L. Mackenzie King: A Bibliography and Research Guide.* Toronto: University of Toronto Press, 2015.

Heyman, Bruce, and Vicky Heyman. *The Art of Diplomacy: Strengthening the Canada–U.S. Relationship in Times of Uncertainty.* New York, Simon and Schuster, 2019.

Hustak, Alan. *Peter Lougheed: A Biography.* Toronto: McClelland & Stewart, 1979.

Hutchison, Bruce. *The Incredible Canadian; A Candid Portrait of Mackenzie King: His Works, His Times, and His Nation.* New York: Longmans Green, 1953.

Ibbitson, John. *Stephen Harper*. Toronto: Signal, 2015.
Johnson, Harry G. *The Canadian Quandary: Economic Problems and Policies*. Ottawa: Institute of Canadian Studies, Carleton University, 1977.
Johnston, David. *Trust – Twenty Ways to Build a Better Country*. Toronto: McClelland & Stewart, 2018.
Ladner, Kiera L., and Myra J. Tait. *Surviving: Canada's Indigenous Peoples Celebrate 150 Years of Betrayal*. Winnipeg: ARP Books, 2017.
LaForest, Guy. *Trudeau and the End of the Canadian Dream*. Montreal: McGill-Queen's University Press, 1995.
Leacock, Stephen. *Economic Prosperity in the British Empire*. Toronto: Macmillan Company of Canada, 1930.
Lewis, J.P., and Joanna Everitt, eds. *The Blueprint: Conservative Parties and Their Impact on Canadian Politics*. Toronto: University of Toronto Press, 2017.
Kenen, Peter B. *Managing the World Economy: Fifty years after Bretton Woods*. Washington, DC: Institute for International Economics, 1994.
Keynes, John Maynard. *The Collected Writings of John Maynard Keynes*. London: Macmillan, 1971.
MacDonald, L. Ian. *Mulroney: The Making of a Prime Minister*. Toronto: McClelland & Stewart, 1984.
MacGuigan, Mark. *An Inside Look at External Affairs during the Trudeau Years: The Memoirs of Mark MacGuigan*. Calgary: University of Calgary Press, 2002.
Macquarrie, Heath. *Red Tory Blues – A Political Memoir*. Toronto: University of Toronto Press, 1992.
Manuel, Arthur, and Grand Chief Ronald M. Derrickson. *Unsettling Canada – A National Wake-up Call*. Toronto: Between the Lines, 2015.
Martin, Lawrence. *Harperland: The Politics of Control*. Toronto: Viking Canada, 2010.
Martin, Paul. *A Very Public Life*. Ottawa: Deneau Publishers, 1983.
McCall-Newman, Christina. *Grits: An Intimate Portrait of the Liberal Party*. Toronto: Macmillan, 1983.
McGregor, Fred A. *The Fall and Rise of Mackenzie King, 1911–1919*. Toronto: Macmillan of Canada, 1962.
McMillan, Charles. *Eminent Islanders*. Bloomington, IL: AuthorHouse, 2009.
McMillan, Tom. *Not My Party: The Rise and Fall of Canadian Tories, from Robert Stanfield to Stephen Harper*. Halifax: Nimbus Publishing, 2016.
McMurtry, Roy. *Memoirs and Reflections*. Toronto: Osgoode Society, 2013.
Miller, J.R. *Compact, Contract, Covenant: Aboriginal Treaty-Making in Canada*. Toronto: University of Toronto Press, 2009.

Moore, Charles. *Margaret Thatcher – The Authorized Biography*. London: Allen Lane, 2005.

Mulroney, Brian. *Memoirs*. Toronto: Emblem Editions, 2007.

– *Where I Stand*. Toronto: McClelland & Stewart, 1983.

Newman, Peter C. *Renegade in Power: The Diefenbaker Years*. Toronto: McClelland & Stewart, 1963.

Nielsen, Erik. *This House Is Not a Home*. Toronto: Macmillan, 1989.

O'Leary, Gratton. *Reflections of People, Press and Politics*. Toronto: McClelland & Stewart, 1977.

Paikin, Steve. *Bill Davis: Nation Builder, and Not So Bland After All*. Toronto: Dundurn, 2016.

Penikett, Tony. *Hunting the Northern Character*. Vancouver: UBC Press, 2017.

Perrin, Andrew. *Social Media Usage: 2005–2015*. New York: Pew Research Center, 2015.

Pinard, Maurice. *The Rise of a Third Party: A Study in Crisis Politics*. Englewood Cliffs, NJ: Prentice-Hall, 1971.

Plamondon, Bob. *Blue Thunder: The Truth about Conservatives from Macdonald to Harper*. Toronto: Key Porter Books, 2009.

Porter, John. *The Vertical Mosaic*. Toronto: University of Toronto Press, 1965.

Pope, Sir Joseph. *Memoirs of the Right Honourable Sir John A. Macdonald*. Toronto: Musson Book Company, 1894.

Pratte, André. *Wilfrid Laurier*. Toronto: Éditions du Boréal, 2011.

Presthus, Robert. *Elite Accommodation in Canadian Politics*. Toronto: MacMillan, 1973.

Rae, Bob. *From Protest to Power: Personal Reflections on a Life in Politics*. Toronto: Viking, 1996.

Robertson, Gordon. *Memoirs of a Very Civil Servant: Mackenzie King to Pierre Trudeau*. Toronto: University of Toronto Press, 2008.

Russell, Peter. *Constitutional Odyssey: Can Canadians Become a Sovereign People?*, 3rd ed. Toronto: University of Toronto Press, 2004.

Schull, Joseph. *Laurier: The First Canadian*. Toronto: Macmillan, 1966.

Segal, Hugh. *No Surrender: Reflections of a Happy Warrior in the Tory Crusade*. Toronto: HarperCollins, 1996.

– *The Right Balance: Canada's Conservative Tradition*. Toronto: Douglas & McIntyre, 2011.

Simpson, Jeffery. *Spoils of Power: The Politics of Patronage*. Toronto: Collins, 1988.

Smith, David E. *The Invisible Crown: The First Principle in Canadian Government*. Toronto: University of Toronto Press, 2013.

Smith, Dennis. *Rogue Tory: The Life and Legend of John G. Diefenbaker.* Toronto: MacFarlane, Walter & Ross, 1955.
Starr, Richard. *Richard Hatfield: The Seventeen Year Saga.* Halifax: Goodread Biography, 1987.
Thompson, Dale. *Louis St. Laurent – Canadian.* Toronto: Macmillan, 1967.
Tupper, Sir Charles. *Recollections of Sixty Years.* London: Cassels, 1914.
Trudeau, Pierre Elliott. *Federalism and the French Canadians.* Toronto: Macmillan, 1968.
– *Memoirs.* Toronto: McClelland & Stewart, 1993.
Turner, John. *Politics of Purpose.* Toronto: McClelland & Steward, 1968.
Van Dusen, Thomas. *The Chief.* Russell, ON: Castor Publishing, 1968.
Vastel, Michel. Trudeau: *Le Québécois.* Montreal: Les Éditions de l'Homme, 1989.
Waite, P.B. *In Search of R.B. Bennett.* Montreal: McGill-Queen's University Press, 2012.
Wells, Paul. *Right Side Up: The Fall of Paul Martin and the Rise of Stephen Harper.* Toronto: Douglas Gibson Books, 2006.
Westell, Anthony. *Paradox: Trudeau as Prime Minister.* Scarborough, ON: Prentice-Hall, 1972.
Whelan, Eugene (with Rick Archibald). *Whelan: The Man in the Green Stetson.* Toronto: Irwin, 1986.
Whitcomb, Ed. *Rivals for Power: Ottawa and the Provinces.* Toronto: James Lorimer, 2017.
Willison, J.S. *Sir Wilfrid Laurier and the Liberal Party,* 2 vols. Toronto, 1903.
Wise, S.F., and R.C. Brown, *Canada Views the United States: Nineteenth Century Political Attitudes.* London: 1967.

Index

Abe, Shinzo 316
abortion 117–19, 359
acid rain 237–8
Adams, John 258
Adams, Michael 352
Adams, Tom 207
Adenauer, Konrad 195
Agreement on Internal Trade (AIT, 1995), western provinces 157
Aiken, Max (Lord Beaverbrook) 212
Airbus 74, 132, 136
Air Canada 71–2, 132, 136
Akaev, Askar 229, 231
Alberta Heritage Fund 141
Alexander, Lincoln 92
Allaire, Jean 183
Almond, Warren 118
Amherst, Jeffery 258
Anderson, Ian 35
Andre, Harvie 38, 129, 362
Andrews, Sharon 70
Andropov, Yuri 208
Angus, David 132
anti-Americanism 359
apartheid 135, 212–13
Arctic Council 233–4, 285–6
Arctic sovereignty 175, 231, 286

Arrow, Ken 101
Asia Pacific Foundation of Canada 217
Atkins, Norman 29, 35, 152
Atlantic Canada Opportunities Agency (ACOA) 55, 149, 152
Atlantic Energy Accord (AEA) 10, 29, 36, 134, 160, 179
Atlantic Gateway 156–8
Attlee, Clement 90, 99, 194
Austin, Jack 217
auto sector 295
Axworthy, Lloyd 70, 142
Axworthy, Tom 217, 234

Badali, Sal 36
Baie James 158, 230
Baird, Patricia 170
Baker, James 231, 303
Balcer, Leon 333, 342
Balfour Declaration (1926) 162, 353
Ballock, Howard 221
Bank of Alberta 52
Bank of Canada 50
Barrette, Antonio 348
Bazin, Jean 25, 29
Beatty, Perrin 109, 321
Bélanger, Michael 47, 183

Bennett, Bill 175, 217
Bennett, Carolyn 286
Bennett, R.B. 4, 152, 286, 337, 342
Bennett, Richard 69
Bennett, W.A.C. 139, 279
Bennett, William 294
Benson, Edgar 69
Berlin, Isaiah 39
Bernard, Hewitt 271
Berstain, William 296
Berstein, Fred 301
Beveridge, William 88. 90
Bevin, Ernest 197
Big Bang financial reform (re City of London, 1986) 93-4
bilateral trade agreements 221, 297
Binns, Pat 189
Bismarck, Otto 91
Bissonnette, André 53, 54, 135
Black, William Anderson 15
Blaikie, Bill 131
Blaine, James 291
Blair, Bob 68
Blais-Grenier, Susan 236
Blake, Edward 95
Blane, Jared 10
Blenkarn, Don 54
Blue Cross 99
Bonnell, Lorne 191
Bordon, Robert 4, 17, 18, 21, 294, 296, 330, 335, 339
Borowski, Joe 117
Bouchard, Lucien 173, 177, 185, 240
Boudria, Don 132
Bouey, Gerald 50-1
Bourassa, Robert 113, 143, 159, 168, 177, 179-80
Bracken, John 338
Brazeau, Patrick 251
Bregan, George W. 132

Brezhnev, Leonid 224
British North America Act 84, 139, 161, 269, 274
Broadbent, Ed 241
Brooks, David 212
Brossard, André 50
Brown, Bob 38
Brown, George 331, 339
Brown, Gordon 315
Browse, Pauline 248
Brundtland, Gro Harlem 239
Brundtland Commission (1983-87) 223, 239
Bryce, Robert 8, 88, 145
Buchanan, John 66
Bullock, John 109
Burke, Alfred 180
Burke, Edmund 180
Burn, Peter 25
Burney, Derek 136, 241, 297
Burns, Jamie 70, 155
Bush, George H.W. 354
Bussières, Pierre 110

Cadman, Chuck 16
Cairncross, Francis 323
Cairns, Alan C. 177
Caisse de dépôt 57
Calder, Frank 251
Cameron, David 243, 316
Camp, Dalton 35, 152, 214, 344
Campbell, Alex 178
Campbell, Kim 89, 185, 309, 345
Campeau, Jean 183
Canada Europe Trade Round (2009-14) 315-16
Canada Health Act 102, 104, 112
Canada Health Social Transfer 143, 146
Canada's trade strategies 314

Canadian Alliance 118
Canadian Commercial Bank 47
Canadian Federation of Independent
  Business 55, 82, 109
Canadian National 71-2
carbon tax 124
Cardinal, Harold 279
Careless, J.M. 339
Carney, Pat 25, 38, 50, 64, 67,
  114, 362
Carson, Rachel 121
Cartier, George-Étienne 188, 231,
  331
Casey, Bill 16
Centres of Excellence 79, 82, 351
chaebols (Korean conglomerates) 218
Chamberlain, Joseph 291
Chambers, Bill 210
Chant, Bob 29
Charest, Jean 185, 187, 240, 309
Charlottetown Accord (1992) 184-5
Charter of Rights and Freedoms
  (1982) 89, 117, 360
Chernenko, Konstantin 47, 208, 224,
  226
China Belt Road 326
Chinese Exclusion Act (1923) 353
Chrétien, Jean 42, 62, 82, 181, 186,
  221, 235, 308, 332, 339-40, 350,
  361
Church, Thomas 164
Churchill, Gordon 334
Churchill, Winston 9, 13, 22, 42,
  194, 203, 209, 289, 309, 330,
  338-9, 363
Churchill Falls 157-9
Cité Libre 199
Citizenship Bill 163
Clark, Clifford 45
Clark, Ed 115, 236

Clark, Ian 37, 73
Clark, Joe 18-19, 36, 109, 118,
  135, 171, 183, 199, 206, 333, 344,
  349, 367
Clark, William 145, 256
Clarkson, Adrienne 92
Claxton, Brooke 145
Coarse, Ronald 283
Cogger, Michel 29, 35, 135
Cohen, Marshal ("Mickey") 50, 57,
  115, 235
Colbert, Jean-Baptiste 255
Collins, Doug 98
Columbus, Christopher 251
Colville, Alexander 261
Commonwealth 206-7, 212-14
competitiveness agenda 34, 244
Confederation Bridge 190-2, 309
Congress of Vienna 265
Copps, Sheila 39, 132, 306
Costigan, John 95
Côté, Michael 136
Côté-O'Hara, Jocelyne 25, 35
Cotler, Irwin 89
Council of the Federation 187, 315
Cowper, William 137
Coyne, James 52, 150
Crane, David 77
Creighton, Donald 339
Crombie, David 112, 129, 250
Crosbie, John 25, 66, 70, 89, 134,
  136, 142, 150, 154, 351
Crossland, Jim 25
Crerar, Thomas 127, 286
Curzon, George 339

da Gama, Vasco 289
Darling, Stan 240
Davidson, George 277
Davies, Lou 161

Davis, William 27, 67, 140, 187, 241, 297, 342
Deaver, Chief Joseph 276
de Cotret, Robert 25, 72, 114
de Gaulle, Charles 209, 354
deindexing 114
Delvoie, Louis 201
Deng Xiaoping 5
Department of the Environment 120
Desmarais, Paul 59
d'Estaing, Valéry Giscard 10
Deutsch, John 9, 145, 296
de Vattel, Emmerich 257
Devine, Grant 38, 140
Dexter, Darryl 9
Dickens, Charles 144
Dickson, Fred 135
Diefenbaker, John 9, 52, 108, 118, 148, 164, 189, 212–13, 275, 334, 344
Dion, Stéphane 346
Disraeli, Benjamin 212
Dodge, David 57
Doha Trade Round (WTO, 2001–08) 298, 311, 312, 313, 323, 325
Domm, Bill 119
Doodie, Bill 188
Doucet, Fred 132–4
Doucet, Gerry 134–5
Douglas, James 269, 279
Douglas, Tommy 101
Drew, George 8, 145, 187, 342
Duffy, Mike 346
Dukakis, Michael 178
Dumont, Mario 183
Duncan, Andrew Rae 151
Dunton, Davidson 165
Duplessis, Maurice 83. 142, 164, 344, 347
Dusseaut, Pierre-Luc 15

Dutil, Marcel 47

Early, Mary Two-Axe 290
Earth Day 122
Economic Council of Canada 132, 299
Economist magazine 9–10
Eisenhower, Dwight D. 139, 197
Epp, Jake 25, 68, 103, 234
equalization 145–7, 348
Established Program Financing (EPF) 89, 146
Estey, William 56
Evershed, Phil 70, 155

Faibish, Roy 88, 232, 356
Fairclough, Ellen 279, 286
Fairhome, C.I. 277
Fast, Ed 316
Favreau, Guy 166, 168
Federal Business Development Bank (FBDB) 46
Ferns, H.E. 337
Fielding, William 293
FIFA 209
Filman, Gary 176, 181
financial services: reforms 44–7, 48, 59–61
Flaherty, Jim 106
Flanagan, Tom 283, 285
Fleming, Don 40
Fonds de Solidarité 79
Ford, Gerald 10, 22
foreign aid 204, 351
Fowler, Robert 212
Fox, Bill 29, 35, 136, 234
Francis, Brian 251
Franco, Emile 25
Franklin, Benjamin 258, 261
Fraser, Graham 342

Fraser, John 62
Fraser, Whit 287
Friedland, Sy 26
Friedman, Milton 108
Frost, Leslie 342
Fulton, E. Davie 166, 168, 277

Gagnier, Dan 315
Galbraith, John Kenneth 23, 358
Galt, Thomas 138, 293
Gandhi, Indira 202
Gardiner, James 366
George III 258
Getty, Don 175
Ghiz, Joe 156, 179–80
Gillies, James 19, 367, 375
Gladstone, James 256, 275
Gladstone, William Ewart 291
Globe and Mail 285, 291, 331
Godbout, Gerald 35
Goldfarb, Martin 227
Good, Jim 36
Good, Len 198
Goods and Service Tax (GST) 75, 111–12, 115–16, 125
Gorbachev, Mikhail 209, 225, 226, 233, 306, 330
Gorbet, Fred 37, 57
Gordon, Walter 8, 40, 297, 305, 355
Gordon Commission (1955–57) 8, 147
Gore, Al 230
Gotlieb, Allan 202, 240, 241, 305, 385
Gratton, Michel 29
Gray, Jim 68, 140
Green Book (August 1945) 8, 88
Griffiths, Franklin 224
Grosart, Allister 88
Grossman, Larry 103

Guilbault, Camilla 29
Gwyn, Richard 242

Halifax Declaration (1989) 83
Hall, Emmett 101, 308
Hamilton, Alvin 20
Harder, Peter 27, 55
Harper, Stephen 13, 18, 61, 73, 116, 160, 282, 313, 317, 333, 346, 362
Harries, Hu 358
Harris, Anne 25, 35
Harris, Michael (Mike) 187, 342, 362
Harris, Walter 148, 273, 286
Hartt, Stanley 50, 115, 297
Hatfield, Michael 255
Hatfield, Richard 113, 140, 153
Hawkes, Jim 362
Hawthorn, Harry 278
Head, Ivan 356
Healey, Denis 198, 379
Heath, Edward 14
HEC ([École des] Haute Études Commericales), Montreal 47
Hedlin, Ralph 140
Heinz, Senator John (R–Penn.) 240
Hepburn, Mitchell 145
Higdon, Lorna 25
Hnatyshyn, Ray 38, 56, 89, 92, 98, 308
Hockin, Tom 57–8
Hofstadter, Richard 4
Howe, C.D. 8, 69, 287, 295
Howe, Geoffrey 216
Hudson's Bay Company 161, 231, 257–68, 279, 289
Hugo, Victor 237
Huntington, Ron 110
Hydro-Québec 157, 165
Hyndman, Doug 61

immigration 164–5, 357
Indian Act 172, 174, 248, 274, 279
Iron Ore Company of Canada 34, 343, 359
Isautier, Bernard 68
Israel 195

James, F. Cyril 163
Jamieson, Don 251
Japan 58, 76, 80, 121, 140, 189, 209, 216, 219–20, 301–2, 317–18, 326–7
Japanese-Canadian redress 125–8
Jarislowsky, Stephen 58
Jelinek, Otto 362
Jenkins, Roy 336
Jenkins, Tom 82
John Paul II, Pope 36, 135, 205, 208, 277
Johnson, Daniel 166, 187
Johnson, Janis 35
Johnson, Jon 25, 155
Johnson, Lynden 108, 355
Johnson, Pierre-Marc 315
Johnson, William 251, 259–60
Johnston, David 363
Johnston, Harry 299
Journal of Economic Literature 75

Kahn, Herman 198
Keenleyside, Hugh 127
Kelleher, James 236, 241, 305, 308
Kelowna Accord (2005) 282
Kennedy, Edward 93
Kennedy, John F. 336
Kennett, William 49, 51
Kent, Tom 9
Keynes, John Maynard 339
Khrushchev, Nikita 187
Kikuchi, Kiyoaki 209

King, William Lyon Mackenzie 4, 21, 88, 104, 129, 145, 191, 294, 331, 352–3
Kirby, Michael 170
Kissinger, Henry 198
Klein, Ralph 283
Kohl, Helmet 210, 213, 230
Komagata Maru, SS 96
Kreiger, Ronald 365
Kroeger, Arthur 297
Kuptana, Rosemary 234
Kwinter, Monte 228
Kyoto Protocol (1997) 240
Kyrgyzstan 229

Labarge, Louis 26, 68, 343
L'Abbé, Paul 38
Laird, David 270–2
Lalonde, Marc 46, 89, 109, 110, 175
Lamontagne, Maurice 149
Lang, Otto 46
Langevin, Hector 286
Lapointe, Ernest 341, 353
Laskin, Bora 168, 174
Lauren, Pierre 47
Laurendeau, André 165
Laurier, Wilfrid 4, 21, 23, 95, 138, 144, 291, 297, 331, 337, 350
Lavigeur, Guy 54
Laxer, James 304
Layton, Jack 341, 346
Le Bloc Québec 185, 341
Lee, Jim 154
Lesage, Jean 25, 141, 145, 165, 348
Lévesque, René 143, 158, 170, 173, 342, 378
Lewis, Doug 29
Lewis, Drew 241
Lewis, Merriwether 256
Lewis, Stephen 216

Li Kai Shing 60
Lloyd George, David 14, 42
lobbying 131–3
London Stock Exchange 213
Lougheed, Peter 28, 38, 66, 113, 139, 297, 299
Louis XIV 356
Lumley, Ed 53, 358

MacAdam, Lane 30
MacAdam, Pat 30
Macdonald, Donald S. 169, 297, 305, 358
MacDonald, Flora 25, 98
Macdonald, John A. 3, 4, 23, 95, 132, 188, 212, 271, 291–2, 329
Macdonald, L. Ian 35
MacDougall, Barbara 43, 50, 57, 73
MacDougall, Don 135
MacEachen, Alan J. 53, 66, 109, 118, 142, 150
MacEachern, Jim 25
Machiavelli, Niccolò 164
machinery of government, Aboriginal Affairs 274
MacInnis, S. Lyman 109
MacIntosh, Robert 56
MacKay, Elmer 25, 150, 191
MacKay, Peter 89, 346
Mackenzie, Alexander 13, 220, 293, 337
Mackenzie, Ian 127, 129
MacKinnon, Frank 18
MacLaren, Roy 315
Macmillan, Harold 301
MacMillan, Margaret 329
Macmillan Commission (banking, 1933) 45
Macphail, Agnes 327

MacPhail, Don 13
Macquarrie, Heath 14, 191
Macrae, Norman 196
Major, John 42, 228
Maloney, Arthur 118
Mandela, Nelson 212, 216–19
Mandelson, Peter 315
Manhattan, USS 232
Manion, Jack 39
Manley, Michael 211
Manning, Ernest 101, 139, 340
Manning, Preston 176–7, 186, 282, 340, 375
Marchand, Jean 69, 168, 349
Maritime union 151–2
Marsh, Leonard 163
Marshall, Donald 119
Marshall, William 67
Martin, Lawrence 339, 351
Martin, Paul, Jr 5, 13, 18, 61, 75, 105, 114, 177, 282, 310, 333
Martin, Paul, Sr 163, 203, 233
Masse, Marcel 112
Matheson, Alex 148
Max Planck Institutes 79
Mayer, Charles 38, 345
Mazankowski, Don 25, 38, 50, 69, 98, 119, 190, 345, 362
McClelland, Jack 203
McDermott, John 26, 68
McGrath, James 42
MacGuigan, Mark 201
McGuinty, Dalton 168
McIlwraith, George 118
McKenna, Frank 152, 156, 176, 179, 185
McKeough, Darcy 25
McKnight, Bill 50, 176, 345
McLaughlin, Gerald 47, 49, 51
McLellan, Anne 89

McMillan, Charles 25, 67, 73, 114, 129, 154, 189, 207, 217–18, 222, 228–9, 298, 320–323
McMillan, Tom 53, 123, 240
McMurtry, Roy 341
McPherson, Don 50
McTeer, Maureen 120
McWhinney, Edward 174
Medicare 349, 361
Medlin, Ted 57
Meech Lake Accord (1987) 97, 174, 282, 345
Meekinson, Peter 140
Meighen, Arthur 286, 338, 342
Menzies, Marshall 88
Menzies, Merrill 232
Meyboom, Peter 55
Miele, Perry 29
Miki, Art 130–1
Miliband, David 182
Miller, Frank 297, 342
Mitterrand, François 230, 361
Monahan, Patrick 172
Monroe Doctrine 207, 293
Montagu, Kyra 234
Montreal Protocol (1987) 56, 123, 193, 240
Montreal *Star* 290
Moores, Frank 132, 136
Morgentaler, Henry 117
Mowat, Oliver 142
Mulholland, Bill 307
Mulroney, Brian: as opposition leader 18, 26–8, 66, 109, 132, 149, 153, 189, 227, 296, 343; personal background 20, 151, 358, 362; as prime minister 14, 34, 92, 130–1, 142, 173, 192, 205, 221–2, 234-5, 280, 302. 307–9, 331, 333
multicultural policy 357–8

Murphy, Peter 307
Murray, Lowell 112, 117, 153, 175, 191
Murta, Jack 129
Muskrat Falls 159
Mustard, Fraser 78

NAFTA 308, 314, 359
NAFTA II 324
Nakasone, Yasuhiro 189, 209, 220, 221, 223, 303
National Advisory Board on Science and Technology 98, 120
National Energy Program 60, 64, 71, 193
National Indian Council 249
NATO 191–9
Nault, Bob 285
Naylor, David 83–5
Near, Harry 68, 114
Newman, Peter 203, 339–40
Nichols, Marjorie 79
Nielsen, Erik 27, 55–6, 199, 275
Nielsen Task Force 36, 54, 206
Nixon, Richard 22, 199, 232, 355
Northlands Bank 47
North-West Mounted Police 231
Norquay, Geoff 25, 35, 39
Noseworthy, Joseph 353
Nowlan, Pierre-Claude 25, 35
Nunavut 188, 232
Nunziata, John 132, 281
Nye, Joseph 242
Nyerere, Julius 202

Oberle, Frank 53, 77
Oki, Jack 130
Okita, Saburo 223
Oliver, Joe 283
Olson, Clifford 119

OpenText 78, 85, 311
operations committee of cabinet 70–1
Osbalderston, Gordon 36, 115, 149
Ostry, Sylvia 297

Pacific Rim 297
pandemics 124
Paris Agreement on Climate Change (2015) 122, 327
Parizeau, Jacques 47, 184, 186
Parker, Bob 70
Parsons, T.W.S. 127
Pasteur, Louis 358
Pearson, Lester B. 9, 91, 102, 165, 191, 201, 242, 277, 349
Peckford, Brian 67, 154
Péclet, Ève 15
Pelletier, Gérard 168, 349
Penikett, Tony 387
Pépin, Jean-Luc 69
perestroika 6
Peterson, David 57, 142, 178, 228, 348
Petro Canada 64, 71, 98
Phillips, Orville 191
Pickersgill, Jack 142, 274, 345, 356
pipeline politics 124, 283–4
Pitfield, Michael 149, 201, 356
Pitt, William, the Younger 14
Planck, Max 79
Plaxton, C.B. 162
Plaza Accord (1985) 220, 381
Polanyi, John C. 78
Policy Analysis Group (PAG) xx, 25, 26, 27, 34, 35, 129
Pope, Joseph 21, 339
Pope, Maurice 128
Porter, John 366
Powell, Enoch 214

Prentice, James 282, 285
privatization policy 71–5
Putin, Vladimir 231, 330

Quebec Act (1774) 253, 261
Quiet Revolution 336, 349–50

Rambouillet, France 208
Rat Pack (Liberal) 39, 132, 306
Reagan, Ronald 10, 133, 203, 224–5, 299, 302
Reform Party 118, 281, 345
Reichman, Paul 114, 234
Reid, Escott 128
Reid, Ross 29, 155
Reid, Tom 127
Reisman, Simon 110, 306
residential schools 232–3
Revenue Canada 109, 114
Richardson, Lee 25, 140, 207
Richardson, Lynn 25
Richie, Nancy 78
Rickford, Greg 286
Riddell, Peter 336
Riel, Louis 182
Rigma, Bob 98
Ritchie, Cedric 56, 59
Ritchie, Gordon 53, 68, 306
Robarts, John 102. 166, 342, 349
Robertson, Gordon 163, 175, 177
Robertson, Norman 127, 356
Robinette, J.J. 169
Robinson, Jackie 359
Rock, Alan 120
Rockefeller, David 296
Romanow, Roy 186
Roosevelt, Franklin 88, 142, 193
Roscoe, Elizabeth 74
Rossiter, Eileen 191
Rotstein, Abe 203

Rowell, Newton 8
Rowell–Sirois Commission
  (Dominion–Provincial Relations,
  1937–40) 8, 147
Roy, Barnard 51, 55–6, 136
Royal Commission on Aboriginal
  Peoples (1991–96) 248, 250, 272,
  281, 380
Royal Commission on Canada's
  Economic Prospects (Gordon
  Commission, 1955--57) 8, 147
Royal Commission on Health
  Services (Hall Commission, 1961–
  64) 101
Royal Commission on New
  Reproductive Technologies (Baird
  Commission, 1989–93) 120
Royal Commission on Taxation
  (Carter Commission, 1962–66)
  64, 108
Royal Canadian Mint 78
Russell, Peter 167
Ryan, Claude 177, 203

St Francis Xavier University,
  Antigonish, NS ii, xvii, 20,
  133, 151
St Germain, Gerry 49, 282
St Laurent, Louis 8, 20, 88, 99, 102,
  162, 194, 287, 341
St. Louis, MS 97
Sampson, Anthony 64
Samuelson, Paul 88, 289, 368
Sauvé, Paul 348
Savoie, Donald 153
Schlesinger, Arthur, Sr 336
Schmidt, Helmut 350
Schreiber, Karlheintz 136
Schumpeter, Joseph 358
Science Council of Canada 76
Scott, Anthony 129

Scott, Frank 338
Scott, Graham 103
Seaga, Edward 207–8
Service, Robert 287
Shamrock Summit (Quebec City,
  March 1985) 47, 133, 240
Shannon, Gerry 37, 297
Shannon, Joe 53
Sharp, Mitchell 186, 201, 366
Shaw, Walter 191
Shortliffe, Glen 70
Shugart, Ian 25, 284
Shultz, George 238
Sifton, Clifford 95
Simon, Mary 235, 285
Skelton, O.D. 145
Smallwood, Joey 66
Smiley, Donald 169
Smith, Adam 63, 87, 161, 292
Smith, Denis 339
Smith, Gordon 201
soft power 242
Solage, Denis 114
South Africa 214–15
Specter, Norman 176
Speyer, Chris 110
Spicer, Keith 183, 357
Spragge, William 271
Stanfield, Robert 20, 91, 109, 150,
  153, 333, 342, 350
Steers, Barry 217
Stevens, Sinclair 25, 53, 77, 110,
  212, 218
Stewart, Barbara 134
Stewart, David 134
Strategic Defense Initiative (SDI) 224
Strom, Harry 340
Stronach, Frank 25
Sumner, William Graham 229
Swain, Harry 37, 54
Symons, T.H.B. (Tom) 242

Tarnopolky, Walter 128
Taschereau, Henri-Thomas 337
Taylor, Alan 56
Taylor, Claude 74
Team Canada 310
Tecumseh 263
Tellier, Paul 68
terra nullius 257–8
Thatcher, Denis 215
Thatcher, Margaret 43, 71, 170, 203, 215–16, 361
Thomson, Roy 135
Tobin, Brian 306
Tolstoy, Leo 96
Toronto Stock Exchange 45
Toyota 217
Trans-Pacific Partnership (TPP) 311, 317, 320
Trbovitch, Tom 36
Treasury Board 42, 53, 114
Tremblay, M.A. 278
Trudeau, Justin 17, 20, 86, 124, 316, 331
Trudeau, Pierre Elliott 13, 30, 38, 88–9, 117, 129, 134, 149, 167, 186, 199, 225–6, 238, 249, 278–9, 332
Truman, Harry 196
Trump, Donald 9, 122, 292, 318–19, 359
Tsechie, Bill 53
Tupper, Charles 334
Turner, John 12, 40, 42, 46, 52, 89, 117, 132, 307

Wagenast, David 25
Wakely, Wilf 315
Walsh, Jack 54, 56
Walters, Alan 26
Wampum diplomacy 254–60
War Measures Act 128–9

Warren, Earl 265
Washington, George 262, 338
Watkins, Mel 304
Wayne, Elsie 185
Weinberger, Caspar 205–6, 239
Wells, Clyde 178, 185
western Canada economic diversification 155, 175
Whelan, Eugene 225, 388
White, Bob 26, 68
White, Jodi 236
White, Nancy 14
White, Peter 223
Whitman, Walt 330
Whitney, James 142
Wilde, Oscar 236
Williams, Danny 160
Wilson, Michael 25, 40, 50–1, 56, 68, 78, 108, 110, 114, 142, 256
Wilson-Raybould, Judy 89, 251
Wolf, Walter 134–5
Wright, Doug 79
Wright, Nigel 35, 175, 207, 316, 320, 346
Wrong, Hume 195

Valcourt, Bernard 283, 286
Vanderlaw, Louis 120
VanDusen, Lisa 29
VanDusen, Tom 88
Veilleux, Gérard 37, 176, 379
venture capital 80–1
Viner, Jacob 323
Volcker, Paul 49, 178, 210, 301

Yakovlev, Alexander 225
Yeltsin, Boris 227, 231

Zakaria, Fareed 42
Zaozirny, John 67